Native American Sovereignty ON TRIAL

Other books in ABC-CLIO's On Trial Series
Charles Zelden, Series Editor

Constitutional Change on Trial, Richard Bernstein

Gay Rights on Trial, Lee Walzer

The Human Body on Trial, Lynne Curry

Pornography on Trial, Thomas C. Mackey

Racial Violence on Trial, Christopher Waldrep

Voting Rights on Trial, Charles L. Zelden

Waging War on Trial, Brian R. Dirck

Native American Sovereignty ON TRIAL

A Handbook with Cases, Laws, and Documents

Bryan H. Wildenthal

ABC CLIO

Santa Barbara, California • Denver, Colorado • Oxford, England

Library of Congress Cataloging-in-Publication Data
Wildenthal, Bryan H.
Native American sovereignty on trial : a handbook with cases, laws, and documents / Bryan H. Wildenthal.
p. cm. — (On trial)
Includes bibliographical references and index.
ISBN 1-57607-624-5 (hardcover : alk. paper) ISBN 1-57607-625-3 (e-book)
1. Indians of North America—Legal status, laws, etc. 2. Indians of North America—Legal status, laws, etc.—Cases. I. Title. II. Series.
KF8205.Z9W55 2003
342.73'0872—dc21 2003001840

07 06 05 04 03 10 9 8 7 6 5 4 3 2 1

ABC-CLIO, Inc.
130 Cremona Drive, P.O. Box 1911
Santa Barbara, California 93116-1911

This book is printed on acid-free paper.
Manufactured in the United States of America

Contents

PART TWO

Series Foreword

The volumes in the On Trial series explore the many ways in which the U.S. legal and political system has approached a wide range of complex and divisive legal issues over time—and in the process defined the current state of the law and politics on these issues. The intent is to give students and other general readers a framework for understanding how the law in all its various forms—constitutional, statutory, judicial, political, and customary—has shaped and reshaped the world in which we live today.

At the core of each volume in the series is a common proposition: that in certain key areas of American public life, we as a people and a nation are "on trial" as we struggle to cope with the contradictions, conflicts, and disparities within our society, politics, and culture. Who should decide if and when a woman can have an abortion? What rights, if any, should those with a different sexual orientation be able to claim under the Constitution? Is voting a basic right of citizenship, and if so, under what rules should we organize this right—especially when the application of any organizing rules inevitably results in excluding some citizens from the polls? And what about the many inconsistencies and conflicts associated with racial tensions in the country? These are just some of the complex and controversial issues that we as a people and a nation are struggling to answer—and must answer if we are to achieve an orderly and stable society. For the answers we find to these disputes shape the essence of who we are—as a people, community, and political system.

The concept of being "on trial" also has a second meaning fundamental to this series: the process of litigating important issues in a court of law. Litigation is an essential part of how we settle our differences and make choices as we struggle with the problems that confront us as a people and a nation. In the 1830s, Alexis de Tocqueville noted in his book *Democracy in America*, "There is hardly a political question in the United States which does not sooner or later turn into a judicial one" (Tocqueville 1835, 270). This insight is as true today as it was in the 1830s. In *The Litigious Society*, Jethro K. Lieberman notes: "To express amazement at American litigiousness is akin to professing astonishment at learning that the roots of most Americans lie in other lands. We have been a litigious nation as we have been an immigrant one. Indeed, the two are related" (Lieberman 1983, 13). Arriving in the United States with different backgrounds, customs, and lifestyle preferences, we inevitably clashed as our contrasting visions of life in United States—its culture, society, and politics—collided. And it was to the courts and the law that we turned as a neutral forum for peaceably working out these differences. For, in the United States at least, it is the courthouse that provides the anvil on which our personal, societal, and political problems are hammered out.

The volumes in this series therefore take as their central purpose the important task of exploring the various ways—good and bad, effective and ineffective, complex and simple—in which litigation in the courts has shaped the evolution of particular legal controversies for which we as a people are "on trial." And, more important, the volumes do all this in a manner accessible to the general reader seeking to comprehend the topic as a whole.

These twin goals—analytical and educational—shape the structure and layout of the volumes in the series. Each book consists of two parts. The first provides an explanatory essay in four chapters. Chapter 1 introduces the issues, controversies, events, and participants associated with the legal controversy at hand. Chapter 2 explores the social, economic, political and/or historical background to this topic. Chapter 3 describes in detail the various court decisions and actions that have shaped the current status of the legal controversy under examination. In some cases that will be done through a close examination of a few representative cases; in others by a broader but less detailed narrative of the course of judicial action. Chapter 4 discusses the impact of these cases on U.S. law—their doctrinal legacy—as well as on U.S. society—their historical, sociological, and political legacy.

Part 2, in turn, provides selective supplementary materials designed to help readers more fully comprehend the topics covered in the chapters of Part 1. First are documents aimed at helping the reader better appreciate both the issues and the process by which adjudication shaped these matters. Selected documents might include court opinions (excerpted or whole), interviews, newspaper accounts, or selected secondary essays. Next comes an alphabetically formatted glossary providing entries on the people, laws, cases, and concepts important to an understanding of the topic. A chronology next provides the reader an easily referenced listing of the major developments covered in the book, and a table of cases lists the major court decisions cited. And lastly, an annotated bibliography describes the key works in the field, directing a reader seeking a more detailed examination of the topic to the appropriate sources.

In closing, as you read the books in this series, keep in mind the purposefully controversial nature of the topics covered within. The authors in the series have not chosen easy or agreeable topics to explore. Much of what you read may trouble you, and should. Yet it is precisely these sorts of contentious topics that need the most historical analysis and scrutiny. For it is here that we are still "on trial"—and all too often, as regards these matters, the jury is still out.

Charles L. Zelden
Ft. Lauderdale, Florida

Preface and Acknowledgments

This book is designed to introduce the general university-level or advanced high school reader to the history and status of Native American (American Indian) societies as governmental bodies within the United States and to the law governing this area. Law students and lawyers will also find it a useful general reference work, though not a substitute for the more detailed and technical treatises on American Indian law. It is my hope that it will provide a compelling and accessible introduction to this endlessly fascinating and profoundly important field of law. It is an area laden with a complex and tragic history, incomparably rich with legal, political, sociological, and cultural interest.

In this book, I ultimately seek to tell a story. Storytelling is a central art of most human societies and very distinctively so in Native American communities. Any American, Indian or non-Indian, who is not familiar with at least the basics of the story of Native American sovereignty lacks a full understanding of the nation of which he or she is a citizen and (to borrow from the title of the 1984 book by Vine Deloria, Jr., and Clifford M. Lytle) of "the nations within" that nation.

The book's approach to this dauntingly rich and fascinating subject is necessarily in the form of a selective overview and proceeds in several steps. Part 1 consists of four narrative chapters surveying the background and development of Native American sovereignty. Chapter 1 introduces, in a general way, what "Native American sovereignty" is and how it came to be, that is, what exactly the

Native American nations or tribes are in a legal sense. It also outlines five historic legal controversies that have shaped Native American sovereignty as it exists today. In each of these historic controversies, Native American sovereignty has quite literally been "on trial." The U.S. Supreme Court, as so often with the deepest issues affecting our system of government, has been the ultimate arbiter of these trials, and so U.S. Supreme Court decisions provide the main fodder for discussion. But the Court shares center stage in one of these controversies with state institutions (California and its state supreme court). And in another of these controversies, a Native American tribal court (the Navajo Nation Supreme Court) has emerged, very fittingly, as a major player. (The "Supreme Court," or simply the "Court," when no further specification is provided, refers to the U.S. Supreme Court.)

Chapter 2 of Part 1 surveys the historical background of Native American sovereignty generally to set the stage for what follows. Chapter 3, the heart of the book, then discusses in depth the five historic controversies outlined in Chapter 1. Devoting a section to each, it explores how these controversies arose, analyzes their key issues and players, and critically examines their resolution. Finally, Chapter 4 offers an overview and reflection on these struggles over American Indian sovereignty, asking: What is the legacy of these controversies for our constitutional system? And what does the future hold in store for Indian tribal governments?

Part 2 provides background reference materials to be consulted at any appropriate point while reading Part 1. It includes a chronology of key events and the actual text of the key legal documents discussed in Part 1. I recommend that the reader tackle the documents pertaining to each section of Chapter 3 *after* reading each relevant section or whenever doing so is suggested within each section. Part 2 also features a glossary explaining and summarizing key concepts, laws, cases, and people. Whenever you encounter a legal term or other specialized word with which you may be unfamiliar, please check the glossary. Part 2 concludes with an annotated bibliography, a comprehensive table of all laws and cases cited, and a general index.

A digression on terminology is necessary. I use "Native American" and "American Indian" (or "Indian" for short, since it should be understood that I am not referring to Indians from South Asia) fairly interchangeably throughout the book. Both terms are, strictly speaking, somewhat inaccurate, imprecise, and problematical.

Non-Indians often assume that Indians prefer "Native American," but in fact that is not usually true. "Indian" is far more commonly used by Indians themselves. Both terms are considered broadly acceptable and not offensive to most. Although "Native American" has a "progressive" or "politically correct" ring to many non-Indian ears, however, some Indians object to what they see as its assimilationist implications. I must stress that I use both terms simply as a recognition of their wide current use, with no ideological implications intended.

"American Indian" is generally understood to refer to the descendants of the peoples indigenous (at the time of Columbus's voyage in 1492) to what are now the mainland "lower forty-eight" United States. "Native American" (and the unqualified terms "Indian" or "native") may be more broadly construed to include the indigenous peoples of Alaska (usually referred to as "Alaska Natives," "Eskimo" having fallen out of favor) and Hawaii (usually referred to as "Native Hawaiians"), and also Canada, Mexico, and other nations of North, Central, and South America. "First Nations" is an increasingly popular term, originating as a reference to the native peoples of Canada. "Indigenous peoples" is itself an attractive and useful term, though it might refer very broadly to the original peoples (typically conquered or colonized by Europeans or others) of lands anywhere on Earth, such as the Aborigines of Australia, the Maori of New Zealand, the Khoisan of South Africa, the native Siberian peoples of eastern Russia, and so on. This book generally does not venture beyond the Indian experience within the mainland lower forty-eight United States.

It should also be noted that American Indians typically describe their own societies as "nations," a usage entirely sensible and appropriate (and not at all vainglorious or "politically correct," as some might suppose) on various legal, political, and historical grounds, as this book discusses throughout. The terms "tribe" and "tribal" are also commonly used to describe Native American societies and governments. This latter usage is certainly troubling. I myself (like many others, Indian and non-Indian) find it rather condescending and even pejorative. But it is so widely used (including by most Indians themselves) as to be effectively unavoidable. It also has the virtue of providing a short and simple term to clearly distinguish American Indian governments from "federal" and "state" governments in the United States. The tripartite federal-tribal-state structure of U.S. politics is a recurrent theme of this book. So, with these caveats understood, "tribe" and "tribal" are used freely here.

One challenge in writing any book focusing on Indian matters generally is that generalizations are hazardous and often misleading. American Indian nations constitute more than 300 different tribes (in the lower forty-eight states) legally recognized as such by the U.S. government. These communities are vastly diverse in geography, culture, and language, often as different from each other as any one of them is from European American society. Most, though not all, have their own territories within the various states (in a few cases stretching over state lines), generally referred to as "reservations." Collectively, the land within the boundaries of Indian reservations is generally referred to as "Indian country." Additional Indian tribes exist that, for various reasons, are no longer legally recognized as such. Since this book focuses on the legal relationship between established Indian tribes and the federal and state governments, the latter groups are mostly not dealt with here. It would be hopeless for a book of this sort to try to survey the social geography of the tribes. Although the book discusses and refers to many specific tribes involved in various legal controversies, the goal is always to draw broader insights applicable to the U.S.-Indian relationship in general. Students desiring more understanding of Native American cultures may refer to many of the books and articles cited in the notes following the various chapters.

How did I come to write this book? I myself am not a Native American in any meaningful sense, being primarily of English, German, Scottish, and Irish stock. Like so many Americans, however, I do have some Indian ancestry; it appears from a recently discovered family tree on my mother's side, impossible to verify or disprove at this late date, that I am one-sixty-fourth Cherokee. And like so many Americans, regardless of ancestry, I have long felt a haunting fascination with the original peoples and nations of this continent that my European ancestors invaded and conquered. At Stanford Law School I was inspired by the Federal Indian Law course taught in 1987 by Adjunct Professor (and Indian law practitioner) Logan Slagle. Having long been interested in constitutional law and the freedoms of speech and religion, I leaped at Professor Paul Finkelman's invitation (in 1995, when he and I were visiting professors at Illinois Institute of Technology, Chicago-Kent

College of Law) to coauthor a chapter on Native American religious rights in his edited volume, *Religion and American Law: An Encyclopedia* (New York: Garland, 2000). No sooner had I joined the faculty of Thomas Jefferson School of Law in San Diego in 1996 (where I still teach) than our enthusiastic dean, Kenneth J. Vandevelde (aware of my work in the area and himself a former practitioner of Indian law) encouraged me to teach the Federal Indian Law course that our students had recently petitioned the school to offer. And I did so that very autumn of 1996.

The rest, as they say, is history. I have enjoyed the course (now called American Indian Law) more every time I've taught it. Teaching in this field as a non-Indian "outsider" has its challenges. These include constantly educating myself about the ways in which Indians themselves experience and view the legal issues affecting their lives and avoiding the ever-present danger of projecting my own non-Indian assumptions. But I try to use my personal detachment to foster a rigorously critical and objective approach to the subject. I have found it rewarding beyond measure to convey to my students the enthusiasm and fascination I feel for this subject. It is of central importance to U.S. history, and I think an understanding of it is essential to a full appreciation of U.S. constitutional law (another of my primary teaching and scholarly interests, along with the law of sexual identity and gay, lesbian, bisexual, and transgender rights) and indeed of U.S. law and history generally.

Every author has the pleasant duty of acknowledging those without whom the book could never have been written. First on the list must be Professor Charles Zelden of Nova Southeastern University, who invited me to write the thing in the first place. He, as the "On Trial" series editor, along with Alicia Merritt and Melanie Stafford at ABC-CLIO, have been the sort of editors every author dreams about: patient, helpful, supportive, and constantly encouraging. I also thank Toki Sandoval (J.D., Thomas Jefferson School of Law, 2002) for her assistance with checking citations. She and my uncle (and fellow sometime law teacher) Bill Lockhart reviewed parts of the manuscript for readability and offered several helpful suggestions. I am also grateful to all the students in my Indian law classes since 1996, who have constantly rekindled my enthusiasm for the subject, as well as to my fellow parishioners at First Unitarian Universalist Church of San Diego, who participated in a discussion I led on Indian law and history at our church camp retreat at De Benneville Pines in June 2002. In all my endeavors, I have had the unstinting love and support of a wide circle of family and friends, including (but not limited to) my parents, Joyce and Hobson; my sisters and brothers, Becky, Lora, Kerry, Andrea, Carl, and Larry; and (especially for their hospitality as I stayed with them in West Texas over the summer of 2002 while finishing the manuscript), my Uncle Bill and Aunt Mary Bell.

Last but not least, I dedicate this book to Patricia Nell Warren (a.k.a. Badger Woman): friend, writer, artist, Montana ranch girl, Earth mother; descendant of Irish, Germans, Melungeons, and American Indians (including both Cherokee and Lakota); and all-around inspiration . . . for teaching me about the circle of law and so much more.

Bryan H. Wildenthal
San Diego, California, and Alpine, Texas

Part One

Old Grandma shook her head slowly, and closed her cloudy eyes again. . . . "It seems like I already heard these stories before . . . only thing is, the names sound different."

—**Leslie Marmon Silko,** ***Ceremony***

1
Introduction

The origins and development of Native American (American Indian) sovereignty in the United States form an essential part of U.S. history and are necessary for a full understanding of U.S. law. The survival of Indian sovereignty in the United States today is one of the most fascinating paradoxes of our history and law.

What exactly is "Native American sovereignty" and how did it come to be? What exactly are the Native American nations or tribes, in the eyes of the law? The term "tribe" suggests a mere private association defined by membership, yet (as we shall see) American Indian communities have always been (and remain) much more than that. They are often referred to (especially by themselves) as "nations," and indeed they are the legal descendants and cousins of foreign states or nations as known under international law and still retain some of those attributes. And yet (as we shall see) they have long been much less than that.

The American Indian tribes are part of and subordinate to the nation or polity we know as the United States of America. They are ultimately subject, like all people, governments, and private entities within the boundaries of the United States, to federal law. And yet they are not states like California or Michigan. Nor are they counties or cities or other units of local government, nor U.S. "territories" like Guam, nor U.S. "commonwealths" like Puerto Rico or the Northern Mariana Islands. They stand within the territorial boundaries of the states, as any child perusing a map can see. The acreage of the various tribal reservations is counted as part of the land area of the various states in which they are located. And tribal members or citizens are today (though they have not always been) full-fledged voting citizens of both the United States and of the states wherein they reside.

And yet, the tribes also stand apart from the states—and in some ways, even from the United States itself. Although now subject to state law in some respects, they are historically immune from state authority in many important ways. They each enact, enforce, and follow their own tribal laws to deal with most local issues that would otherwise be covered by state law. And even though they have long been subject to the ultimate power of federal law on issues within the national government's powers, they are *not* (paradoxical and amazing though it may seem) directly subject to some of the most important provisions of the U.S. Constitution itself.

Specifically, tribal governments are not directly subject to the individual rights set forth in the Constitution, most notably in the Bill of Rights (the first ten constitutional amendments adopted in 1791). Those guarantees apply only to the federal government created by the Constitution and (for the most part, under the Fourteenth Amendment adopted in 1868) to the states that entered into the Constitution. The tribal governments (or their ancestors) existed before the formation of the federal and state governments and do not derive their powers from the Constitution that was adopted without consulting them. It is important to be precise about these matters. It is sometimes loosely said that the Constitution and the Bill of Rights do not apply to Indians or on Indian reservations, but that is not true. The Constitution as a framework of governmental powers most certainly *does* apply, in all respects. And the individual rights guaranteed by the Constitution and Bill of Rights also apply, but only (directly) as limitations on federal or state powers exercised within Indian country, not as limitations on tribal powers. Congress can, however, limit tribal powers by statute and has done so on numerous occasions. For example, by federal law enacted in 1968, Congress did in fact impose most Bill of Rights guarantees as limitations on tribal power.

Although one can no longer realistically say that the tribes enjoy a status generally superior to the states, it would be a mistake to classify them as generally subordinate to the states. Indeed, the tribes still enjoy some powers that state governments have never had under the Constitution. Most notably, they enjoy the classically sovereign power to control travel and immigration by non-Indians into Indian lands, to exclude and expel nonmembers of the tribe as they see fit, and to control who qualifies to be or become a tribal member and how. By contrast, the states are forbidden under the Constitution from prohibiting or even taxing travel or migration across state lines, and they have no control over state citizenship. Under the Fourteenth Amendment, any U.S. citizen choosing to move to a state and set up domicile there becomes automatically entitled to citizenship in that state. Tribal powers in this area are much more akin to the federal government's powers over immigration, naturalization, and international travel.

The tribes, thus, are clearly governments in some sense. They enjoy, to some degree, that quality of governments known to lawyers as "sovereignty" (which basically means "the power to govern"). But why do such sovereign bodies exist within our constitutional framework? What defines them? What exactly are their powers? Exactly whom and what do they govern? What defines the limits of their powers—territory, membership, or (as we shall see) a perplexing combination of both? Will they persist within this nation's constitutional and political structure? Should they?

It is best to begin with the basic structure of the U.S. Constitution. Most U.S. schoolchildren are taught that the Constitution defines a two-tier federal-state system, with the national or federal government at the top and the state governments as component parts below. The federal government enjoys the full sovereignty possessed by any independent nation under international law. The state governments possess a reservoir of limited state sovereignty, to the extent they have not delegated certain powers to the federal government. Keep in mind that the original thirteen colonies broke free from Great Britain not as a single unified nation but, in the words of the Declaration of Independence in 1776, as "Free and Independent States." They did not formally yield any of their full original sovereignty until the Articles of Confederation (drafted in 1777) were ratified in 1781. That first, weak central government of the United States was then replaced by the Constitution drafted at the Philadelphia Convention of 1787, which took effect in 1789. Indeed, the states of Vermont and Texas, as their citizens often proudly note, each existed for about a decade as independent republics before yielding their full sovereignty to join the Union (in 1791 and 1845, respectively).

This standard account, however, leaves a gaping omission. What about the American Indian tribes? Where do they fit in? They also possessed full sovereignty as independent nations, until they were forcibly deprived of it by the European powers that conquered the New World. The United States, upon its independence, inherited Great Britain's claim to ultimate sovereignty over the Indian tribes then within its territory and later inherited similar claims over tribes occupying lands ceded by France, Spain, and Mexico. Chief Justice John Marshall articulated what came to be known as the "Discovery Doctrine"—describing this basic trumping of full Native American sovereignty upon the "discovery" of the New World by the Europeans—in the foundational Supreme Court decisions of *Johnson v. M'Intosh* (1823), *Cherokee Nation v. Georgia* (1831), and *Worcester v. Georgia* (1832).

But the American Indian nations still retain a part of the full sovereignty they once possessed. That is what we now refer to as Native American (or American Indian or tribal) sovereignty, which this book is devoted to exploring. As the Supreme Court has summarized:

> The powers of Indian tribes are, in general, "*inherent powers of a limited sovereignty which has never been extinguished*" (Cohen 1941, 122; emphasis by Cohen).
>
> Indian tribes are, of course, no longer "possessed of the full attributes of sovereignty" (*United States v. Kagama* 1886, 381). . . .
>
> The sovereignty that [they] retain is of a unique and limited character. It exists only at the sufferance of Congress and is subject to complete defeasance. But until Congress acts, the tribes retain their existing sovereign powers. In sum, Indian tribes still possess those aspects of sovereignty not withdrawn by treaty or statute, or by implication as a necessary result of their dependent status. (*United States v. Wheeler* 1978, 322–323)

As the Court has pointed out on several occasions, American Indians were not parties to the Constitutional Convention of 1787. Like women and African Americans, they had no voice in framing or agreeing to the founding documents of the United States. Indeed, one finds in the Constitution, as in the Articles of Confederation before it, no explicit recognition of the tribes as a part of our governmental structure and little mention of them at all. But the Indians, like the African slaves who were subjected to the Constitution's fugitive slave clause (U.S. Const., art. IV, § 2, cl. 3), were not ignored altogether. A careful reading reveals hints about their status.

The Articles of Confederation contained two brief references to Indians. Although generally prohibiting individual states from engaging in war "without the consent of the United States in Congress assembled," the Articles allowed self-defense in cases of "imminent" danger, such as when a state learns "of a resolution being formed by some nation of Indians to invade such state" (Art. Conf., art. VI). This clause is noteworthy for its use of the term "nation." The Articles also gave Congress the power of "regulating the trade and managing all affairs with the Indians" (Art. Conf., art. IX).

In the Constitution, instead of being defined (like slaves) as "three-fifths" of a person for purposes of apportioning "representatives and direct taxes," the Indians were "exclud[ed]" altogether from the basis of apportionment. And this exclusion seemed to offer some kind of recognition of their politically distinct status because the clause described them as "not taxed" (U.S. Const., art. I, § 2, cl. 3), perhaps in keeping with the well-known cry of "no taxation without representation."

We next see a reference to the Native Americans in the clause of the Constitution granting Congress the power "[t]o regulate commerce with foreign Nations, and among the several States, and with the Indian Tribes" (U.S. Const., art. I, § 8, cl. 3). This mention of the tribes is especially interesting. Not only is the organized, communal status of the Indians as "tribes" explicitly recognized, but they seem to be treated as comparable to "foreign nations" and the "states." It does not seem a terrible stretch to take this language (in combination with the earlier language in the Articles of Confederation) as an implicit recognition, by the white men gathered in Philadelphia, of some form of Native American sovereignty.

It is also noteworthy that the Constitution expressly grants the president the "power, by and with the advice and consent of the Senate, to make treaties" (U.S. Const., art. II, § 2, cl. 2). Under the supremacy clause (U.S. Const., art. VI, cl. 2), all such treaties, upon ratification by the Senate, have the full force of federal law, becoming part of "the supreme law of the land" and trumping any contrary state law. As the Framers in 1787 knew full well, the United States was already in the regular business of making treaties with those very same "Indian tribes" referred to elsewhere in the same document.

And with whom else does one make a treaty but a sovereign government of some kind? Indeed, the United States had just negotiated in 1785 the very important Treaty of Hopewell with the Cherokee Nation, one of seven treaties with Indian tribes concluded prior to the 1787 convention. The supremacy clause was carefully worded to include "all treaties made, or which shall be made, under the authority of the United States," precisely in order to remove any doubts about the continuing legal force of treaties entered into prior to the adoption of the Constitution.

Beyond these references, however, the Constitution falls silent on the subject of the Indians. The only later mention is in the Fourteenth Amendment, ratified in 1868, which repeated the reference to "Indians not taxed" in the context of congressional apportionment (U.S. Const., amend. XIV, § 2). As discussed in Chapter 2, those particular provisions were later rendered obsolete by the conferral of U.S. citizenship on Indians.

How has Native American sovereignty developed and evolved from these beginnings? The five historic controversies chosen as the focus of this book illustrate and dramatize that process. The following is a summary outline; details are left to the full treatment set forth in Chapter 3, which builds on the historical background set forth in Chapter 2. This account describes, in many ways, a one-way journey of continual encroachment and ever-tightening limitations on a narrowing domain of residual Indian tribal sovereignty. But some of these controversies have also involved defiant assertions of renewed and reinvigorated American Indian sovereignty. The ultimate outcome remains very much in doubt. But the sheer survival of Indian sovereignty in the United States up to the present day is a stunning, remarkable fact.

Laying the Foundation: Chief Justice Marshall and the Cherokee Cases

The Cherokee Cases of 1831–1832 brought to a head the first great legal and constitutional crisis over the competing rights to the land of the Native Americans and the European-American settlers. The cases were about not just property ownership but, more fundamentally, sovereignty—the power to *govern* the land and its inhabitants. The immediate cause of the crisis was the desire of white settlers for the rich Appalachian lands claimed by the Cherokee Nation, at one time extending to parts of what are now Kentucky, Tennessee, Alabama, Georgia, South Carolina, North Carolina, and Virginia. Cherokee rights to much of this land were guaranteed by the Treaty of Hopewell in 1785, one of the first treaties entered into by the United States following the conclusion of the war of independence from Great Britain by the Treaty of Paris in 1783.

Later treaties between the Cherokee and the United States reaffirmed Cherokee rights to an ever-dwindling area of their ancestral domain (most of it in northern Georgia) while yielding up portions of it under pressure from constant encroachments and treaty violations by white settlers. In the late 1820s, the Cherokee adoption of a national constitution and the discovery of gold on Cherokee land led to a dramatic escalation of the conflict. Georgia asserted direct state power over the area. Congress passed and President Andrew Jackson signed the Removal Act of 1830. This federal law did not, however, purport to abrogate any of the Cherokee treaties. It merely authorized a grant of federal territorial land west of the Mississippi (the "Indian Territory" in what is now Oklahoma) to any Indians who "may choose to exchange the lands where they now reside, and remove there."

The Cherokee did not so "choose," but faced with menacing state neighbors and a hostile president and Congress, their only recourse was to turn to the third branch of the government with which they had dealt as a fellow sovereign for almost fifty years: the Supreme Court, led by Chief Justice John Marshall. *Cherokee Nation v. Georgia* (1831) and *Worcester v. Georgia* (1832) thus posed a direct conflict between the sovereignty and power of the state of Georgia and the Cherokee Nation. The Cherokee did not directly confront the power of the United States itself in these cases. On the contrary, they relied on federal power in the form of the federal treaty guarantees.

Marshall's opinions in the Cherokee Cases may be viewed, at least in the context of his society and time, as a thoughtful and courageous defense of Native American sovereignty, albeit in limited form. After initially rebuffing the Cherokee appeal in the *Cherokee Nation* case, he and his Court awarded a dramatic legal victory to the Cherokee in *Worcester.* He defined Indian tribes as "domestic dependent nations" entitled to territorial integrity, political self-government, and legal immunity from intrusions of state power.

But Marshall also recognized sweeping *federal* power over the tribes and their relationships with both the state and federal governments. Indeed, his opinions can largely be viewed within the context of other great decisions of the Marshall Court, which decisively subordinated state to federal power, generally expanded the prerogatives of the federal government, and specifically asserted the power and independence of the federal courts. This federal power would come to be viewed as "plenary" (meaning "total" or "unlimited") in the field of Indian affairs, and it carried with it the seeds of the later erosion of Native American sovereignty and the constant threat of its total extinction.

To the extent that the Cherokee Cases ruled against Georgia and upheld Cherokee sovereignty, they went tragically unenforced at the time. The infamous Trail of Tears ensued, which forced most of the Cherokee people to Oklahoma and led eventually to the loss of most of their sovereign tribal powers. But the principles Chief Justice Marshall set forth were vindicated in the court of history. They laid the foundation for the legal framework that has governed, ever since, the triangular relationship of the states, the tribes, and the federal government and their respective rights, powers, and duties toward each other.

Indian Treaty Rights

The Cherokee Cases laid the basic foundation for Native American sovereignty and American Indian law generally. Chief Justice Marshall's opinion in *Worcester* was, in particular, the classic and prototypical model of Indian treaty interpretation by the Supreme Court. He pioneered what became known as the "canons of construction," under which Native American treaty rights have (at least in theory) been generously construed in their favor and strictly against the unnecessary erosion of tribal sovereignty. This approach has (with notable omissions and deviations) spilled over into the interpretation of most laws affecting Indians. Closely related to the canons of construction is the notion that the U.S. government has a "trust relationship" with Indian nations, in which it is supposed to act as "trustee" for their interests.

The Supreme Court ruled in *Lone Wolf v. Hitchcock* (1903) that Congress has the ultimate, so-called plenary power to abrogate Indian treaties, without (or so it appeared at the time) any limits or duty of compensation. Treaty making with the Indian tribes had ceased altogether in 1871, although treaties ratified before then remain valid until and unless abrogated. Congress later offered by statute to provide some compensation for takings of Indian land and other property interests, instituting a claims process that has proved, at best, only partly satisfactory.

The potential and limits of this claims and compensation process were illustrated by the 1980 Supreme Court decision in *United States v. Sioux Nation*, which upheld a monetary award for the seizure of treaty-guaranteed land encompassing much of South Dakota. The Sioux have thus far refused to collect on the judgment, finding it no substitute for at least a partial recognition of their rights under the Fort Laramie Treaty of 1868. Another 1868 treaty, with the Navajo (Diné) Nation, has enjoyed greater durability and continues to provide the basis for the vigorous modern assertions of tribal sovereignty by the Navajo. One such treaty-based assertion, dealing with tribal criminal jurisdiction over nonmembers of the tribe, is discussed below and in the third section of Chapter 3.

The Supreme Court's interpretation of Native American treaty rights has taken a meandering and inconsistent course in the 170 years since the Cherokee Cases, especially toward the end of the twentieth century. Some decisions, even dating back a century or more, have construed treaty provisions with surprising breadth and firmness, notably in the area of hunting and fishing rights. Other decisions, even in modern times, especially those dealing with land rights and jurisdiction over nonmembers of tribes, have arguably failed to honor the canons of construction. A common bone of contention has been the impact on treaty rights of the sovereign powers assumed by states upon their admission to the Union on an "equal footing" with other states.

Against this backdrop, the Court's 1999 decision in *Minnesota v. Mille Lacs Band of Chippewa Indians* took on an importance going beyond the seemingly narrow issues it raised concerning hunting, fishing, and gathering rights under an 1837 treaty. The Court was tugged in opposite directions by the tensions of its earlier case law. As it happened, a 5–4 majority ruled in favor of the Indian treaty rights, thus suggesting at least the possibility of stronger enforcement of such rights in the twenty-first century.

Tribal Criminal Jurisdiction

One area in which Native American sovereignty has been most sharply curtailed in modern times—and controversially so—is tribal criminal jurisdiction over non-Indians and over Indians who happen to be members of other tribes. The infamous 1978 Supreme Court case of *Oliphant v. Suquamish Indian Tribe* held that criminal prosecution of non-Indians was always outside the inherent sovereign powers of the tribes, as limited under Marshall's conception of their status as "domestic dependent nations."

In *Duro v. Reina* (1990), the Court compounded what many scholars view as the error of *Oliphant* by holding that inherent tribal criminal jurisdiction did not extend to Indians of other tribes, even when they reside within the reservation of the prosecuting tribe and commit crimes against tribal members. This decision posed a very serious threat to effective law enforcement in Indian country. Congress quickly purported to reverse by statute the effect of the *Duro* decision, but that "*Duro* fix" has only raised new issues.

The Navajo Nation Supreme Court confronted the issues raised by *Oliphant* and *Duro* in its landmark 1999 decision in *Means v. Chinle District Court,* possibly the most important decision ever issued by a tribal court. The question raised was whether the Navajo Nation could lawfully prosecute Russell Means, the well-known American Indian activist and member of the Oglala Sioux Nation, for a crime allegedly committed within the Navajo Nation against (in part) a Navajo tribal member. The Navajo court upheld tribal jurisdiction, partly on the basis of a broad reading of the Navajo-U.S. Treaty of 1868. The U.S. Supreme Court will eventually have the final word on the limits of tribal power, but the Navajo Supreme Court's decision was a bold and pathmarking contribution to this vexing debate.

Tribal Civil Jurisdiction

The civil or regulatory jurisdiction of Native American governments has generally fared better than tribal criminal jurisdiction. The Supreme Court's decision in *Williams v. Lee* (1959) dramatically reaffirmed the foundational tribal sovereignty principles of Chief Justice Marshall's opinions in the Cherokee Cases. *Williams* upheld exclusive tribal jurisdiction over civil lawsuits against Indians arising within Indian country (including suits brought by non-Indians) that would otherwise be litigated in state court. This case was especially significant coming during the 1950s, an era when the notion of terminating tribal sovereignty altogether was again enjoying a brief heyday in Congress.

The Supreme Court, in the decades since *Williams,* has often upheld tribal jurisdiction to tax, regulate, and exercise jurisdiction over civil lawsuits, even those involving non-Indians, regarding activities within Indian country that affect tribal members. But the Court's denial in *Oliphant* of tribal criminal jurisdiction over non-Indians has had increasingly important spillover effects in the area of tribal civil jurisdiction over nonmembers. The Court's decision in *Montana v. United States* (1981) appears especially pivotal in retrospect. The *Montana* case rejected a tribe's power to regulate hunting and fishing by non-Indians on non-Indian-owned land within the reservation and seemed to reverse the historic presumption in favor of tribal sovereignty unless and until clearly taken away by treaty or statute.

An especially troubling application of *Montana* was the Court's splintered decision in *Brendale v. Yakima Indian Nation* (1989), which severely undermined tribal authority over land-use zoning on the reservation. The Court's unanimous decision in *Strate v. A-1 Contractors* (1997) was another important step in this post-*Oliphant* trend. *Strate* involved a lawsuit against non-Indian defendants over an accident on a state highway within reservation boundaries. The decision extended and solidified the new presumption against tribal jurisdiction over nonmembers in many circumstances. Although *Williams* upheld exclusive tribal civil jurisdiction over the lawsuit involved in that case, *Strate* rejected even concurrent tribal jurisdiction, instead ruling in favor of exclusive state court jurisdiction.

Although *Montana, Brendale,* and *Strate* marked a substantial erosion of Native American sovereignty, they pale in comparison to the Court's recent decision in *Nevada v. Hicks* (2001), probably the most important Indian law case in the quarter century since *Oliphant. Hicks* held that a tribal court lacked jurisdiction over a civil lawsuit against non-Indian state officers, even though the suit involved allegedly lawless conduct by the officers against an Indian in his own home on reservation property otherwise fully subject to normal tribal sovereignty. The Court held that states have "inherent" authority in some circumstances to extend their official power into Indian country, free of any tribal regulation. The majority's reasoning appeared to threaten tribal civil jurisdiction over all non-Indians, state officers or not. The decision exhibited little respect or even understanding of time-honored principles of Indian law and suggested that the boundaries of Native American sovereignty may have entered a new era of increased instability. How far-reaching the ramifications of *Hicks* will be, however, remains unclear.

Tribal Gambling

Tribal authority to conduct gambling operations has become one of the hottest legal controversies of recent years. The modern development of this issue, which combines some of the most difficult issues of state and tribal criminal and civil jurisdiction, began with the Supreme Court's decision in *California v. Cabazon Band of Mission Indians* (1987). Although Indian gambling has exploded in many states around the country, it is useful to focus on the progress of the issue in California. As the most populous state in the nation, with a large number of historically impoverished Native American tribes, California has become a test case for whether legalized gambling may be the long-term economic development boon for Indians that many have predicted.

The *Cabazon* case opened the door to certain forms of legalized gambling within California's Indian country (and nationwide). Congress passed the Indian Gaming Regulatory Act (IGRA) in 1988 to codify and clarify the reach of the *Cabazon* holding. A critical feature of IGRA seemed to require states that did not totally prohibit high-stakes gambling to negotiate compacts with any Indian tribes that might wish to conduct such operations, up to and including full-blown "Nevada-style" casinos.

Two critical developments during the 1990s, however, seemed to severely undermine the promise of *Cabazon* and IGRA for the tribes. First, the Supreme Court ruled, under the theory of state sovereign immunity, that tribes could not sue states to enforce IGRA requirements. Second, some lower courts held (in decisions the Supreme Court declined to review) that a state's duty of negotiation under IGRA was very narrow and extended only to those specific types of gambling that the state *already* allowed anyway.

In California, as the 1990s went on, Indian governments that had been conducting post-*Cabazon* gaming operations (in many cases of doubtful legality) faced a frustrating situation. Governor Pete Wilson refused to negotiate compacts authorizing tribal casino operations. Existing tribal games faced the threat of closure. The tribes then turned to the voters of California via the state's famous initiative and referendum process. The result was a series of stunning victories for Indian gaming.

In November 1998, California voters elected Governor Gray Davis, a pro-Indian-gaming candidate, by a landslide. And by an even greater landslide, they passed Proposition 5, the "Indian Self-Reliance" statutory initiative, which endorsed a model state-tribal compact allowing certain kinds of high-stakes tribal gambling. Then, in *Hotel Employees Union v. Davis* (1999), the California Supreme Court struck down Proposition 5 as a violation of the California Constitution. The 6–1 decision, especially Justice Joyce L. Kennard's lone dissent, highlighted some of the fascinating dilemmas posed by the interaction of the gambling issue with the background principles of Native American sovereignty.

In any event, the ironic and unintended result of the *Davis* decision was to open the door even wider to tribal gaming. The model compact embodied in Proposition 5 would supposedly have drawn a line short of outright "Nevada-style" casino gambling on California Indian reservations. With Proposition 5 set aside, however, Governor Davis negotiated a new compact with California's gaming tribes, which the voters ratified by passing a state constitutional amendment, Proposition 1A, by an even wider landslide margin in the March 2000 election.

The new California-tribal compact allows almost all forms of casino gambling on tribal lands and has led to a boom in reservation casino operations, with no end in sight. For better or worse, California's voters—in a remarkable exercise of democratic power—have given the green light to an experiment in tribal economic development that could have vast national repercussions. It is a profoundly ironic closing of the circle that the doctrine of Native American sovereignty—first defined by struggles against the non-Indian voters and political leaders of Georgia in the Cherokee Cases—has now received a dramatic boost from the non-Indian voters and political leaders of California at the turn of the twenty-first century.

References and Further Reading

See the listing at the end of Chapter 2 for sources and further reading pertaining generally to American Indian law and history and generally informing Chapters 1 and 2 and the Chronology in Part 2. Sources pertaining more particularly to the five controversies outlined in this chapter are set forth at the end of Chapter 3.

2
Historical Background

When the nation-states of Europe—most notably Spain, France, and Great Britain—began their conquest of the Western Hemisphere in 1492, they each had to grapple with the issue of how to deal with the numerous distinct communities of human beings then populating the Americas. One cliché (less than accurate, of course, though not without a grain of truth) is that the Spanish sought mainly to kill them off, the French to intermarry with them, and the British to take their land. That is perhaps too hard on the Spanish, whose formerly colonized lands (along with formerly Portuguese Brazil) today contain vastly greater and more influential populations of Native Americans (or people partaking heavily of such ancestry) than do the areas colonized by their northern European neighbors. For example, Alejandro Toledo, an Andean Indian, was recently elected president of Peru. It is certainly too easy on the British, whose record contains brutality and coercion to rival Spain's. For that matter, contrary to some patronizing and romanticized accounts, brutality and violence were hardly unknown among the Native Americans, who frequently warred with each other before and after Europeans arrived on the scene and sometimes gave as good as they got to their European adversaries afterward.

The European powers hungered for American land and the mineral and agricultural riches it contained. They worked ceaselessly, by whatever means seemed most convenient, to obtain and secure it. The Indians were viewed by many Europeans as objects for religious conversion, in line with the prevailing, proselytizing theology of

Christianity. But many Europeans cared more for material than spiritual matters, focusing on land, power, and gold. Indeed, one need not be a cynic to estimate that they were in the vast majority, starting with Christopher Columbus himself. They viewed the Indians simply as obstacles to be exterminated or, at the very least, pushed out of the way.

It is beyond the scope of this book to attempt any in-depth historical survey of the almost incredibly rich, fascinating, and tragic history of European–Native American interaction. The Chronology provided in Part 2 sketches the basic sequence of events. Interested students may go from there to the sources noted at the end of this chapter. It suffices here to summarize those aspects of the history necessary to place in context the development of the law of American Indian sovereignty.

Human beings seem to have a deep-seated need to justify their actions, and law is a primary means for us to formulate and codify rationales for what we do. Thus, it is not surprising that Europeans, almost as soon as word of Columbus's encounter spread, began debating the philosophical and legal implications of the impending conquest of America and its native peoples. And this was, at its core, a religious debate. Robert A. Williams, Jr., in his brilliant study *The American Indian in Western Legal Thought: The Discourses of Conquest* (1990), has demonstrated that it is impossible to fully understand modern American Indian law without considering the religious Crusades launched by Christian Europeans against the Muslims of the Middle East, as long before Columbus sailed as we now stand after his voyages.

Lest this focus seem unduly Eurocentric, it should be noted that American Indians doubtless began philosophical debates among themselves, at the same time or soon after, about how to respond to the European invaders. Sadly, because the Indians then had no written historical tradition, those debates are mostly invisible to us today. More crudely, one might note that the European debate is more salient today since European power and force prevailed. Our task is to dissect and understand—and, of course, criticize where appropriate—the legal regime that has in fact governed European–Native American relations and still does so today. And the fact is, for better or worse, it is a legal regime created and imposed mostly by white men long dead. Even those who would therefore reject the entire edifice as illegitimate need to study it, for one cannot effectively oppose or criticize without understanding.

European Christians during the time of the Crusades felt that they had a legal and moral entitlement to conquer peoples who did not share their religious beliefs—people therefore deemed "infidels" or "pagans"—and to rule their lands. This attitude fit rather neatly with the prevailing belief that earthly kings and rulers governed only by "divine right." The Roman Catholic popes during this era occasionally issued edicts authorizing wars or crusades against "infidels" to be carried out by various Christian rulers who had the military means to do so. Although the Crusades against Islam ended in the thirteenth century, similar religious and legal theories were applied to the New World.

In 1493, the year after Columbus's first voyage, Pope Alexander VI issued an edict purporting to grant Spain the exclusive right to colonize most of the Americas. On the basis of this papal order, the Spanish government in 1513 concocted a document known as the *Requerimiento* (Requirement), which was formally required "to be read aloud to any group of Indians newly discovered . . . before any hostilities could legally be commenced against them in the New World." The *Requerimiento* informed the Indians that God had granted governance of "the whole human race" to the pope in Rome, who had in turn "donated" their lands to the rulers of Spain:

> Wherefore . . . we ask and require that you consider what we have said to you, and that you take the time that shall be necessary to understand and deliberate upon it. . . . But if you do not do this or if you maliciously delay in doing it, I certify to you that with the help of God we shall forcefully enter into your country and shall make war against you in all ways and manners that we can, and shall subject you to the yoke and obedience of the Church and of their highnesses [the Spanish rulers]; we shall take you and your wives and your children and shall make slaves of them, and as such shall sell and dispose of them as their highnesses may command; and we shall take away your goods and shall do to you all the harm and damage that we can, . . . and we protest that the deaths and losses which shall accrue from this are your fault, and not that of their highnesses, of ours, or of these soldiers who come with us. And that we have said this to you and made this *Requerimiento* we request the notary here present to give us his testimony in writing, and we ask the rest who are present that they should be witnesses of this *Requerimiento.* (Getches, Wilkinson, and Williams 1998, 47–48; Williams 1990, 88–93)

Williams, quoting historian Lewis Hanke, noted that the manner in which the *Requerimiento* was executed "might tax the reader's patience and credulity, for [it] was read to trees and empty huts when no Indians were to be found. Captains muttered its theological phrases into their beard on the edge of sleeping Indian settlements, or even a league away before starting the formal attack" (Williams 1990, 92). One doubts, in any event, that it was often (if ever) translated into any language understood by the Indians.

The holocaust of enslavement, disease, and mass murder that swept across the natives of the West Indies in the early years of European colonization, beginning with Columbus's governorship of Hispaniola, was so horrific as almost to defy imagination. Entire tribes were wiped out, and the final death toll may have been in the millions, rivaling in scale the worst mass killings of the twentieth century. This barbarity did not go unchallenged at the time. Catholic Dominican clergymen (ironically, the order feared as the most harshly orthodox proponents of the Spanish Inquisition) landed in Hispaniola in 1510 and promptly condemned the blatant cruelties of the profit-driven settlers. The Dominican priest Bartolomé de las Casas, the first Christian cleric to be ordained in the New World, returned to Spain and made a career of chronicling and protesting the rapacious conduct he had witnessed. Las Casas condemned the *Requerimiento* as "diabolical and most unrighteous" (Williams 1990, 173).

Even the most humane and liberal Christian thinkers of the time tended, however, to endorse the European powers' ultimate right to colonize and rule the American Indians. Franciscus de Victoria, a Dominican priest and professor at the University of Salamanca, published in 1532 an influential analysis of the principles of natural law thought to govern relations with the Indians. Victoria conceded that Indians were rational beings morally equivalent to Europeans and entitled to basic natural rights. He rejected the validity of the *Requerimiento* and the papal "donations" of America to European rulers. He has been hailed by some modern scholars as one of the founders of the "law of nations" (principles governing international relations). But as Williams demonstrated, Victoria's legal theories, albeit in more sophisticated and secularized form than the *Requerimiento*,

> justified the extension of Western power over the American Indians as an imperative of the Europeans' vision of truth. In Victoria's system,

the Indians might be subjected to Spanish rule for denying the Spanish conquistadors free passage in their territory, preventing Spanish merchants from making their profit, refusing to share communally held wealth, or hindering the propagation of Christianity. Any of these actions by the Indians would constitute transgressions of the Law of Nations for which the Spaniards could wage a just war and assume all the rights of conquest. In Victoria's view, the Indian's consent to this Law of Nations was immaterial, since the majority of the world's civilized states (that is, European Christian states) had already consented . . . to the[se] norms." (Williams 1990, 107)

The British and other European powers adopted much of the theory of the Spanish religious and legal rationales for conquering the Americas and subjecting the native inhabitants to their rule. In practice, however, the power of the Indian nations dictated a more prudent course. In most cases, the early British colonists in North America made at least some effort to purchase Indian lands with the consent of the Indians. And European governments found it strategically convenient to cultivate alliances with Indian nations, for example, during the French and Indian War (1754–1763) (known in Europe as the Seven Years' War of 1756–1763). Britain defeated France in that war, acquiring French claims to Canada and the lands between the American colonies and the Mississippi River. But Britain had not actually conquered all the powerful Indian nations occupying most of that territory. Although the European colonists in North America wanted to settle those lands, the British government was tired of the expense and bloodshed of fighting the Indians.

As a result, British King George III issued a royal proclamation in 1763 prohibiting the American colonists from settling or encroaching on Indian lands west of the Appalachians. The colonists greatly resented this order, and it became one of the prime causes of the American war for independence a decade later. One of the many disputes arising out of the 1763 proclamation led to the first U.S. Supreme Court decision touching on Indian law issues, *Fletcher v. Peck* (1810). In 1795, in what became known as the Yazoo Land Grant (or more bluntly, the Yazoo Fraud), Georgia purported to grant to private speculators an area within what is now Mississippi, though nominally within Georgia's westward boundaries during that time. Western Georgia, including what are now Mississippi and Alabama, was occupied entirely by the original Indian inhabitants at the end of the 1700s, and it was generally agreed that they retained "Indian title" to these lands under the 1763 proclamation, title that Chief Justice John Marshall declared was "certainly to be respected by all courts, until it be legitimately extinguished" (*Fletcher v. Peck* 1810, 142–143). Furthermore, many of the Georgia state legislators who approved the grant were bribed with promises of profits from the land deal.

Responding to popular outrage, a later Georgia legislature tried to repeal the grant, but people who had innocently bought land from the original speculators defended their title in court. No Indians were parties to the *Fletcher* case, which involved only the competing property claims of non-Indians. Marshall's majority opinion upheld the original land grant. The greatest legal significance of his opinion (which only briefly glossed over the Indian title issue) was that he struck down Georgia's attempt to repeal its land grant as a violation of the contracts clause (U.S. Const., art. I, § 10, cl. 1).

Justice William Johnson's partial dissent (*Fletcher v. Peck* 1810, 146–147) pointed out the obvious awkwardness of finding Georgia authorized to dispose of the Yazoo lands as if the state owned them outright ("in fee simple," to use the legal term), when in fact "the right of soil" (i.e., actual and lawful possession of the lands of western Georgia) belonged to the Indian nations, as recognized by "innumerable treaties . . . [which] acknowledge them to be an independent people." As Johnson noted, "how could [Georgia's property right] be called a fee-simple, [when it] was nothing more than a power to acquire a fee-simple by purchase, when the proprietors [i.e., the Indians] should be pleased to sell?" (*Fletcher v. Peck* 1810, 147).

Chief Justice Marshall did not pretend to find any moral justification for the raw assertion of European colonial power over Native Americans, whatever its religious roots may have been. Indeed, he hinted at contrary views in the first important Indian law case decided by the Supreme Court, *Johnson v. M'Intosh* (1823). In this decision, a decade before the Cherokee Cases, Marshall commented:

> We will not enter into the controversy, whether agriculturists, merchants, and manufacturers, have a right, on abstract principles, to expel hunters from the territory they possess, or to contract their limits. Conquest gives a title which the courts of the conqueror cannot deny, whatever the private and speculative opinions of individuals may be,

respecting the original justice of the claim which has been successfully asserted. . . . (*Johnson v. M'Intosh* 1823, 588)

[T]he tribes of Indians inhabiting this country were fierce savages, whose occupation was war, and whose subsistence was drawn chiefly from the forest. To leave them in possession of their country, was to leave the country a wilderness; to govern them as a distinct people, was impossible, because they were as brave and as high spirited as they were fierce, and were ready to repel by arms every attempt on their independence.

What was the inevitable consequence of this state of things? The Europeans were under the necessity either of abandoning the country, and relinquishing their pompous claims to it, or of enforcing those claims by the sword. . . .

Frequent and bloody wars, in which the whites were not always the aggressors, unavoidably ensued. European policy, numbers, and skill, prevailed. As the white population advanced, that of the Indians necessarily receded. The country in the immediate neighborhood of agriculturists became unfit for them. The game fled into thicker and more unbroken forests, and the Indians followed. . . .

However extravagant the pretension of converting the discovery of an inhabited country into conquest may appear; if the principle has been asserted in the first instance, and afterwards sustained; if a country has been acquired and held under it; if the property of the great mass of the community originates in it, it becomes the law of the land, and cannot be questioned. So . . . the Indians are to be considered merely as occupants, to be protected, indeed, while in peace, in the possession of their lands, but to be deemed incapable of transferring the absolute title to others [without U.S. government authorization]. However this restriction may be opposed to natural right, and to the usages of civilized nations, yet, if it be indispensable to that system under which the country has been settled, and be adapted to the actual condition of the two people[s], it may, perhaps, be supported by reason, and certainly cannot be rejected by courts of justice. (*Johnson v. M'Intosh* 1823, 590–92)

Johnson v. M'Intosh, like *Fletcher v. Peck,* was devoted to sorting out the competing claims of non-Indians to land previously taken from Indians and did not raise any direct conflict between Indians and non-Indians. It did, however, define the nature of Indian title, first explored in *Fletcher v. Peck* (1810), as noted earlier. This was a peculiar legal concept under which the Indian nations, absent any treaty or other law either affirming or divesting their ownership, were deemed not to own ordinary title to their ancestral lands. Rather, they were said to enjoy a mere right of "occupancy." The Indians were deemed entitled to continue enjoying this right of occupancy (also called "aboriginal title") until and unless divested by the U.S. government.

The Supreme Court ruled much later that the government could legally expropriate such Indian title without incurring any constitutional obligation of compensation (*Tee-Hit-Ton Indians v. United States* 1955). By that time, however, Congress had chosen to provide a partial and decidedly imperfect means of statutory redress for such claims in the Indian Claims Commission Act of 1946. Federal law, such as a treaty with the United States, has been held capable of upgrading Indian title to the status of legally secure ownership, from which Indians can be divested only with "just compensation," as required by the takings clause of the Fifth Amendment (U.S. Const., amend. V; *United States v. Sioux Nation* 1980). *Johnson v. M'Intosh,* however, deemed Indian tribes to lack (and they still lack to this day) the legal authority to sell their lands, except to the U.S. government itself or to others with U.S. government permission. This situation is discussed at greater length in the second section of Chapter 3.

The notion of Indian title grew out of the equally peculiar Discovery Doctrine. This principle, derived from the early Spanish legal theories discussed above, was asserted by the European colonial powers as they competed to settle and develop the New World. Under this doctrine, whichever European nation first "discovered" a given piece of American territory had sovereignty over it, to the exclusion of any other European power and trumping the preexisting sovereignty of whatever Indian nation or nations might actually govern the area. Chief Justice Marshall, in *Johnson v. M'Intosh,* accepted the Discovery Doctrine as a bedrock principle of American Indian law. But he defined it merely as a rule of priority among Europeans and emphasized that it did not resolve the rights of the Indians who actually occupied the land.

The Supreme Court first decided a direct conflict between Indians and non-Indians in the second of the Cherokee Cases, *Worcester v. Georgia* (1832) (discussed in the first section of Chapter 3), in which

Marshall offered this sardonic addition to his discussion in *Johnson v. M'Intosh:*

> Did these [European] adventurers, by sailing along the coast, and occasionally landing on it, acquire for the several governments to whom they belonged . . . a rightful property in the soil, from the Atlantic to the Pacific; or rightful dominion over the numerous people who occupied it? Or has nature, or the great Creator of all things, conferred these rights over hunters and fishermen [i.e., the Indians], on agriculturists and manufacturers [i.e., the European settlers]?
>
> But war, power, conquest, give rights, which, after possession, are conceded by the world; and which can never be controverted by those on whom they descend. We proceed, then, to the actual state of things, having glanced at their origin; because holding it in our recollection might shed some light on existing pretensions. (*Worcester v. Georgia* 1832, 543)

Marshall's analysis of the Discovery Doctrine thus had a distinctly ironic, detached, and skeptical tone. He spoke as a legal realist and positivist, unwilling to use his power as a judge to enforce notions of natural justice, but still somewhat sensitive to the situation of the Indians. Of course, as these passages indicate, Marshall's view of Native American culture and society was also colored by the racist attitudes of his time, which presumed as a given the superiority of European culture and society.

The history of European-Indian relations in the United States, following American independence in 1776, can be broken into five broad eras. First, from 1776 to 1871, was a period during which U.S.-Indian relations were governed by treaties between the U.S. government and the various Indian nations. This Treaty Era, and its legacy for American Indian law, is discussed in the first two sections of Chapter 3.

Between 1871 and 1933, the U.S. government pursued a systematic policy aimed, in the long run, at eradicating Indian tribes as independent governments and assimilating Indians into the mass of U.S. citizens. Three key acts of Congress underscored this new approach. In an 1871 statute, Congress called a halt to any new treaty negotiations with the tribes. The Major Crimes Act of 1885 extended federal criminal jurisdiction over Indians in Indian country, a topic discussed in the third section of Chapter 3. And the Allotment (Dawes) Act of

1887 began breaking up Indian reservations into small plots "allotted" to individual Indians, with the remaining lands, deemed "surplus," opened up to non-Indian settlement and commercial exploitation. As a result, Indian nations eventually lost about two-thirds of the land they possessed in 1871, together with incalculable mineral riches and other natural resources. Many supporters of the allotment policy viewed themselves as reform-minded liberals and sincerely believed that such policies were in the best long-term interests of the Indians. Sheer greed and the desire to exploit Indian land and resources, however, also clearly played a role.

The oppressive policies pursued during the Assimilation Era are likely to startle most modern U.S. readers. The U.S. Department of the Interior, without any statutory authorization, created "Courts of Indian Offenses" on most Indian reservations. Among other measures, these courts attempted to ban most Native American religions, along with Indian dances and other cultural practices. At the same time, the federal government placed local Indian agencies under the supervision of various religious missionaries charged with "Christianizing" and "civilizing" the Indians. All this proceeded in astonishing and blatant disregard of the First Amendment's protection of religious freedom and prohibition of any governmental establishment of religion. Federal regulations of Indian customs ranged from efforts to wipe out polygamy as practiced by some tribes to almost incredibly petty and intrusive matters, such as forcing Indian men and boys to cut their hair short, contrary to deeply held beliefs in many Indian cultures.

Indian children were coerced into attending English-language schools at which they were punished for speaking their native languages. Many of these were remote boarding schools, and sending children there had the effect of breaking up Indian families and the avowed purpose, as expressed by the military superintendent of one such school, to "kill the Indian and save the man." The effects of the boarding schools and related policies on the cultural vitality of Indian nations were, of course, devastating. Only in recent decades, especially with the passage of the Indian Child Welfare Act of 1978, which gave tribes more control over Indian children, have the effects of these policies been ameliorated to some extent.

It was not just the cultural survival of Indians that was in doubt during the Assimilation Era. The combined effects of disease and outright genocide continued to devastate the Indian population. It is believed that Indians in what are now the lower forty-eight United States may have numbered around 5 million when Columbus landed (estimates vary widely). As the scholar C. Blue Clark has described:

> By 1800, that population had dwindled to 600,000. In the period 1890–1900, the American Indian population in the United States hit bottom, with the total number falling to only 248,000 in the census of 1890. By 1900, the census figure for native peoples nationwide showed a slight increase to just under 270,000. During the same period of time that the native population was dropping, the non-Indian population skyrocketed from five million in 1800 to over 75 million in 1900. (Clark 1998, 177)

The question of Indian citizenship, always something of a puzzle, was another issue tackled during the Assimilation Era. At the time of the framing of the U.S. Constitution and throughout the Treaty Era, most Indians were not considered U.S. citizens. Despite being born and living within territory deemed to constitute part of the United States, they were generally exempt from direct federal or state jurisdiction or taxation, as long as they resided within tribal territories and were governed by tribal governments. Indeed, as noted in Chapter 1, the Constitution of 1787 excluded "Indians not taxed" from the population-based apportionment of the U.S. House of Representatives (U.S. Const., art. I, § 2, cl. 3). The Civil Rights Act of 1866 likewise excluded "Indians not taxed" from U.S. citizenship while otherwise generally conferring citizenship on all persons born in the United States without regard to race. A number of federal statutes had already been passed in prior decades conferring citizenship on Indians in a handful of specific tribes.

In 1868, the Fourteenth Amendment was ratified, declaring that "All persons born or naturalized in the United States, and subject to the jurisdiction thereof, are citizens of the United States and of the State wherein they reside" but retaining the exclusion of "Indians not taxed" from congressional apportionment (U.S. Const., amend. XIV, §§ 1, 2). It is fairly clear that the understanding of those who supported and opposed the 1866 Civil Rights Act and the Fourteenth Amendment (a prime purpose of which was to confirm the constitutionality of the 1866 law) was that Indians in "tribal relations" were not viewed as "subject to the jurisdiction" of the United States and therefore were not intended to be made U.S. citizens. By logical inference, however (an inference explicitly stated by some), that understanding supported the citizenship of Indians who had (at least by 1868) separated themselves from any tribe and merged into the mass of U.S. society.

In truth, it is difficult to reconcile the notion that *any* Indians, by 1868, were not "subject to the jurisdiction" of the United States, with the sheer fact of U.S. power over Indians. "Jurisdiction" means literally the power to "say what the law is." Although the federal government had not yet sought, by 1868, to comprehensively regulate internal tribal affairs, it both claimed and exercised ultimate legal power over Indians. Chief Justice Marshall's opinion in the first of the Cherokee Cases declared that Indians generally were "in a state of pupilage" and that "[t]heir relation to the United States resembles that of a ward to his guardian" (*Cherokee Nation v. Georgia* 1831, 17). A ward is obviously subject to the jurisdiction of his guardian by any practical, commonsense understanding. The federal Trade and Intercourse Act (Indian Country Crimes Act) subjected Indians within Indian country to federal criminal jurisdiction over crimes committed against non-Indians, starting at least as early as 1817. The Supreme Court upheld that assertion of federal power in *United States v. Rogers* (1846). In the 1871 *Cherokee Tobacco* case, the Supreme Court ruled that Congress, in an 1868 statute, had subjected Indians within Indian country to the federal tobacco tax, thus undermining their tax-free status.

Nevertheless, the Supreme Court, when faced with the issue in the landmark case of *Elk v. Wilkins* (1884), rejected citizenship not only for tribal Indians but all Indians, absent specific legislative authorization. The plaintiff in that case, John Elk, had left his tribe and settled in Omaha, Nebraska, and sought to register to vote. But the majority, employing a frankly racist rationale, held that because he had been born a tribal Indian, he could not qualify:

> The national legislation has tended more and more toward the education and civilization of the Indians, and fitting them to be citizens. But the question whether any Indian tribes, or any members thereof, have become so far advanced in civilization that they should be let out of the state of pupilage, and admitted to the privileges and responsibilities of citizenship, is a question to be decided by the nation whose wards they are and whose citizens they seek to become, and not by each Indian for himself. (*Elk v. Wilkins* 1884, 106–107)

Such reasoning was, of course, surreal, given that the very purpose of the 1866 Civil Rights Act and the Thirteenth, Fourteenth, and Fifteenth Amendments (ratified in 1865, 1868, and 1870, respectively) was to grant full citizenship and voting rights without regard to race. The Court at least acknowledged that purpose with regard to African Americans, who were not only in a state of "pupilage" but mostly owned as property prior to 1865. As a practical matter, of course, African Americans fared little better than Indians at the hands of the prevailing Court majority during this era, which struck down a federal law banning segregation (*Civil Rights Cases* 1883) and upheld state laws mandating segregation (*Plessy v. Ferguson* 1896). It was thus not surprising that the first Justice John Marshall Harlan, who dissented alone in those cases, angrily dissented in *Elk* as well. Joined in *Elk* by Justice William B. Woods, Harlan pointed out that the majority's decision created "a despised and rejected class of persons with no nationality whatever, who, born in our territory, owing no allegiance to any foreign power, . . . are yet not members of any political community, nor entitled to any of the rights, privileges, or immunities of citizens of the United States" (*Elk v. Wilkins* 1884, 122–123).

Exactly four months after the Court decided *Elk,* Congress passed the Major Crimes Act of 1885, which subjected Indians within Indian country to federal jurisdiction over major crimes committed even against other Indians. It seems difficult to dispute that, at least from that time on, Indians have been "subject to the jurisdiction" of the United States. But the Court did not reconsider *Elk* (which never has been overruled), and the Indian exemption from the Fourteenth Amendment persisted. Congress did continue granting U.S. citizenship on a piecemeal basis to Indians, such as those to whom land was distributed under the Allotment Act of 1887. One statute, still on the books though now obsolete, conferred citizenship on Indian women who married non-Indian men.

Not until the Indian Citizenship Act of 1924, however, did Congress finally confer U.S. citizenship on all Indians, including those maintaining active tribal citizenship. Even then, some states persisted in denying Indians the right to vote in state elections on the theory that they were still largely exempt from state laws, despite the plain language of the Fourteenth Amendment that all U.S. citizens are automatically citizens "of the State wherein they reside" (U.S. Const., amend. XIV, § 1). It was not until lower court decisions as late as the 1940s and 1950s that Indians finally gained the universal right to vote.

It must be noted that many Indians did not and still do not regard the acquisition of U.S. citizenship as a liberating event. To the contrary, many condemn it as an imposition without their consent, as yet another colonial act contributing to the undermining of tribal governments. At the same time, citizenship and its attendant voting rights have been valuable to many Indians who have fought for their rights and for preserving tribal sovereignty and who continue to do so within the U.S. political system. In several states, such as Arizona, New Mexico, Oklahoma, and South Dakota, the Indian vote is quite significant. As a few tribes have become wealthy through gambling revenues in recent years, as discussed in the fifth section of Chapter 3, they have also become influential political campaign contributors.

The inauguration of President Franklin D. Roosevelt and his Democratic "New Deal" administration in 1933 marked an epochal shift in federal Indian policy. He appointed John Collier, a reformist advocate of Indian rights, as commissioner of Indian affairs, and soon obtained passage of the Indian Reorganization (Wheeler-Howard) Act of 1934, which sought to strengthen tribal governments. Collier reversed repressive policies toward Indian religions and actually sought to promote Native American cultures. Felix S. Cohen, who served as a lawyer for the Department of the Interior during Collier's tenure, published his landmark *Handbook of Federal Indian Law* in 1941, which amounted to a watershed scholarly defense of Native American sovereignty. Despite all these good intentions, however, modern critics have noted that this first "Self-Determination Era" involved many intrusions into internal tribal governance. Tribes were pressured to adopt constitutions and tribal governments modeled on European American traditions, often exacerbating internal divisions. And the Interior Department retained the power to approve or reject many tribal laws.

Following World War II, the federal policy pendulum swung in the other direction. After President Dwight D. Eisenhower, a Republican, took office in 1953 along with a Republican-controlled Congress, assimilation of Indians again became the order of the day. Congress passed House Resolution 108, which declared the "termination" of tribal governments to be the guiding principle of federal Indian policy. Also in 1953, Congress passed Public Law 280, which unilaterally extended state criminal jurisdiction over Indian reservations in several states and offered that option to others. A number of tribes were dissolved during this Termination Era, generating lasting grievances and distrust, but this period proved short-lived. By 1959, the Eisenhower administration backed off any further pursuit of termination without Indian consent, which was decidedly lacking.

The Democratic administrations of Presidents John F. Kennedy and Lyndon B. Johnson emphasized social welfare programs to benefit impoverished Indians. Johnson, in a landmark message to Congress describing Indians as the "forgotten" Americans, rejected termination and emphasized economic development (Johnson Message 1968). That same year, Congress passed and Johnson signed the Indian Civil Rights Act. One important feature of that law required tribal consent for any further expansion of state jurisdiction under Public Law 280. No tribe has ever granted such consent. The 1968 law also applied most of the Bill of Rights to tribal governments. Although welcomed by many as a protection of individual Indian rights, this law also amounted to yet another limitation on tribal sovereignty without the tribe's consent. The law also sharply limited the scope of tribal criminal jurisdiction. Some Indians opposed it on those grounds. The Supreme Court later made it difficult for anyone not facing criminal or civil tribal court sanctions to gain relief under the law (*Santa Clara Pueblo v. Martinez* 1978).

The Termination Era was decisively laid to rest in 1970, surprisingly, by Republican president Richard M. Nixon, who had taken office as Eisenhower's vice president in 1953. Nixon strongly supported tribal sovereignty and self-determination, albeit in limited form (Nixon Message 1970). That has remained, more or less, the bipartisan consensus ever since. This second Self-Determination Era has seen a number of important legislative milestones. The Indian Self-Determination and Education Assistance Act of 1975 sought to delegate more authority to tribal governments to administer federal programs. In 1978, Congress passed the American Indian Religious Freedom Act (AIRFA). Although essentially symbolic, it was widely hailed within Indian country as supporting Native American religious practices. Later court cases proved disappointing. For example, the Supreme Court rejected any First Amendment right to use peyote in Native American rituals (*Oregon Department of Human Resources v. Smith* 1990). Congress, however, protected religious peyote use by an amendment to AIRFA passed in 1994.

The Indian Child Welfare Act of 1978 has had much greater importance for Native American sovereignty. It dramatically expanded tribal powers to intervene in adoption and parental-rights termination cases affecting Indian children. The Native American Graves Protection and Repatriation Act of 1990 extended somewhat similar tribal powers over Indian religious and cultural artifacts and human remains. Huge amounts of such artifacts and remains have languished for years in museums, including the Smithsonian Institution, deeply offending Indian religious sensibilities. The enforcement of both of these laws has proved controversial, but they have been strongly welcomed and defended by Indians. Each of these landmark statutes merits book-length treatment by itself, but they are unfortunately beyond the necessarily selective scope of this book. Excellent overviews and citations to further sources may be found in the 1998 treatises by William C. Canby, Jr., coauthored by David H. Getches, Charles F. Wilkinson, and Robert A. Williams, Jr.

Native Americans have been less successful in preventing more insidious forms of cultural conquest. These include the faddish appropriation of Indian religious imagery by "New Age" enthusiasts and the offensive commercial exploitation of Indian names and stereotypical images by sports teams and mascots. Scholars such as Philip J. Deloria, in his book *Playing Indian* (1998), and Shari M. Huhndorf, in her book *Going Native: Indians in the American Cultural Imagination* (2001), have analyzed such phenomena in U.S. film, literature, and culture.

The disputes over Indian citizenship that marked the Assimilation Era of 1871–1933 have found a modern echo in controversies over "preferential" treatment for Indians in the post-1970 Self-Determination Era. Some have argued that special treatment of Indians under the law amounts to a form of racial "affirmative action" or "reverse discrimination" violating the Fourteenth Amendment's guarantee of "equal protection of the laws." That issue has continued to percolate for other racial minorities such as African Americans. The Supreme Court, however, sought to lay it to rest with regard to Indians in *Morton v. Mancari* (1974), which held that Indians with tribal membership are not simply members of racial or ethnic groups but have a distinct, quasi-*political* status. The Court unanimously held that special legal treatment of Indians (at least those who are members of legally recognized tribes) is justified and proper on this basis and does not amount to unlawful racial discrimination. Some scholars continue to debate the issue, noting that tribal citizenship itself (a matter governed by each tribe's own laws) is typically based to some degree on Indian racial ancestry.

The dilemma of Indian racial and political identity is only one of many issues affecting Native American sovereignty as the United States moves into the twenty-first century. Many of these issues are explored in more depth in the chapter that follows.

References and Further Reading

Cabeza de Vaca, Álvar Nuñez. [1542] 1983. *Adventures in the Unknown Interior of America.* Reprint, Albuquerque: University of New Mexico Press (translated and annotated by Cyclone Covey; epilogue by William T. Pilkington; first written as *La Relacion,* a report to the King of Spain).

Canby, William C., Jr. 1998. *American Indian Law in a Nutshell.* 3d ed. St. Paul, MN: West.

Clark, C. Blue. 1998. "How Bad It Really Was before World War II: Sovereignty." *Oklahoma City University Law Review* 23: 175.

Cogan, Neil H., ed. 1999. *Contexts of the Constitution: A Documentary Collection on Principles of American Constitutional Law.* New York: Foundation.

Cohen, Felix S. 1941. *Handbook of Federal Indian Law.* Washington, DC: U.S. Government Printing Office.

Debo, Angie. 1970. *A History of the Indians of the United States.* Norman: University of Oklahoma Press.

Deloria, Philip J. 1998. *Playing Indian.* New Haven, CT: Yale University Press.

Deloria, Vine, Jr., and Clifford M. Lytle. 1983. *American Indians, American Justice.* Austin: University of Texas Press.

———. 1984. *The Nations Within: The Past and Future of American Indian Sovereignty.* New York: Pantheon.

Deloria, Vine, Jr., and David E. Wilkins. 1999. *Tribes, Treaties, and Constitutional Tribulations.* Austin: University of Texas Press.

Dussias, Allison M. 1997. "Ghost Dance and Holy Ghost: The Echoes of Nineteenth-Century Christianization Policy in Twentieth-Century Native American Free Exercise Cases." *Stanford Law Review* 49: 773.

Getches, David H., Charles F. Wilkinson, and Robert A. Williams, Jr. 1998. *Cases and Materials on Federal Indian Law.* 4th ed. St. Paul, MN: West.

Goldberg, Carole. 2002. "American Indians and 'Preferential' Treatment." *UCLA Law Review* 49: 943.

Goldberg-Ambrose, Carole. 1991. "Not 'Strictly' Racial: A Response to 'Indians as Peoples.'" *UCLA Law Review* 39: 169.

Huhndorf, Shari M. 2001. *Going Native: Indians in the American Cultural Imagination.* Cornell: Cornell University Press.

Jackson, Helen Hunt. 1995 [1881]. *A Century of Dishonor: A Sketch of the United States Government's Dealings with Some of the Indian Tribes.* New York: Harper. Reprint, Norman: University of Oklahoma Press.

Loewen, James W. 1995. *Lies My Teacher Told Me: Everything Your American History Textbook Got Wrong.* New York: Simon and Schuster.

Prucha, Francis Paul. 1984. *The Great Father: The United States Government and the American Indians.* 2 vols. Lincoln: University of Nebraska Press (abridged 1-vol. ed., 1986).

———. 1994. *American Indian Treaties: The History of a Political Anomaly.* Berkeley: University of California Press.

———, ed. 2000. *Documents of United States Indian Policy.* 3d ed. Lincoln: University of Nebraska Press.

Richter, Daniel K. 2001. *Facing East from Indian Country: A Native History of Early America.* Cambridge, MA: Harvard University Press.

Thomas, David Hurst, Jay Miller, Richard White, Peter Nabokov, and Philip J. Deloria. 1993. *The Native Americans: An Illustrated History.* Atlanta: Turner Publishing.

Urofsky, Melvin I., and Paul Finkelman. 2002a. *A March of Liberty: A Constitutional History of the United States.* 2 vols. 2d ed. Oxford: Oxford University Press.

———, eds. 2002b. *Documents of American Constitutional and Legal History.* 2 vols. 2d ed. Oxford: Oxford University Press.

Wilkins, David E. 1997. *American Indian Sovereignty and the U.S. Supreme Court: The Masking of Justice.* Austin: University of Texas Press.

———. 2002. *American Indian Politics and the American Political System.* Lanham, MD: Rowman and Littlefield.

Wilkinson, Charles F. 1987. *American Indians, Time, and the Law: Native American Societies in a Modern Constitutional Democracy.* New Haven, CT: Yale University Press.

Williams, David C. 1991a. "The Borders of the Equal Protection Clause: Indians as Peoples." *UCLA Law Review* 38: 759.

———. 1991b. "Sometimes Suspect: A Response to Professor Goldberg-Ambrose." *UCLA Law Review* 39: 191.

Williams, Robert A., Jr. 1990. *The American Indian in Western Legal Thought: The Discourses of Conquest.* Oxford: Oxford University Press.

Wunder, John R. 1994. *"Retained by the People": A History of American Indians and the Bill of Rights.* Oxford: Oxford University Press.

———, ed. 1996. *Native Americans and the Law: Contemporary and Historical Perspectives on American Indian Rights, Freedoms, and Sovereignty.* 6 vols. New York: Garland.

Zelden, Charles L. 2002. *Voting Rights on Trial: A Handbook with Cases, Laws, and Documents.* Santa Barbara, CA: ABC-CLIO.

3
Cases

Laying the Foundation: Chief Justice Marshall and the Cherokee Cases

The Cherokee Cases decided by the U.S. Supreme Court—*Cherokee Nation v. Georgia* (1831) and *Worcester v. Georgia* (1832)—brought to a head the first great legal conflict over the competing land rights of the Native Americans and the European American settlers. As described in Chapter 2, the Supreme Court in two earlier cases—*Fletcher v. Peck* (1810) and *Johnson v. M'Intosh* (1823)—had dealt with disputes between non-Indians over ownership of property that once had belonged to Indians. What made the Cherokee Cases new and important was that they involved something more than mere land ownership. They involved the more fundamental issue of sovereignty: the power to *govern* both the land and its inhabitants.

What makes the story of the Cherokees and these cases especially poignant and ironic is that the Cherokees had already, by the 1820s, proven far more successful than any other Indian tribe at adapting to the European culture of the white settlers. Most Cherokees converted to Christianity while also proudly adhering to their ancestral traditions, which included a vastly more respected and influential status for women than in European American society. Indeed, a Cherokee woman delivered the closing remarks at the signing ceremony of the Treaty of Hopewell in 1785, which is quite remarkable, considering that not until the twentieth century did any women serve as U.S.

diplomats. By the 1820s, most Cherokees adopted a farming lifestyle and agricultural economy not unlike that of the European settlers. Ownership of African slaves was another practice of the European American South adopted by some Cherokees. The Cherokees, like many Indians, had long enslaved enemy captives, but the plantation system of chattel slavery was something new. With the invention of a written alphabet for the Cherokee language by the great Cherokee teacher Sequoyah, literacy spread like wildfire. The fact that most Cherokees were now literate in their own language and thus less dependent on the white man's English for written communication, added immeasurably to their cultural pride and national self-confidence.

Few could have predicted this Cherokee renaissance in the aftermath of the American Revolution. In 1783, as the United States secured its independence from Britain in the Treaty of Paris, the Cherokee Nation seemed ruined and destitute. The Cherokees, like most eastern Indian nations, had sided with the British during the American Revolution and had suffered considerable wartime casualties and ravaging of their lands. All the eastern Indians quite rightly feared the territorial ambitions and thirst for settlement of the new United States of America. The United States, however, only precariously independent from European despots, also felt vulnerable at this stage of its history. From the European American perspective, powerful and well-armed Indian tribes remained in actual possession and control of vast stretches of land from the Appalachians westward. This fact helps to explain the surprisingly respectful and egalitarian tone and substance of the U.S.-Indian treaties negotiated during this early era.

The very first treaty between the United States and an Indian nation was concluded with the Delaware tribe in 1778. This treaty went out of its way to disavow the "false suggestion" of which "the enemies of the United States have endeavored, by every artifice in their power, to possess the Indians," namely, that the United States intended to seize Indian lands and perhaps exterminate the Indians outright. Mocked in retrospect by all the later treaty violations and genocidal encounters that proved such fears right, this inaugural treaty solemnly implored the Indians to "hold fast the chain of friendship now entered into" (Delaware-U.S. Treaty of 1778, art. VI).

The Treaty of Hopewell, concluded by the United States and the Cherokee Nation in 1785, reaffirmed a generous territorial domain for the Cherokees, including most of what is now the region of Tennessee southeast of Nashville, the western tips of North and South Carolina, a goodly part of northern Alabama, and almost all of the chunk of Georgia that lies north of Atlanta (art. IV). The treaty explicitly recognized Cherokee criminal jurisdiction over any non-Indian who settled in or refused to remove from this territory in violation of the treaty (art. V). It also included some vague and condescending language that provided fodder for later disputes, referring to Cherokee lands as merely "allotted . . . for their hunting grounds" (art. IV) and at one point seeming to grant Congress the power of "managing all [Cherokee] affairs in such manner as they [Congress] think proper" (art. IX). It concluded, in the manner of the Delaware Treaty of 1778, by declaring that "[t]he hatchet shall be forever buried" and that "peace" and "friendship" between the United States and the Cherokee Nation "shall be universal" (art. XIII).

The Cherokee-U.S. Treaty of Holston River, in 1791, reaffirmed the guarantees of Hopewell in crisper and more unequivocal terms, though at the price of new land cessions by the Cherokees. Dispensing with talk of "hunting grounds," this treaty simply defined "the boundary between the United States and the Cherokee nation" (art. IV). It granted to Congress the sole power of regulating the Cherokee Nation's external trade but omitted any language threatening Cherokee self-government (art. VI). The pattern set by the 1791 treaty continued in future years. The recurrent problem was treaty violations by white settlers hungry for the rich Cherokee lands. The recurrent solution was new negotiations and new treaties, each solemnly reaffirming Cherokee rights but over an ever-dwindling domain.

The wave of the future was foreshadowed most ominously in 1802, when Georgia reluctantly ceded to the federal government its claims to lands west of its present boundaries. This concession was made only in return for President Thomas Jefferson's promise, spelled out in the 1802 compact, to secure the extinction of all remaining Indian title to lands in what was left of Georgia. Most European Americans understood this agreement as part of a general call for the removal of eastern Indians to lands west of the Mississippi. The Cherokees, naturally, were not consulted. Indeed, Jefferson was the first in a line of presidents who openly endorsed removal as the only feasible "solution" to the Indian "problem." It was a notable shift from the policy of the first U.S. president, George Washington, who had sternly condemned violations of Indian treaties and sought in vain to effectively prevent and punish them.

The saving catch for the Cherokees, or so it seemed, was that the 1802 compact provided that the dispossession of the Indians could only be done "peaceably . . . upon reasonable terms" (Carter 1976, 28). Furthermore, the compact could not legally trump the federal treaties guaranteeing Cherokee land rights. So if the Cherokees simply stood firm and refused to go "peaceably," it seemed they were safe. But practically speaking, a collision course had been set.

A strange prelude to the coming tragedy of the 1830s transpired during the War of 1812 between the United States and Britain. Many Creek Indians (among others) sided again with the British, but the Cherokees gallantly came to the aid of their new U.S. treaty allies. In one of the towering ironies of U.S. history, they not only fought alongside General Andrew Jackson (who as president would prove the implacable advocate of their westward exile), but a Cherokee warrior saved his life during the Alabama campaign of 1814. At the climactic Battle of Horseshoe Bend on the Tallapoosa River, in March 1814, Jackson routed the Creeks with the decisive help of the Cherokee fighters.

The last of the early line of Cherokee-U.S. treaties was signed in Washington in 1819. The Cherokee Nation's reward for helping defend the United States against the British was bitter indeed. Having already lost their bit of South Carolina (including Hopewell, the site of the 1785 treaty), the Cherokees now gave up all but a tiny portion of far western North Carolina, a small slice of southeastern Tennessee (including Chattanooga), and smaller but still significant chunks of northeastern Alabama and northwestern Georgia. They were determined not to yield another square foot.

As Cherokee culture and commerce bloomed during the 1820s, the nation's political development kept pace. The Cherokees established democratic institutions, including an elected principal chief and legislative council, as well as a court system. A capital city was built at New Echota, Georgia. In 1827, the nation adopted a written constitution, and 1828 saw the inaugural publication of the *Cherokee Phoenix,* an influential newspaper published in both Cherokee and English. Around the same time, the Reverend Samuel Austin Worcester and his wife arrived in New Echota. Worcester, a Vermonter and young Congregationalist minister, became a leader among the white missionaries spreading Christianity in Cherokee country. With the support of their sponsoring churches in New England and elsewhere, they also became fierce advocates on behalf of the Cherokee Nation.

The new assertiveness of the Cherokees as a political body and their success in adapting to European ways while enhancing their power and independence were alarming enough to white Georgians. But the final log on this building fire in the late 1820s was the discovery of gold in Cherokee country within Georgia. It raised to a fever pitch the demand among whites for access to Cherokee land. Illegal incursions by non-Indians escalated. Conflicts with Cherokees led to violence on both sides. Federal and state officials seemed unable and were certainly unwilling to stem the tide. Georgia responded in 1828 and 1829 by enacting a series of laws purporting to abolish the Cherokee government, nullify all Cherokee laws, and extend Georgia state law over the Cherokee Nation.

The Georgia laws, however, did more than that. They dispelled any notion that Cherokees might remain in Georgia even as private individuals under any tolerable conditions. They denied Cherokees the right to testify in any court case involving a white person, leaving them helpless victims of crimes and breaches of contract by whites, and white hoodlums promptly took advantage of this immunity. They banned all political assemblies by Cherokees except for the purpose of negotiating land cessions and removal. In a sort of pièce de résistance, they prohibited Cherokees from mining gold on Cherokee-owned land, on the laughable ground of preventing Cherokees from "appropriating riches to themselves which of right equally belong to every other citizen of the state" (Carter 1976, 90; Ehle 1988, 225). There is no record of Georgia requiring white citizens to share mineral wealth found on white-owned lands with all others in the state (least of all Cherokees), a curiously Marxist notion predating the *Communist Manifesto* by almost twenty years. Nor, indeed, did Georgia make any effort to prevent the flood of white prospectors from mining and exploiting that same Cherokee land (in violation of treaty, of course), without sharing it "equally" with others.

Andrew Jackson, elected president of the United States in 1828, took office in March 1829. In his first message to Congress in December 1829, he advocated passage of a federal law authorizing removal of the Cherokees and the other four "Civilized Tribes" (the Choctaw, Chickasaw, Creek, and Seminole) to the west. The debate on this bill consumed Congress and the nation for most of the spring of 1830. Northeasterners, especially New Englanders (areas where Indians had mostly long since been defeated or removed), generally opposed the bill. Southerners and westerners facing active disputes with Indians mostly supported it. Party divisions were more opportunistic, as many National Republicans (soon to be known as Whigs, not to be confused with Lincoln's Republican Party, founded in 1854) opposed Jackson's Democrats on the issue. These Whigs included such leading statesmen as Daniel Webster and Henry Clay. Clay would exploit the issue in his presidential race against Jackson in 1832.

The Senate and House of Representatives both divided bitterly on the Removal Act, with oratory at white heat. It passed the House by 102–99, a margin that could have been reversed had only two members switched their votes. President Andrew Jackson signed it into law on May 28, 1830. The act explicitly provided, however, that it should not "be construed as authorizing . . . the violation of any existing [Indian] treaty" (Removal Act, sec. 7). Instead, it authorized grants of federal land west of the Mississippi (the "Indian Territory" in what is now Oklahoma) to any Indians who "may choose to exchange the lands where they now reside, and remove there" (sec. 1).

The Cherokees, obviously, did not so "choose," but faced with a hostile president and Congress, their only remaining option was to turn to the courts. They could not have found a better lawyer: William Wirt, who had served twelve years as U.S. attorney general under Presidents James Monroe and John Quincy Adams (1817–1829). The problem was how to obtain a judicial forum. The first vehicle was the case of a Cherokee man convicted in Georgia state court of a murder committed on Cherokee land. Wirt asked Chief Justice John Marshall for a writ to halt the man's execution and require Georgia to show cause why its claimed jurisdiction did not violate federal law. Marshall granted the writ in December 1830, but Georgia hastily carried out the execution, rendering the case brutally moot.

Wirt's next gambit was *Cherokee Nation v. Georgia,* a lawsuit invoking the Supreme Court's original jurisdiction over disputes to which any state was a party. The problem with this approach was that it framed the case as a generalized challenge to Georgia's laws rather than litigating the legal rights or status of some specific person or property. Courts are much more likely to find the latter kind of case justiciable (i.e., suited to judicial review). Thus it was not surprising that the justices, by a 4–2 majority, dismissed the Cherokee claim. The Court decided the case on March 18, 1831, just days after oral arguments at which Wirt was unopposed, since Georgia refused even to dignify the suit by appearing.

You should read at this point, if you have not already, the *Cherokee Nation* opinions in the Documents section, along with the Treaty of Hopewell. Consider the somewhat contradictory tone of Marshall's lead opinion for himself and Justice John McLean. Marshall scarcely concealed his sympathy for the Cherokees, but he avoided deciding the merits. Instead, he concluded on rather technical grounds that the suit did not fall within the Court's jurisdiction because the Cherokee Nation was not a "foreign state."

Although plausible, Marshall's conclusion was hardly compelled. The Court unquestionably would have had jurisdiction if the Cherokees had been citizens of (or if the Cherokee Nation had been) another state of the United States, or if they had been a foreign nation such as France (or citizens or subjects thereof). Indians living under tribal governments were not considered U.S. citizens at this time, so by simple deductive logic they arguably had to be foreign citizens and, in the aggregate, a foreign state (at least for jurisdictional purposes). For the Court to have heard the case on the merits would have stretched constitutional language only a little and the spirit of the document not at all. Marshall admitted these arguments were "imposing" (*Cherokee Nation v. Georgia* 1831, 16). Indeed, consider whether Justice Smith Thompson's dissenting opinion, joined by Justice Joseph Story, is more persuasive. Curiously, it was Marshall who encouraged Thompson and Story to publish their dissent. Historical study of personal correspondence has revealed the strong sympathy of both Marshall and Story for the Cherokee cause, and their moral horror at the policy pursued by Jackson and Georgia and reflected in the Removal Act.

But Marshall evidently felt that *Cherokee Nation* was not the right vehicle for judicial relief. State sovereign immunity might also have thwarted the Cherokee claim in any event. The Supreme Court ruled much later that neither Indian tribes nor foreign nations may bring direct civil lawsuits against states without their consent. In any event, Marshall avoided jurisdiction by finding that Indian tribes constituted a different, hybrid sort of "state," one falling between the cracks of the Court's jurisdiction. They were, he found in *Cherokee Nation*, "domestic dependent nations" with a relationship to the United States "resembl[ing] that of a ward to his guardian" (17). He also concluded his opinion by suggesting doubt whether the relief the Cherokees sought was a "proper subject for judicial inquiry and decision," or perhaps "savours too much of the exercise of political power" (20).

Justices William Johnson and Henry Baldwin, in separate opinions, agreed with Marshall's result but were openly contemptuous of any sovereign status for the Cherokees. Johnson asked mockingly whether "every petty kraal of Indians" could declare themselves a government and suggested that the Cherokees enjoyed political status only in that "[t]heir condition is something like that of the Israelites, when inhabiting the deserts" (25, 27). He was indifferent to the impact of the Georgia laws, asserting without apparent irony that the Cherokees had not been "subjugat[ed] . . . as a people, or restrain[ed] [in] their personal liberty, except as to their land and trade" (27). Of course, it was the removal policy itself that threatened to convert the Cherokees into forlorn wanderers like the Israelites, in search of a homeland.

The same month that *Cherokee Nation* was decided, Georgia arrested Worcester and several other missionaries for remaining in Cherokee country without obtaining a license or swearing allegiance to Georgia, as required by one of Georgia's recent laws. Worcester was quite willing to provide a test case to enable the Cherokees to again bring their grievances before the Supreme Court, but a curious procedural minuet ensued. The charges against Worcester were initially dismissed because he also served as postmaster for New Echota, and federal employees were exempted from the Georgia law. President Jackson fixed that by firing him at the request of Georgia's governor. Worcester was rearrested, separated from his wife and a newborn baby who both lay ill, and in September 1831 was sentenced to four years in prison. The governor, hoping to avoid a test case and sensitive to the public relations downside of jailing men of the cloth, offered all the convicted missionaries pardons if they agreed to comply with the law. Only Worcester and one other refused. Wirt had his case, and he promptly brought an appeal that the Supreme Court could not refuse to hear. Georgia again disdainfully boycotted the proceedings.

It doubtless helped the Cherokee cause among non-Indians that *Worcester v. Georgia* involved the personal liberty of a flesh-and-blood white minister, rather than the seemingly abstract tribal sovereignty at issue in *Cherokee Nation.* But the case still pitted Cherokee sovereignty and power squarely against that of Georgia. It is critical to understanding *Worcester,* however, to keep in mind that the Cherokees in this case did not confront—and could not successfully have done so—their ultimate and most dangerous adversary: the federal government of the United States. On the contrary, they necessarily *relied upon* federal power in the form of the federal treaty guarantees, Jackson and the Removal Act notwithstanding. This necessity both explains their victory in court and why it was tragically and inevitably fruitless in reality.

On March 3, 1832, Chief Justice Marshall gave the Cherokees what seemed a dramatic victory in *Worcester.* He wrote for a united majority of himself, Justices Story and Thompson, and Justice Gabriel Duvall (who had not participated in *Cherokee Nation*). Justice McLean's separate concurrence made it a 5–1 decision, with only Justice Baldwin dissenting (in a brief statement simply referring to his *Cherokee Nation* opinion) and Justice Johnson not participating. As you read the *Worcester* opinions, you may find Marshall's defense of the Cherokees to have a somewhat condescending ring. But in historical context, it was a thoughtful and courageous defense of Native American sovereignty, albeit in limited form. As a "domestic dependent nation," he found the Cherokees entitled to territorial integrity, political self-government, and immunity from state law. He therefore threw out Worcester's conviction as "repugnant to the Constitution, treaties, and laws of the United States" (*Worcester v. Georgia* 1832, 562–563).

But what was the *source* of this Native American sovereignty? In terms of morality and natural justice, as Marshall himself seemed to believe, Indian sovereignty rightfully derived from their prior tenure on the land, from the sheer fact of their preexisting independence. Those who believe in natural law might have rested on that. But Marshall had already conceded, nine years before, the fait accompli of European and then European American conquest. "It has never been doubted," he had asserted then, "that either the United States, or the several States, had a clear title to all the lands within the boundary lines described in the treaty [of 1783 with Great

Britain], subject only to the Indian right of occupancy, and that the exclusive power to extinguish that right, was vested in that government which might constitutionally exercise it" (*Johnson v. M'Intosh* 1823, 584–585). In cruelly positivist terms, he had concluded simply: "Conquest gives a title which the courts of the conqueror cannot deny" (588).

So what was the *legal* basis for Cherokee title? As Marshall saw it, only the treaty guarantees that the United States—the European American latecomers—had seen fit to offer their Cherokee predecessors. And those treaties trumped Georgia's pretensions only because the U.S. Constitution made them supreme federal law, "anything in the constitution or laws of any state to the contrary notwithstanding" (U.S. Const., art. VI, cl. 2). As Marshall saw it, the federal government's constitutional "powers of war and peace; of making treaties, and of regulating commerce . . . with the Indian tribes . . . comprehend all that is required for the regulation of our intercourse with the Indians" (*Worcester v. Georgia* 1832, 559).

Marshall, we should never forget, was fundamentally a nationalist. His most important Supreme Court opinions promoted federal judicial review (*Marbury v. Madison* 1803) and expansive federal powers to regulate commerce (*McCullough v. Maryland* 1819). Seen in this light, *Worcester* was simply another decisive subordination of state to federal power. And in typically Marshallian fashion, it asserted the power and independence of the federal courts. As further discussed in this chapter, this federal power would come to be viewed as virtually unlimited ("plenary") in the field of Indian affairs, and it carried with it the seeds of further erosion of Native American sovereignty and the constant threat of its total extinction.

But Marshall's opinion in *Worcester* was not just a celebration of federal power. The sympathy of Marshall and his colleagues for the justice of the Cherokee claim was real, and in the hands of less sympathetic judges, the outcome and tenor of the case could have been far different. Whether the Cherokee treaties provided a legal shield against Georgia's aggression depended entirely on how they were interpreted. Marshall and his majority colleagues read them generously. *Worcester* remains the original and classic model of Indian treaty interpretation by the Supreme Court. It pioneered what became known as the "canons of construction," under which Native American treaty rights have (at least in theory) been generously construed in their favor and strictly against the erosion of tribal sovereignty. It was also the basis for the U.S. government's "trustee" relationship toward Indian nations, founded on Marshall's rather condescending formulation of that relationship as one "resembl[ing] that of a ward to his guardian" (*Cherokee Nation v. Georgia* 1831, 17). This approach has (with notable omissions and deviations) spilled over into the interpretation of most laws affecting Indians, as discussed later in this chapter. It suffices here to note the contrast between Marshall's approach in *Worcester* and that of Justices Johnson and Baldwin in their *Cherokee Nation* opinions.

One problem for the Cherokees was the often patronizing language of the treaties, especially the first at Hopewell, which smacked very much of the "ward-guardian" relationship asserted by Marshall himself in *Cherokee Nation.* But in *Worcester* Marshall emphasized that the treaties should be interpreted as the Indians themselves probably understood them, and he was appropriately sensitive to the fact that probably they "were not very critical judges of the [English] language" and "the treaty was interpreted to them" (*Worcester v. Georgia* 1832, 551). Consider also Justice McLean's concurrence in *Worcester.* He declined to join Marshall's opinion and insisted that Indian sovereignty by its nature was "temporary" and that Indians must "eventually, consent to become amalgamated in our political communities" (593). But he articulated even more clearly than Marshall why "[t]he language used in treaties with the Indians should never be construed to their prejudice.... How the words of the treaty were understood by this unlettered people ... should form the rule of construction" (582). One might add that although the Cherokees were indeed mostly "unlettered" when the first treaties were signed, many, if not most, were literate by 1832, in the Cherokee alphabet created by Sequoyah.

With regard to the Treaty of Hopewell's preamble stating that "the United States give peace to all the Cherokees, and receive them into the favour and protection of the United States," Marshall asked wryly: "When the United States gave peace, did they not also receive it?" Were not the Americans "at least as anxious to obtain it as the Cherokees?" Marshall asked: Who came to whom to obtain peace? "The treaty was made at Hopewell, not at New York" (551). Where the treaty placed the Cherokees "under the protection of the United States" (art. III), Marshall emphasized the benefits of such protection for the Cherokees and noted that "[p]rotection does not imply the destruction of the protected" (551–552).

Marshall dismissed any significance in the treaty's reference to "hunting grounds" (art. IV) in defining the boundaries of the Cherokee Nation. He observed: "Hunting was at that time the principal occupation of the Indians" (553) and it was not reasonable to infer any limitation on their future use of the land. With regard to the treaty's most troubling language, suggesting that Congress would have power to manage all Cherokee affairs "in such manner as [it] think[s] proper" (art. IX), Marshall found that this language applied only to the tribe's external trade, the main subject of that article. Otherwise, he pointed out, "It would convert a treaty of peace covertly into an act annihilating the political existence of one of the parties" (554).

Marshall went on to artfully exploit the language of the 1791 Treaty of Holston River, which provided even stronger support for Cherokee sovereignty. It is especially revealing to compare the legal reasoning of the Thompson-Story dissent in *Cherokee Nation,* whose publication Marshall had encouraged, with Marshall's discussion of the sovereign status of the Cherokees in *Worcester.* Consider whether Marshall simply adopted much of the reasoning of Thompson and Story, who after all formed half of Marshall's majority in *Worcester.*

In sum, having surveyed the treaties and other federal and state interactions with the Cherokees over the past fifty years, Marshall found "evidence of a settled purpose to fix the Indians in their country by giving them security at home" (557). This interpretation was fully consistent with a just reading of treaty obligations to the Cherokees. But as a flat rejection of the removal philosophy, it was at best an optimistic reading of U.S. Indian policy taken as a whole up to that time.

Johnson and Baldwin, by contrast, read the treaties and other evidence in a light far more restrictive of Cherokee sovereignty. Baldwin even blatantly misstated the language of the Treaty of Hopewell, falsely claiming that "[t]he word nation is not used in . . . any part of the treaty" and that it did not even refer to itself as a "treaty" except once toward the end, in Article 13 (*Cherokee Nation v. Georgia* 1831, 38). In fact, Articles 5 and 8 also referred to "this treaty," and Article 6 referred twice to the Cherokee "nation."

The epilogue to the Cherokee Cases was, of course, continued defiance by Georgia and, more significantly, by President Jackson. Jackson may never have said the exact words (in the famous apocryphal quotation), "John Marshall has made his decision; now let him enforce it." And some scholars have emphasized that technical flaws in federal court jurisdictional laws delayed the issuance of the Court's mandate and made it impossible to directly order Jackson to protect the Cherokees. But that amounts to quibbling. Jackson could have fulfilled his constitutional obligation to "take care that the laws be faithfully executed" (U.S. Const., art. II, § 3) by seeking to enforce the Court's ruling. Instead, he openly encouraged Georgia's contemptuous defiance. Invasions of Cherokee territory by white settlers and gold seekers increased.

Worcester continued to languish in prison, until he was pardoned by the governor in December 1832. By that time, Jackson had been reelected, defeating Clay by a crushing margin. Many Cherokees had already emigrated west; a western branch of the tribe had been in existence for some years, based in what is now Oklahoma. Some leading stalwarts of the eastern nation began to question whether they should accept wholesale removal while they could still obtain halfway decent terms. The Cherokee fell into bitter division over the issue.

A tiny rump faction of the eastern Cherokee endorsed the Treaty of New Echota in December 1835, which was ratified by the U.S. Senate in May 1836. It called for removal of all remaining Cherokees to Oklahoma, with some compensation for their eastern property. Repudiated by the vast majority of Cherokees, it was nevertheless treated as the new law of the land. John Marshall, who died in July 1835, did not live to see it. In accordance with the fraudulent new treaty and under the prodding bayonets of the U.S. Army called out by President Martin Van Buren, the Cherokee embarked on the Trail of Tears in 1838. Thousands, perhaps one-fourth of the entire nation, died along the way from disease and hardship.

In one of the many strange side-chapters of the Cherokee saga, Sam Houston, adopted son of the western Cherokee chief John Jolly, was engaged during this time in founding the Republic of Texas. Houston twice served as president of Texas during its nine-year independence (1836–1845) and later as a U.S. senator and governor of Texas. In February 1836, a small band of Cherokee who had settled along the Sabine River entered into a treaty negotiated by Houston on behalf of the Texas provisional government. But despite Houston's efforts, it was never ratified, and in 1839, while he was out of office, the Texas Cherokees were also driven out, again mostly to Oklahoma.

Despite the solemnly renewed promises of the U.S. government, the Indian Territory in Oklahoma would not prove a permanent refuge for the transplanted Cherokee Nation. Non-Indian settlers eventually swamped the western territories as well. The Curtis Act of 1898 and Oklahoma statehood in 1907 dissolved the main Cherokee Nation as a territorial entity, though it lives on as a federally recognized tribe with an elected government, the largest tribe in the United States measured by total membership. Not all the eastern Cherokees, however, had submitted to removal. A few hundred holdouts remained in the remote mountains of western North Carolina, where their descendants today have a small reservation and separate tribal recognition as the Eastern Band of Cherokee Indians. Other small groups of Cherokees also remain scattered throughout the old eastern domain. And what of Sequoyah, the great teacher who brought the power of writing to his people? In 1842, when he was more than seventy years old, he embarked on a quixotic journey through the Republic of Texas and across the Rio Grande into Mexico, in search of rumored remnants of the Texas Cherokees. He reportedly "died somewhere along the trail" (Carter 1976, 276).

Despite the defeat of the Cherokee in the 1830s, the principles Chief Justice Marshall set forth in the Cherokee Cases have been vindicated in the court of history. Later Supreme Courts have continued to cite and build upon them in resolving Indian law cases from across the country. They laid the foundation for the legal framework that continues to govern the triangular relationship of the states, the tribes, and the federal government and their respective rights, powers, and duties toward each other.

Indian Treaty Rights

The Cherokee Cases came in the middle of the Treaty Era of U.S.-Indian relations. Just two years after American independence was declared in 1776, the United States entered into its first treaty with an Indian nation: the Delaware-U.S. Treaty of 1778. Ninety years later, it entered into its last: the Nez Percé–U.S. Treaty of 1868. Three years later, Congress decreed that no more such treaties would be negotiated, though it preserved the validity of those that had already taken effect (1871 Act of Congress). In practice, the U.S. government continued entering into numerous "agreements" with Indian tribes for several decades after 1871, and modern times have seen a revival of this approach. Such agreements often differ from treaties only in that they are ratified by legislation adopted by both houses of Congress, rather than by the Senate alone.

During the ninety-five years of the Treaty Era, more than 350 Indian treaties became part of U.S. law. There is no question that they became a valid part of "the supreme law of the land" on a par with federal statutes (U.S. Const., art. VI, cl. 2). The Constitution, framed in 1787, expressly provided for the continuing force of treaties previously "made . . . under the authority of the United States" (U.S. Const., art. VI, cl. 2), which were known to include the seven treaties with Indian nations entered into from 1778 to 1786.

And yet, the Indian treaties were obviously different in important ways from the treaties the United States negotiated with foreign nations such as Britain and France. As Francis Paul Prucha, one of the greatest scholars of American Indian law, has noted:

> It will not do to insist on univocal definitions while ignoring the multifaceted historical reality of the use of treaties in the relationships between the United States and the Indian communities. Only a detailed historical account will display the nature of the treaties and the many changes through which the understanding and use of the treaties passed in the course of American history. (Prucha 1994, 2)

The United States never recognized the Indian nations within its borders as foreign sovereigns enjoying complete independence. To the contrary, the United States asserted ultimate sovereignty over them, to the exclusion of any foreign power. The Indian treaties were thus not part of or governed by international law, at least in the view of the United States. As time went on, the U.S. attitude toward the Indian tribes became more and more patronizing and supervisory. In the early years, during the Revolutionary War and the War of 1812, Americans had good cause to fear the military power of the Indian nations, which often allied themselves with Britain. Thus, the early treaties were negotiated on a more equal basis.

But as U.S. power increased relative to that of the tribes, the relationship became increasingly unequal. Treaties became less about true negotiation and more about implementing U.S. policies and goals, whether the Indians liked them or not. Bribery and coercion became common, corrupting many treaties. President Jefferson, in an 1803 letter to Indian fighter and future president William Henry

Harrison, commented: "We presume that our strength and their weakness is now so visible that they must see we have only to shut our hand to crush them" (Prucha 2000, 6).

Many U.S.-Indian treaties have turned out to have remarkable longevity, as discussed in this section and indeed throughout this book. And they have played an immeasurably important role in preserving Indian sovereignty, both as an enduring aspiration of Native Americans and as reality on the ground. But this is partly a testament to the law of unintended consequences. The original intent behind many treaties, at least on the part of the United States and especially as to the later treaties, was to transform and eventually dissolve the Indian nations:

> [C]ontributing to the anomalous character of the Indian treaties was the persistent drive of white society and its government to change—indeed, to revolutionize—Indian societies by the promotion of white civilization. The treaties themselves, to a remarkable degree, were instruments intended to transform the cultures of the tribes. (Prucha 1994, 9)

Evaluate Prucha's comment above by comparing the Cherokee-U.S. Treaty of 1785 and the Navajo-U.S. Treaty of 1868, set forth in the Documents section. Can you identify which provisions, if any, support Prucha's theory? Then, after you have had an opportunity to finish this chapter and the associated documents in Part 2, consider which treaty has actually endured as a stronger shield of Indian sovereignty. Which tribe has become more assimilated, culturally and territorially? Do the experiences of the Cherokee and Navajo confirm Prucha's belief, suggested by the quotation above, that understanding Indian treaty law depends less on legal theory and more on appreciating the actual course of history, in all its particular twists and turns? Geography and economics also doubtless play a very influential role, as much if not more so than the language in legal documents.

The most important question regarding Indian treaty rights is whether and how they can legally be abrogated. The Cherokee Cases, especially *Worcester,* established that states have no such power. But what about the federal government? Chief Justice Marshall's eloquent defense of Cherokee treaty rights in *Worcester* was built upon a foundation of asserted federal power over Indian affairs.

What if that power were turned *against* the Indians, as it was against the Cherokee following the *Worcester* decision?

In the decades after *Worcester*, the Court had a chance to build upon Marshall's reasoning. The Supreme Court first clearly endorsed Congress's power to abrogate an Indian treaty in the *Cherokee Tobacco* case, decided on May 1, 1871, less than two months after the March 3, 1871, act of Congress terminating any new Indian treaty making. An 1868 federal law had expanded the federal tobacco tax without making any reference to Indian lands or treaties. The Cherokee-U.S. Treaty of 1866 had expressly guaranteed the right of Cherokee farmers to market their produce within the Cherokee Nation exempt from federal tax. The Court held 4–2 (three justices not participating) that the 1868 statute must have implicitly abrogated that part of the 1866 treaty.

Justice Joseph P. Bradley's dissent, joined by Justice David Davis, strikingly foreshadowed modern scholarly arguments that statutes should not be construed to abrogate Indian treaty rights unless the intent to do so is expressly stated on the face of the law. Bradley pointed out that while

> Congress has occasionally passed laws affecting [the Indian territory], yet by repeated treaties the government has in effect stipulated that in all ordinary cases the Indian populations shall be autonomies, invested with the power to make and execute all laws for their domestic government. Such being the case, all laws of a general character passed by Congress will be considered as not applying to the Indian territory, unless expressly mentioned. (*Cherokee Tobacco* 1871, 622)

Furthermore, Bradley noted,

> The exempt jurisdiction here depends on a solemn treaty . . . in which the good faith of the government is involved. . . . In such a case there are peculiar reasons for applying with great strictness the rule that the exempt jurisdiction must be expressly mentioned in order to be affected. (*Cherokee Tobacco* 1871, 623)

In *United States v. Kagama* (1886), the Court considered Congress's assertion, in the Major Crimes Act of 1885, of jurisdiction over certain crimes committed by Indians on Indian lands. The Court discussed which clauses of the Constitution, if any, might confer power on the federal government to regulate the affairs of Indian nations. Recall that Marshall, in *Worcester,* had referred to a combination of the war power, the treaty power, and the power to regulate commerce with the Indian tribes.

The *Kagama* Court noted that "it would be a very strained construction" of Congress's commerce power to impose a criminal code "without any reference to . . . commerce" (*United States v. Kagama* 1886, 378–379). The treaty power could not apply, since no tribe had consented by treaty to this expansion of non-Indian power over internal Indian affairs. In any event, as noted above, Congress had recently terminated Indian treaty making. Nor did Congress or the Court invoke the war power. Most tribes had long been at peace with the United States. The Apache under Geronimo, the last to surrender on the battlefield, were defeated the very year *Kagama* was decided.

The *Kagama* Court suggested reliance on a constitutional clause that Marshall had not mentioned in *Worcester:* the territory clause, granting Congress the "power to dispose of and make all needful rules and regulations respecting the territory or other property belonging to the United States" (U.S. Const., art. IV, § 3, cl. 2). This clause may be a plausible textual source of federal constitutional power over the Indian nations, even if those who framed and adopted the Constitution probably did not contemplate applying it in that way. At the time the Constitution was adopted, relations with eastern Indian tribes were governed by a handful of early treaties, and the United States had not yet sought to exercise any power over their internal affairs. The United States had not yet even acquired the territories encompassing the vast bulk of western tribes. How to handle relations with the Indians over the long term was mostly an unresolved puzzle at that point. But according to *Johnson v. M'Intosh* (1823), the fact of conquest, however unjustly, brought the Indian nations and their lands within U.S. territory and under ultimate U.S. sovereignty and ownership. Marshall had confirmed in *Cherokee Nation* that "Indian territory is admitted to compose a part of the United States" (17). Indian lands are thus analogous for some purposes to other tracts of territory subject to direct and comprehensive federal jurisdiction, such as military bases and national parks.

The *Kagama* Court did not rely, however, on the territory clause. Instead, it argued rather vaguely that Congress's power rested not so much on constitutional language as on "the ownership of the country in which the territories are, and the right of exclusive sovereignty which must exist in the national government, and can be found nowhere else" (380). Emphasizing the "dependent" nature of the Indians as "wards of the nation," the Court unanimously concluded:

> The power of the [federal] government over these remnants of a race once powerful, now weak and diminished in numbers, is necessary to their protection, as well as to the safety of those among whom they dwell. It must exist in that government, because it never has existed anywhere else; because the theater of its exercise is within the geographical limits of the United States; because it has never been denied; and because it alone can enforce its laws on all the tribes. (383–385)

In the course of all this, the *Kagama* Court (in dicta, i.e., discussion not essential to the Court's holding) seemed to dismiss the very existence of Native American sovereignty: "The soil and the people within [the United States] are under the political control of the government of the United States, or of the states of the Union. There exists within the broad domain of sovereignty *but these two*" (379; emphasis added).

It should be kept in mind, as mentioned in Chapter 2, that the period from about 1870 to 1930 was the all-time low point for Native American sovereignty and the political, cultural, and material status of American Indians generally. Perhaps the very nadir of this era, from the standpoint of Indian sovereignty, was the Supreme Court's ruling in *Lone Wolf v. Hitchcock* (1903). *Lone Wolf* is probably the most infamous and harshly criticized Indian law decision in the history of U.S. courts. It held that Congress did indeed have the power to abrogate Indian treaties and that it could do so practically at will, without any judicially enforceable duty of compensation.

Read the *Lone Wolf* opinion in the Documents section at this point, but be aware that the opinion does not tell the entire story. Under the terms of the Kiowa-Comanche-U.S. Treaty of 1867, a reservation was set aside for those tribes in the Indian Territory (later Oklahoma). By a later treaty, some Apache Indians were settled there along with the Kiowa and Comanche. The treaty provided that no cession of any tribal land on the reservation would be valid without the signed consent of at least three-fourths of all the adult male Indians. In 1892, however, U.S. commissioners negotiated an agreement under which part of the reservation would be divided up into individual allotments for tribal members and the remainder, treated as "surplus," would be opened up to white settlement in return for a lump-sum payment.

Even as the 1892 agreement was submitted to Congress for approval, the Indians hotly objected that it was a swindle. Although the agreement purported to have been signed by more than three-fourths of the Indians on the reservation, the U.S. secretary of the interior confirmed that it had not. The Indians claimed deception and fraudulent misrepresentation. Once the terms were widely understood, they were almost unanimously opposed. They testified before Congress against it and submitted a protest memorial signed by more tribal members than had allegedly signed the agreement itself. The secretary of the interior urged Congress to reject the agreement, noting the Indian opposition and that, in any event, the allotments should be at least doubled in size because of the poor quality of the land. The agreement provided for "compensating" the tribes for their "surplus" lands at the rate of one dollar an acre, far below their true value. A few years later, white settlers were charged $1.75 an acre for homesteads on the land, and even that was doubtless a highly subsidized rate.

The Senate was more reluctant than the House of Representatives to endorse the agreement. An 1899 Senate resolution requested the secretary of the interior's feedback, and the agreement died in the Senate during that session of Congress. The House remained enthusiastic to pass it, however, so much so that during the following Congress it was tacked on to an unrelated bill whose title remained deceptively unchanged. The bill incorporated changes in the 1892 agreement, which had been made without any pretense of further consultation with the Indians. In this form, it slipped by both Houses of Congress and became law in 1900. The Indians promptly brought a lawsuit and lost in the trial court. Even as the appeal was pending, President William McKinley ordered the "surplus" lands opened to white settlement. By the time the case reached the Supreme Court, 13,000 non-Indian homesteads had already been established.

The Court's opinion, written by Justice Edward D. White (who was appointed chief justice seven years later), conceded most of these objections to the 1892 agreement and the dodgy manner in which it passed Congress. The same Court, during this same era, zealously guarded property rights in other areas and usually strictly enforced the constitutional requirement of "just compensation" for governmental takings of property (U.S. Const., amend. V). But in *Lone Wolf* it held Indian property rights of little account. Although conceding the "sacred" nature of Indian title, the Court found that Congress enjoyed "[p]lenary authority" over Indian land rights (564–565).

To the extent that the *Cherokee Tobacco* and *Lone Wolf* Courts held that a treaty may be abrogated by an act of Congress, they were (at first glance) not wildly out of line with generally accepted legal principles. Federal statutes and treaties have always been considered to be on the same plane of authority. Both are trumped by the U.S. Constitution, but either may be modified or repealed by any subsequent federal statute or treaty. Both *Cherokee Tobacco* and *Lone Wolf* cited earlier cases so holding as to treaties with foreign nations. Foreign policy reasons may often arise that require disengagement from a treaty entered into with a foreign nation. Indeed, many foreign treaties have express provisions allowing either party, under certain procedures usually involving advance notice, to walk away.

This reasoning, however, begs the question whether such a raw power of unilateral treaty abrogation could be justified in the case of an Indian treaty, contrary to procedures set forth in the treaty, given that it amounted to a deprivation of the property interests of people residing within the United States. As one leading Indian law scholar has aptly observed,

> a power to unilaterally abrogate treaties with foreign nations involves no potential enlargement of American sovereignty over foreign nations or their subjects, merely a potential violation of international law. By contrast, . . . in *Lone Wolf*, the United States abrogated the Indian treaty so that it could appropriate and redistribute *tribal* land. (Clinton 2002, 186; emphasis in original)

Even if Congress's power to abrogate an Indian treaty were properly conceded, one would think the *Lone Wolf* Court would have enforced or at least reviewed the Indian claim to compensation for the property seized against their will. But the Court found this to be a "political" question, purely a matter of "governmental policy" beyond the reach of judicial review (565). Because, taken on its face, the 1892 agreement "purported to give an adequate consideration for the surplus lands not allotted among the Indians," the Court viewed it as "a mere change in the form of investment of Indian tribal property. . . . We must presume that Congress acted in perfect good faith in the[se] dealings with the Indians . . . , and that the legislative branch of the government exercised its best judgment" (568).

Recall, as discussed previously, that a corollary of the canons of treaty construction, rooted in the Cherokee Cases, is the notion that the U.S. government has a "trust relationship" with Indian nations. Under well-established legal principles, a trust relationship implies that the "trustee" has "fiduciary duties" toward the "ward"—meaning essentially that the U.S. government has a duty to protect Indian interests. But instead of using this "trust" doctrine to scrutinize the U.S. government's conduct as trustee in *Lone Wolf*, the Court (as noted above) simply assumed the government's "perfect good faith." The Court's conclusion, astonishingly callous under the circumstances detailed in its own opinion, was that "[i]f injury was occasioned, which we do not wish to be understood as implying, by the use made by Congress of its power, relief must be sought . . . [from] that body" (568). Although the *Lone Wolf* decision was unanimous, the opinion may have been too much to stomach for Justice John Marshall Harlan, the great dissenter in the *Elk* and *Plessy* cases, as discussed in Chapter 2. He concurred only in the result.

Quite clearly, if *Kagama* heralded a doctrine of federal plenary power over Indians, *Lone Wolf* suggested plenary power on steroids. Even if there were some theoretical basis for such federal power, the issue of limitations on that power was not satisfactorily resolved. *Lone Wolf* simply announced a policy of judicial abdication. Although the Constitution contains no express protection for tribal sovereignty, it does expressly authorize treaty making, and it expressly preserved the validity of previously made treaties. As discussed above, that was clearly understood to encompass Indian treaties. Although Indian treaty making was terminated in 1871 and many individual treaties have been modified or abrogated, the United States has never gone so far as to renounce wholesale the century's worth of Indian treaty obligations it undertook as a nation between 1778 and 1868. Could the Constitution tolerate such a massive breach of national faith? Would it be legal in a strictly positivist sense but immoral and wrong in terms of natural justice? Or does the Constitution itself embody principles of natural justice?

A related question is whether treaty making (along with just wars, perhaps) may be the *only* constitutionally legitimate means for the U.S. government to carry on relations with the Indian nations. In other words, perhaps the "plenary power" doctrine is purely a phantom—an invented, post hoc rationalization for conquest without any legitimate constitutional basis. Modern scholars have pointed out that *Johnson v. M'Intosh, Kagama, Lone Wolf,* and many other Indian law cases from that era are deeply, perhaps irretrievably, tainted by racist and colonialist ideologies and presumptions of Indian inferiority. They are premised on the notion of "conquest," which amounts to little more than an arbitrary assertion of raw power. The Supreme Court has long since rejected other relics from that same era, such as *Plessy v. Ferguson* (1896), which endorsed racial segregation. How can the Court continue (as it does) to cite and rely upon cases like *Kagama* and *Lone Wolf?*

Several modern scholars of Indian law have argued, indeed, that the Court *cannot* properly do so. Some urge a return to treaty making as the only legitimate means to handle Indian relations. One recent law review article by a leading Indian law scholar is entitled simply, "There Is No Federal Supremacy Clause for Indian Tribes" (Clinton 2002). But are such advocates quixotically tilting at windmills? Given how far Native American sovereignty has eroded as a historical fact, is it realistic to try to resurrect a treaty relationship between what remains of the Indian nations and the world's only superpower? Is there any point, at this late date, in challenging the legality of the conquest?

There may be no clear or satisfactory answers to the foregoing questions. The best-informed legal scholars continue to debate them. But consider them as you read the remainder of this section and the rest of this book. At this point, read the opinions in *United States v. Sioux Nation* (1980) in the Documents section and compare them to *Lone Wolf.* You will see that Justice Harry A. Blackmun's 8–1 majority opinion in *Sioux Nation* provided a very thorough narrative of the facts of that case, which involved Congress's 1877 expropriation of the Black Hills of South Dakota in violation of the Sioux-Arapaho-U.S. Treaty of Fort Laramie of 1868. For that reason, the background of *Sioux Nation* is not set forth in detail here.

In comparing *Lone Wolf* and *Sioux Nation,* consider whether and in what ways the *Sioux Nation* Court reaffirmed or rejected *Lone Wolf* as a guiding precedent. Obviously, *Lone Wolf* was not overruled outright. Courts only rarely take such a drastic step with regard to prior judicial decisions, under the principle of stare decisis (a Latin phrase meaning literally, "let the decision stand"). But did the Court in 1980 get around or undermine the *Lone Wolf* holding? How carefully and skeptically did the *Sioux Nation* Court scrutinize the U.S. government's conduct as "trustee" for the Indians?

Note that the *Sioux Nation* Court discusses the Indian Claims Commission Act of 1946. This statute was passed by Congress to give Indian tribes a judicial forum in which to seek compensation for past treaty violations, seizures of land, and other cases of unjust treatment by the U.S. government. It was necessary to pass a law authorizing such court claims because normally the United States enjoys "sovereign immunity," a doctrine that prevents the government from being sued for money damages in court. There are other ways in which governmental conduct can be contested in court, such as when the government seeks to prosecute someone for a crime or to enforce an allegedly unconstitutional law or policy. In cases like that, sovereign immunity may not apply since the government itself chooses to go to court. But as a general matter, oddly enough, it is very difficult to simply bring a lawsuit challenging some alleged governmental misdeed and seeking compensation without first getting the government's own permission. Both state governments and Indian tribal governments also enjoy sovereign immunity, although the federal government has the power in some cases to override their immunity.

In 1923, Congress had passed a special law allowing the Sioux to file a claim contesting the Black Hills seizure. The Sioux lost that lawsuit, and when they refiled under the 1946 law, the Court of Claims eventually ruled against them, citing the earlier decision. It was on appeal from that decision that the Supreme Court reversed the Court of Claims and found the Sioux entitled to more than $17.5 million in compensation for the land and gold they lost in 1877. With interest accrued over more than a century, the award came to more than $100 million in 1980. The Sioux, however, have never collected the award, which continues to sit in a government bank account, accruing more interest every year (it is now worth several hundred million dollars). The Sioux insist they are entitled to a return of at least some of the land itself and fear that accepting the cash award might forever destroy such a possibility.

Another aspect of *Sioux Nation* is worth commenting upon. You will note that the Court said: "Only if the acquisition of the Black Hills amounted to an unconstitutional taking would the Sioux be entitled to interest" (387). That is because the 1946 law offered compensation for two different kinds of Indian property seizures by the

U.S. government. If the property was land to which the Indian tribe could claim only "Indian title" —that is, a claim that they were the original occupants of the land without any other legal basis for ownership recognized by U.S. law (see Chapter 2)—then the Indians might receive compensation for the value of the land at the time it was taken but not the interest accrued since then. Only if the tribe could show that the property seized was guaranteed to them by treaty or some other formality recognized by U.S. law would they be entitled to interest on the value of the property taken. Luckily for the Sioux, they were able to show that Congress's seizure of the Black Hills did indeed violate the terms of the 1868 Treaty of Fort Laramie.

In *Tee-Hit-Ton Indians v. United States* (1955), a case less famous than *Lone Wolf* but in some ways even more shocking, the Supreme Court held that Congress was not strictly obliged to provide *any compensation at all* for seizures of Indian land supported only by Indian title. Even *Lone Wolf* had not gone so far. The *Lone Wolf* Court said in essence that it would trust Congress's good faith in providing some fair equivalent for the value of seized Indian land, whether supported by Indian title alone or (as in *Lone Wolf*) by treaty guarantees. The *Tee-Hit-Ton* Court upheld in principle the legality of refusing to provide *any* equivalent for the value of Indian title standing alone. Only if Indian land were guaranteed by treaty or some other formal recognition by European Americans would its seizure be considered a "taking" for which the Constitution would require "just compensation" (U.S. Const., amend. V). This reasoning amounted to saying that Indians had no land rights—even on lands that they had occupied for uncounted generations before Columbus arrived—except those that European Americans might deign to grant them.

The *Tee-Hit-Ton* Court claimed to derive this principle from Chief Justice Marshall's opinion in *Johnson v. M'Intosh* (1823). It phrased the rule as follows:

> After conquest [Indians] were permitted to occupy portions of territory over which they had previously exercised "sovereignty," as we use that term. This is not a property right but amounts to a right of occupancy which the sovereign grants and protects against intrusion by third parties but which right of occupancy may be terminated and such lands fully disposed of by the sovereign itself without any legally enforceable obligation to compensate the Indians. (279)

In fact, the final quoted words, "without any legally enforceable obligation to compensate the Indians," went well beyond Marshall's reasoning. *Johnson v. M'Intosh* merely required a decision as to whom Indians could legally convey their land title. A priority rule was needed to resolve a title dispute between non-Indians. Johnson held title originating in grants by certain Indian tribes to private land speculators, and M'Intosh held title based on a grant by the U.S. government, which had obtained the lands from the tribes by treaty. Marshall held that Indian tribes could convey full legal title only to the U.S. government. Although inherently patronizing, this rule—also rooted in the Trade and Intercourse Act of 1790—has at least served the valuable purpose of helping to protect Indian lands, to a certain extent, from being alienated over the years to mostly hostile state governments or private land speculators and swindlers. Indeed, this nonalienation rule led to one of the most striking Indian legal victories in the modern Supreme Court. In *Oneida County v. Oneida Indian Nation* (1985), the Court ruled 5–4 that a transfer of Indian land to the state of New York in 1795 was invalid because it was not approved by the federal government. A number of eastern tribes have been able to negotiate generous settlements as a result of successful claims like this.

Marshall certainly held in *Johnson v. M'Intosh*, as discussed in Chapter 2, that the Indian tribes lost full sovereignty and the full power to dispose of their lands as a result of the European American conquest. He conceded the power of the United States to extinguish the Indians' remaining land rights—their aboriginal Indian title. But he never suggested that the United States was free to do so *without any legal consequences.* To the contrary, Marshall asserted that "the exclusive power to extinguish that right [of Indian occupancy], was vested in that government which might *constitutionally* exercise it" (585; emphasis added). He added that even though the "title by conquest is acquired and maintained by force, . . . humanity demands, and a wise policy requires, that the rights of the conquered to property should remain unimpaired" (589). Marshall, in this passage, was speaking of conquest in a generic and theoretical sense. He was not called upon to decide in that case whether the European American conquest of North America could constitutionally justify the dispossession without compensation of the American Indians. What "humanity" and "a wise policy" might require of some hypothetical conqueror, the *Constitution* surely requires of the United States.

All sovereign governments have traditionally enjoyed the power to extinguish property rights held by anyone under their rule, when necessary for some overriding public purpose. That reflects the ancient principle of "eminent domain." But the very purpose of the takings clause of the Fifth Amendment was to place a constitutional condition on the exercise of this sovereign power. It is impossible to conceive of any legitimate basis for excluding Indian nations from the benefit of that constitutional principle.

The actual basis for the Court's 1955 *Tee-Hit-Ton* decision was perhaps best revealed in a footnote to the majority opinion, which noted the U.S. government's contention "that if aboriginal Indian title was compensable . . . , there were claims with estimated interest already pending . . . aggregating $9,000,000,000" (283, n. 17). With remarkably crude candor, the Court concluded:

> [T]he savage tribes of this continent were deprived of their ancestral ranges by force and . . . even when the Indians ceded millions of acres by treaty in return for blankets, food and trinkets, it was not a sale but the conquerors' will that deprived them of their land. . . .
>
> [N]o other course would meet the problem of the growth of the United States. . . . Our conclusion . . . leaves with Congress, where it belongs, the policy of Indian gratuities for the termination of Indian occupancy of Government-owned land rather than making compensation for its value a rigid constitutional principle. (289–291)

Tee-Hit-Ton thus culminated the nakedly colonialist theory of plenary power developed in *Kagama* and *Lone Wolf.* Although derived to a certain extent from Marshall's opinions, it was also a grotesque perversion of his respect for the legal rights of Native Americans as reflected in *Worcester. Tee-Hit-Ton* was a 5–3 decision, but Justice William O. Douglas's dissent, joined by Chief Justice Earl Warren and Justice Felix Frankfurter, did not challenge the majority's theory of Congress's power. The dissenters merely argued that Congress had, in fact, granted legal recognition to the Indian title at issue in an 1884 law organizing the territory of Alaska. Even a Justice like Hugo L. Black, a notable defender of Indian rights in other cases, joined silently with the majority. Needless to say, cases like *Lone Wolf* and *Tee-Hit-Ton* demonstrate that the U.S. government's fiduciary duties as "trustee" for the Indians have often been honored more in the breach than in the observance.

In *Sioux Nation,* the Supreme Court did not overrule either *Lone Wolf* or *Tee-Hit-Ton.* Indeed, although the *Sioux Nation* Court was certainly much more skeptical and critical than the *Lone Wolf* Court in analyzing Congress's actions, it was Congress itself that was mostly responsible for the different outcome in 1980. The Supreme Court was able to hear the *Sioux Nation* case only because Congress, in 1946, had passed the Indian Claims Commission Act and, in 1978, had passed another law authorizing the Court of Claims to reconsider the Sioux claim. Thus, although *Sioux Nation* did suggest that the modern Supreme Court is more sympathetic to Indian treaty claims, it was also a reminder that Congress ultimately possesses plenary power over the issue. It would be wishful thinking to suppose that *Sioux Nation* reflects any willingness by the Court to challenge Congress's ultimate power to abrogate Indian treaties or Congress's power to control whether and how any compensation may be obtained by Indian nations for seizures of their lands, even when guaranteed by treaty.

Another aspect of *Sioux Nation* deserving consideration is Justice William H. Rehnquist's lone dissent. Although he was isolated in that case, he was appointed chief justice in 1986 and has generally played an influential role in Indian law cases on the modern Supreme Court. When you reach that point in your reading, compare his *Sioux Nation* dissent with his dissenting opinion in the much closer 5–4 decision in *Minnesota v. Mille Lacs Band of Chippewa Indians* (1999) (discussed later in this section) and his majority opinion in *Oliphant v. Suquamish Indian Tribe* (1978) (discussed in the following section). How would you summarize Rehnquist's attitude toward Indian sovereignty?

The discussion so far in this section has focused on the power to abrogate Indian treaty rights. But even if Congress has that raw power, it may often be reluctant to exercise it. And the courts may be equally reluctant to conclude that Congress has done so. As is so often true in law, the issue becomes one of interpretation. The courts must interpret treaty provisions to decide what rights, if any, they conferred on the Indians. And the courts must interpret both the treaties and Congress's legislation in order to decide whether a given Indian treaty right has in fact been abrogated. It is here that the "canons of construction" pioneered in the Cherokee Cases become extremely important. The canons are essentially rules of interpretation. In theory, they guide courts toward a generous reading of Indian rights under treaties and other sources of Indian law and create a presumption against abrogation or dilution of Native American sovereignty. In practice, things have not been quite that simple.

The Supreme Court's approach to Indian treaty rights has taken a meandering and inconsistent course in the 170 years since *Worcester* was decided. Some older decisions have construed treaty provisions with surprising breadth and firmness. Indeed, one of the most striking early applications of the canons of construction by the Supreme Court came just two years after *Lone Wolf.* In *United States v. Winans* (1905), the Court generously construed treaty language guaranteeing Indians "the right of taking fish at all usual and accustomed places, in common with citizens of the territory" that later became Washington state (378). In response to the argument that this language merely assured the Indians equal rights with non-Indians, the Court observed that this interpretation would afford the Indians "no rights but such as they would have without the treaty. This is certainly an impotent outcome to negotiations and a convention which seemed to promise more" (380).

The *Winans* Court found the Indians entitled under the treaty, among other things, to cross privately owned non-Indian land to gain access to traditional fishing places. The Court pointed out that such rights were merely "a part of larger rights possessed by the Indians" prior to their loss of full sovereignty over the land, rights "not much less necessary to the[ir] existence . . . than the atmosphere they breathed" (381). Indian treaties were properly seen, the Court said, "not [as] a grant of rights to the Indians, but a grant of rights from them—a reservation [by the Indians] of those not granted" (381). That is, although the Indians had agreed by treaty to give up some of their rights, which they had exercised since time immemorial, they reserved by default those that were not clearly surrendered. This was consistent with non-Indian property rights and the state's ability, upon its admission to the Union, to exercise its authority on an "equal footing" with other states. The state's authority and the property rights of non-Indian citizens were properly limited from the outset by the federal government's decision "to secure to the Indians such a remnant of the great rights they [once] possessed" (384). It "only fixe[d] in the land such easements as enable the right[s] to be exercised" (384). Any state's authority might be so limited, as indeed that of Georgia (one of the original thirteen) had been found to be in *Worcester.*

Modern courts have followed the *Winans* approach in several high-profile and controversial lawsuits over Indian fishing rights. Litigation over salmon fishing in the Pacific Northwest led to a Supreme Court decision upholding Indian treaty rights to up to half the available catch, in *Washington v. Washington State Commercial Passenger Fishing Vessel Association* (1979). Lower court decisions in the 1980s upholding Indian treaty fishing rights in Wisconsin led to ugly outbreaks of violence and racist anti-Indian rhetoric. Other Supreme Court decisions have arguably failed to honor the canons of construction. Perhaps the most notorious example is *Federal Power Commission v. Tuscarora Indian Nation* (1960). The state of New York sought to condemn and inundate (albeit with compensation) part of the Tuscarora reservation for a federally funded dam project. The Tuscarora claimed that this violated rights stretching back to a 1794 treaty between the United States and the Six Nations of Iroquois (Haudenosaunee) Indians (the Tuscarora, Oneida, Mohawk, Onondaga, Cayuga, and Seneca). It was far from clear that Congress ever intended to override the land rights of the Tuscarora. But the Court, 6–3, held that federal legislation implicitly did so. The dam was built, and the reservation flooded.

Justice Black's impassioned dissent in *Tuscarora,* joined by Chief Justice Warren and Justice Douglas, is one of the most often quoted in American Indian law. Black did not challenge Congress's power to authorize the dam, but he argued that courts should not infer such authorization without evidence that Congress clearly, specifically, and intentionally abrogated tribal rights. That way, Congress would not be able to dodge the issue and leave the dirty work to the courts or administrative agencies. Black quoted the words of Senator Sam Houston of Texas in an 1854 speech regarding promises made to other Indians:

> As long as water flows, or grass grows upon the earth, or the sun rises to show your pathway, or you kindle your camp fires, so long shall you be protected by this Government, and never again removed from your present habitations. (140)

Black dissected the legal issues in the case with a pithy eloquence recalling John Marshall. "The solemn pledge of the United States," he asserted, "is not to be construed like a money-lender's mortgage" (137).

> It may be hard for us to understand why these Indians cling so tenaciously to their lands and traditional tribal way of life. The record does not leave the impression that the lands of [the Tuscarora] reservation are the most fertile, the landscape the most beautiful or their homes the most splendid specimens of architecture. But this is their home—their ancestral home. There, they, their children, and their forebears were born. They, too, have their memories and their loves. Some things are worth more than money and the costs of a new enterprise.
> . . . Great nations, like great men, should keep their word. (142)

That this was the same Justice Black who concurred silently in the 1955 *Tee-Hit-Ton* decision illustrates the contradictory tensions in the Court's Indian treaty cases.

There has been persistent tension and dispute over exactly how strong a presumption should exist in favor of reserved Indian treaty rights. In *Menominee Tribe v. United States* (1968), the Court suggested that only an explicit statement by Congress would suffice to abrogate an Indian treaty. The Court's membership by then had become notably more liberal than in 1955 or 1960, and Justice Douglas, who had dissented in *Tee-Hit-Ton* and *Tuscarora,* wrote the *Menominee* opinion for a 6–2 majority. In 1975, a major law review article by two leading Indian law scholars advocated strict and universal application of the *Menominee* approach. This "rule of express legislative action," they argued, would ensure that "no [treaty] abrogation would occur without full notice and disclosure to the affected tribes" (Wilkinson and Volkman 1975, 659). But the Court has declined to adopt such a strict rule. In *United States v. Dion* (1986), the Court found that a federal law generally banning the hunting of eagles overrode a claimed treaty hunting right. Although Congress had not explicitly abrogated any treaty hunting rights in the law, a limited exemption written into the law allowed some taking of eagles by Indians for religious purposes. This, along with the legislative history of the law, provided clear evidence that Congress must have considered Indian treaty rights and (aside from the express religious exemption) intentionally decided to override them.

Dion may have departed only slightly from the rule suggested by *Menominee* and scholars like Wilkinson and Volkman. But other cases have veered farther away. In *South Dakota v. Bourland* (1993), the Supreme Court dealt with another case involving Sioux rights under the Fort Laramie Treaty of 1868. The 7–2 majority held that the

Cheyenne River Sioux Tribe had lost the treaty right to regulate non-Indian hunting and fishing on land taken for a federal dam project. Congress did not expressly abrogate the tribe's regulatory rights, but the majority found that result to be fairly implied. Justice Blackmun (the author of *Sioux Nation*) dissented, joined by Justice David H. Souter. Blackmun protested that to "imply an intent to abrogate Indian rights from . . . congressional silence . . . ignores the principles [of *Dion*]" (*South Dakota v. Bourland* 1993, 703).

Against this backdrop, the Supreme Court's decision in *Minnesota v. Mille Lacs Band of Chippewa Indians* (1999) may have been an important turning point. *Mille Lacs* upheld treaty rights claimed by the Chippewa to hunt, fish, and gather plants (collectively referred to as "usufructuary" rights), on lands in Minnesota that they had ceded to the United States in the Chippewa-U.S. Treaty of 1837. Just as in the 1905 *Winans* case, a central issue in *Mille Lacs* concerned the impact on Indian treaty rights of the sovereign powers assumed by states upon their admission to the Union on an "equal footing" with other states.

Read the *Mille Lacs* opinions set forth in the Documents section at this point. You may find them somewhat difficult going. The sequence of events is rather complex, and both Justice O'Connor's majority opinion and Chief Justice Rehnquist's dissent make a series of clever arguments. The 1837 treaty gave the president the power to terminate at his or her pleasure the Chippewa treaty rights on the lands ceded by that treaty. There is no dispute that the president still has that power today. The issue is whether that presidential power has ever actually been effectively exercised. The Chippewa, in another treaty concluded in 1842, ceded ownership of some additional lands but continued to live in the general area. The 1842 treaty expressly gave the president the power to actually remove (at his or her pleasure) the Chippewa from the lands covered by that treaty. In 1850, President Zachary Taylor ordered the removal of the Chippewa from the lands covered by both the 1837 and 1842 treaties and purported to revoke all their privileges under both treaties. Because of Chippewa resistance, however, the removal order was never carried out, and it was abandoned when President Franklin Pierce took office in 1853.

Justice O'Connor concluded in *Mille Lacs* that the 1850 removal order was invalid with regard to the lands covered by the 1837 treaty because that treaty only gave the president power to revoke the treaty rights to hunt, fish, and gather, not to actually force the removal of the Indians. However, as Chief Justice Rehnquist pointed out in dissent, the 1850 order *did* expressly revoke *all* privileges under *both* treaties, and there was no dispute that the president had the power to wipe out the 1837 usufructuary rights, even if he could not validly force the Chippewa to actually leave the 1837 lands. From Rehnquist's standpoint, Minnesota had an airtight case that the treaty rights were extinguished in 1850, even though removal was never carried out.

As icing on the cake, Rehnquist argued that yet a third Chippewa-U.S. Treaty, that of 1855, which ceded still more Chippewa lands to the United States, *independently* extinguished the 1837 treaty rights. The 1855 treaty provided generally that the Chippewa "fully and entirely relinquish . . . any and all right, title, and interest, of whatsoever nature the same may be . . . to any other lands in the Territory of Minnesota or elsewhere" (Chippewa-U.S. Treaty of 1855, 1166). Rehnquist also found the 1837 treaty rights null and void on yet a *third* ground. Because such usufructuary rights are typically "temporary and precarious" by nature, they were, he argued, implicitly abrogated by Congress's admission of Minnesota as a state in 1858. In support, Rehnquist cited an 1896 Supreme Court decision that relied on the theory that Indian treaty rights are generally inconsistent with a newly admitted state's right to exercise power over all of its territory on an "equal footing" with other states (*Minnesota v. Mille Lacs Band of Chippewa Indians* 1999, 219–220; *Ward v. Race Horse* 1896, 515).

Not so fast, argued O'Connor for the majority. Would President Taylor have intended to revoke the 1837 treaty rights had he known that his 1850 order was invalid as to removal and, indeed, that the removal would never actually be carried out? No, she concluded, applying the canons of construction. Closely reviewing the history of the botched removal, she found that the 1850 order had to "stand or fall as a whole" (191). Because it was partly invalid to begin with and never carried out, it could not be construed to abrogate the 1837 treaty rights. The majority also stringently applied the canons to the 1855 treaty. Yes, the language at first glance appeared to relinquish "all" Chippewa rights on "any" lands in Minnesota. But the language was vague and general. The focus of the 1855 treaty was on selling lands entirely separate from those covered by the 1837 treaty. There was no explicit mention of the 1837 treaty or of hunting, fishing, and gathering rights. Nor was there any mention of separate compensation for any such abrogated rights. "These omissions are telling," O'Connor found, "because the United States treaty drafters had the sophistication and experience to use express language for the abrogation of treaty rights" (195). She went on to again review the historical record in remarkable detail and with meticulous sensitivity to the Indian perspective.

As for the abrogation argument based on Minnesota statehood in 1858, O'Connor found that completely contrary to the canons of construction. Congress made no mention of any Indian treaty rights in admitting Minnesota. Citing the 1905 *Winans* decision and many later cases, O'Connor rejected as obsolete the main premise of the 1896 *Race Horse* decision. "Treaty rights," she concluded simply, "are not impliedly terminated upon statehood" (207). The majority did not technically overrule *Race Horse,* because O'Connor noted it could be supported on a narrower alternative ground set forth in the 1896 opinion: that the specific treaty rights at issue there were not intended to survive statehood (in that case, of Wyoming).

The approach of the *Mille Lacs* majority may signal a return to stricter judicial adherence to Indian treaty and related land rights. Two years later, by the exact same 5–4 division, the Supreme Court upheld the Coeur d'Alene tribe's title to a lakebed and riverbed in Idaho, against the argument that Idaho had acquired such navigable waterbeds upon statehood in 1890 (*Idaho v. United States* 2001). Although the Coeur d'Alene reservation was not created by treaty, but rather (after 1871) by presidential executive order and an agreement ratified by Congress, the majority employed the same sensitive canons of construction and historical review that marked *Mille Lacs.* Chief Justice Rehnquist again wrote a dissent on behalf of the same justices who dissented in *Mille Lacs.*

The close votes in both the *Mille Lacs* and *Idaho* cases are a reminder of the precarious knife-edge on which Native American sovereignty rests. It is especially illuminating to look closely at Rehnquist's *Mille Lacs* dissent. It is remarkable enough that Rehnquist sought to revive and convert into a general rule of Indian treaty interpretation the *Race Horse* decision of more than 100 years ago. *Race Horse* was a relic of the *Lone Wolf* era whose basic theory was rejected by the Court only nine years later—and ninety-four years before *Mille Lacs*—in the *Winans* case. Even more startling is how Rehnquist went out of his way to construe President Taylor's 1850 executive order as properly terminating the Chippewa treaty rights. He found the rights-terminating and removal portions of the order severable, so that even if the removal portion was invalid, the treaty rights would still be nullified.

But Rehnquist did not stop there. Read carefully the third-to-last paragraph in Part II of his dissent. He found the president legally empowered to remove the Chippewa from the area of the lands ceded in 1837, based merely on alleged *implications* in the 1837 treaty itself. That treaty, of course, only ceded *ownership* of the land while *preserving* (subject to presidential termination) special Chippewa rights to hunt, fish, and gather on it. As Justice O'Connor noted for the majority, "the revocation of [the 1837 treaty] rights would not have prevented the Chippewa from hunting, fishing, and gathering on the ceded territory; . . . [it] would merely have subjected Chippewa hunters, fishers, and gatherers to territorial, and later, state regulation" (192). Rehnquist, by contrast, seemed to assume that simply because tribal property rights were ceded and special treaty usufructuary privileges were revoked (if indeed they were), the Indians properly became subject to forcible relocation to a distant territory. Yet there are many examples throughout U.S. history in which Indians ceded tribal property rights and gave up (or never had) special treaty rights, without being subject to removal.

In *Mille Lacs,* Rehnquist strained to interpret the language of an Indian treaty to authorize Indian removal, one of the most horrific and genocidal policies in U.S. history, apart from slavery. Not only that, he strained to uphold the legal validity and effectiveness of a presidential removal order that was abandoned by that president's successor within three years, precisely because of the practical problems, hardships, and injustices typical of removal generally. It is difficult to imagine an approach in greater conflict with the canons of construction. And Rehnquist spoke for four justices—just one short of a majority of the Court.

Tribal Criminal Jurisdiction

The field in which American Indian sovereignty has been most sharply curtailed in modern times—and controversially so—is tribal criminal jurisdiction over non-Indians and over Indians who happen to be members of other tribes. To set the stage for considering this issue, it is necessary first to survey the overall framework of criminal law on Indian reservations. This is a somewhat convoluted area of law, one that many law students and even experienced lawyers find confusing. A full treatment is well beyond the scope of this book or the needs of a college-level course in this area, but a brief outline is useful.

There are three possible sources of criminal jurisdiction or law enforcement power in any given part of Indian country: the federal government, the government of whatever state in which the Indian tribe is located, and the relevant tribal government. To start with federal criminal jurisdiction, that in turn comes in three broad varieties. First, certain crimes uniquely federal in nature (treason, espionage, theft from U.S. mails, federal drug offenses, federal tax evasion, etc.) are universally punished directly by the federal government, against Indians in Indian country just as against anyone anywhere else within the United States.

Second, serious felonies committed by Indians within Indian country (such as murder, rape, robbery, arson, and kidnapping) are directly punished by the federal government under the Major Crimes Act of 1885. Ordinarily, these are not federal crimes and are prosecuted by state authorities. But as treaties and the Cherokee Cases established early on, states generally cannot extend their jurisdiction into Indian country. This fact was dramatized by the famous case of *Ex parte Kan-Gi-Shun-Ca (Crow Dog)* (1883), in which the Supreme Court found that the Sioux Nation had exclusive jurisdiction to punish a Sioux Indian for killing a fellow tribal member. The Sioux had already handled the matter under their traditional customs of mediation and restitution between the affected families. The Court thus reversed the conviction and death sentence imposed on the Indian defendant by a Dakota territorial court. Congress, following the somewhat hysterical public reaction to this decision (orchestrated by the Bureau of Indian Affairs), decided that the tribes themselves were not up to the task of controlling such serious and violent crimes on the reservation. So it gave the federal government that power in the Major Crimes Act. The Supreme Court upheld this assertion of "plenary" federal power in *United States v. Kagama* (1886).

Third, the federal government, under the Assimilative Crimes Act, directly punishes most criminal offenses, major or minor, committed on federally controlled lands such as military bases and national parks. The definitions and penalties for many of these offenses, especially the minor ones, are borrowed from the law of whatever state in which the federal land is located, but the crimes are handled by federal prosecutors in federal courts. This "federal enclave" criminal law has long been applied to Indian reservations, which are under federal rather than state supervision, *but only with regard to crimes committed by Indians against non-Indians or by non-Indians against Indians.* This is done under the Indian Country Crimes Act, which originated in the 1790 Trade and Intercourse Act generally governing relations with Indian tribes. This federal law has been amended various times over the years, but it has always expressly exempted purely "intra-Indian" crimes, that is, crimes in which both the alleged perpetrator and victim are Indians. Serious felonies committed between Indians *are* federally prosecuted under the Major Crimes Act mentioned above. But minor crimes between Indians are generally left for tribal governments to deal with.

The states traditionally have had very limited criminal jurisdiction (in any direct sense) within Indian country, even when Indian reservations fall within a state's borders. The major historical exception was for crimes committed within Indian country by one non-Indian against another non-Indian. The federal Major Crimes Act was no help in those cases, because it applied only to Indian defendants. The Indian Country Crimes Act might have been construed to support federal jurisdiction, and indeed it was often used in such cases during the 1800s. But in a series of cases starting with *United States v. McBratney* (1882), the Supreme Court (without any basis in statutory or treaty law) held that state power in this situation follows the non-Indian status of the parties rather than stopping at the geographical boundary of the Indian reservation. Thus, the states directly prosecute such crimes, on the theory (somewhat awkward and fictitious) that, even though committed within Indian country, they do not directly affect Indian people.

A second major enlargement of state criminal jurisdiction within Indian country took place in 1953, when Congress passed Public Law 280. This statute granted full criminal jurisdiction over Indians and Indian country (with certain exceptions not relevant here) to six specified states: Alaska, California, Minnesota, Nebraska, Oregon, and Wisconsin. It offered other states the option of assuming such jurisdiction. Under the Indian Civil Rights Act (ICRA) of 1968, Congress required tribal consent for any further expansions of state Public Law 280 jurisdiction. No tribe has granted such consent since 1968, but between 1953 and 1968, seven states in addition to the first six asserted such criminal jurisdiction: Florida (in full) and, to a limited extent (sometimes contingent on tribal consent), Idaho, Montana, Nevada, South Dakota, Utah, and Washington. Public Law 280 has particular relevance to the origins of the Indian gambling issue (as discussed later in this chapter).

That leaves tribal criminal jurisdiction. The Major Crimes Act, Indian Country Crimes Act, and Public Law 280, while asserting federal or state jurisdiction over the most serious Indian crimes and all crimes involving non-Indians, did not clearly oust tribal governments from jurisdiction over those crimes. Thus, it is arguable that tribal governments, at least in theory, have "concurrent" jurisdiction over them. That is, the tribe and the federal government or the tribe and the state could theoretically *both* prosecute such crimes. The federal and state governments have similar concurrent jurisdiction in some areas, such as illegal drug crimes. And outside the states covered by Public Law 280, with regard to offenses not covered by the Major Crimes Act, the Indian tribes still have their ancestral, *exclusive* jurisdiction over "Indian-on-Indian" crimes.

A major practical obstacle to tribal criminal jurisdiction (whether concurrent or exclusive) was imposed, however, by the ICRA in 1968. That law limited the severity of criminal punishments that any Indian tribe may impose. As currently amended, such penalties are capped, for any one offense, at no more than one year in jail and a $5,000 fine. For all practical purposes, that prevents tribes from prosecuting serious felonies. Partly for this reason, Indian tribes have never developed the law enforcement resources to prosecute and punish serious crimes in the formalized manner of modern federal and state criminal justice systems.

Tribal court systems have, however, developed dramatically in the last few decades. Historically, Indian nations handled criminal behavior within their societies by various traditional methods, most often social and religious pressure, mediation, and restitution. The first court systems in Indian country, in the sense familiar to Anglo-American law, were the "Courts of Indian Offenses" imposed on many reservations by the U.S. Department of the Interior, starting in the 1880s. After the passage of the Indian Reorganization Act of 1934, many tribes adopted written legal codes and modernized their governments. Some, like the Navajo (Diné) Nation, did so outside the auspices of the 1934 law, which was viewed by many Indians as meddlesome and intrusive.

The Navajo Nation, the second-largest American Indian tribe in population (the Cherokee Nation is the largest) and by far the largest in terms of reservation land area, has developed the most extensive Indian judicial system. It has numerous trial courts and a Navajo Nation Supreme Court, which has published many important decisions, including the historic case of *Means v. Chinle District Court* (1999), discussed later in this section. But many other tribes, by the 1970s, also had tribal courts and tribal police.

Modern times have brought increased travel and business activities by nonmembers, including many non-Indians, on Indian reservations. In fact, many non-Indians and especially Indians of other tribes now reside within the boundaries of many Indian nations. Thus, the issue inevitably arose whether tribal governments, with their increasingly sophisticated court and police systems, could prosecute and punish such nonmembers for at least the minor crimes falling under the penalty cap imposed by ICRA. It is, after all, a familiar legal principle that visitors to another jurisdiction, unless they enjoy diplomatic immunity, are fully subject to the local criminal law. Thus, U.S. citizens crossing the border into Mexico or Canada become immediately subject to Mexican or Canadian criminal jurisdiction, notwithstanding that they are not citizens of those nations. By the same token, the United States itself and all state governments have always asserted the right to prosecute crimes by foreign or out-of-state visitors.

The Supreme Court, however, rejected tribal criminal jurisdiction over non-Indians in *Oliphant v. Suquamish Indian Tribe* (1978). Then, in *Duro v. Reina* (1990), the Court extended *Oliphant* by finding that Indian nations lack any inherent criminal jurisdiction over Indians who are members of other tribes, even when such Indians (as is very common in Indian country) intermingle with members of the prosecuting tribe and establish permanent residence within the prosecuting tribe's reservation. Few, if any, Supreme Court decisions in modern times have aroused such an angry reaction from Indians and advocates of Indian sovereignty.

Duro, in particular, posed a very serious threat to effective law enforcement in Indian country. With regard to crimes by non-Indians within Indian country, there is always (in theory) federal or state jurisdiction, depending on who the victim is. Tribes, however, have complained bitterly that such crimes are often not effectively prosecuted. Congress has never moved to grant or reinstate (depending on one's perspective) the jurisdiction rejected by *Oliphant.* But *Duro* created both a theoretical and actual jurisdictional void. Crimes by nonmember Indians against tribal members, unless they were serious enough to qualify for Major Crimes Act prosecution, could not be prosecuted by *any* government in most cases. The Indian Country Crimes Act did not apply, since it exempted all Indian-on-Indian crimes, regardless of tribal membership. Thus, it was not surprising that Congress quickly "fixed" the *Duro* void by statutorily declaring that Indian tribes *did* have the power over nonmember Indians that the *Duro* Court had found they lacked.

Before considering the issues raised by Congress's *Duro* Fix Act, pause to read the majority and dissenting opinions in both *Oliphant* and *Duro,* set forth in the Documents section. The underlying issue in both cases was the proper baseline or default presumption about Indian power over nonmembers. Was such power presumptively part of the ancestral sovereignty of the Indian nations? Was the U.S. assertion of ultimate national and territorial sovereignty over the tribes, by which they were treated as "domestic dependent nations" (as defined by Chief Justice Marshall in the Cherokee Cases), automatically sufficient to extinguish such power over outsiders? If so, then tribes cannot exercise such powers until and unless the United States specifically revives them in some fashion by granting or delegating them to the tribes. Or does tribal power over outsiders remain a presumptive and inherent part of limited tribal sovereignty, until and unless the United States specifically revokes all or part of it?

One way to answer that question is to examine the historical record for actual instances in which the United States purported to specifically either authorize or prohibit tribal power over non-Indian criminals. Thus, Justice Rehnquist, in the main text of Part I of his *Oliphant* majority opinion, placed great weight on a single instance in which the Choctaw Nation requested that Congress grant it the power to punish non-Indian criminals entering its territory. As he argued, such a request might arguably imply, by default, that tribes were otherwise generally understood to lack such power. But then consider the other historical evidence set forth by Rehnquist himself in footnote 8 in Part I (set forth in the text in brackets, as is all footnote material sufficiently important to include in the Documents section). Does he draw the fairest and most logical conclusion from that evidence? Was his analysis internally consistent?

As Rehnquist conceded, numerous early treaties with Indian tribes expressly removed from them the power to punish non-Indian wrongdoers, typically promising instead that such criminals would be "punished according to the laws of the United States." Rehnquist insisted that "these provisions were not necessary to remove criminal jurisdiction over non-Indians from the Indian tribes" but "served an important function . . . by clarifying jurisdictional limits of the Indian tribes" (197, n. 8). But why were such provisions so "important" to "clarify" tribal power, if the general understanding was as Rehnquist insisted? Such provisions certainly *were* important if the presumed alternative was that tribes *did* have such power.

Many of those same early treaties, as Rehnquist noted, expressly *recognized* tribal power to "punish . . . as they please" non-Indian intruders into Indian treaty lands, declaring that such intruders would "forfeit the protection of the United States" (197, n. 8). Review, for example, Article 5 of the Cherokee-U.S. Treaty of Hopewell. Rehnquist insisted that such provisions were merely "a means of discouraging non-Indian settlements on Indian territory" (197, n. 8). That was doubtless true in part, but did they not also recognize a background presumption that tribes actually were in the business of punishing non-Indian offenders? One might also argue, using the logic suggested above, that such affirmative authorizations of tribal power over non-Indians implied by default a *lack* of preexisting power. But Rehnquist did not make such an argument, and it would not hold up very well. These provisions went beyond merely authorizing such tribal power and explicitly promised that the United States would wash its hands of such non-Indian intruders and make no protest when the tribes exercised such power against them.

It is one thing to recognize the presumptive power of another sovereign government to try one's own citizens while reserving the right to protest unjust exercises of such power and seeking to provide protection for such citizens. Diplomatic envoys do that all the time. But these Indian treaty provisions were apparently deemed necessary to clarify that no such protective efforts would be made on behalf of illegal non-Indian intruders. Rehnquist noted that later treaties dropped such provisions (which could hardly have been popular among non-Indian settlers of the day) and instead typically promised that illegal settlers "would be removed by the United States upon complaint being lodged by the tribe" (197, n. 8). That too, of course, implied (though Rehnquist did not acknowledge it) that tribes might otherwise enforce their own penalties against such non-Indians.

Rehnquist made special note of what he asserted was the only Indian treaty that "ever provided for any form of tribal criminal jurisdiction over non-Indians (other than in the illegal-settler context noted above)" (197, n. 8). It was the Delaware-U.S. Treaty of 1778, the very first Indian treaty ever contracted by the United States. Oddly, Rehnquist seemed to think this treaty supported his overall argument. But as Rehnquist's own description of the relevant treaty provision made clear, it was not so much an *authorization* of tribal jurisdiction over non-Indians as a *limitation* on such jurisdiction. The treaty prohibited *either* the United States *or* the Delaware tribe from punishing the other's citizens except by a "fair and impartial trial" according to procedures "to be hereafter fixed" by the Continental Congress in consultation with the Delaware (197, n. 8). This stipulation no more suggested that the Delaware tribe lacked inherent criminal jurisdiction over non-Indians than it implied the United States lacked inherent criminal jurisdiction over Indians. Quite the contrary: the apparent need for such an affirmative limitation and clarification of tribal and U.S. criminal jurisdiction in this particular treaty logically supported a background understanding that *both* parties (like Indian and other nations generally) would otherwise enjoy such traditional sovereign power without limitation.

Rehnquist canvassed other scattered indications about tribal criminal jurisdiction in Part I of his *Oliphant* majority opinion. Overall, he was on strong ground in noting that there was little or no actual historical practice of non-Indians being criminally prosecuted, in a formal sense, by Indian tribes. Of course, there was little or no historical practice of Indian tribes formally prosecuting anyone, even their own citizens, until the modern development of tribal courts as discussed here. But Indian tribes always, of course, exercised the actual power to restrain, punish, and otherwise deal with violent or antisocial acts by their own members, and history does not suggest that they were shy about or reluctant to deal with violent or antisocial non-Indian intruders. The treaty provisions discussed previously provided clear recognition of that. The particular means or methods by which a sovereign enforces its laws or social norms might well change over time. That would seem to have little relevance to the existence or nonexistence of inherent sovereign power itself.

However strong or weak the arguments in Part I of Rehnquist's *Oliphant* opinion, Part II of his opinion remains the most controversial. In that section, he argued that tribal criminal jurisdiction over non-Indians was simply inconsistent with the tribes' status as limited sovereigns dependent on the United States. Why? Rehnquist cited the Bill of Rights and the "great solicitude" the United States has always had "that its citizens be protected . . . from unwarranted intrusions on their personal liberty" (210). The Bill of Rights, as discussed in Chapter 1, does not directly apply to Indian tribes. Therefore, Rehnquist argued, the tribes "necessarily [gave] up their power to try non-Indian citizens of the United States except in a manner acceptable to Congress" (210).

As Rehnquist conceded, Congress had in fact applied most of the Bill of Rights to the tribes in the Indian Civil Rights Act of 1968. One might argue that is evidence that Congress was sensitive to concerns about the quality of tribal justice and had already imposed the safeguards it felt were necessary. Yet again, that actually supports by implication the background presumption that tribes otherwise enjoy the inherent power to criminally prosecute anyone coming within their lands. Rehnquist pointed in particular to a provision of Suquamish tribal law excluding non-Indians (of whom there were many living on the tribe's Port Madison reservation) from service on tribal court juries. But it is quite likely that if that provision were specifically litigated (the *Oliphant* decision made that unnecessary), it would be struck down as a violation of ICRA.

Consider also whether the outcome in *Oliphant* was driven by the facts of that particular tribe and reservation. What were the relative populations of Suquamish Indians and non-Indians living within the Port Madison reservation? Did the Court see this is a "tail wagging the dog" situation? A common saying among lawyers is that "bad facts make bad law." Even many advocates of tribal sovereignty have conceded that *Oliphant* did not present the most appealing context for assertion of tribal criminal jurisdiction over non-Indians. Would the case have been decided differently if it had arisen, say, in the Navajo Nation? Consider that when you read *Means v. Chinle District Court* (1999), discussed hereafter.

The *Oliphant* majority opinion was pervaded by distrust and suspicion of tribal courts, though Rehnquist grudgingly conceded that they "have become increasingly sophisticated and resemble in many respects their state counterparts" (211–212). He also admitted "the prevalence of non-Indian crime on today's reservations" (212). But he concluded that "these are considerations for Congress to weigh in deciding whether Indian tribes should finally be authorized to try non-Indians. They have little relevance to the principles which lead us to conclude that Indian tribes do not have inherent jurisdiction to try and punish non-Indians" (212).

One might just as well argue, of course, that Congress could weigh such considerations in deciding whether to *divest* Indian tribes of some or all of their inherent criminal jurisdiction, as Congress has repeatedly demonstrated the willingness to do. This argument captures the fundamental break of the *Oliphant* majority from the Court's general approach with regard to Native American sovereignty over the previous 150 years. Under the canons of construction, tribes were traditionally presumed to *retain* sovereign power *unless and until* Congress clearly and affirmatively *divested* some part of it from them. But according to *Oliphant,* at least with regard to tribal criminal jurisdiction over non-Indian visitors, the background presumption was that tribes *lacked* sovereign power unless and until Congress clearly and affirmatively *granted* it to them. Of course, to the extent Indian nations become dependent on Congress to affirmatively delegate powers to them, that tends to erode their inherent sovereign character. They would become little more than appendages of the federal government.

If concerns about the sophistication and fairness of tribal courts had as "little relevance" to the Court's *Oliphant* decision as Rehnquist claimed, why did Part II of his opinion rely so heavily on exactly such concerns? In truth, such concerns, although entirely legitimate, would not seem to have any logical relevance to the issue of inherent jurisdiction—any more than concerns about the quality of justice in, say, Russian courts have any relevance to Russia's inherent and presumptive criminal jurisdiction over U.S. and other foreign citizens visiting there. Furthermore, to the extent concerns do exist about tribal courts, why should there be any greater concern for criminal defendants who happen to be non-Indian as opposed to Indian? In waxing eloquent about the need to protect the personal liberties of U.S. citizens, Rehnquist seemed to forget that American Indians themselves had long been U.S. citizens!

The Court in *Oliphant* conceded that *Indians* fall within tribal criminal jurisdiction, yet the Court suggested no concern for their rights and liberties in this regard. One might argue, of course, that Indians have chosen to maintain and submit to the ancestral sovereignty of their own tribes and thus are in no position to complain about any risks that poses to their rights and liberties. But by the same token, one might argue that non-Indians who choose to go on an Indian reservation and commit crimes there have also voluntarily consented to the jurisdiction of the tribal courts. As noted above, that is the standard rule of criminal jurisdiction when foreigners enter the United States or when Americans travel abroad or across state lines. Indeed, it is the rule when Indians leave Indian country. One might argue that Indians who live on reservations deserve *greater* concern than non-Indians in this regard. Such Indians can only escape tribal criminal jurisdiction by uprooting themselves and leaving their homelands. Non-Indians concerned about possibly unfair treatment by tribal courts must merely choose not to reside in or enter Indian country or do business there.

It is in this light that some critics have attacked *Oliphant* as based on blatant anti-Indian racism. Of course, as discussed in Chapter 2, distinctions between tribal member Indians and non-Indians have been held to be not racial, strictly speaking, but rather political. That is, they are analogous to distinctions based on nationality. Many such distinctions as to Indians are justified by the historical and present status of Indian nations as quasi-sovereign political entities. In the same way, discriminatory treatment by the United States of some or all foreign citizens may be justifiable, for reasons of war, national security, or political policy. Since the terrorist attacks of September 11, 2001, for example, it has been reported that the U.S. State Department has raised the level of scrutiny of foreign visitors from certain nations found to have supported or to have been infiltrated by terrorist groups. Such policies may or may not be sound or just, but they are not necessarily "racist" in any simple sense. But rank favoritism based on national affiliation, for no articulated reason, is surely just as offensive as pure racism.

Consider, finally, the analogy Rehnquist attempts to draw between *Oliphant* and the 1883 *Ex parte Kan-Gi-Shun-Ca* case. Was *Kan-Gi-Shun-Ca* "almost the inverse of" *Oliphant,* as Rehnquist argues? Do the considerations cited in *Kan-Gi-Shun-Ca* really "speak equally strongly against" tribal criminal jurisdiction over non-Indians entering Indian lands? Where did the crime in *Kan-Gi-Shun-Ca* take place? Can you come up with a better hypothetical analogy?

The Court's decision in *Duro* was, if possible, even more harshly criticized by many Indian law scholars and historians than *Oliphant.* It is interesting to note that Justice Kennedy, the author of the *Duro* majority opinion, had (while still a lower court judge) dissented from the Ninth Circuit U.S. Court of Appeals decision in *Oliphant,* which had upheld tribal jurisdiction (only to be reversed by the Supreme Court, as discussed earlier). To a certain extent, Kennedy's *Duro* opinion suggested sheer ignorance about the history and realities of Indian law and Indian country. For example, Kennedy claimed that the historical record on tribal jurisdiction over nonmember Indians was "less illuminating" than in *Oliphant* and "tend[ed] to support" rejection of jurisdiction over nonmember Indians (*Duro v. Reina* 1990, 688). In fact, as pointed out by Justice Brennan's dissent (joined by Justice Marshall), the evidence regarding nonmember Indians is far stronger and clearer and plainly supports tribal jurisdiction over such persons.

It has been common throughout much of U.S. history for Indians to settle or mingle with Indians of other tribes, often because of deliberate U.S. government policies relocating different tribes together on artificially created reservations. As discussed previously, there has never been federal jurisdiction over minor crimes between Indians in Indian country. Major crimes only came under federal jurisdiction after 1885. Nor has state jurisdiction ever existed over any such crimes, except since 1953 in the handful of states that have jurisdiction under Public Law 280. So how did tribes handle such crimes by nonmember Indians during all those years? Kennedy offered no answer in *Duro.* As to how such crimes would be handled in the future, given the jurisdictional void created by *Duro,* Kennedy weakly suggested that perhaps the Indian Country Crimes Act could be reinterpreted to cover them.

Even more astonishingly, Kennedy blithely suggested that state criminal jurisdiction under Public Law 280 might be expanded. The vast majority of Indians have never been subject to Public Law 280, which has been intensely unpopular with both states and tribes (in the few states where it applies) ever since it was passed at the height of the Termination Era in 1953. States have resented the costs of criminal jurisdiction over territories and peoples not otherwise subject to state taxation, and tribes have resented the consequent loss of sovereignty and intrusion by non-Indian state authorities into their affairs. This problem is discussed further in this chapter with regard to the gambling situation in California, a Public Law 280 state.

And yet, it must be conceded that there is a certain logic to Justice Kennedy's *Duro* majority opinion. If one first accepts *Oliphant* as a given (and the Court has shown no inclination to overrule it), then the question becomes whether a distinction may be drawn between tribal criminal jurisdiction over nonmembers who are Indians of other tribes and nonmembers who are non-Indians. Although Rehnquist in *Oliphant* seemed to find unimportant the fact that Indians are now U.S. citizens, Kennedy emphasized it. He refused to "adopt a view of tribal sovereignty that would single out another group of citizens, nonmember Indians, for trial by political bodies that do not include them" (*Duro v. Reina* 1990, 693).

For example, suppose the author of this book (a non-Indian living in California) were to visit the Navajo Nation (which covers parts of Arizona, New Mexico, and Utah) with a friend who happens to be a member of the Oglala Sioux Nation, located hundreds of miles away in South Dakota. Suppose our judgment temporarily deserts us, and we commit a petty crime of some sort within Navajo country. Why should the Navajo Nation have criminal jurisdiction over my friend but not me? He is no more a citizen of the Navajo Nation than I am. Yes, he happens to be ethnically an Indian, but "Indians" actually comprise hundreds of different ethnic groupings with different languages, cultures, and religions, just as non-Indians hail from such diverse ethnic backgrounds as Irish, Jewish, African, and Chinese. I myself (as noted in the Preface) have one-sixty-fourth Cherokee blood. Suppose I had one-sixty-fourth Navajo blood? That (although not qualifying me for Navajo citizenship) might arguably give me a *stronger* ethnic connection to the Navajo Nation than my friend.

But, you may point out, my friend is an official member of at least *some* Indian nation, whereas I am not. But there is no treaty between the Navajo and Oglala Sioux Nations pertaining to criminal jurisdiction. Indian nations might in theory enter into reciprocal agreements in this regard (another suggestion offered by Kennedy in *Duro*), but that would be a complicated matter given that there are more than 300 Indian tribes and reservations in the lower forty-eight United States. Each Indian nation enjoys whatever sovereignty it does independently, as a separate government. There is no obvious justification for lumping them or their members all together, except with regard to common obligations or relationships that exist between them and the U.S. government.

Even more troublingly, if my friend and I are treated differently, would that amount to sheer ethnic or racial discrimination in violation of the equal protection clause of the Constitution? That clause does not directly apply to Indian nations, but Congress legislatively applied its principles to the tribes in the Indian Civil Rights Act of 1968. Furthermore, the principles of the clause *do* apply to Congress itself, which enacted the *Duro* Fix Act. This issue is no longer hypothetical, because the *Duro* Fix Act, made permanent in 1991, dictates that my friend and I *would* be treated differently. He would be subject to Navajo criminal jurisdiction, but I would not.

Justice Kennedy was clearly bothered by such issues in *Duro.* And yet, there was something bizarrely oblivious about his previously quoted argument that recognizing tribal criminal jurisdiction over nonmember Indians would "single out another group of citizens." Tribes have never sought to "single out" anyone, either non-Indians or nonmember Indians, for criminal jurisdiction. They have simply sought to do what all sovereign governments traditionally do: apply their laws to *all people* entering their lands. It was the Court's own decisions in *Oliphant* and *Duro* that singled out certain groups, first non-Indians generally and then all nonmember Indians, for special immunity from tribal jurisdiction. Although Rehnquist expressed concern for the rights of non-Indian U.S. citizens in tribal courts in *Oliphant* and Kennedy expressed concern for nonmember Indian U.S. citizens in *Duro,* they both ignored the fact that tribal member Indians are *themselves* U.S. citizens. Neither explained why, if it is tolerable for *any* U.S. citizen to be prosecuted by a tribe, *all* U.S. citizens choosing to reside in or enter Indian country should not be treated the same.

Another issue arising from the *Duro* Fix Act concerns "double jeopardy" for criminal offenses. The double jeopardy clause of the Constitution generally protects a person from being prosecuted more than once for the same offense. But it does not apply to prosecutions by different sovereigns, such as by the United States and a particular state or by two different states. Thus, if the same criminal conduct happens to violate federal, state, and tribal law (or the law of more than one state, as sometimes happens when criminals cross state lines during a crime spree), then any or all of those separate governments may bring separate prosecutions against the accused criminal. But if tribal power to prosecute a nonmember Indian is not based on inherent tribal sovereign power but is simply delegated to the tribes by act of Congress, then the tribe is simply acting as an arm of the federal government and may not bring a separate tribal prosecution if the federal government has already prosecuted the defendant for that offense.

So, is the *Duro* Fix Act a mere "delegation" of federal power to the tribes? Everyone concedes that Congress has the power to delegate federal power in that manner. But if that is what Congress is doing, then it raises the troubling specter, as noted earlier, that tribes may become mere appendages or agencies of the federal government. Or is the *Duro* Fix Act properly seen as a restoration of *inherent* tribal sovereign power? Was Congress, in effect, "fixing" the mistake the Supreme Court arguably made in *Duro?* Does Congress have the *power* to fix or correct what it perceives as "mistaken" Supreme Court rulings on the scope of inherent tribal sovereignty? Could Congress similarly "correct" the *Oliphant* decision by ordinary legislation? Or would that violate the principles of separation of powers or judicial review? Would it constitute an improper intrusion by Congress into the Supreme Court's ultimate right to interpret the law?

The Navajo Nation Supreme Court confronted some of the issues raised by *Oliphant* and *Duro* in *Means v. Chinle District Court* (1999). The question raised was whether the Navajo Nation could lawfully prosecute Russell Means, a member of the Oglala Sioux Nation, for a crime allegedly committed within the Navajo Nation against (in part) a Navajo tribal member. The case thus raised the hypothetical issue set forth above. Means has a colorful and controversial personal history. He is one of the founders of the modern American Indian Movement and a longtime activist for Indian rights. But his own criminal prosecution by the Navajo Nation put him in the unaccustomed position of *challenging* Indian sovereignty. He claimed that the Navajo Nation lacked criminal jurisdiction over him and that any assertion of Navajo jurisdiction would violate the principle of equal protection of the laws, since (under *Oliphant*) he would not be subject to Navajo jurisdiction if he were non-Indian.

Read the Navajo-U.S. Treaty of 1868 and Chief Justice Robert Yazzie's opinion in *Means,* set forth in the Documents section. Yazzie upheld Navajo jurisdiction over Means, partly on the basis of a broad reading of this treaty. Did he rely on the *Duro* Fix Act to uphold Navajo jurisdiction? Why or why not, do you think? Why do you think Yazzie included in Part I of the opinion the extensive factual discussion of law enforcement and social problems on the Navajo reservation? Do you find Yazzie's analysis in Part II, based on the 1868 treaty, persuasive? Explain why or why not, with reference to the principles of treaty interpretation (i.e., the canons of construction discussed earlier).

Also consider Yazzie's argument in Part III, based on his conclusion that Means had established himself as a *hadane* or in-law, thus implicitly consenting to Navajo criminal jurisdiction under Navajo common law principles. This argument is one of the most subtle aspects of Yazzie's thoughtful opinion. Yazzie was, in legal terms, trying to thread a needle here. The U.S. Supreme Court in *Duro* had rejected tribal jurisdiction over a male nonmember Indian who had lived on a reservation for three months with a "woman friend" tribal member and suggested that even "close ties . . . through marriage or long employment" would not suffice to subject non-Indians or nonmember Indians to tribal jurisdiction (*Duro v. Reina* 1990, 679, 695). And yet, the *Duro* majority opinion seemed to endorse tribal power to provide for membership by adoption and intermarriage with tribal members, citing with approval several older cases from the 1800s. Yazzie seized on this ambiguous opening and exploited it skillfully to argue that the Navajo Nation maintained inherent criminal jurisdiction over such adoptive tribal members.

Finally, on what basis did Yazzie, in Part IV, reject Means's equal protection argument? Did he try to resolve the equal protection problem posed by *Oliphant* and the *Duro* Fix Act? Was Yazzie defying *Oliphant* itself in this part of his opinion? Since the Navajo Nation Supreme Court's decision, handed down in May 1999, Means has gone to federal court to challenge the nation's prosecution of him. He lost in federal trial court, and as this book went to press, the case is currently pending before the U.S. Court of Appeals for the Ninth Circuit. The Ninth Circuit, which supervises all federal courts in a large area of the Pacific West of the United States, has already upheld the *Duro* Fix Act as a restoration of inherent tribal sovereignty in *United States v. Enas* (2001), a case the U.S. Supreme Court declined to review. Other lower federal courts, however, have held that the *Duro* Fix Act is only valid as a delegation of federal power.

The issue presented by *Means* that was not presented by *Enas*, however, concerns equal protection of the laws. Does it violate that principle for an Indian tribe to prosecute nonmember Indians while nonmember non-Indians stand exempt? Justice Brennan's dissent in *Duro* itself suggested it was not a problem. Rather cleverly, Brennan pointed out that equal protection only prohibits discrimination among people who are within a given government's jurisdiction. If non-Indians are simply outside a tribe's inherent jurisdiction (as *Oliphant* held), then they are not part of the equation. It is not the tribe's fault that they are treated differently from nonmember Indians. Unless a tribe discriminates between people who are *within* tribal jurisdiction, no claim *against the tribe* can even arise under equal protection principles.

But such reasoning may not justify *Congress's own* discriminatory treatment of non-Indians and nonmember Indians in the *Duro* Fix Act. The Court and Congress together have effectively drawn a line around each tribe's criminal jurisdiction that discriminates among nonmembers of the tribe based on Indian or non-Indian status. Given the concerns expressed by the majority in *Duro,* it seems doubtful that the Court will tolerate this state of affairs. The Court may eventually strike down the *Duro* Fix Act. The only way for Congress to avert that outcome may be to legislatively overturn *Oliphant* as well as *Duro,* to recognize tribal criminal jurisdiction over *all* persons, Indian or non-Indian, tribal members or nonmembers, who venture within Indian country.

That, in turn, raises the broader question of how far tribal criminal law enforcement powers should be extended in general. Should the "penalty cap" currently imposed by the Indian Civil Rights Act be raised? Should tribes be allowed to or attempt to prosecute more serious felonies? Would they have the resources to do so? These are all difficult questions with no clear answers. But they remain open questions as Indian nations enter the new millennium.

Tribal Civil Jurisdiction

One reason that criminal cases like *Oliphant v. Suquamish Indian Tribe* (1978) and *Duro v. Reina* (1990) came as such a shock to many advocates of tribal sovereignty is that the Supreme Court has been far more likely to uphold the *civil* or "regulatory" jurisdiction of Native American governments. This type of jurisdiction refers to a tribe's power to impose taxes on economic activities within Indian country and to regulate matters such as land use, zoning, health and safety, family law, and environmental protection. It also refers to the power of tribal courts to hear civil lawsuits arising within Indian country over such matters as breaches of contract, personal injuries (what the law refers to as "torts"), domestic disputes, and property disputes. Starting with *Williams v. Lee* (1959), it appeared that the

Court accepted that tribal *civil* jurisdiction *did* extend to non-Indians, at least those who chose to enter or do business on an Indian reservation.

Read the *Williams* opinion set forth in the Documents section. The facts were quite simple. Lee, a non-Indian shopkeeper who ran a store in the Navajo Nation, tried to sue a Navajo couple (the Williamses) who allegedly failed to pay for goods bought on credit. Justice Black's unanimous opinion strongly reaffirmed the foundational principles of the Cherokee Cases, especially *Worcester v. Georgia* (1832). He found that (outside the handful of states covered by Public Law 280) state courts had *no* jurisdiction over such lawsuits and tribal courts had *exclusive* jurisdiction. The historical timing of the decision was especially significant, coming right around the time that the Eisenhower administration was backing away from the "termination" policy that otherwise dominated the 1950s. *Williams* was thus a key turning point in the return to a policy of self-determination and greater respect for tribal sovereignty.

The Supreme Court, in the decades since *Williams,* has often upheld tribal power to tax, regulate, and exercise jurisdiction over civil lawsuits, even involving non-Indians, regarding activities within Indian country that affect tribal members. At the same time, consistent with *Worcester* and *Williams,* it has generally excluded the states from exercising such jurisdiction in Indian country. For example, in *Fisher v. District Court* (1976), the Supreme Court rejected state jurisdiction over the adoption of an Indian child, where all parties resided on a reservation. Two years later, in the Indian Child Welfare Act of 1978, Congress expanded tribal jurisdiction over Indian adoption and related cases, even when they occurred outside Indian country. Even in cases in which state courts retain jurisdiction, the child's tribe usually has the right to participate in the proceedings, and the law created a preference in favor of placing such children with Indian foster or adoptive parents. In *New Mexico v. Mescalero Apache Tribe* (1983), consistent with this general approach, the Court rejected state authority to regulate hunting and fishing within tribally owned reservation lands.

But the Court's denial in *Oliphant* of tribal *criminal* jurisdiction over non-Indians was in obvious tension with the *Williams* line of cases. After all, when push comes to shove, the only way for any government to enforce "civil" or "regulatory" authority may be the threat of criminal sanctions. The trend was not entirely clear at the time. But it is now obvious, in retrospect, that the Court's reasoning in *Oliphant* soon started to spill over and affect tribal civil jurisdiction over non-Indians and nonmember Indians.

Read the Court's opinion in *Montana v. United States* (1981), set forth in the Documents section. Notice that the case involved land on the Crow Indian Reservation owned by Indians (either individually or by the tribe and "held in trust" by the U.S. government) and by non-Indians (548). It might seem surprising and confusing that non-Indians could own land that is still within an Indian reservation (and thus legally part of "Indian country"). Because of the allotment policy launched in the 1880s, however, and discussed in Chapter 2, non-Indians were allowed to settle within many Indian reservations. Although the vast bulk of Indian country remains owned by the tribes or individual tribal members, a significant fraction of it is non-Indian-owned. As a result, of course, substantial numbers of non-Indians and nonmember Indians live within the outer territorial boundaries of many Indian reservations. Indeed, recall the facts of *Oliphant*, which showed that Indians were actually in a tiny minority on their own reservation in that case. And recall that the Navajo Nation Supreme Court in the *Means* case emphasized the large number of Indians living on the reservations of tribes of which they are not members.

Montana involved the hunting and fishing rights of non-Indians within the Crow Reservation. What did the *Montana* Court say about inherent tribal regulatory power over non-Indians on tribally or Indian-owned reservation land? *Montana*, it should be noted, also involved *treaty-based* tribal powers, but we will not attempt to discuss that issue here. What did the Court say about inherent tribal power over non-Indians on non-Indian-owned reservation land? Read especially carefully the next-to-last paragraph in *Montana*. It has become one of the most hotly disputed passages in all the Supreme Court's Indian law opinions. This paragraph sets forth a "general proposition that the inherent sovereign powers of an Indian tribe do not extend to the activities of nonmembers of the tribe" (565). However, the Court said there were two exceptions to this general presumption, and it seemed to phrase the exceptions in rather broad terms. Also, it must be emphasized that this *Montana* presumption was never meant to apply to any tribal powers based on treaties.

The first *Montana* exception was that a tribe retains inherent power to "regulate . . . the activities of nonmembers who enter consensual relationships with the tribe or its members, through commercial dealing, contracts, leases, or other arrangements" (565). The second *Montana* exception was that a tribe retains inherent power to regulate "the conduct of non-Indians on fee lands within its reservation when that conduct threatens or has some direct effect on the political integrity, the economic security, or the health or welfare of the tribe" (566).

The rule and exceptions stated in *Montana* raise three interesting questions. First, recall that under the canons of construction (at least prior to *Oliphant* and outside the criminal context), it was generally presumed that tribes *retained* sovereignty and jurisdiction until and unless clearly *divested* of any of it by Congress. Did *Montana* reverse that basic presumption and, if so, was that a logical or justifiable step? If *Montana* did reverse the basic presumption, that brings us to the second question: in which cases, exactly, did *Montana* reverse the presumption in favor of tribal sovereignty? Did the *Montana* rule apply to *all* inherent tribal powers over nonmembers of the tribe? Or did it apply only to inherent tribal powers over nonmembers *on nonmember-owned land?* What do you think, based on your own reading of the opinion? The third question is this: exactly how broadly should the *Montana* "exceptions" be interpreted?

The *Montana* decision itself and later cases have tended to answer the third question. The Court has construed the exceptions to the *Montana* rule very narrowly. One might think, for example, that a nonmember engages in a "consensual" relationship with a tribe simply by choosing to own and reside on land within an Indian reservation. And almost any kind of land use by such property owners arguably has some potential impact on the economy or environment of the tribe. That is the general basis on which local governments exercise zoning authority over land and regulate such activities as hunting and fishing. But the Court in *Montana* itself rejected the Crow Tribe's power to regulate hunting and fishing by non-Indians on land they owned within the reservation.

However, the *Montana* Court "readily agree[d]" that the tribe could regulate non-Indian hunting and fishing on *tribally owned land* (557). This language seemed to imply that the *Montana* rule and exceptions did not even apply to tribally owned land. Otherwise, it would be difficult to explain why the same test would yield such dramatically different results. Since wildlife crosses property lines all the time, hunting and fishing anywhere within an Indian reservation could easily affect the environmental health of the entire reservation. It should also be noted, however, that the Court's "ready agreement" may have been based largely on tribal treaty-based powers, a separate issue discussed in the case.

An especially troubling application of *Montana* was the Court's decision in *Brendale v. Yakima Indian Nation* (1989). *Brendale* concerned the inherent power of the Yakima Nation to impose zoning regulations on its reservation lands. Two different parcels of property owned in fee simple by nonmembers were at issue in the case, one owned by Philip Brendale (an Indian but nonmember of the Yakima Nation) and the other by Stanley Wilkinson (a non-Indian). The Brendale property was located in a mostly undeveloped area of the reservation that was formerly closed to the general public. Aside from Brendale's and a few other isolated parcels, it was almost entirely owned by the tribe. The Wilkinson property was located in a more developed, historically "open" area of the reservation dotted with numerous nonmember-owned parcels in a "checkerboard" pattern.

The justices in *Brendale* could not agree on a coherent resolution of the case, ending up in a confusing 4–2–3 split. Justice Byron R. White, joined by Chief Justice William H. Rehnquist and Justices Antonin Scalia and Anthony M. Kennedy, found that the tribe retained the power to zone reservation lands owned by the tribe or tribal members but not the Brendale, Wilkinson, or other parcels owned by nonmembers. They said the state of Washington and its local government agency, Yakima County, had authority to zone those parcels of land. Justice John Paul Stevens, joined by Justice Sandra Day O'Connor, awkwardly tried to split the difference. They concluded that the tribe retained the power to zone the Brendale property, in order to preserve the undeveloped character of that portion of the reservation, which was almost entirely tribally owned. But they agreed with the White-Rehnquist-Scalia-Kennedy plurality that the state, not the tribe, had the power to zone the Wilkinson property and other nonmember-owned parcels within the "open" area of the reservation.

Justice Harry A. Blackmun, joined by Justices William J. Brennan, Jr., and Thurgood Marshall, objected that this outcome would destroy the ability of either the tribe or the state to develop any kind of coherent or comprehensive zoning plan for the reservation. As they pointed out, "concurrent zoning jurisdiction by its very nature is unworkable" (466). "This, in practice, will be nothing short of a nightmare, . . . exacerbating the already considerable tensions that exist between local and tribal governments . . . about the best use of reservation lands" (461). Blackmun, Brennan, and Marshall concluded that the tribe retained authority to zone all reservation lands, including nonmember-owned property. "It would be difficult to conceive of," they argued, "a power more central to 'the economic security, or the health or welfare of the tribe,' than the power to zone" (458, quoting *Montana v. United States* 1981, 566).

Although the Stevens-O'Connor and Blackmun-Brennan-Marshall opinions created a 5–4 majority in *Brendale* upholding tribal zoning power over the historically "closed" portion of the reservation, Blackmun expressed particular dismay at Stevens's analysis. Not only did Stevens and O'Connor endorse the unworkable "checkerboard" of state and tribal zoning authority in the "open" area of the reservation, their approach "require[d] an intrinsically standardless threshold determination as to when a section of a reservation contains sufficient non-Indian land holdings to warrant an 'open' classification" (464). Furthermore, Blackmun argued, Stevens's approach

> betrays a stereotyped and almost patronizing view of Indian and reservation life. [Stevens] describes the "closed area" of the Yakima Reservation as "pristine," and emphasizes that it is spiritually significant to the Tribe and yields natural foods and medicines. [He] then contrasts this unadulterated portion of the reservation with the "open area," which is "marked by 'residential and commercial developmen[t].'" (464–465)

But according to Blackmun, it could not be true that Indian nations could maintain control of land use within their reservations "only if they forgo economic development and maintain those reservations according to a single, perhaps quaint, view of what is characteristically 'Indian' today" (465).

Perhaps the most notable aspect of Blackmun's opinion in *Brendale* was that it represented what was, in retrospect, a last-chance effort to correct what he (along with many Indian law scholars) had come to view as the Court's wrong turn in the *Montana* case. Ironically, Blackmun, Brennan, and Marshall had all concurred in the relevant (unanimous) portion of the *Montana* opinion. But in *Brendale*, the Blackmun trio castigated the *Montana* Court for having "missed its usual way" and the *Montana* opinion as "flatly inconsistent with . . . prior decisions defining the scope of inherent tribal jurisdiction" (*Brendale v. Yakima Indian Nation* 1989, 455). Blackmun described as "anomalous" the fact that the *Montana* Court "strangely reversed the otherwise consistent presumption in favor of inherent tribal sovereignty over reservation lands" (456). He depicted the 1978 *Oliphant* decision (which he, unlike Brennan and Marshall, had joined) as a unique exception to inherent tribal sovereignty.

The Court's decision in *Strate v. A-1 Contractors* (1997) was another important step in the post-*Oliphant*, post-*Montana* trend. *Strate* involved a civil lawsuit against non-Indian defendants over an accident on a state highway within reservation boundaries. The decision extended and solidified the *Montana* presumption against tribal jurisdiction over nonmembers. Although *Williams* upheld exclusive tribal civil jurisdiction over the lawsuit involved in that case, *Strate* rejected even concurrent tribal jurisdiction, instead ruling in favor of exclusive state court jurisdiction. Most foreboding for tribal sovereignty advocates, the decision was unanimous and was written by Justice Ruth Bader Ginsburg, appointed by President Clinton and widely considered the most liberal member of the current Court.

Perhaps the most important civil or regulatory power of any government is the power to tax. The Court's rulings on tribal tax powers have veered back and forth at times, but some consistent principles seemed to emerge in the decades after *Williams*. The Court has generally rejected state efforts to tax Indians living on reservations with regard to their on-reservation economic activities. For example, in *McClanahan v. Arizona State Tax Commission* (1973), the Court ruled unanimously that Arizona could not tax the income of a member of the Navajo Nation earned on the Navajo reservation. At the same time, the Court has generally supported tribal power to tax not only tribal members but also nonmembers doing business on tribally owned land. For example, in *Merrion v. Jicarilla Apache Tribe* (1982), the Court upheld inherent tribal power to impose a severance tax on oil and gas extracted from the reservation, even though the oil companies subjected to the tax were already required to pay royalties to the tribe.

In *Washington v. Confederated Tribes of the Colville Indian Reservation* (1980), the Court faced a collision between state and tribal tax powers. The key issue in *Colville* was whether the state of Washington, the Indian tribes who were parties to the case, or both enjoyed the power to tax cigarette sales to nonmembers by tribal smokeshops on the reservations. The Court, consistently with cases like *Merrion,* unanimously upheld *tribal* power to tax such sales. But it then drained that tribal victory of any practical value by *also* upholding *state* power to tax such sales. Only Justices Brennan and Marshall dissented from the latter holding. Justice Stewart argued that the state should at least have to credit the tribal taxes against its own taxes, but the majority rejected that accommodation.

The tribes, of course, hoped to attract outside purchasers to the reservation by taxing cigarette sales at a lower rate than the prevailing state tax. The state, for its part, feared the loss of revenues and the loss of business by off-reservation shops that would be caused by any general tribal exemption from state taxes. The Court agreed with the state in *Colville,* holding that the tribes were properly prevented "from marketing their tax exemption to nonmembers . . . who would otherwise purchase their cigarettes outside the reservations" (157). The unfortunate result was to eliminate a valuable source of tribal revenue. By upholding the state tax without any credit for tribal taxes, the Court effectively destroyed tribal power to collect any revenues from such sales. "Double taxation" by the tribe would simply make on-reservation sales hopelessly noncompetitive.

The most recent major Supreme Court decision on tribal tax powers is *Atkinson Trading Co. v. Shirley* (2001). *Atkinson* combined the issues presented by cases like *Montana, Colville,* and *Merrion.* The question was whether the Navajo Nation could impose a hotel occupancy tax on nonmember guests at a hotel operated by a nonmember-owned company on nonmember-owned land within the reservation. Despite the tribal tax powers upheld in *Colville* and in post-*Montana* cases like *Merrion,* the *Atkinson* Court applied the *Montana* rule and unanimously struck down the Navajo tax. Illustrating the narrow scope allowed for the *Montana* exceptions, the Court found that such hotel guests do not enter into any relevant "consensual relationship" with the Navajo Nation, even though they obviously choose to visit the reservation and rent hotel rooms there and benefit from the police, fire, and emergency medical services maintained by the Navajo Nation and supported by Navajo taxpayers. The Court also rejected as irrelevant or insufficient the extensive voluntary ties between the hotel itself and the Navajo Nation. Furthermore, the Court concluded that operation of a hotel on nonmember-owned land within a reservation does not sufficiently implicate the health, economic, or political interests of the tribe.

As much as decisions like *Brendale, Strate,* and *Atkinson* expanded the *Montana* rule and eroded tribal sovereignty over nonmembers, they still seemed to preserve the basic distinction of *Montana* itself between tribally owned land and nonmember-owned land. *Brendale, Strate,* and *Atkinson* denied tribal authority only over land owned by nonmembers (or, as in *Strate,* land controlled by non-Indian state authorities). These cases, even as late as *Atkinson,* decided on May 29, 2001, all seemed consistent with respect for tribal authority over nonmembers on lands owned and controlled by the tribe.

The *Atkinson* case, however, contained a foreboding portent. Justice David H. Souter, joined by Justice Kennedy and Justice Clarence Thomas, wrote a concurring opinion stating his view that the *Montana* rule should apply "regardless of whether the land at issue is [nonmember-owned] fee land, or land owned by or held in trust for an Indian tribe" (660). Souter's concurrence turned out to be the early warning tremor of a major earthquake in the Court's Indian law jurisprudence. Less than a month after *Atkinson,* on June 25, 2001, the Court decided *Nevada v. Hicks,* probably one of the three most important Indian law cases (along with *Oliphant* and *Montana*) in the more than forty years since *Williams.*

Hicks held that a tribal court lacked jurisdiction over a civil lawsuit against several Nevada state game wardens. The suit alleged lawless conduct by the state officers while searching the home of Floyd Hicks, a member of the Fallon Paiute-Shoshone Tribes. Hicks lived on tribal land within the Fallon reservation, located in Nevada but fully subject to normal tribal sovereignty. He was suspected of having killed a bighorn sheep off the reservation, in violation of Nevada state law. The search was conducted jointly by state and tribal officers, based on search warrants obtained from both a state court judge and a judge of the Fallon Tribal Court. At this point, read the opinions in *Hicks* set forth in the Documents section.

Justice Scalia wrote the majority opinion in *Hicks,* joined by Chief Justice Rehnquist and Justices Kennedy, Souter, Thomas, and Ginsburg. Scalia said in a footnote: "Our holding . . . is limited to the question of tribal-court jurisdiction over state officers enforcing state law" and added that the Court left "open the question of tribal-court jurisdiction over nonmember defendants in general" (358, n. 2). But the reasoning Scalia employed to reach that holding was far-reaching.

He applied the *Montana* rule, despite the fact that the case arose on tribally owned land. And he endorsed sweeping, "inherent" state power to enter Indian reservations without tribal permission or regulation, whenever deemed necessary by state officials to investigate or enforce state law.

Read carefully Part II.A of Scalia's *Hicks* opinion, in which he concluded that *Montana* provided the governing rule for the case. Did he fairly quote and describe the Court's opinion in *Montana*? Can you construct an argument that he did not? Is it plausible to say that *Montana*'s language (quoted by Scalia), stating that "Indian tribes retain inherent sovereign power to exercise some forms of civil jurisdiction over non-Indians . . . , even on non-Indian fee lands" (*Montana v. United States* 1981, 565), "clearly impl[ies] that the general rule of *Montana* applies to both Indian and non-Indian land" (*Nevada v. Hicks* 2001, 360)? What other implications might be drawn from that language in *Montana*? Recall that in *Montana* itself, the quoted language came right before the Court set forth the two exceptions to the *Montana* rule, which the Court then applied to the *non-Indian-owned* land involved in that case. Go back and review the *Montana* opinion if necessary. Did the *Montana* Court itself apply the *Montana* rule or its exceptions to the *Indian-owned* land in that case? Note that Justice Ginsburg claimed, in her concurring opinion, that Scalia's opinion did "not reach out definitively to answer the jurisdictional questions left open in *Strate*" (*Nevada v. Hicks* 2001, 386), such as the question whether the *Montana* rule applies to tribally owned and controlled land. Can her claim be reconciled with Part II.A of Scalia's opinion, which she joined in full?

Part II.B of Scalia's *Hicks* opinion was in some ways even more far reaching than Part II.A. Scalia admitted that it was "not entirely clear" from the Court's past decisions whether states had the legal authority "to enter a reservation . . . for [state law] enforcement purposes" without either tribal or federal permission (363). That was certainly an understatement. In fact, the prevailing assumption had long been that state officials generally have little more authority within an Indian reservation than they do outside their own state lines in another state or within federally controlled territory such as a military base or national park. Of course, law enforcement officials have traditionally cooperated in cases reaching across jurisdictional lines. And the Supreme Court has long carved out certain exceptions in which state authorities *do* enjoy law enforcement powers within

Indian country. For example, under *United States v. McBratney* (1882), states have long exercised the power to investigate and prosecute state-law crimes committed within Indian country by non-Indians against other non-Indians.

But it appears quite likely that the Nevada state game wardens sought (and obtained with no apparent difficulty) tribal court approval and tribal police cooperation for the raid on Hicks's home, for the same reasons that they would have sought the approval and cooperation of California state police if Hicks had resided across Lake Tahoe in California. And state officials would doubtless have sought the approval and cooperation of federal authorities before raiding Hicks's home if he had resided, say, on a federal military base. But Scalia's reasoning made it clear that, in the majority's view, Nevada need never have bothered with the tribal-court warrant it obtained and need not have given tribal police the courtesy of so much as a phone call to let them know a state raid would be carried out on the reservation.

In fact, as Justice O'Connor pointed out in her opinion (joined by Justice Stevens and Justice Stephen G. Breyer), *Hicks* appeared to be a model example of tribal-state law enforcement cooperation. It was thus more than a little puzzling why Scalia and the majority went out of their way to give states a green light to play lone ranger in asserting state law enforcement power within Indian country. And it seemed an astonishingly rude and gratuitous slap at Indian nation law enforcement for Scalia to suggest such state power was necessary "to 'prevent [such areas] from becoming an asylum for fugitives from justice'" (364).

Having found that the *Montana* rule applied, Scalia barely bothered to consider the two *Montana* exceptions. He asserted that it was simply impossible for state law enforcement officers to endanger tribal self-government or have any "'direct effect on the political integrity, the economic security, or the health or welfare of the tribe'" because that was "guaranteed by the limitations of federal constitutional and statutory law to which the officers are fully subject" (371, quoting *Montana v. United States* 1981, 566). This was rather like arguing that it is simply impossible for criminals to endanger public safety because, of course, criminals are "fully subject" to laws prohibiting any unlawful conduct in which they might engage. The very issue in *Hicks* was whether the state officers violated federal, state, and tribal law while raiding Hicks's home on the reservation. Of course, there is no guarantee that obtaining a tribal court warrant (which these very officers did) would prevent them from violating the law, and there are (fortunately) other forms of legal redress if they did so. But some degree of tribal control obviously enhances the security of the tribe against possible abuses of state power. Such abuses might well include lax control of state executive officials by state judges. In many states, officials in all three branches of government have been notoriously hostile or callous to Indian interests and concerns. Scalia in *Hicks* seemed completely oblivious to such historical and social realities.

In any event, Scalia totally missed (or chose to ignore) the deeper point. The fact that federal law might provide some redress for state violations of *individual* rights completely failed to address the undermining of tribal *governmental* authority blatantly evident if state authorities are free to unilaterally assert power within tribal territory, against tribal members, on tribally owned land. The state court warrant could not possibly substitute for the tribal court warrant, because the state court simply had no proper jurisdiction over tribally owned land. The only way in which federal law might protect tribal integrity in that sense would be to maintain the very kind of rule that Scalia rejected in *Hicks*, a rule of respect for tribal sovereignty requiring some form of tribal or federal permission or consultation before state authorities reach the long arm of state law enforcement into Indian country.

Scalia, of course, argued that tribal "self-government" and "internal relations" were not implicated because Hicks was, after all, accused of violating state law while off the reservation. The state officers, he implied, would have transgressed tribal sovereignty only if they had sought to investigate or punish Indian conduct originating on the reservation itself and thus totally beyond the reach of state law. But under this reasoning, Nevada state officials would be perfectly free to roam about California carrying out raids and searches and arresting criminal suspects without seeking permission from (or even consulting) California authorities, as long as the suspects being pursued were accused of committing some crime in Nevada. According to Scalia's logic, such actions would not pose any threat whatsoever to California's political integrity as a state or the security or welfare of its citizens.

Scalia argued that federal law can provide any needed protection against abuses of state officials operating on Indian reservations. But one can just as easily argue that federal law can provide any remedy that might be needed for Scalia's claimed concerns about tribal noncooperation with state law enforcement. Note also how Scalia cleverly extended the reversed presumption of *Oliphant* and *Montana.* He argued in *Hicks:* "Nothing in the federal statutory scheme prescribes, or even remotely suggests, that state officers cannot enter a reservation (including Indian-[owned] land) to investigate or prosecute violations of state law occurring off the reservation" (366). Thus, he found states free to invade and curtail tribal sovereignty because they have not been expressly forbidden from doing so. One might argue, more consistently with the presumption of *Worcester* and *Williams,* that states do not have such unilateral power over Indians within Indian country because there is nothing in federal statutory or treaty law clearly (or to use Scalia's phrase, "even remotely") authorizing such a power grab.

These decisions all bring into sharp focus the fact that Scalia—and the majority of the U.S. Supreme Court in *Hicks*—simply do not view tribal sovereignty as analogous to state sovereignty. The single most shocking statement in Scalia's *Hicks* opinion was that state enforcement of state law on the reservation "no more impairs the tribe's self-government than federal enforcement of federal law impairs state government" (364). This statement is shocking because it appears ignorant of or willfully hostile to the entire structure, logic, and history of American Indian law. Federal enforcement of federal law obviously must take place almost entirely within the boundaries of the states, since (with a few exceptions like the District of Columbia and several overseas commonwealths) the states constitute the territorial extent of U.S. federal jurisdiction. Of course, such federal law enforcement does not improperly "impair" state sovereignty because the states are constitutionally subordinate to federal law, which trumps state law under the supremacy clause (U.S. Const., art. VI, cl. 2). The states are mere components of the United States.

The Indian nations, by contrast, are most emphatically *not* mere components of the states, nor are they legally subordinate to the states. According to the "plenary power" doctrine, the tribes *are* mere components of the United States and are, like the states, fully subject to federal enforcement of federal law. But that doctrine as applied to the tribes actually has a far shakier basis than the explicit text of the supremacy clause as applied to the states. Scalia's statement in *Hicks* implied a mythical supremacy clause under which state law somehow trumps tribal law. In fact, as established by *Worcester* 170 years ago and almost unquestioned by the Supreme Court until *Hicks*, *tribal* sovereignty, as rooted and recognized in federal law, trumps *state* power under the Supremacy Clause!

If the Court actually intended Scalia's statement to be taken seriously—that the tribes bear the same relationship to the states as do the states to the federal government—then American Indian law as we know it is dead. It seems difficult to believe the Court would follow through on such an apocalyptic suggestion. But that a justice could throw out such an off-the-wall statement, in an opinion speaking for the U.S. Supreme Court, suggests how uncertain and unstable Indian sovereignty has become, at least before that Court.

Justice Souter's concurrence in *Hicks*, joined by Justices Kennedy and Thomas, was in some ways even more far-reaching than Scalia's majority opinion. As in *Atkinson*, the Souter trio called forthrightly for the *Montana* rule to be applied throughout Indian country on tribally owned as well as non-Indian land, and they expressly would not limit this rule to tribal power over state officials. Souter's opinions in these cases were especially surprising, given that he has generally upheld Indian treaty rights. For example, he dissented in *South Dakota v. Bourland* (1993) and provided one of the crucial majority votes in *Minnesota v. Mille Lacs Band of Chippewa Indians* (1999).

In *Hicks*, Souter specifically endorsed and relied upon "one of the principal policy considerations underlying *Oliphant*, namely, an overriding concern that citizens *who are not tribal members* be 'protected . . . from unwarranted intrusions on their personal liberty'" (384, quoting *Oliphant v. Suquamish Indian Tribe* 1978, 210; emphasis added). He indicated no awareness of the withering criticism *Oliphant* has rightly faced for exactly that troubling analysis. He expanded on the deep suspicion *Oliphant* expressed toward tribal courts, stating that ICRA had made only "a handful of [Bill of Rights] safeguards enforceable in tribal courts" (384). In fact, ICRA applied *all but* a handful of such rights to tribal courts, and the few exceptions do not differentiate them from state courts at all for purposes of civil lawsuits. More fairly, Souter also noted that "[t]ribal courts . . . differ . . . in their structure, in the substantive law they apply, and in the independence of their judges" (384). Even so, like Rehnquist in *Oliphant* and Kennedy in *Duro*, Souter made no attempt to explain why any deficiencies counseled greater concern for nonmembers choosing to subject themselves to tribal court jurisdiction, as opposed to tribal members themselves who are *also* U.S. citizens and who have far less realistic choice about being subject to tribal jurisdiction.

Souter generally seemed ill-informed about the factual realities of Indian country. He argued in *Hicks* that expanding the *Montana* rule "serves sound policy . . . [b]ecause land on Indian reservations constantly changes hands (from tribes to nonmembers, from nonmembers to tribal members, and so on)," thus rendering the original *Montana* rule "extraordinarily difficult to administer" (382–383). Indian lands do not, in fact, frequently change ownership in this fashion. For the most part, non-Indian-owned parcels within Indian reservations are long-established relics of the Allotment Era. It is true that they form something of a "checkerboard" on some reservations.

But of course, as critics have pointed out, it was the *Montana* rule itself that needlessly tied tribal power to the occasional crazy quilt of land ownership in Indian country, and it was *Montana* that partly reversed the long-established presumption of tribal civil jurisdiction. It is thus ironic, at best, to see *Montana* described as a source of "coherence" in Indian law, as both Souter in *Atkinson* and O'Connor in *Hicks* have done (*Atkinson Trading Co. v. Shirley* 2001, 659; *Nevada v. Hicks* 2001, 388). In this regard, even though O'Connor's concurrence in *Hicks* criticized some of the more obvious flaws in Scalia's opinion, it was hardly anything for Indians to cheer about. She too (joined by Justices Stevens and Breyer) agreed that *Montana* should be expanded to cover all tribal land, and she offered far less in the way of explanation.

The Court in *Hicks* appears to unanimously agree that tribal land ownership is at best a mere "factor" to be considered in applying the *Montana* rule. O'Connor's main protest was that the majority did not treat it as a sufficiently "*important* factor" (389; emphasis added). But given how narrowly all the justices (including O'Connor, Stevens, and Breyer) have construed the *Montana* exceptions, this offered very little protection for tribal sovereignty, even (now) on tribally owned lands. How *Montana* can be a source of "coherence" when all nine justices have thus ripped it out of its carefully limited original context is a deep mystery.

Despite the shaky reasoning of *Hicks,* the specific outcome of the case was not terribly surprising. Actually ruling in favor of tribal jurisdiction against the state officials would have been almost equally radical and unprecedented. The precise issue presented was whether state officials could be held personally liable as defendants in a civil lawsuit. Such officers are ordinarily entitled to qualified immunity from lawsuits for actions taken in the course of their official duties, if they acted in the good faith belief that their conduct was lawful. As O'Connor noted in Part II of her opinion, the Fallon Tribal Courts failed to promptly address the officers' immunity claims. She argued that on remand, instead of just dismissing the lawsuit as required under the majority's reasoning, the lower federal court should itself address the immunity issue.

Review at this point the second-to-last paragraph of Scalia's opinion. He was on strong legal ground in criticizing O'Connor's opinion in this regard. O'Connor argued, in effect, that tribal courts could be denied jurisdiction as a sort of punishment for not adequately addressing the immunity issue. But normally, federal courts must make an all-or-nothing decision as to whether tribal courts have jurisdiction. If tribal courts *do* have jurisdiction, *they* would seem to have authority to decide the immunity issue under tribal law. That could, in theory, place state officials at the mercy of tribal courts. Indeed, a general problem highlighted by the *Hicks* case, as Souter noted, is that "there is no effective review mechanism in place" over tribal court decisions (385). Tribal court judgments cannot be formally removed or appealed to any state or federal court. The only (and rather cumbersome) recourse for tribal court defendants like the Nevada state officials is to bring a separate lawsuit in federal court, seeking either a writ of habeas corpus or a "declaratory judgment" that the tribal courts lack jurisdiction.

Now review the final paragraph in Scalia's opinion. He recapped first the broad and sweeping rationale the Court chose to employ in deciding *Hicks,* that tribes "lac[k] . . . authority to restrict, condition, or otherwise regulate" the on-reservation conduct of state officials enforcing state law (374). He then stated the narrower ground on which the Court *could* have relied: "State officials operating on a reservation . . . are properly held accountable . . . in either state or federal court, but not in tribal court" (374). The Court could have upheld tribal jurisdiction and left it to Congress to provide any needed controls on tribal courts. Or the Court could have denied tribal jurisdiction over Hicks's lawsuit while still maintaining legal limits on state authority and legal protections for tribal sovereignty within Indian country. Such limits could then be enforced, with any added remedies Congress might find appropriate, in federal court.

Instead, Scalia and the majority threw out the baby with the bathwater.

How much of Native American sovereignty remains after *Hicks?* In reality, a great deal, largely because Congress and even many states are now more respectful of tribal sovereignty than the U.S. Supreme Court. Congress has already held hearings on whether to reverse by statute some aspects of the *Hicks* decision. The author of this book attended the Federal Bar Association's annual Indian Law Conference in April 2002, at which tribal leaders and Indian law practitioners and scholars from around the country were still reeling from the decision. But the state attorney general of Nevada, Frankie Sue Del Papa, spoke at the conference and offered her personal assurance that Nevada would not alter its practice of seeking tribal permission for on-reservation search warrants and tribal cooperation generally on law enforcement matters. She viewed *Hicks* as merely offering defensive protection for state officers against potentially ruinous civil liability.

The impact of *Hicks* should not be exaggerated. But it does, perhaps, mark the end of an era. The forty-two years between *Williams* and *Hicks* were, to a large extent, a time of vigorous renewal of American Indian sovereignty, often led by the U.S. Supreme Court. That era revived the spirit of John Marshall and the Cherokee Cases. But the Court no longer fulfills any such role. As Justices Blackmun, Brennan, and Marshall lamented in *Brendale,* the Court seems to have lost its way. Barring a fundamental shift in attitude among the justices, further development of Indian sovereignty will have to come from the other branches of government and from the Indian nations themselves.

Tribal Gambling

Driving east from San Diego on Interstate 8, if one exits at El Cajon and then heads east on Dehesa Road, the urban sprawl starts to thin out, and shopping malls give way to arid brown hills. Just past the Singing Hills golf course, an opulent splash of green in the desert, signs point to the reservation of the Sycuan Band of the Kumeyaay Nation. The Sycuan are one of dozens of tiny Indian tribes scattered along the back roads of California. Many of these bands are also known as "Mission Indians" because they were mostly colonized and converted to Christianity by the Spanish Catholic monks who established the famed California missions. The first of these, in San

Diego, was founded in 1769 by Father Junípero Serra, just a few miles west of the present Sycuan reservation. It was the first European settlement in what is now California.

The American Indian experience throughout the United States was largely one of hardship and genocide during the nineteenth century, as discussed in Chapter 2. The Indian experience in California was especially brutal. California passed from Spain to Mexico upon Mexican independence in 1821 and then in 1848 was ceded to the United States at the end of the Mexican-American War. That followed a brief interlude of nominal independence during the "Bear Flag" revolt staged by U.S. settlers and explorers such as John C. Frémont. The infamous gold rush began in 1848 and reached flood tide in 1849. Statehood followed quickly in 1850. California, today the wealthiest state in the Union, with its population of more than 30 million dwarfing any other state, produced two of our last seven presidents. It leads the United States into the twenty-first century. But there is another side to the vaunted "California dream."

In 1769, more than 300,000 Indians are estimated to have lived in California. The number was cut in half to about 150,000 by the 1830s. By 1900, the Indian population in all the lower forty-eight United States had sunk to less than 300,000 and that in California to as little as 15,000. Where did they all go? Disease and starvation killed many, as entire tribes were driven from their homes by the flood of gold seekers and other settlers. Several treaties were negotiated with California tribes during the 1850s but never ratified. The tribes were dispossessed of most of their lands without compensation and often exiled to barren, remote corners of California's back country. Outright extermination was practiced on a wide scale, as white vigilantes murdered whole families and communities. The slaughter was widely encouraged by state authorities. It was one of the most evil chapters in U.S. history and is scarcely remembered today. And it forms the backdrop for the final section of this book's exploration of the trials of Native American sovereignty.

Just a few years ago, the Sycuan reservation, inhabited by fewer than 100 adult tribal members, was typical of much of California Indian country: a bleak place on a road to nowhere. Today, visitors turning off Dehesa Road and entering the reservation might be forgiven for imagining that they are seeing a mirage. A fabulous palace painted in fantastical pastel colors rises from the scrubby valley floor. Seven days a week, twenty-four hours a day, visitors flock to the gambling casino housed in this fairyland castle. Although Indian casinos are reluctant to publicize their earnings, the monthly take is surely many millions of dollars. That fancy golf course and country club before the reservation turnoff? The Sycuan bought it in 2001, the same year they opened the new casino. Across California, more than sixty Indian tribes already operate casinos, or are in the process of building or expanding them. Money has flowed into tribal coffers at an astounding rate, making the members of many of the small tribes quite wealthy. More important, money for health care, schools and other tribal government programs, and higher education of the next generation of Indians is now plentiful, at least for these fortunate tribes.

It should be emphasized that, nationwide, only a small minority of Indians has yet benefited from the gambling boom. The vast majority of Indian reservations remain places of grinding, discouraging poverty and unemployment, high crime, and endemic social problems, including alcoholism and domestic violence. The statistics summarized in the *Means* case about the Navajo (Diné) Nation, by far the largest Indian reservation, starkly illustrate that reality. Some tribes, like the Navajo, maintain deeply held moral and religious beliefs that preclude resorting to gambling. But from the old woodland tribes of New England to the adobe pueblos of New Mexico, from the Chippewa of northern Wisconsin and Minnesota to the Sycuan of southern California, gambling has remade much of Indian country and appears to hold out extraordinary promise. How did that come about?

The story begins with one of the most controversial federal laws passed during the Termination Era of the 1950s: Public Law 280. Signed with misgivings in 1953 by President Dwight D. Eisenhower, Public Law 280 granted full criminal jurisdiction over Indians and Indian country (with certain exceptions not relevant here) to six specified states: Alaska, California, Minnesota, Nebraska, Oregon, and Wisconsin. Public Law 280 also granted those states "jurisdiction over civil causes of action" involving Indians on the same terms as state jurisdiction over all civil lawsuits, and it purported to apply to Indian country all "civil laws of such State . . . of general application to private persons or private property" (P.L. 280, 28 U.S.C. § 1360). The scope and distinctions between these two aspects of Public Law 280 jurisdiction—criminal and civil—would turn out to be critical to the issue of Indian gambling.

Public Law 280 offered other states the option of assuming jurisdiction over Indian country within their borders. Under the Indian Civil Rights Act of 1968, however, Congress required tribal consent for any further expansions of Public Law 280. No tribe has granted such consent since 1968, but between 1953 and 1968, several states in addition to the first six asserted various degrees of criminal or civil jurisdiction or both. Most states remain unaffected by Public Law 280, but because California, the largest, is a Public Law 280 state, the law has had great national importance. This section focuses on California with regard to the gambling issue because of its sheer size and importance, because it produced the leading Supreme Court decision in the field, and because political and legal developments in the late 1990s make it a fascinating and highly instructive case study in the battles over Indian sovereignty.

A casual reading of the text of Public Law 280 would suggest that the affected states obtained comprehensive legal authority, both criminal and civil, over Indian country within their borders. Surprisingly, it was not until twenty-three years after the law was passed that the Supreme Court first tested that proposition. In *Bryan v. Itasca County* (1976), the State of Minnesota and Itasca County sought to levy a personal property tax on a mobile home owned by a member of the Minnesota Chippewa Tribe and located on the tribe's Leech Lake Reservation. But the Court unanimously struck down the state tax, prominently citing and relying on a 1975 law review article by Carole Goldberg, one of the nation's leading Indian law scholars and a professor at the University of California at Los Angeles.

Goldberg's theory, adopted by the Court, was that Congress was primarily concerned in Public Law 280 with perceived criminal lawlessness in Indian country. Under the canons of construction requiring clear evidence of legislative intent to override tribal sovereignty, Public Law 280 was clear enough in extending state jurisdiction over criminal prosecutions and state court jurisdiction over civil lawsuits. But it was far less clear that Congress ever intended to allow Public Law 280 states to exercise comprehensive regulatory jurisdiction over Indian country, covering such matters as taxation, zoning, public health, safety, and morals. Thus, under the historic presumption of Indian law, Public Law 280 was found not to have disturbed tribal immunity and autonomy in those areas.

Even as limited by the *Bryan* decision, Public Law 280 has been bitterly resented by affected Indian tribes and often by affected state and local governments as well. As Goldberg noted, "the Indians ... did not want state jurisdiction thrust upon them against their will, [and] the states ... resented the remaining federal protection which seemed to deprive them of the ability to finance their newly acquired powers" (Goldberg 1975, 538). As Goldberg documented in a major book and article published in 1997, Public Law 280 has actually been a source of lawlessness in Indian country.

Eleven years after *Bryan*, the Supreme Court addressed the issue of gambling on a Public Law 280 Indian reservation. Read the opinions in *California v. Cabazon Band of Mission Indians* (1987) in the Documents section. The Cabazon band, like many small California tribes consigned to essentially worthless and remote parcels of rural land, sought to make a living by running a bingo parlor and a card club offering games like poker. But California state law limited bingo games to nonprofit charitable organizations like churches, with a $250 prize cap per game, and some California counties prohibited certain card games. Violations of these laws were prosecuted as criminal misdemeanors. The issue, as framed by the *Cabazon* Court, was whether California's gambling laws amounted to criminal prohibitions within its Public Law 280 powers or merely a "civil/regulatory" scheme analogous to the tax laws in *Bryan*. The Court reasoned in *Cabazon* that

> if the intent of a state law is generally to prohibit certain conduct, it falls within [Public Law 280] ..., but if state law generally permits the conduct at issue, subject to regulation, it must be classified as civil/regulatory and [Public Law 280] does not authorize its enforcement on an Indian reservation. The shorthand test is whether the conduct at issue violates the State's public policy. (209)

The Court concluded that California did not, in fact, have any public policy generally prohibiting gambling. The Court noted that California allowed many forms of bingo and card games, as well as horse-race betting. The Court placed especially heavy emphasis on the fact that California "actually *promote[d]* gambling through its state lottery" (211; emphasis added). Furthermore, "that an otherwise regulatory law is enforceable by criminal as well as civil means does not necessarily convert it into a criminal law within the meaning of [Public Law 280]" (211). Most tax laws, after all (which the Court found to be "civil/regulatory" in *Bryan*), are enforced, if need be, by criminal prosecution for tax evasion. Perhaps the most surprising thing about *Cabazon* was that Chief Justice William H. Rehnquist, no friend of Indian sovereignty in most cases, joined fully in Justice Byron R. White's 6–3 majority opinion. Justice John Paul Stevens, joined by Justice Sandra Day O'Connor (usually more friendly to tribal sovereignty than Rehnquist), and Justice Antonin Scalia, dissented.

But were there important factual differences between *Bryan* and *Cabazon*? Exactly who was being subjected to the state laws in each case? Recall that in the 1980 *Colville* cigarette tax case, the Court had upheld state taxation of non-Indians buying cigarettes on the reservation. That was consistent with *Bryan* because *Bryan* involved direct taxation of an Indian tribal member. Furthermore, *Colville* enunciated a general rule of Indian law not limited to the Public Law 280 context. *Colville* arose in Washington State, which had only partly implemented Public Law 280 and did not claim that the law authorized the tax. The Cabazon gambling operation, like other such establishments and the tribal smokeshops in *Colville,* catered to an overwhelmingly non-Indian clientele. How did the majority in *Cabazon* get around the *Colville* precedent? What did Stevens's dissent say about that?

Strictly speaking, *Cabazon* applied only to California and possibly to other Public Law 280 states, depending on each state's gambling laws. But even outside the Public Law 280 states, there has long been debate about the application of state laws to gambling and other issues of public health, safety, and morals within Indian country. The federal Indian Country Crimes Act (ICCA) and Assimilative Crimes Act (ACA) effectively borrow the substance of state criminal law and apply it (via the federal court system) to crimes on Indian reservations not covered by the federal Major Crimes Act. (In Public Law 280 states, of course, Public Law 280 itself generally eliminates the need for federal law enforcement under the Major Crimes Act, ICCA, or ACA.) Generally speaking, ICCA and ACA apply only to crimes involving non-Indians. But what about minor, so-called victimless crimes, such as prostitution or sale of illegal fireworks? The courts have generally ruled that such crimes nevertheless threaten the public safety or morals of the non-Indian community and therefore fall within ICCA and ACA.

For example, in *United States v. Marcyes* (1977), a case not governed by Public Law 280, the U.S. Court of Appeals for the Ninth

Circuit found that Washington State's criminal laws against illegal fireworks reflected a prohibitory public policy. Thus, *Marcyes* held that these laws fell within ICCA and ACA, and upheld the federal government's power to enforce these state laws in Indian country. But the *Marcyes* court was sensitive to the concern that ICCA and ACA might swamp tribal self-government if they applied to all the criminal enforcement provisions of every state regulatory law, such as those dealing with taxation or hunting and fishing licenses. ICCA and ACA might become a backdoor method to subject tribes to the full range of state civil and regulatory laws, contrary to basic principles of tribal sovereignty. Therefore, *Marcyes* adopted the same criminal/civil or "prohibitory/regulatory" distinction adopted by the Supreme Court's *Bryan* decision just the year before. *Marcyes* even cited *Bryan,* though *Bryan* technically did not govern non–Public Law 280 issues.

In *Cabazon,* Stevens argued in dissent that the majority's reasoning would open the door to "cockfighting, tattoo parlors, nude dancing, houses of prostitution, and other illegal but profitable enterprises" on Indian reservations (222). The majority dismissed that in a footnote, asserting that state laws in each case had to be examined individually. The majority cited *Marcyes* as a good example, thus indicating that *Cabazon* had implications stretching well beyond the Public Law 280 states.

At this point, read the opinions in the California Supreme Court's landmark decision in *Hotel Employees Union v. Davis* (1999), set forth in the Documents section. The *Davis* majority opinion provides a useful overview of California gambling laws and, in particular, Congress's response to the *Cabazon* decision in the federal Indian Gaming Regulatory Act of 1988 (IGRA). Before getting into the issues raised by California's Proposition 5, passed in 1998, it is important to review the development of Indian gambling in the decade after *Cabazon.*

Although Congress took over the issue of Indian gambling in passing IGRA, the influence of the Supreme Court's reasoning in *Cabazon* was obvious. To some extent, IGRA simply codified *Cabazon* and extended its principles nationwide, to both Public Law 280 and non–Public Law 280 states. In one sense, IGRA federalized gambling regulation in Indian country. The federal government now borrows and enforces all state laws regarding gambling (even in Public Law 280 states) in much the same manner as it borrows and enforces state criminal laws generally through ICCA and ACA. To whatever extent gambling may still be unlawful in a given state, it is the U.S. government, not the state, that enforces the law within Indian country.

But IGRA is a complex statute and generated many new legal issues. Like *Cabazon,* it gave state gambling laws great influence in Indian country. Even though the tribe won in *Cabazon,* the potential threat to Indian sovereignty was clear. IGRA also perpetuated a key ambiguity of *Cabazon.* At what point, exactly, did a state open the door to tribal gambling operations by allowing or promoting some types of gambling outside Indian country? And what types of Indian gambling are we talking about? *Cabazon* itself involved a relatively modest bingo and card-club operation, a far cry from the full-scale casinos familiar to gambling enthusiasts visiting Nevada or Atlantic City, New Jersey.

The most lucrative kinds of casino gambling are classified by IGRA as "Class III gaming." As explained in the *Davis* majority opinion, there are several hurdles that a tribe has to surmount before conducting Class III gambling. First, such gambling is only allowed in a state that itself, outside Indian country, "permits such gaming for any purpose by any person, organization, or entity" (Indian Gaming Regulatory Act, § 2710). IGRA did not explain whether "such gaming" refers to *any* Class III gambling, the same general types of Class III gambling, or only *exactly the same specific* types of Class III gambling that a tribe might seek to offer. This issue is critically important, since Class III includes several types of gambling commonly legalized in most states, such as race-track betting and lotteries, as well as types historically available only in places like Nevada or Atlantic City, such as slot machines and high-stakes casino games like blackjack, craps, and roulette. Did every state that allowed race-track betting or ran a state lottery now face the prospect of full-blown Las Vegas–style casinos on Indian reservations within the state?

Furthermore, IGRA requires that a tribe and the state in which it is located negotiate a compact to govern any tribal Class III gambling. Upon a tribe's request, the state is obligated to "negotiate with the Indian tribe in good faith" (Indian Gaming Regulatory Act, § 2710). IGRA authorized tribes to sue states that violated their duties under IGRA. As a backup enforcement provision in case a state refused to negotiate in good faith, the U.S. secretary of the interior was authorized to directly impose regulations allowing Class III gambling, but that drastic power has never been used.

In the first few years following *Cabazon* and IGRA, California Indian tribes continued to win some important victories in court. In *Sycuan Band v. Roache,* a lawsuit brought by the Sycuan, Viejas, and Barona tribes near San Diego, a federal district judge in 1992 ordered a halt to raids and prosecutions of tribal gambling operations carried out by the San Diego County sheriff and district attorney. The state authorities had seized a number of electronic gambling devices that they regarded as slot machines. The U.S. Court of Appeals for the Ninth Circuit affirmed the district judge's ruling in September 1994, in an opinion written by Judge William C. Canby, Jr., a noted Indian law scholar and author of a major treatise on the subject. The Supreme Court, in 1995, declined to review that decision.

Just two months after the 1994 *Sycuan* ruling, however, a different three-judge panel of the Ninth Circuit, in *Rumsey Indian Rancheria v. Wilson,* rejected a lawsuit brought by a larger coalition of California gambling tribes, including the Sycuan, Viejas, Barona, and other bands. The tribes objected to then California governor Pete Wilson's refusal to negotiate compacts authorizing casino-style card games and electronic slot machines. But the *Rumsey* panel held that "IGRA does not require a state to negotiate over one form of gambling activity simply because it has legalized another, albeit similar form of gambling" (427). Judge Canby was not on the panel that heard *Rumsey,* but he issued a strong dissent when the full Ninth Circuit, in August 1995, declined to rehear the panel's decision. Canby, joined by five other Ninth Circuit judges, pointed out that the panel's decision "frustrate[d] IGRA's entire plan" (1253) by relieving the state of any duty to even negotiate over any specific form of Class III gambling disallowed by existing state law.

Rumsey blatantly conflicted with the Supreme Court's reasoning in *Cabazon,* which upheld the tribe's right to conduct specific types of gambling that were illegal under California law, pointing out that California *did* allow *other* types of gambling. Some of the other types of gambling that the *Cabazon* Court pointed to, like racetrack betting and the state lottery, were not even that similar to the bingo games conducted by the Cabazon Band. Under the *Rumsey* interpretation of IGRA, Congress might as well have simply granted states direct and comprehensive control over Class III gambling. IGRA's negotiation process was rendered pointless. Nevertheless, the Supreme Court, in 1997, declined to review the *Rumsey* decision.

A U.S. Supreme Court decision around this time struck another crushing blow to Indian hopes under *Cabazon* and IGRA. In *Seminole Tribe v. Florida* (1996), the Court ruled that tribal lawsuits against states to enforce IGRA violated the principle of state sovereign immunity. *Seminole Tribe* was a bitterly divided 5–4 decision. Chief Justice Rehnquist wrote for the Court, joined by Justices O'Connor, Scalia, Kennedy, and Thomas. Justices Stevens, Souter, Ginsburg, and Breyer vehemently dissented. But none of the justices were especially focused on Indian law issues. Rather, the decision was one of a series of similar 5–4 rulings by which the Rehnquist Court has enhanced state sovereignty and limited the scope of federal power. In any event, the tribes were left with little leverage to enforce IGRA.

Yet another setback to California gambling tribes was the California Supreme Court's decision in *Western Telcon v. California State Lottery* (1996). At first glance, this case involved a rather technical dispute about whether a "Keno" game offered by the state lottery complied with state law. The court found that Keno constituted an unlawful "house-banked" game, not a true "lottery" as allowed by state law. Because *Cabazon* and IGRA (and especially the *Rumsey* decision) tied Indian gambling to the types of games permitted under state law, *Western Telcon* posed a serious threat to many of the games the tribes were already operating.

The result of all these decisions was a period of frustration and uncertainty for California tribes. Many were conducting gambling operations of doubtful legality. The historically impoverished tribes were heavily dependent on the revenues from such operations. Federal authorities were reluctant to stage confrontational raids on such operations, but they signaled that it was only a matter of time before they would crack down. Governor Wilson remained adamantly opposed to widespread casino-style gambling. His administration did negotiate, in early 1998, a limited compact with the Pala Band of Mission Indians in northern San Diego County. Other California tribes, however, overwhelmingly rejected the Pala compact, which they viewed as a sellout to Wilson.

The California tribes themselves then resorted to a series of high-stakes political gambles. Relying largely on revenues already earned from gambling operations, they sponsored a statewide ballot initiative (Proposition 5) for the November 1998 election and advertised heavily to win its passage. Proposition 5 endorsed a model state-tribal compact that would have allowed many but not all types of Class III gambling on California Indian reservations. Nevada gambling interests, alarmed by the prospect of competition from California tribes, fought Proposition 5 furiously, along with antigambling groups. But the opponents were still outspent about 2 to 1 overall. The total campaign spending of around $100 million broke all records for such ballot propositions.

California voters, however, have often not been swayed by heavy spending on such campaigns. In 1988, they overwhelmingly rejected several propositions supported by the insurance industry, despite tens of millions of dollars spent on advertising. Proposition 5, appealingly titled the "Indian Self-Reliance Initiative," seemed to generate a genuine groundswell of sympathy and support among the overwhelmingly non-Indian electorate. It passed by a landslide margin, with about 63 percent voting in favor. Perhaps equally important, California Indian tribes also spent heavily on other political campaigns, including the victorious candidates for governor and state attorney general, Democrats Gray Davis and Bill Lockyer, who generally supported tribal gambling. Davis defeated the Republican candidate, Dan Lungren, by a margin almost as lopsided as Proposition 5's victory. Lungren was the incumbent state attorney general and (like Wilson) viewed as hostile to gambling. (Wilson was barred by term limits from running for governor again.)

Just nine months later, however, in August 1999, the California Supreme Court temporarily derailed any expansion of Indian gambling in the *Davis* decision. By a vote of 6–1, the state justices struck down Proposition 5 as a violation of the California Constitution. The problem was that in 1984, when California voters authorized the state lottery, they also amended the state constitution to expressly prohibit Nevada-style casinos. Proposition 5 was merely a statutory initiative because its backers ran out of time to gather sufficient petition signatures to qualify it as a state constitutional amendment. Thus, it could not legally override the 1984 Lottery Amendment. The lawyers on both sides and the majority and dissenting justices engaged in a heated and highly technical debate about whether the types of gambling authorized by Proposition 5 actually amounted to "Nevada-style casinos." That aspect of the case has little enduring interest, however, and has been edited out of the *Davis* opinions set forth in the Documents section.

The more interesting question posed by *Davis* was whether California voters, by approving a compact allowing tribal gambling, were "authorizing" casino gambling in the sense prohibited by the Lottery Amendment. The majority devoted only a footnote to this issue, but read carefully Justice Joyce L. Kennard's dissent. Kennard framed the issue of Indian gambling in its proper historical context, as an aspect of inherent Native American sovereignty. She argued that the state or voters of California had no power to "authorize" Indian casinos because that was governed by federal law (IGRA) and its recognition of the Indian nations' ancestral power to govern their own lands.

True, as Kennard conceded in *Davis,* IGRA delegated to the states considerable influence to "shape the contours of the federal authorization" (620). Proposition 5's own language purported to "authorize" the model compact that it offered. But that "authorization," in Kennard's view, was ultimately effective only as part of a scheme of federal law based on recognition of limited Indian sovereignty. Thus, it could not logically be controlled by the Lottery Amendment, which, as she saw it, merely limited California state law outside Indian country.

Kennard illustrated her point by noting that California had "entered into a compact with . . . Nevada . . . regulating the number and size of gaming facilities located in Nevada within the Lake Tahoe basin" (621). Yet no one had ever suggested *that* compact "authorized" casinos in violation of the Lottery Amendment. In Kennard's view, California had no more sovereignty over "gambling on Indian lands than it . . . [did over] gambling in another state" (621). This was a vision of Native American sovereignty and its relation to state sovereignty far closer to the historical understanding than U.S. Supreme Court Justice Scalia's in *Nevada v. Hicks* (2001).

In any event, the ironic and unintended result of the *Davis* decision was to open the door even wider to Indian gambling. The model compact embodied in Proposition 5 would have drawn a line short of full-scale Nevada-style casino gambling on California reservations. With Proposition 5 set aside, however, newly elected Governor Davis negotiated and signed a new compact with fifty-nine tribes in September 1999. The state legislature proposed it to the voters as a state constitutional amendment in the March 2000 primary election, as Proposition 1A. The people of California clearly had few second thoughts about Indian gambling, at least at that point. Proposition 1A was ratified by an even wider landslide margin (65 percent) than Proposition 5. The final step required by IGRA, approval by the U.S. Department of the Interior, followed two months later (Gover Notice 2000).

Read the California-Tribal Gaming Compact in the Documents section. Section 4.1 dealt with the types of gaming devices permitted. By allowing slot machines and "banking or percentage card game[s]," the new compact essentially opened the door to the full range of Nevada-style casino gambling, except for craps and roulette. Note that section 4.1(c) also permitted negotiation of separate compacts allowing off-track betting at Indian casinos, which has occurred. Section 4.3, dealing with the number of slot machines each tribe is allowed to operate, was somewhat confusingly worded and has generated continued controversy. Governor Davis insisted at first that the compact would only allow about 45,000 slot machines statewide. Fewer than 20,000 were in operation in September 1999. By comparison, Nevada had about 200,000 slot machines. But in June 2002, the California Gambling Control Commission (see section 2.2), which Davis appointed, raised its estimate of the statewide limit to 51,000. That was contested by the tribes, however, and may well be a conservative figure.

Davis, perhaps concerned that the growth of Indian gambling was getting out of control, suddenly called a halt in May 2001 to negotiations for any new tribal compacts. The official excuse was a recently filed lawsuit claiming that the legal framework of California gambling unconstitutionally discriminated against non-Indians. Davis claimed this suit created too much legal uncertainty and required an indefinite suspension of negotiations. But the lawsuit was plainly frivolous under the U.S. Supreme Court's decision in *Morton v. Mancari* (1974) (discussed in Chapter 2). Davis's announcement angered the many nongambling California tribes that had already requested new compacts. They have yet to share in any major way from the gambling boom. Indeed, the uneven benefits of Indian gambling, both in California and nationwide, are a source of major concern.

Review sections 4.3.2 and 4.3.2.1 of the 2000 compact, which provided for revenue sharing with tribes not yet operating casinos. It was a widely hailed aspect of the compact, mitigating the impression that it might benefit only a few wealthy tribes. But it has also predictably led to controversy. The first payments under this provision, only about $300,000 to each nongambling tribe, were not made until the summer of 2001. Some have criticized the payments as inadequate, and some leaders of both gambling and nongambling tribes have advocated scrapping the revenue-sharing program.

There is no doubt that Indian gambling has generally boosted the state's economy for both Indians and non-Indians. Given the small populations of most California tribes, the casinos necessarily employ large numbers of non-Indians. The total payrolls of the largest casinos rival those of Fortune 500 companies. Note also section 5 of the compact. Although the state does not tax Indian casinos, which the tribes would view as a violation of their sovereignty, they did agree to share a portion of their revenues with state and local governments. And, of course, state and local governments levy taxes on the many non-Indian employees of Indian casinos. Congress has also refrained so far from taxing tribal government income from gambling, though individual Indians are generally subject to the same federal income taxes as anyone else. The conferral of U.S. citizenship on all Indians in 1924 (as discussed in Chapter 2), and the development of modern federal tax laws, have superseded (at least at the federal level) the old constitutional presumption that Indians were "not taxed."

One key provision of the compact was section 9.4, in which both the state and the tribes partly waived their respective sovereign immunity for disputes arising under the compact. This concession was important because the U.S. Supreme Court, in *Kiowa Tribe v. Manufacturing Technologies, Inc.* (1998), had recently reaffirmed, 6–3, the immunity of Indian nations from civil lawsuits, even when such lawsuits arise from off-reservation commercial ventures. Four of the five justices who supported state sovereign immunity in the 1996 *Seminole Tribe* case (Chief Justice Rehnquist and Justices O'Connor, Scalia, and Kennedy) supported tribal immunity in *Kiowa Tribe.* Two of the dissenters in *Seminole Tribe* also dissented in *Kiowa Tribe* (Justices Stevens and Ginsburg); Justice Thomas was the third dissenter in *Kiowa Tribe.* Even Kennedy's majority opinion questioned the wisdom of preserving tribal immunity, however, and there have been proposals in Congress to limit or abolish it.

Politically speaking, one of the most critical provisions of the compact—insisted upon by Governor Davis, who enjoyed heavy labor union support—was buried in section 10.7. Although Indian nations are exempt from many labor laws, they agreed in this provision to enter into union contracts with casino workers. Section 10.8 was also critical to mollify the environmental concerns of local communities adjoining casino developments.

But other troubling questions about the compact remain. Sections 6 and 7 provided for stringent licensing of casino employees and regulatory oversight of casino operations, largely by tribal regulatory agencies in cooperation with the state. Recall that in *Cabazon,* one of the primary concerns of Justice Stevens's dissent was that organized crime might gain a foothold in tribal gambling operations. Although there is no evidence that such infiltration has yet occurred, the practical reality is that tribes have largely been trusted to police themselves. Federal and state regulatory agencies exist, but their resources are spread very thin.

As noted in Chapter 1, it is profoundly ironic that the doctrine of Indian sovereignty—first defined by struggles against the non-Indian state voters and political leaders of Georgia in the 1830s—has now received a dramatic boost from the non-Indian state voters and political leaders of California at the turn of the twenty-first century. The spectacle of Indians as wealthy operators of lucrative businesses may conflict, of course, with stereotypical images that many non-Indians have of native peoples. In point of fact, the Indian nations that have chosen gambling as a path to economic development have not abandoned their ancient cultures. To the contrary, the resources provided by gambling have enabled many tribes to better preserve and enhance their cultural identities.

But in any event, if Native American sovereignty is taken seriously, it must mean the right of Indian nations to pursue whatever course of development and self-government suits their own vision. It must mean the freedom to evolve and change. As Justices Blackmun, Brennan, and Marshall reminded us in *Brendale v. Yakima Indian Nation* (1989), "it must not be the case that tribes can retain the 'essential character' of their reservations . . . only if they forgo economic development and maintain those reservations according to a single, perhaps quaint, view of what is characteristically 'Indian'" (465). Ray Halbritter, a leader of the Oneida Indian Nation of New York, perhaps best summed up the ongoing experiment of Indian gambling: "We had tried poverty for 200 years, so we decided to try something else" (Halbritter and McSloy 1994, 568).

References and Further Reading

Laying the Foundation: Chief Justice Marshall and the Cherokee Cases

Baker, Leonard. 1974. *John Marshall: A Life in Law.* New York: Macmillan.

Burke, Joseph C. 1969. "The Cherokee Cases: A Study in Law, Politics, and Morality." *Stanford Law Review* 21: 500 (reprinted in Wunder 1996, 1: 136).

Carr, Waggoner, Attorney General of Texas (with J. S. Bracewell and Milton Richardson). March 3, 1964. *Memorandum to Governor John Connally Concerning Cherokee Indian Claim Relating to Lands in Texas.*

Carter, Samuel III. 1976. *Cherokee Sunset: A Nation Betrayed.* Garden City, NY: Doubleday.

Debo, Angie. 1984 [1940]. *And Still the Waters Run: The Betrayal of the Five Civilized Tribes.* Norman: University of Oklahoma Press.

Ehle, John. 1988. *Trail of Tears: The Rise and Fall of the Cherokee Nation.* New York: Doubleday.

Mankiller, Wilma, and Michael Wallis. 1993. *Mankiller: A Chief and Her People.* New York: St. Martin's.

Newmyer, R. Kent. 1985. *Supreme Court Justice Joseph Story: Statesman of the Old Republic.* Chapel Hill: University of North Carolina Press.

Indian Treaty Rights

Canby, William C., Jr. 1998. *American Indian Law in a Nutshell.* 3d ed. St. Paul, MN: West.

Clinton, Robert N. 2002. "There Is No Federal Supremacy Clause for Indian Tribes." *Arizona State Law Journal* 34: 113.

Getches, David H., Charles F. Wilkinson, and Robert A. Williams, Jr. 1998. *Cases and Materials on Federal Indian Law.* 4th ed. St. Paul, MN: West.

Kades, Eric. 2000. "The Dark Side of Efficiency: *Johnson v. M'Intosh* and the Expropriation of American Indian Lands." *University of Pennsylvania Law Review* 148: 1065.

Klein, Christine A. 1996. "Treaties of Conquest: Property Rights, Indian Treaties, and the Treaty of Guadalupe Hidalgo." *New Mexico Law Review* 26: 201.

Newton, Nell Jessup. 1980. "At the Whim of the Sovereign: Aboriginal Title Reconsidered." *Hastings Law Journal* 31: 1215.

———. 1984. "Federal Power over Indians: Its Sources, Scope, and Limitations." *University of Pennsylvania Law Review* 132: 195.

Prucha, Francis Paul. 1994. *American Indian Treaties: The History of a Political Anomaly.* Berkeley: University of California Press.

———. ed. 2000. *Documents of United States Indian Policy.* 3d ed. Lincoln: University of Nebraska Press.

Wilkinson, Charles F., and John M. Volkman. 1975. "Judicial Review of Indian Treaty Abrogation: 'As Long as Water Flows or Grass Grows upon the Earth'—How Long a Time Is That?" *California Law Review* 63: 601.

Wilkinson, Charles F. 1991. "To Feel the Summer in the Spring: The Treaty Fishing Rights of the Wisconsin Chippewa." *Wisconsin Law Review* 1991: 375.

Tribal Criminal Jurisdiction

Bailey, Lynn R. 1964. *The Long Walk: A History of the Navajo Wars, 1846–1868.* Los Angeles: Westernlore Press.

Benedek, Emily. 1992. *The Wind Won't Know Me: A History of the Navajo-Hopi Land Dispute.* New York: Knopf.

Canby, William C., Jr. 1998. *American Indian Law in a Nutshell.* 3d ed. St. Paul, MN: West.

Clinton, Robert N. 1976. "Criminal Jurisdiction over Indian Lands: A Journey through a Jurisdictional Maze." *Arizona Law Review* 18: 503.

Deloria, Vine, Jr., and Clifford M. Lytle. 1983. *American Indians, American Justice.* Austin: University of Texas Press.

Forbes, Jack D. 1994. *Apache, Navajo, and Spaniard.* 2d ed. Norman: University of Oklahoma Press.

Getches, David H., Charles F. Wilkinson, and Robert A. Williams, Jr. 1998. *Cases and Materials on Federal Indian Law.* 4th ed. St. Paul, MN: West.

Gould, L. Scott. 1994. "The Congressional Response to *Duro v. Reina:* Compromising Sovereignty and the Constitution." *U.C. Davis Law Review* 28: 53.

Jones, B. J. 1998. "Welcoming Tribal Courts Into the Judicial Fraternity: Emerging Issues in Tribal-State and Tribal-Federal Court Relations." *William Mitchell Law Review* 24: 457.

Locke, Raymond Friday. 1992. *The Book of the Navajo.* 5th ed. Los Angeles: Mankind.

O'Connor, Sandra Day. 1997. "Lessons from the Third Sovereign: Indian Tribal Courts." *Tulsa Law Journal* 33: 1.

Pommersheim, Frank. 1995. *Braid of Feathers: American Indian Law and Contemporary Tribal Life.* Berkeley: University of California Press.

Shebala, Marley. 2002. "No Rights for Nonmember Indians, Means Says." *Navajo Times,* June 13.

Valencia-Weber, Gloria. 1994. "Tribal Courts: Custom and Innovative Law." *New Mexico Law Review* 24: 225.

Yazzie, Robert. 1994. "'Life Comes from It': Navajo Justice Concepts." *New Mexico Law Review* 24: 175.

———. 1996. "'Hozho Nahasdlii'—We Are Now in Good Relations: Navajo Restorative Justice." *St. Thomas Law Review* 9: 117.

———. 1997. "Navajo Peacekeeping: Technology and Traditional Indian Law." *St. Thomas Law Review* 10: 95.

Tribal Civil Jurisdiction

Canby, William C., Jr. 1998. *American Indian Law in a Nutshell.* 3d ed. St. Paul, MN: West.

Dussias, Allison M. 1993. "Geographically-Based and Membership-Based Views of Indian Tribal Sovereignty: The Supreme Court's Changing Vision." *University of Pittsburgh Law Review* 55: 1.

Federal Bar Association. April 4–5, 2002. "Twenty-seventh Annual Indian Law Conference: Reaffirming Tribal Sovereignty in an Era of Judicial Activism: Course Materials." Albuquerque, NM.

Frickey, Philip P. 1999. "A Common Law for Our Age of Colonialism: The Judicial Divestiture of Indian Tribal Authority over Nonmembers." *Yale Law Journal* 109: 1.

Getches, David H. 1996. "Conquering the Cultural Frontier: The New Subjectivism of the Supreme Court in Indian Law." *California Law Review* 84: 1573.

———. 2001. "Beyond Indian Law: The Rehnquist Court's Pursuit of States' Rights, Color-Blind Justice and Mainstream Values." *Minnesota Law Review* 86: 267.

Getches, David H., Charles F. Wilkinson, and Robert A. Williams, Jr. 1998. *Cases and Materials on Federal Indian Law.* 4th ed. St. Paul, MN: West.

O'Connor, Sandra Day. 1997. "Lessons from the Third Sovereign: Indian Tribal Courts." *Tulsa Law Journal* 33: 1.

Skibine, Alex Tallchief. 2001. "Making Sense Out of *Nevada v. Hicks:* A Reinterpretation." *St. Thomas Law Review* 14: 347.

Tribal Gambling

Barfield, Chet. 2001. "Sycuan Band Purchases Country Club." *San Diego Union-Tribune,* May 26, p. B7.

Canby, William C., Jr. 1998. *American Indian Law in a Nutshell.* 3d ed. St. Paul, MN: West.

Clark, C. Blue. 1998. "How Bad It Really Was before World War II: Sovereignty." *Oklahoma City University Law Review* 23: 175.

Cornell, Stephen. 1997. "Sovereignty, Prosperity, and Policy in Indian Country Today." *Community Reinvestment* (Federal Reserve Bank of Kansas City) 5: 5.

Ellis, Virginia. 1998. "Tribes Emerge as Powerful Players in State Politics." *Los Angeles Times,* November 9, p. A3.

Getches, David H., Charles F. Wilkinson. and Robert A. Williams, Jr. 1998. *Cases and Materials on Federal Indian Law.* 4th ed. St. Paul, MN: West.

Goldberg, Carole. 1975. "Public Law 280: The Limits of State Jurisdiction over Reservation Indians." *UCLA Law Review* 22: 35.

Goldberg-Ambrose, Carole. 1997a. *Planting Tail Feathers: Tribal Survival and Public Law 280.* Los Angeles: UCLA American Indian Studies Center.

———. 1997b. "Public Law 280 and the Problem of Lawlessness in California Indian Country." *UCLA Law Review* 44: 1405.

Gorman, Tom. 1998. "Decision '98—the Final Count; Tribes Behind Prop. 5 Seek State Recognition of Casinos." *Los Angeles Times,* November 5, p. S4.

Halbritter, Ray, and Steven Paul McSloy. 1994. "Empowerment or Dependence? The Practical Value and Meaning of Native American Sovereignty." *New York University Journal of International Law and Policy* 26: 531.

Heizer, R. F., and M. A. Whipple. 1971. *The California Indians: A Source Book.* Berkeley: University of California Press.

Howe, Kenneth. 1998. "State Initiatives—Most Costly Campaign Ever." *San Francisco Chronicle,* November 5, p. A19.

Jordan, David B. 2000. "Rolling the Dice on the Cyber-Reservation: The Confluence of Internet Gaming and Federal Indian Law." *American Indian Law Review* 24: 455.

Katzanek, Jack. 2002. "Casinos Help Build Inland Work Force; American Indian Tribes Already Employ Thousands and Are Adding Jobs." *Riverside Press-Enterprise,* February 24, p. A1.

Kroeber, Theodora. 1961. *Ishi in Two Worlds: A Biography of the Last Wild Indian in North America.* Berkeley: University of California Press.

Levy, Guy. 1997. "*Western Telcon v. California State Lottery:* Will Native Americans Lose Again?" *Thomas Jefferson Law Review* 19: 361.

May, James. 2002. "California Indian Tribes Fight over Proposed Revenue Sharing Fund." *Indian Country Today,* March 22.

Miller, Robert J. 2001. "Economic Development in Indian Country: Will Capitalism or Socialism Succeed?" *Oregon Law Review* 80: 757.

Nakao, Annie. 1998. "Heavy Spending Pays Off for Tribal Casino Backers; with $70 Million, Proponents Won Right to Keep Slots." *San Francisco Examiner,* November 4, p. A28.

"Nongaming Tribes Get Their Cut." 2001. *San Diego Union-Tribune,* August 28, p. A3.

Pollack, Andrew. 2000. "Las Vegas Glitz Is Set to Go West; Tribes in California Scramble to Expand Casinos after Vote." *New York Times,* March 10, p. C1.

Rand, Kathryn R. L. 2002. "There Are No Pequots on the Plains: Assessing the Success of Indian Gaming." *Chapman Law Review* 5: 47.

Rand, Kathryn R. L., and Steven A. Light. 1997. "Virtue or Vice? How IGRA Shapes the Politics of Native American Gaming, Sovereignty, and Identity." *Virginia Journal of Social Policy and the Law* 4: 381.

"State Propositions." 1998. *San Francisco Chronicle,* November 5, p. A26.

"State Propositions." 2000. *San Francisco Chronicle,* March 9, p. A8.

Sweeney, James P. 2001a. "Governor Halts New Gambling Compacts; Moratorium Leaves Some Tribes in Limbo." *San Diego Union-Tribune,* May 23, p. A1.

———. 2001b. "A New Payout Urged in Indian Revenue Sharing." *San Diego Union-Tribune,* May 31, p. A3.

———. 2001c. "Gaming Tribes Police Themselves; It's a Bad Policy, Some Critics Say." *San Diego Union-Tribune,* July 22, p. A8.

———. 2002. "State OKs More Slots for Indian Casinos." *San Diego Union-Tribune,* June 20, p. A1.

4
Impact and Legacy

Charles F. Wilkinson, one of the most distinguished scholars in the history of American Indian law, wrote in 1987: "Now, two and a half decades after *Williams v. Lee* (1959), most branches of Indian law have stabilized." Indeed, Wilkinson expressed the hope that "[p]erhaps, at last, the tribes can begin to withdraw from the judicial system and train their energies on fulfilling their historic task of creating workable islands of Indianness within the larger society" (122). But from the perspective of 2003, only sixteen years later, that vision of legal stability no longer appears true, if it ever was. The law governing Indian nations and their relationship with the United States continues to evolve in dramatic and unpredictable ways. The current majority of the U.S. Supreme Court veers from undermining Native American sovereignty in some cases to shakily reaffirming it in others. Many state governments remain unremittingly hostile to Indian sovereignty, even as the people of California have given Indian economic self-determination a stunning electoral endorsement.

Many Indian nations, in line with Wilkinson's suggestion in 1987, have attempted to shift their focus away from constant litigation battles to the task of internal development. Indeed, given the attitude of the Rehnquist Court, many Indian nation lawyers actively discourage bringing any major test cases for the foreseeable future. But as the cases surveyed in Chapter 3 demonstrate, the U.S. legal system is far too decentralized and far too empowering of individual litigants for such a strategy ever to work. That is part of the genius of our system. It is impossible to prevent any individual or tribe from seeking justice as they see it. They may win or lose, but our legal system guarantees at least the right to be heard. Even if the outcome in *Nevada v. Hicks* (2001), for example, could have been predicted, who was to tell Floyd Hicks that he could not seek redress for the wrong he felt was done to him?

As Wilkinson noted, "The field of Indian law rests mainly on the old treaties" (Wilkinson 1987, 120). The history of the Indian treaties is deeply paradoxical. The subject is clouded by popular misconceptions, such as that all or most Indian treaties have been broken or discarded. The U.S. government's conduct *has* been shameful, when one considers the many treaty obligations that have indeed been abrogated or ignored. A central and entirely justifiable strand of modern American Indian activism centers on the theme of broken treaties. A major Indian protest march in 1972 was even called the "Trail of Broken Treaties." But many people on the street, unfamiliar with the details of Indian law and history, would be surprised at how many Indian treaties are still in force, still honored in very important ways. They still provide the bedrock of support for the exercise of many real powers by Indian governments on Indian land. The cases surveyed in Chapter 3 are a testament to the continued vitality of Native American sovereignty, based largely on the old treaties.

Yet, when all is said and done, has the U.S. legal system been, on balance, an ally or an enemy to Native American sovereignty? It is a very difficult and complex question. Wilkinson (1987) hazarded the conclusion that "the thrust" of U.S. law in this field "has hewed to principle in the face of agonizingly powerful forces to abandon principle in the name of societal change" (122). Many would dispute the generosity of that conclusion. Robert A. Williams, Jr., as discussed in Chapter 2, is one of many who have taken a far darker view of the racist and colonialist roots of American Indian law. That Wilkinson and Williams are two of the three coauthors of the leading modern textbook on Indian law (Getches, Wilkinson, and Williams 1998) illustrates the healthy and productive coexistence of these differences in outlook. There is deep truth to both.

Vine Deloria, Jr. (1989), a renowned Indian scholar whose expertise spans history, political science, and law, has mocked Indian law as

> a mythical creature . . . composed of badly written, vaguely phrased and ill-considered federal statutes; hundreds of self-serving [Interior

> Department] Solicitor's Opinions and regulations; and state, federal, and Supreme Court decisions which bear little relationship to rational thought and contain a fictional view of American history that would shame some of our country's best novelists. (203)

Deloria also complained about "the propensity of legal scholars to avoid the historical context in which events occurred and to concentrate instead on the documents themselves and the federal courts' interpretation of them" (210). It is, indeed, almost impossible to overstate the importance of historical context in understanding Native American sovereignty and the legal status of Indians generally. This book is devoted to studying "the documents themselves" that govern that status and to doing so in historical context. Law is ultimately composed of words, of competing stories. The stories told by the documents set forth in Part 2 and discussed in Part 1 are of surpassing importance.

Petra T. Shattuck and Jill Norgren (1991) described a "two-tier structure" of American Indian law. On the "higher" tier, this field is frankly governed by the old maxim, "might makes right." U.S. courts, without necessarily endorsing the justice of the U.S. government's treatment of Indians, have, when push comes to shove, "condoned a system of rule in which the power of the federal government was limited neither by concepts of the inherent rights of Indians nor the imposition of external constitutional standards or institutional restraints" (190–191). One need only read the first important case in this field, Chief Justice Marshall's opinion in *Johnson v. M'Intosh* (1823) and then jump to any number of modern opinions by Chief Justice Rehnquist or his Court to appreciate the continuity in this regard.

Shattuck and Norgren also identified a second and lower tier in which U.S. courts have often subjected "the implementation and administration of such policies *as the federal government had chosen to adopt*" to various rules "consistent with liberal principles of formal legal rationality" (191; emphasis in original). This theme also pervades the documents studied in this book, for example, with regard to the canons of treaty construction and the U.S. government's asserted duties as "trustee" for the rights of Indian nations. But as Shattuck and Norgren argued and as the cases studied in Chapter 3 starkly illustrate, what legal victories the Indians have achieved have been precarious at best. Thus, for example, Indians have won damages for wrongful takings of land in such cases as *United States v. Sioux Nation* (1980)—but only because the sovereign trustee consented to be sued. Indians have won hard-fought battles over treaty interpretation in cases like *Minnesota v. Mille Lacs Band of Chippewa Indians* (1999)—but only against the backdrop of the Court's recognition of the U.S. government's ultimate "plenary" power to abrogate such treaty obligations at any time.

Shattuck and Norgren conceded that the U.S. judicial system "has allowed Indians at times to hold the law to its own promises and pretensions of justice—and to win" (196). But, they said, the "paradox" for Indians is that "the legal gains they make are never final nor are they secure from political manipulation." This was a recipe, they argued, "for partial but not lasting justice." Indeed, they concluded with harsh irony:

> It is . . . not without meaning that Indians have relied on the law and have articulated their grievances and needs in terms of rights thought to be promised or owed by law. The faith in the law of a disenfranchised and dominated people nourishes the mystique of the neutrality and autonomy of the law, even as it denies them justice. Federal Indian law ought to be praised for inspiring the Indians' faith in the law but cursed for betraying the believer. (197)

It is difficult to deny the power of Shattuck's and Norgren's perspective, but their view is arguably too despairing. The maintenance of a legal and judicial system in which wronged peoples may demand and obtain at least partial justice does far more than "nourish the mystique of the law." The "courts of the conqueror," to borrow Marshall's phrase (*Johnson v. M'Intosh* 1823, 588), may indeed operate under certain limitations. They do not have the power to undo centuries of dominance and dispossession. They may often betray the hopes of those inspired to believe in them. But they do not simply ease the conqueror's conscience. To the contrary, they are a constant goad and a constant reproach. Just the latest example of this capacity in our court system is the current class-action lawsuit, *Cobell v. Norton.* In this truly epic case, more than 300,000 Indians are seeking to hold the U.S. government responsible for mismanagement of trust funds deriving from the allotment of Indian lands starting in 1887. The secretary of the interior and other top federal officials have been held in contempt of court. Estimates of the government's ultimate potential liability range up to a staggering total of $10 billion.

The very belief in justice that a constitutional system under the rule of law inspires is a constant thorn in the conqueror's side. Courts provide a forum in which the memory of injustice may be kept alive and constantly refreshed, thereby increasing the odds of justice's eventual triumph, even if it is only a partial and imperfect triumph. They teach us lessons from our own history, if we only choose to learn from them. From these lessons, we may avoid more injustice in the future.

What is really surprising is the degree to which the Indian treaties are still in force. Hardly any other nation on Earth even has any such treaty tradition with its indigenous populations or accords such peoples any quasi-sovereign status. There are, of course, some exceptions, like New Zealand's relationship with its indigenous Maori people. But even Canada, which in recent years has pursued notably liberal policies toward its native inhabitants, has no continuous treaty tradition even remotely comparing to that of the United States. None of this excuses, of course, the repeated failure of the United States to live up to its legal obligations. Any nation that asserts it lives by honorable principles of law should and will be judged by those principles.

As discussed in the second section of Chapter 3, many modern scholars and activists advocate restoring a government-to-government relationship between the United States and American Indian nations. Such a relationship would be modeled on the old treaty-making relationship that prevailed before 1871. This approach is not as far-fetched as it may seem. Indeed, it is already practiced as official policy to some extent. Robert N. Clinton, in the course of forcefully advocating such a shift, has pointed out that the Indian Gaming Regulatory Act of 1988 is built on the concept of state-tribal compacts governing Indian gambling (see the fifth section of Chapter 3). And he noted that recent amendments to the Indian Self-Determination and Education Assistance Act of 1975 rely on federal-tribal compacts (Clinton 2002, 252–260).

President Bill Clinton's administration placed especially strong emphasis on respecting Indian sovereignty. In April 1994, following a historic summit meeting at the White House with Indian leaders from across the United States, President Clinton issued an order seeking "to ensure that the Federal Government operates within a government-to-government relationship with federally recognized Native American tribes." He declared himself "strongly committed to building a more effective day-to-day working relationship reflecting respect for the rights of self-government due the sovereign tribal governments" (Clinton Memorandum 1994). Toward the end of his tenure, Clinton enshrined this policy in a formal executive order (Clinton Order 1998). He also ordered federal agencies to try to accommodate Indian concerns over sacred religious sites on federal land (Clinton Order 1996).

Wilkinson has cited a 1997 order by Secretary of the Interior Bruce Babbitt and Secretary of Commerce William Daley, on tribal rights and endangered species protection, "as one major example of how the government-to-government relationship between the United States and Indian tribes can be successfully implemented" (Wilkinson 1997, 1063). The 1997 order was inspired in part by an agreement negotiated in 1994 between Ronnie Lupe, chairman of the White Mountain Apache Tribe of Arizona, and Mollie Beattie, director of the U.S. Fish and Wildlife Service (Getches, Wilkinson, and Williams 1998, 728–736). The U.S. Environmental Protection Agency has long delegated certain environmental enforcement powers to states, as authorized by various federal laws. In 1984, under the Reagan administration, the EPA adopted a policy of developing government-to- government relationships with Indian tribes. In 1987, amendments to federal clean water laws authorized the EPA to delegate enforcement powers to qualified tribes. In one famous example, the Isleta Pueblo in New Mexico, 5 miles downstream from Albuquerque on the Rio Grande, imposed water pollution standards that forced expensive improvements in Albuquerque's wastewater treatment. As a result of this remarkable equalization of state and tribal sovereignty, "states in which [such] tribes are located do not have complete control over water quality" (Baker 1997, 390).

Some Indian scholars and activists have debated whether such renewed government-to-government relationships are inconsistent with Indian participation in U.S. politics as voters and campaign supporters. Robert B. Porter is one of the most outspoken advocates of Indian disengagement from the individual political rights of U.S. citizenship. John P. LaVelle and David E. Wilkins, however, have strongly rebutted Porter's arguments, maintaining that Indian participation in U.S. politics can strengthen tribal sovereignty and is probably essential (LaVelle 2001; Porter 1999; Wilkins 2000).

As discussed in Chapter 3, some Indian nations have enjoyed the benefits of explosive economic development through gambling enterprises. The revenue produced by these enterprises and tribal dependence on non-Indian politics to maintain and develop them virtually guarantee that Indians, both as tribes and as individuals, will become more, not less, involved in the often expensive game of U.S. politics. Such participation may indeed muddy the theoretical clarity of the principle of Native American sovereignty. But as Wilkins (2000) has suggested, "Such efforts, while not guaranteed to produce success, will be in keeping with the adaptive and flexible activist tradition that has enabled Indian peoples to sustain themselves despite the oppressive odds they have faced throughout history" (748–749). Longtime Indian lawyer and activist Sam Deloria (2002) has warned against "yearn[ing] for a time which never existed, when Indian sovereignty was like Superman in a universe without kryptonite. That never even happened for Superman." Indian sovereignty, like that of the United States itself, he pointed out, has always been limited, both constitutionally and by "political and economic reality" (55).

As the controversies chronicled in this book illustrate, the trends regarding Native American sovereignty do not all point the same way. As the twenty-first century dawns, the story of Indian tribal governments and their place within the U.S. constitutional framework is becoming ever more complex and paradoxical. As noted in the Introduction, the ultimate outcome for the tribes remains very much in doubt. But especially in light of the recent boom in tribal economic development through gambling, one would not be wise to lay odds against them.

American Indians, as peoples and as governments, have survived horrendous ordeals and hardships over the last five centuries. They have persevered through pandemic disease, military conquest, genocide, and dispossession of their lands at the hands of the European Americans who now dominate their ancestral continent. Their governments have faced defeat and betrayal countless times—in war, at the treaty table, and in the courts and legislatures. But by working within the constitutional system that is the proudest achievement of the European American invaders, Indians and their ancient governments have persevered and survived. The story is not over yet, not by a long shot.

The storyteller keeps the stories
all the escape stories
she says "With these stories of ours
we can escape almost anything
with these stories we will survive."

The old teller has been on every journey
and she knows all the escape stories
even stories told before she was born.
She keeps the stories for those who return
but more important
for the dear ones who do not come back
so that we may remember them
and cry for them with the stories.

"In this way
we hold them
and keep them with us forever
and in this way
we continue."

Leslie Marmon Silko,
Excerpt from "The Storyteller's Escape," in *Storyteller*

References and Further Reading

Baker, Janet K. 1997. "Tribal Water Quality Standards: Are There Any Limits?" *Duke Environmental Law and Policy Forum* 7: 367.

Clinton, Robert N. 2002. "There Is No Federal Supremacy Clause for Indian Tribes." *Arizona State Law Journal* 34: 113.

Deloria, Philip J. 1998. *Playing Indian.* New Haven, CT: Yale University Press.

Deloria, Sam. 2002. "Commentary on Nation-Building: The Future of Indian Nations." *Arizona State Law Journal* 34: 55.

Deloria, Vine, Jr. 1989."Laws Founded in Justice and Humanity: Reflections on the Content and Character of Federal Indian Law." *Arizona Law Review* 31: 203.

Getches, David H., Charles F. Wilkinson, and Robert A. Williams, Jr. 1998. *Cases and Materials on Federal Indian Law.* 4th ed. St. Paul, MN: West.

Gibeaut, John. 1999. "Another Broken Trust." *American Bar Association Journal* 85 (September): 40.

Huhndorf, Shari M. 2001. *Going Native: Indians in the American Cultural Imagination.* Cornell: Cornell University Press.

LaVelle, John P. 2001. "Strengthening Tribal Sovereignty through Indian Participation in American Politics: A Reply to Professor Porter." *Kansas Journal of Law and Public Policy* 10: 533 (see Porter 1999).

Porter, Robert B. 1999. "The Demise of the *Ongwehoweh* and the Rise of the Native Americans: Redressing the Genocidal Act of Forcing American Citizenship upon Indigenous Peoples." *Harvard BlackLetter Law Journal* 15: 107 (see LaVelle 2001).

Prucha, Francis Paul. 1994. *American Indian Treaties: The History of a Political Anomaly.* Berkeley: University of California Press.

Shattuck, Petra T., and Jill Norgren. 1991. *Partial Justice: Federal Indian Law in a Liberal Constitutional System.* New York: Berg.

Silko, Leslie Marmon. 1977. *Ceremony.* New York: Viking.

———. 1981. *Storyteller.* New York: Seaver.

Wilkins, David E. 2000. "An Inquiry into Indigenous Political Participation: Implications for Tribal Sovereignty." *Kansas Journal of Law and Public Policy* 9: 732.

Wilkinson, Charles F. 1987. *American Indians, Time, and the Law: Native Societies in a Modern Constitutional Democracy.* New Haven, CT: Yale University Press.

———. 1997. "The Role of Bilateralism in Fulfilling the Federal-Tribal Relationship: The Tribal Rights–Endangered Species Secretarial Order." *Washington Law Review* 72: 1063.

Williams, Robert A., Jr. 1990. *The American Indian in Western Legal Thought: The Discourses of Conquest.* Oxford: Oxford University Press.

Wunder, John R. 2001. "'Merciless Indian Savages' and the Declaration of Independence: Native Americans Translate the *Ecunnaunuxulgee* Document." *American Indian Law Review* 25: 65.

Part Two

Documents

All documents have been edited for space and ease of reading. Omissions are indicated by ellipses, except that citations and footnotes are mostly omitted without indication. Added or modified language not in the original text is enclosed in brackets; any such modifications are consistent with the substance and tenor of the original text and are intended to aid clarity and comprehension. Footnotes present an unusual problem with court opinions. Many courts are in the bad habit of burying some of the most important and interesting substantive discussion in the footnotes, even though it is often worthy of inclusion in the main text. To avoid the clutter and distraction of footnotes in this book, any footnote text deemed worthy of inclusion is presented as regular text, in brackets, following the paragraph where the footnote call appears, or in some cases is simply inserted in the text (in brackets) at the point of the footnote call.

Following the date of each document is a citation to the best available primary source for the full original text and sometimes additional citations to alternative sources (see Annotated Bibliography and Table of Cases and Statutes for more information on all sources cited).

Laying the Foundation: Chief Justice Marshall and the Cherokee Cases

Treaty of Hopewell between the United States and the Cherokee Nation (1785)

November 28, 1785
7 Stat. 18; Kappler 1904, 8; Prucha 2000, 6

ARTICLES

Concluded at Hopewell, on the Keowee, between . . . [the] Commissioners Plenipotentiary of the United States of America . . . and the Head-Men and Warriors of all the Cherokees. . . .

The Commissioners Plenipotentiary of the United States, in Congress assembled, give peace to all the Cherokees, and receive them into the favour and protection of the United States of America, on the following conditions:

ARTICLE I

The Head-Men and Warriors of all the Cherokees shall restore all the prisoners, citizens of the United States, or subjects of their allies, to their entire liberty: They shall also restore all the Negroes, and all other property taken during the late war from the citizens, to such persons, and at such time and place, as the Commissioners shall appoint.

ARTICLE II

The Commissioners of the United States in Congress assembled, shall restore all the prisoners taken from the Indians, during the late war, to the Head-Men and Warriors of the Cherokees, as early as is practicable.

ARTICLE III

The said Indians for themselves and their respective tribes and towns do acknowledge all the Cherokees to be under the protection of the United States of America, and of no other sovereign whosoever.

ARTICLE IV

The boundary allotted to the Cherokees for their hunting grounds, between the said Indians and the citizens of the United States, within the limits of the United States of America, is, and shall be the following . . . [details omitted].

ARTICLE V

If any citizen of the United States, or other person not being an Indian, shall attempt to settle on any of the lands westward or southward of the said boundary which are hereby allotted to the Indians for their hunting grounds, or having already settled and will not remove from the same within six months after the ratification of this treaty, such person shall forfeit the protection of the United States, and the Indians may punish him or not as they please. . . .

ARTICLE VI

If any Indian or Indians, or person residing among them, or who shall take refuge in their nation, shall commit a robbery, or murder, or other capital crime, on any citizen of the United States, or person under their protection, the nation, or the tribe to which such offender or offenders may belong, shall be bound to deliver him or them up to be punished according to the ordinances of the United States; Provided, that the punishment shall not be greater than if the robbery or murder, or other capital crime had been committed by a citizen on a citizen.

ARTICLE VII

If any citizen of the United States, or person under their protection, shall commit a robbery or murder, or other capital crime, on any Indian, such offender or offenders shall be punished in the same manner as if the murder or robbery, or other capital crime, had been committed on a citizen of the United States; and the punishment shall be in presence of some of the Cherokees, if any shall attend at the time and place, and that they may have an opportunity so to do, due notice of the time of such intended punishment shall be sent to some one of the tribes.

ARTICLE VIII

It is understood that the punishment of the innocent under the idea of retaliation, is unjust, and shall not be practiced on either side, except where there is a manifest violation of this treaty; and then it shall be preceded first by a demand of justice, and if refused, then by a declaration of hostilities.

ARTICLE IX

For the benefit and comfort of the Indians, and for the prevention of injuries or oppressions on the part of the citizens or Indians, the United States in Congress assembled shall have the sole and exclusive right of regulating the trade with the Indians, and managing all their affairs in such manner as they think proper.

ARTICLE X

Until the pleasure of Congress be known, respecting the ninth article, all traders, citizens of the United States, shall have liberty to go to any of the tribes or towns of the Cherokees to trade with them, and they shall be protected in their persons and property, and kindly treated.

ARTICLE XI

The said Indians shall give notice to the citizens of the United States, of any designs which they may know or suspect to be formed in any neighboring tribe, or by any person whosoever, against the peace, trade or interest of the United States.

ARTICLE XII

That the Indians may have full confidence in the justice of the United States, respecting their interests, they shall have the right to send a deputy of their choice, whenever they think fit, to Congress.

ARTICLE XIII

The hatchet shall be forever buried, and the peace given by the United States, and friendship re-established between the said states on the one part, and all the Cherokees on the other, shall be universal; and the contracting parties shall use their utmost endeavours to maintain the peace given as aforesaid, and friendship re-established.

In witness of all and every thing herein determined, between the United States of America, and all the Cherokees, We, their underwritten Commissioners, by virtue of our full powers, have signed this definitive treaty, and have caused our seals to be hereunto affixed.

Done at Hopewell, on the Keowee, this twenty-eighth of November, in the year of our Lord one thousand seven hundred and eighty-five.

Cherokee Nation v. Georgia (1831)

U.S. Supreme Court
March 18, 1831
30 U.S. (5 Pet.) 1

Chief Justice John Marshall, appointed by President John Adams in 1801, wrote the lead opinion in Cherokee Nation, *the first of the two great Cherokee Cases. Although identified in the case reports as "the opinion of the Court," it was actually joined only by Justice John McLean, appointed by President Andrew Jackson in 1830, among the six associate justices then sitting with Marshall on the Court. But Marshall controlled the balance of power in the case and his opinion—endorsing limited sovereignty for the Cherokee but finding that the tribe could not directly invoke the Court's jurisdiction—fairly reflected the views of the Court's majority. Two justices—William Johnson, appointed by President Thomas Jefferson in 1804, and Henry Baldwin, appointed by President Jackson in 1830—agreed with Marshall and McLean that the Court lacked jurisdiction to hear the case, although they relied on much more extreme grounds, denigrating any sovereign status for the Cherokee. Two other justices—Smith Thompson, appointed by President James Monroe in 1823, and Joseph Story, appointed by President James Madison in 1812—disagreed with Mar-*

shall's conclusion that the Court lacked jurisdiction. But more importantly, Thompson (joined by Story) agreed with Marshall and McLean that the Cherokee enjoyed at least limited sovereign status; in fact, they went further and would have found the Cherokee legally equivalent to a foreign nation for purposes of invoking the Court's jurisdiction. Justice Gabriel Duvall, appointed by President Madison in 1811, did not participate.

Chief Justice Marshall (joined by Justice McLean):

This [lawsuit] is brought by the Cherokee nation, praying an injunction to restrain the state of Georgia from the execution of certain laws of that state, which, as is alleged, go directly to annihilate the Cherokees as a political society, and to seize, for the use of Georgia, the lands of the nation which have been assured to them by the United States in solemn treaties repeatedly made and still in force.

If courts were permitted to indulge their sympathies, a case better calculated to excite them can scarcely be imagined. A people once numerous, powerful, and truly independent, found by our ancestors in the quiet and uncontrolled possession of an ample domain, gradually sinking beneath our superior policy, our arts and our arms, have yielded their lands by successive treaties, each of which contains a solemn guarantee of the residue, until they retain no more of their formerly extensive territory than is deemed necessary to their comfortable subsistence. To preserve this remnant, the present application is made.

Before we can look into the merits of the case, a preliminary inquiry presents itself. Has this court jurisdiction of the cause? The third article of the Constitution describes the extent of the judicial power. The second section closes an enumeration of the cases to which it is extended, with "controversies" "between a state or the citizens thereof, and foreign states, citizens, or subjects." A subsequent clause of the same section gives the Supreme Court original jurisdiction in all cases in which a state shall be a party. The party defendant may then unquestionably be sued in this court. May the plaintiff sue in it? Is the Cherokee nation a foreign state in the sense in which that term is used in the Constitution?

The counsel for the plaintiffs have maintained the affirmative of this proposition with great earnestness and ability. So much of the argument as was intended to prove the character of the Cherokees as a state, as a distinct political society, . . . has . . . been completely successful. . . .

A question of much more difficulty remains. Do the Cherokees constitute a foreign state in the sense of the Constitution? The counsel have shown conclusively that they are not a state of the union, and have insisted that individually they are aliens, not owing allegiance to the United States. An aggregate of aliens composing a state must, they say, be a foreign state. Each individual being foreign, the whole must be foreign.

This argument is imposing, but we must examine it more closely before we yield to it. The condition of the Indians in relation to the United States is perhaps unlike that of any other two people in existence. . . .

The Indian territory is admitted to compose a part of the United States. In all our maps, geographical treatises, histories, and laws, it is so considered. In all our intercourse with foreign nations, . . . they are considered as within . . . the United States. . . . They acknowledge themselves in their treaties to be under the protection of the United States. . . .

Though the Indians are acknowledged to have [a] . . . right to the lands they occupy, until that right shall be extinguished by a voluntary cession to our government; yet it may well be doubted whether those tribes which reside within the acknowledged boundaries of the United States can, with strict accuracy, be denominated foreign nations. They may, more correctly, perhaps, be denominated domestic dependent nations. They occupy a territory to which we assert a title independent of their will, which must take effect in point of possession when their right of possession ceases. Meanwhile they are in a state of pupilage. Their relation to the United States resembles that of a ward to his guardian.

They look to our government for protection; rely upon its kindness and its power; appeal to it for relief to their wants; and address the president as their great father. They and their country are considered by foreign nations, as well as by ourselves, as being so completely under the sovereignty and dominion of the United States, that any attempt to acquire their lands, or to form a political connexion with them, would be considered by all as an invasion of our territory, and an act of hostility.

These considerations go far to support the opinion, that the framers of our Constitution had not the Indian tribes in view, when they opened the courts of the union to controversies between a state or the citizens thereof, and foreign states.

In considering this subject, the habits and usages of the Indians, in their intercourse with their white neighbours, ought not to be entirely disregarded. At the time the Constitution was framed, the idea of appealing to an American court of justice for an assertion of right or a redress of wrong, had perhaps never entered the mind of an Indian or of his tribe. Their appeal was to the tomahawk, or to the government.... [C]onsiderable aid is [also] furnished by that clause [U.S. Const., art. I, § 8]... which empowers Congress to "regulate commerce with foreign nations, and among the several states, and with the Indian tribes."

In this clause they are as clearly contradistinguished by a name appropriate to themselves, from foreign nations, as from the several states composing the union.... We cannot assume that the distinction was lost in framing a subsequent article....

A serious additional objection exists to the jurisdiction of the Court. Is the matter of the [lawsuit] the proper subject for judicial inquiry and decision? It seeks to restrain a state from the forcible exercise of legislative power over a neighbouring people, asserting their independence; their right to which the state denies.... The propriety of such an interposition by the Court may be well questioned. It savours too much of the exercise of political power to be within the proper province of the judicial department. But the opinion on the point respecting parties makes it unnecessary to decide this question.

If it be true that the Cherokee nation have rights, this is not the tribunal in which those rights are to be asserted. If it be true that wrongs have been inflicted, and that still greater are to be apprehended, this is not the tribunal which can redress the past or prevent the future. The motion for an injunction is denied.

Justice Johnson:

... [T]here are strong reasons for doubting the applicability of the epithet state, to a people so low in the grade of organized society as our Indian tribes most generally are. I would not here be understood as speaking of the Cherokees under their present form of government; which certainly must be classed among the most approved forms of civil government. Whether it can be yet said to have received the consistency which entitles that people to admission into the family of nations is, I conceive, yet to be determined by the [president]. Until then I must think that we cannot recognize it as an existing state....

In the very treaty of Hopewell,... which is appealed to as the leading proof of the existence of this supposed state, we find... the language of sovereigns and conquerors, and not the address of equals to equals. . . . It is clear that it was intended to give them no other rights over the territory than what were needed by a race of hunters; and it is not easy to see how their advancement beyond that state of society could ever have been promoted, or, perhaps, permitted, consistently with the unquestioned rights of the states, or United States, over the territory within their limits. . . .

But it is said, that we have extended to [the Indians] the means and inducement to become agricultural and civilized. It is true. . . . [T]hese people were restless, warlike, and signally cruel in their irruptions during the Revolution. The policy, therefore, of enticing them to the arts of peace, and to those improvements which war might lay desolate, was obvious; and it was wise to prepare them for what was probably then contemplated, . . . to incorporate them in time into our respective governments: a policy which their inveterate habits and deep-seated enmity has altogether baffled. But the project of ultimately organizing them into states . . . could not possibly have entered into the contemplation of our government. . . .

Where is the rule to stop? Must every petty kraal of Indians, designating themselves a tribe or nation, and having a few hundred acres of land to hunt on exclusively, be recognized as a state? . . .

. . . I believe, in one view and in one only, if at all, [the Cherokees] are or may be deemed a state, though not a sovereign state. . . . Their condition is something like that of the Israelites, when inhabiting the deserts. Though without land that they can call theirs in the sense of property, their right of personal self-government has never been taken from them. . . . [No] attempt [has been] made at subjugating them as a people, or restraining their personal liberty, except as to their land and trade. . . .

. . . I think it very clear that the Constitution neither speaks of them as states [n]or foreign states, but as just what they were, Indian tribes; an anomaly unknown to the books that treat of states, and which the law of nations would regard as nothing more than wandering hordes, held together only by ties of blood and habit, and having neither laws [n]or government, beyond what is required in a savage state. . . .

Justice Baldwin:

. . . I concur in the opinion of the Court in dismissing the [lawsuit], but not for the reasons assigned [by Chief Justice Marshall]. In my opinion there is no plaintiff in this suit; and this opinion precludes any examination into the merits. . . .

. . . The word "nation" is not used in the preamble or any part of the treaty [of Hopewell], so that we are left to infer the capacity in which the Cherokees contracted, whether as an independent nation or foreign state or a tribe of Indians. . . .

This treaty is in the beginning called "Article": the word "treaty" is only to be found in the concluding line, where it is called "this definitive treaty." But article or treaty, its nature does not depend on the name given it. It is not negotiated between ministers on both sides representing their nations; the stipulations are wholly inconsistent with sovereignty; the Indians acknowledge their dependent character; hold the lands they occupy as an allotment of hunting grounds; give to Congress the exclusive right of regulating their trade and managing all their affairs as they may think proper. . . .

. . . [Georgia's] jurisdiction over the territory in question is . . . supreme. . . . Within her boundaries there can be no other nation, community, or sovereign power. . . . Foreign states cannot be created by judicial construction; Indian sovereignty cannot be roused from its long slumber, and awakened to action by our fiat. . . .

Justice Thompson (joined by Justice Story):

. . . [H]aving arrived at a conclusion different from that of a majority of the Court, and considering the importance of the case and the constitutional principle involved in it, I shall proceed, with all due respect for the opinion of others, to assign the reasons upon which my own has been formed. . . .

It would very ill become the judicial station which I hold, to indulge in any remarks upon the hardship of the case, or the great injustice that would seem to have been done to the complainants. . . . If they are entitled to other than judicial relief, . . . the responsibility for its denial must rest upon those who have the power to grant it. . . .

. . . [T]he first inquiry is, whether the Cherokee nation is a foreign state within the sense and meaning of the Constitution. . . . Every nation that governs itself . . . is a sovereign state. . . .

We ought . . . to reckon . . . [as] sovereigns those states that have bound themselves to another more powerful, although by an unequal alliance. The conditions of these unequal alliances may be infinitely varied; but . . . provided the inferior ally reserves to itself the sovereignty or the right to govern its own body, it ought to be considered an independent state. . . . Tributary and feudatory states do not thereby cease to be sovereign and independent states, so long as self-government, and sovereign and independent authority is left in the administration of the state.

Testing the character and condition of the Cherokee Indians by these rules, . . . they form a sovereign state. They have always been dealt with as such by the government of the United States; both before and since the adoption of the present Constitution. . . .

. . . The progress made in civilization by the Cherokee Indians cannot surely be considered as in any measure destroying their national or foreign character, so long as they are permitted to maintain a separate and distinct government. . . .

And what possible objection can lie to the right of the complainants to sustain [this] action? The treaties made with [the Cherokee] nation purport to secure to it certain rights. These are not gratuitous obligations assumed on the part of the United States. They are obligations founded upon a consideration paid by the Indians by cession of part of their territory. And if they, as a nation, are competent to make a treaty or contract, it would seem to me to be a strange inconsistency to deny to them the right and the power to enforce such a contract. . . .

The next inquiry is, whether . . . this Court [is warranted] in granting any relief. . . . The injuries complained of are violations committed and threatened upon the property of the complainants, secured to them by the laws and treaties of the United States. Under the Constitution, the judicial power of the United States extends expressly to all cases in law and equity, arising under the laws of the United States, and treaties made or which shall be made, under the authority of the same. . . .

That the Cherokee nation of Indians have, by virtue of these treaties, an exclusive right of occupancy of the lands in question, and that the United States are bound . . . to protect . . . the enjoyment of such occupancy, cannot, in my judgment, admit of a doubt: and that some of the laws of Georgia . . . are in violation of, and in conflict with those treaties . . . , is to my mind equally clear. . . .

Worcester v. Georgia (1832)

U.S. Supreme Court
March 3, 1832
31 U.S. (6 Pet.) 515

In Worcester, *the second and more important of the two Cherokee Cases, Chief Justice Marshall wrote the opinion of the Court (the membership of which had not changed) for a majority composed of himself and Justices Duvall, Story, and Thompson. This time, the Court found that it had jurisdiction, and it strongly reaffirmed Cherokee tribal sovereignty. Justice McLean wrote a concurring opinion, endorsing a more limited and temporary vision of tribal sovereignty. Justice Baldwin dissented in a brief statement referring to his opinion in* Cherokee Nation. *Justice Johnson did not participate.*

Chief Justice Marshall (for the Court):

This cause, in every point of view in which it can be placed, is of the deepest interest. The defendant is a state . . . which has exercised the powers of government over a people who deny its jurisdiction, and are under the protection of the United States. The plaintiff is a citizen of the state of Vermont, condemned to hard labour for four years in the penitentiary of Georgia, under colour of an act which he alleges to be repugnant to the Constitution, laws, and treaties of the United States. The legislative power of a state, the controlling power of the Constitution and laws of the United States, the rights, if they have any, the political existence of a once numerous and powerful people, the personal liberty of a citizen, are all involved in the subject now to be considered. . . .

The indictment charges . . . [Samuel A. Worcester] and others, being white persons, with the offence of "residing within the limits of the Cherokee nation without a license," and "without having taken the oath to support and defend the constitution and laws of the state of Georgia."

[Worcester] . . . filed the following plea [in the Georgia state court]:

" . . . [T]hat . . . he . . . is, a resident in the Cherokee nation; and that the said supposed crime or crimes, . . . were committed, if committed at all, at the town of New Echota, in the said Cherokee nation . . .

" . . . that he . . . entered the aforesaid Cherokee nation in the capacity of a duly authorised missionary . . . [and] that he was, at the time of his arrest, engaged in preaching the gospel to the Cherokee Indians, and in translating the sacred scriptures into their language, with the permission and approval of the said Cherokee nation, and in accordance with the humane policy of the government of the United States for the civilization and improvement of the Indians . . .

" . . . that . . . several treaties have . . . been entered into between the United States and the Cherokee nation of Indians . . . which . . . acknowledge the said Cherokee nation to be a sovereign nation, authorised to govern themselves, and all persons who have settled within their territory. . . .

"[T]herefore, [the state] court has no jurisdiction to . . . try and punish this defendant for the said supposed offence or offences alleged. . . ."

This plea was overruled by the [Georgia state] court. And the prisoner, being arraigned, plead[ed] not guilty. The jury found a verdict against him, and the court sentenced him to hard labour, in the penitentiary, for the term of four years. . . .

It is . . . too clear for controversy, that . . . this Court . . . [has] jurisdiction in this case. This duty, however unpleasant, cannot be avoided. . . . We must inquire and decide whether the act of the legislature of Georgia, under which [Worcester] has been prosecuted and condemned, be consistent with, or repugnant to, the Constitution, laws and treaties of the United States.

. . . [T]he acts of the legislature of Georgia seize on the whole Cherokee country, parcel it out among the neighbouring counties of the state, extend her code over the whole country, abolish its institutions and its laws, and annihilate its political existence. . . .

America, separated from Europe by a wide ocean, was inhabited by a distinct people, divided into separate nations, independent of each other and of the rest of the world, having institutions of their own, and governing themselves by their own laws. It is difficult to comprehend the proposition, that the inhabitants of either quarter of the globe could have rightful original claims of dominion over the inhabitants of the other, or over the lands they occupied; or that the discovery of either by the other should give the discoverer rights in the country discovered, which annulled the pre-existing rights of its ancient possessors.

After lying concealed for a series of ages, the enterprise of Europe, guided by nautical science, conducted some of her adventurous sons into this western world. They found it in possession of a people who had made small progress in agriculture or manufactures, and whose general employment was war, hunting, and fishing.

Did these adventurers, by sailing along the coast, and occasionally landing on it, acquire for the several governments to whom they belonged, or by whom they were commissioned, a rightful property in the soil, from the Atlantic to the Pacific; or rightful dominion over the numerous people who occupied it? Or has nature, or the great Creator of all things, conferred these rights over hunters and fishermen, on agriculturists and manufacturers?

But power, war, conquest, give rights, which, after possession, are conceded by the world; and which can never be controverted by those on whom they descend. We proceed, then, to the actual state of things, having glanced at their origin; because holding it in our recollection might shed some light on existing pretensions. . . .

. . . [O]ur history furnishes no example . . . of any attempt on the part of the [British] crown to interfere with the internal affairs of the Indians, farther than to keep out the agents of foreign powers. . . .

This was the settled state of things when the . . . [American] revolution commenced. The influence of . . . [the British] was established; her resources enabled her to keep up that influence; and the colonists had much cause for the apprehension that the Indian nations would, as the allies of Great Britain, add their arms to hers. . . . Far from advancing a claim to their lands, or asserting any right of dominion over them, Congress resolved "that the securing and preserving the friendship of the Indian nations appears to be a subject of the utmost moment to these colonies."

The early journals of Congress exhibit the most anxious desire to conciliate the Indian nations. . . . The most strenuous exertions were made to procure those supplies on which Indian friendships were supposed to depend; and everything which might excite hostility was avoided.

The first treaty was made with the Delawares, in September 1778. The language of equality in which it is drawn, evinces the temper with which the negotiation was undertaken, and the opinion which then prevailed in the United States. . . . The sixth article is entitled to peculiar attention, as it contains a disclaimer of designs which were, at that time, ascribed to the United States, by their enemies, and from the imputation of which Congress was then peculiarly anxious to free the government. It is in these words: "Whereas the enemies of the United States have endeavoured, by every artifice in their power, to possess the Indians in general with an opinion that it is the design of the states aforesaid to extirpate the Indians, and take possession of their country: to obviate such false suggestion the United States do engage to guaranty to the aforesaid nation of Delawares, and their heirs, all their territorial rights, . . . as long as the said Delaware nation shall abide by, and hold fast the chain of friendship now entered into. . . ." . . .

During the war of the revolution, the Cherokees took part with the British. After its termination, the United States, though desirous of peace, did not feel its necessity so strongly as while the war continued. Their political situation being changed, they might very well think it advisable to assume a higher tone, and to impress on the Cherokees the same respect for Congress which was before felt for the King of Great Britain. This may account for the language of the treaty of Hopewell. There is the more reason for supposing that the Cherokee chiefs were not very critical judges of the language, from the fact that every one makes his mark; no chief was capable of signing his name. It is probable the treaty was interpreted to them.

The treaty is introduced with the declaration, that "the commissioners plenipotentiary of the United States give peace to all the Cherokees. . . ." When the United States gave peace, did they not also receive it? Were not both parties desirous of it? If we consult the history of the day, does it not inform us that the United States were at least as anxious to obtain it as the Cherokees? We may ask, further: Did the Cherokees come to the seat of the American government to solicit peace; or, did the American commissioners go to them to obtain it? The treaty was made at Hopewell, not at New York. The word "give," then, has no real importance attached to it.

The first and second articles stipulate for the mutual restoration of prisoners, and are of course equal. The third article acknowledges the Cherokees to be under the protection of the United States . . . and of no other power. This stipulation is found in Indian treaties, generally. It was introduced into their treaties with Great Britain. . . . It merely bound the nation to the British crown, as a dependent ally, claiming the protection of a powerful friend and neighbour, and receiving the advantages of that protection, without involving a surrender of their national character. . . . The same stipulation entered into with the United States, is undoubtedly to be construed in the same manner. . . . Protection does not imply the destruction of the protected. . . .

The fourth article draws the boundary between the Indians and the citizens of the United States. But, in describing this boundary, the term "allotted" and the term "hunting ground" are used. Is it reasonable to suppose, that the Indians, who could not write, and most probably could not read, who certainly were not critical judges of our language, should distinguish the word "allotted" from the words "marked out"? . . .

So with respect to the words "hunting grounds." Hunting was at that time the principal occupation of the Indians, and their land was more used for that purpose than for any other. It could not, however, be supposed, that any intention existed of restricting the full use of the lands they reserved. To the United States, it could be a matter of no concern, whether their whole territory was devoted to hunting grounds, or whether an occasional village, and . . . corn field, interrupted, and gave some variety to the scene. . . .

The fifth article withdraws the protection of the United States from any citizen who has settled, or shall settle, on the lands allotted to the Indians, for their hunting grounds; and stipulates that, if he shall not remove within six months the Indians may punish him. The sixth and seventh articles stipulate for the punishment of the citizens of either country, who may commit offences on or against the citizens of the other. The only inference to be drawn from them is, that the United States considered the Cherokees as a nation.

The ninth article is in these words: "for the benefit and comfort of the Indians, and for the prevention of injuries or oppressions on the part of the citizens or Indians, the United States, in Congress assembled, shall have the sole and exclusive right of regulating the trade with the Indians, and managing all their affairs, as they think proper." To construe the expression "managing all their affairs," into a surrender of self-government, would be, we think, a perversion of their necessary meaning, and a departure from the construction which has been uniformly put on them. The great subject of the article is the Indian trade. The influence it gave, made it desirable that Congress should possess it. The commissioners brought forward the claim, with the profession that their motive was "the benefit and comfort of the Indians, and the prevention of injuries or oppressions." This may be true, as respects the regulation of their trade, . . . but cannot be true, as respects the management of all their affairs. . . .

Is it credible, that they should have considered themselves as surrendering to the United States the right to dictate their future cessions, and the terms on which they should be made? Or to compel their submission to the violence of disorderly and licentious intruders? It is equally inconceivable that they could have supposed themselves, by a phrase thus slipped into an article, on another . . . subject, to have divested themselves of the right of self-government on subjects not connected with trade. Such a measure could not be "for their benefit and comfort," or for "the prevention of injuries and oppression." Such a construction would be inconsistent with the spirit of this and of all subsequent treaties; especially of those articles which recognise the right of the Cherokees to declare hostilities, and to make war. It would convert a treaty of peace covertly into an act annihilating the political existence of one of the parties. . . .

The treaty of Hopewell seems not to have established a solid peace. To accommodate the differences still existing between the state of Georgia and the Cherokee nation, the treaty of Holston was negotiated in July 1791. The existing Constitution of the United States had been then adopted, and the government, having more intrinsic capacity to enforce its just claims, was perhaps less mindful of . . . expressions denoting superiority. We hear no more of giving peace to the Cherokees. The mutual desire of establishing permanent peace and friendship, and of removing all causes of war, is honestly avowed, and, in pursuance of this desire, the first article declares, that there shall be perpetual peace and friendship between all the citizens of the United States of America and all the individuals composing the Cherokee nation.

The second article repeats the important acknowledgement, that the Cherokee nation is under the protection of the United States. . . . The meaning of this has been already explained. . . . The third article contains a perfectly equal stipulation for the surrender of prisoners. The fourth article declares, that "the boundary between the United States and the Cherokee nation shall be as follows. . . ." We hear no more of "allotments" or of "hunting grounds." A boundary is described, between nation and nation, by mutual consent. The national character of each, the ability of each to establish this boundary, is acknowledged by the other. . . .

By the sixth article, it is agreed, on the part of the Cherokees, that the United States shall have the sole and exclusive right of regulating their trade. No claim is made to the management of all their affairs. This stipulation has already been explained. . . .

By the seventh article the United States solemnly guaranty to the Cherokee nation all their lands not hereby ceded. The eighth article relinquishes to the Cherokees any citizens of the United States who may settle on their lands; and the ninth forbids any citizen of the United States to hunt on their lands, or to enter their country without a passport. The remaining articles are equal, and contain stipulations which could be made only with a nation admitted to be capable of governing itself.

This treaty, thus explicitly recognizing the national character of the Cherokees, and their right of self government; thus guarantying their lands; assuming the duty of protection, and of course pledging the faith of the United States for that protection; has been frequently renewed, and is now in full force. . . .

From the commencement of our government, Congress has passed acts to regulate trade and intercourse with the Indians; which treat them as nations, respect their rights, and manifest a firm purpose to afford that protection which treaties stipulate. All these acts . . . manifestly consider the several Indian nations as distinct political communities, having territorial boundaries, within which their authority is exclusive, and having a right to all the lands within those boundaries, which is not only acknowledged, but guarantied [sic] by the United States.

In 1819, Congress passed an act for promoting . . . humane designs of civilizing the neighbouring Indians. . . . This act avowedly contemplates the preservation of the Indian nations as an object sought by the United States, and proposes to effect this object by civilizing and converting them from hunters into agriculturists. Though the Cherokees had already made considerable progress in this improvement, it cannot be doubted that the general words of the act comprehend them. . . . This act furnishes strong additional evidence of a settled purpose to fix the Indians in their country by giving them security at home.

The treaties and laws of the United States contemplate the Indian territory as completely separated from that of the states; and provide that all intercourse with them shall be carried on exclusively by the government of the union. . . .

. . . [O]ur . . . Constitution . . . confers on Congress the powers of war and peace; of making treaties, and of regulating commerce with foreign nations, and among the several states, and with the Indian tribes. These powers comprehend all that is required for the regulation of our intercourse with the Indians. They are not limited by any restrictions on their free actions. . . .

. . . The Constitution, by declaring treaties already made, as well as those to be made, to be the supreme law of the land, has adopted and sanctioned the previous treaties with the Indian nations, and consequently admits their rank among those powers who are capable of making treaties. The words "treaty" and "nation" are words of our own language, selected in our diplomatic and legislative proceedings, by ourselves, having each a definite and well understood meaning. We have applied them to Indians, as we have applied them to the other nations of the earth. They are applied to all in the same sense. . . .

. . . [Georgia's claims] can derive no aid from the articles so often repeated in Indian treaties, extending to them . . . the protection . . . of the United States. These articles are associated with others, recognizing their title to self-government. The very fact of repeated treaties with them recognizes it; and the settled doctrine of the law of nations is, that a weaker power does not surrender its independence, its right to self-government, by associating with a stronger, and taking its protection. A weak state, in order to provide for its safety, may place itself under the protection of one more powerful, without stripping itself of the right of government, and ceasing to be a state. Examples of this kind are not wanting in Europe. "Tributary and feudatory states," says Vattel [a widely cited scholar and expert on the law of nations], "do not thereby cease to be sovereign and independent states, so long as self-government and sovereign and independent authority are left in the administration of the state." . . .

The Cherokee nation, then, is a distinct community occupying its own territory, . . . in which the laws of Georgia can have no force, and which the citizens of Georgia have no right to enter, but with the assent of the Cherokees themselves, or in conformity with treaties, and with the acts of Congress. . . . The act of the state of Georgia, under which [Worcester] was prosecuted, is consequently void, and the judgment a nullity. . . .

. . . [T]he acts of Georgia are repugnant to the Constitution, laws, and treaties of the United States. They interfere forcibly with the relations established between the United States and the Cherokee nation, the regulation of which, according to the settled principles of our Constitution, are committed exclusively to the government of the union. . . .

. . . [Worcester] was apprehended, tried, and condemned, under colour of a law which has been shown to be repugnant to the Constitution, laws, and treaties of the United States. Had a judgment, liable to the same objections, been rendered for property, none would question the jurisdiction of this Court. It cannot be less clear when the judgment affects personal liberty, and inflicts disgraceful punishment, if punishment could disgrace when inflicted on innocence. . . .

It is the opinion of this Court that the judgment of the superior court for the county of Gwinnett, in the state of Georgia, condemning . . . Worcester to hard labour, in the penitentiary of the state of Georgia, for four years, was pronounced by that court under colour of a law which is void, as being repugnant to the Constitution, treaties, and laws of the United States, and ought, therefore, to be reversed and annulled.

Justice Baldwin dissented, stating that . . . his opinion remained the same as was expressed by him in the case of *Cherokee Nation v. Georgia,* at the last term. . . .

Justice McLean (concurring in the judgment):

. . . With the decision just given, I concur. . . . It is apparent that [Georgia's] laws are repugnant to the treaties with the Cherokee Indians. . . .

The language used in treaties with the Indians should never be construed to their prejudice. If words be made use of which are susceptible of a more extended meaning than their plain import, as connected with the tenor of the treaty, they should be considered as used only in the latter sense. To contend that the word "allotted," in reference to the land guarantied to the Indians in certain treaties, indicates a favour conferred, rather than a right acknowledged, would, it would seem to me, do injustice to the understanding of the parties. How the words of the treaty were understood by this unlettered people, rather than their critical meaning, should form the rule of construction. . . .

The stipulation made in [the 1802 compact] of cession [with Georgia], that the United States should extinguish the Indian title to lands within the state, was a distinct recognition of the right in the federal government, to make the extinguishment; and also, that, until it should be made, the right of occupancy would remain in the Indians. . . .

Under the act of cession, the United States were bound, in good faith, to extinguish the Indian title to lands within the limits of Georgia, so soon as it could be done peaceably and on reasonable terms. . . .

The exercise of . . . independent power [by Indians] surely does not become more objectionable, as it assumes the basis of justice and the forms of civilization. Would it not be a singular argument to admit, that, so long as the Indians govern by the rifle and the tomahawk, their government may be tolerated; but, that it must be suppressed, so soon as it shall be administered upon the enlightened principles of reason and justice? Are not those nations of Indians who have made some advances in civilization, better neighbours than those who are still in a savage state? . . .

The exercise of the power of self-government by the Indians, within a state, is undoubtedly contemplated to be temporary. . . . [A] sound national policy does require that the Indian tribes within our states should exchange their territories, upon equitable principles, or, eventually, consent to become amalgamated in our political communities. . . .

It has been shown, that the treaties and laws referred to . . . throw a shield over the Cherokee Indians. They guarantied [sic] to them their rights of occupancy, of self-government, and the full enjoyment of those blessings which might be attained in their humble condition. But, by the enactments of the state of Georgia, this shield is broken in pieces—the infant institutions of the Cherokees are abolished, and their laws annulled. Infamous punishment is denounced against them, for the exercise of those rights which have been most solemnly guarantied to them by the national faith. . . .

Of the justice or policy of [Georgia's] laws, it is not my province to speak: such considerations belonging to the legislature by whom they were passed. They have, no doubt, been enacted under a conviction of right, by a sovereign and independent state, and their policy may have been recommended, by a sense of wrong. . . . Thirty years have elapsed since the federal government engaged to extinguish the Indian title, within the limits of Georgia. That [Georgia] has strong ground of complaint arising from this delay, must be admitted; but such considerations are not involved in the present case; they belong to another branch of the government. . . .

Indian Treaty Rights

Lone Wolf v. Hitchcock (1903)

U.S. Supreme Court
January 5, 1903
187 U.S. 553

The Court's opinion was written by Justice Edward D. White, appointed by President Grover Cleveland in 1894 (later appointed chief justice by President William Howard Taft in 1910). The decision was unanimous. Joining fully in White's opinion were Chief Justice Melville W. Fuller, appointed by President Cleveland in 1888; Justices David J. Brewer, Henry B. Brown, and George Shiras, appointed by

President Benjamin Harrison in 1890, 1891, and 1892; Justice Rufus W. Peckham, appointed by President Cleveland in 1896; Justice Joseph McKenna, appointed by President William McKinley in 1898; and Justice Oliver Wendell Holmes, Jr., appointed by President Theodore Roosevelt in 1902. Justice John Marshall Harlan (the elder), appointed by President Rutherford B. Hayes in 1877, declined to join White's opinion, concurring only in the result without further elaboration.

Justice White (for the Court):

In 1867 [the Kiowa-Comanche-U.S. Treaty of Medicine Lodge Creek] was concluded[,] . . . setting apart a reservation for the use of such Indians. By a separate treaty the Apache tribe of Indians was incorporated with the two former-named, and became entitled to share in the benefits of the reservation.

The . . . [Medicine Lodge] treaty . . . [provided in part] as follows: "Article 12. No treaty for the cession of any portion or part of the reservation herein described, which may be held in common, shall be of any validity or force as against the said Indians, unless executed and signed by at least three fourths of all the adult male Indians occupying the same. . . ."

The three tribes settled under the treaties upon the described land. On October 6, 1892, 456 male adult members of the confederated tribes signed, with three commissioners representing the United States, an agreement concerning the reservation. The Indian agent . . . represented that there were then 562 male adults in the three tribes. . . . [The signers] therefore constituted more than three fourths of the certified number of total male adults. . . . [T]he agreement . . . provided for a surrender to the United States of the rights of the tribes in the reservation, for allotments out of such lands to the Indians[,] . . . and the payment or setting apart for the benefit of the tribes of two million dollars as the consideration for the surplus of land over and above the allotments which might be made to the Indians. . . .

Soon after the signing of the foregoing agreement it was claimed by the Indians that their assent had been obtained by fraudulent misrepresentations of its terms by the interpreters, and . . . that the agreement should not be held binding upon the tribes because three fourths of the adult male members had not assented thereto. . . .

. . . [V]arious bills were introduced in both Houses of Congress designed to give legal effect to the [1892] agreement. . . . [T]he Indians presented their objections. . . . In 1898 the Committee on Indian Affairs of the House of Representatives unanimously reported a bill for the execution of the [1892] agreement. . . .

The bill . . . did not exactly conform to the agreement as signed by the Indians. It . . . chang[ed] the time for making the allotments, and it also provided that the proceeds of the surplus lands remaining after allotments to the Indians should be held to await the judicial decision of a claim asserted by the Choctaw and Chickasaw tribes of Indians to the surplus lands. . . .

The bill . . . passed the House of Representatives on May 16, 1898. When [it] reached the Senate that body, on January 25, 1899, adopted a resolution calling upon the Secretary of the Interior for information as to whether the signatures attached to the agreement comprised three fourths of the male adults of the tribes. In response the Secretary . . . informed the Senate . . . that the records of the department "failed to show a census of these Indians for the year 1892," but that "from a roll used in making a payment to them in January and February, 1893, it appeared that there were 725 males over eighteen years of age, of whom 639 were twenty-one years and over." The Secretary further called attention to the fact that by the agreement of 1892 a right of selection was conferred upon each member of the tribes over eighteen years of age, and observed: "If 18 years and over be held to be the legal age of those who were authorized to sign the agreement, the number of persons who actually signed was 87 less than three fourths of the adult male membership of the tribes; and if 21 years be held to be the minimum age, then 23 less than three fourths signed the agreement. In either event, less than three fourths of the male adults appear to have so signed." With this information before it the bill was favorably reported by the Committee on Indian Affairs of the Senate, but did not pass [the Senate].

At the first session of the following Congress . . . [substantially similar] bills were introduced in both the Senate and House. . . . In the meanwhile, about October, 1899, the Indians had, at a general council at which 571 male adults of the tribes purported to be present, protested against the execution . . . of the [1892] agreement . . . and adopted a memorial . . . praying that [Congress] should not give [it] effect. . . .

On January 19, 1900, an [unrelated] act was passed by the Senate, entitled "An act to ratify an agreement made with the Indians of the Fort Hall Indian reservation in Idaho, and making an appropriation to carry the same into effect." In February, 1900, the House Committee on Indian Affairs, having before it the memorial of the Indians[,] . . . reported [the unrelated Senate] bill back to the House favorably, with certain amendments[,] [o]ne of [which] . . . add[ed] . . . a provision to execute the [1892] agreement. . . . [But] the title of the bill was not changed, . . . referr[ing] only to . . . the Fort Hall reservation. . . . The bill became a law [on June 6, 1900]. . . .

On June 6, 1901, a [lawsuit] was filed . . . charg[ing] . . . that the [1892] agreement had not been signed as required by the Medicine Lodge treaty, that is, by three fourths of the male adult members of the tribe, and that the signatures thereto had been obtained by fraudulent misrepresentations and concealment. . . . [T]he charge was [also] made that the interpreters falsely represented, when the said [1892 agreement] was being considered by the Indians, that the [agreement] provided "for the sale of their surplus lands at some time in the future at the price of $2.50 per acre"; whereas, in truth and in fact, "by the terms of said [agreement], only $1.00 an acre is allowed for said surplus lands," which sum, it was charged, was an amount far below the real value of said lands. It was also averred that portions of the signed agreement had been changed by Congress without submitting such changes to the Indians for their consideration.

Based upon the foregoing allegations, it was alleged that . . . [the 1892 agreement and the 1900 Act of Congress,] opening to settlement by white men of two million acres . . . , were enacted in violation of the property rights of the . . . Kiowa, Comanche and Apache Indians, and if carried into effect would deprive [the] Indians of their lands without due process of law, . . . contrary to the Constitution of the United States. . . . [The trial court refused to grant a preliminary injunction, and the Indians appealed.]

. . . While this appeal was pending, the President issued a proclamation, dated July 4, 1901, in which it was ordered that the surplus lands ceded by the Comanche, Kiowa and Apache and other tribes of Indians should be opened to entry and settlement on August 6, 1901. Among other things, it was recited . . . that all the conditions required by law to be performed prior to the opening of the lands to settlement and entry had been performed. . . .

The appellants base their right to relief on the proposition that by the effect of the [Medicine Lodge treaty] the . . . Kiowas, Comanches and Apaches were vested with an interest in the lands held in common within the reservation, which interest could not be divested by Congress in any other mode than that specified in . . . [the treaty], and that . . . the interest of the Indians in the common lands fell within the protection of the Fifth Amendment to the Constitution of the United States, and such interest—indirectly at least—came under the control of the judicial branch of the government. We are unable to yield our assent to this view.

The contention in effect ignores the status of the contracting Indians and the relation of dependency they bore and continue to bear towards the government of the United States. To uphold the claim would be to adjudge that the indirect operation of the treaty was to materially limit and qualify the controlling authority of Congress in respect to the care and protection of the Indians, and to deprive Congress, in a possible emergency, when the necessity might be urgent for a partition and disposal of the tribal lands, of the power to act, if the assent of the Indians could not be obtained.

Now, it is true that in decisions of this court, the Indian right of occupancy of tribal lands, whether declared in a treaty or otherwise created, has been stated to be sacred, or as sometimes expressed, as sacred as the fee [i.e., the ownership interest] of the United States in the same lands. [*Johnson v. M'Intosh* 1823; *Cherokee Nation v. Georgia* 1831, 48; *Worcester v. Georgia* 1832, 581]. But in none of these cases was there involved a controversy between Indians and the government respecting the power of Congress to administer the property of the Indians. . . . [T]he cases referred to . . . had relation to . . . the character and extent of [Indian property] rights as respected States or individuals. . . . Congress possesse[s] a paramount power over the property of the Indians, by reason of its exercise of guardianship over their interests, and . . . such authority might be implied, even though opposed to the strict letter of a treaty with the Indians. . . .

Plenary authority over the tribal relations of the Indians has been exercised by Congress from the beginning, and the power has always been deemed a political one, not . . . controlled by the judicial department. . . . Until the year 1871 the policy was pursued of dealing with the Indian tribes by means of treaties, and, of course, a moral obligation rested upon Congress to act in good faith in performing the stipulations entered into on its behalf. But, as with treaties made with foreign nations, the legislative power might pass laws in conflict with treaties made with the Indians.

The power exists to abrogate the provisions of an Indian treaty, though presumably such power will be exercised only when circumstances arise which will not only justify the government in disregarding the stipulations of the treaty, but may demand, in the interest of the country and the Indians themselves, that it should do so. . . .

In upholding the validity of an act of Congress which conferred jurisdiction upon the courts of the United States for certain crimes committed on an Indian reservation within a State, the Court said [in *United States v. Kagama* 1886, 382]:

" . . . These Indian tribes are the wards of the nation. They are communities dependent on the United States. Dependent largely for their daily food. Dependent for their political rights. They owe no allegiance to the States, and receive from them no protection. Because of the local ill feeling, the people of the States where they are found are often their deadliest enemies. From their very weakness and helplessness, so largely due to the course of dealing of the federal government with them and the treaties in which it has been promised, there arises the duty of protection, and with it the power. . . . The power of the general government over these remnants of a race once powerful, now weak and diminished in numbers, is necessary to their protection, as well as to the safety of those among whom they dwell. . . ." . . .

In view of the legislative power possessed by Congress over treaties with the Indians and Indian tribal property, we may not specially consider the contentions pressed upon our notice that the signing by the Indians of the [1892] agreement . . . was obtained by fraudulent misrepresentations . . . , that the requisite three fourths of adult male Indians had not signed, . . . and that the treaty as signed had been amended by Congress without submitting such amendments to the action of the Indians, since all these matters, in any event, were solely within the domain of the legislative authority and its action is conclusive upon the courts.

The act . . . which is complained of . . . dealt with the disposition of tribal property and purported to give an adequate consideration for the surplus lands not allotted among the Indians or reserved for their benefit. . . . [We have] held that full administrative power [is] possessed by Congress over Indian tribal property. In effect, the action of Congress now complained of was but an exercise of such power, a mere change in the form of investment of Indian tribal property. . . . We must presume that Congress acted in perfect good faith in the[se] dealings with the Indians . . . , and that the legislative branch of the government exercised its best judgment. . . . In any event, as Congress possessed full power in the matter, the judiciary cannot question or inquire into the motives which prompted the enactment of this legislation. If injury was occasioned, which we do not wish to be understood as implying, by the use made by Congress of its power, relief must be sought by an appeal to that body for redress and not to the courts. The legislation in question was constitutional. . . .

Justice Harlan concurs in the result.

United States v. Sioux Nation (1980)

U.S. Supreme Court
June 30, 1980
448 U.S. 371

The Court's opinion was written by Justice Harry A. Blackmun, appointed by President Richard M. Nixon in 1970. The decision was 8–1. Joining fully in Blackmun's opinion were Chief Justice Warren E. Burger, appointed by President Nixon in 1969; Justices William J. Brennan, Jr., and Potter Stewart, appointed by President Dwight D. Eisenhower in 1956 and 1958; Justice Thurgood Marshall, appointed by President Lyndon B. Johnson in 1967; Justice Lewis F. Powell, Jr., appointed by President Nixon in 1972; and Justice John Paul Stevens, appointed by President Gerald R. Ford in 1975. Justice Byron R. White, appointed by President John F. Kennedy in 1962, concurred fully in the judgment but joined only part of Blackmun's opinion in a short separate opinion omitted here. Justice William H. Rehnquist, appointed by President Nixon in 1972 (later appointed chief justice by President Ronald W. Reagan in 1986), wrote a dissenting opinion.

Justice Blackmun (for the Court):

This case concerns the Black Hills of South Dakota, the Great Sioux Reservation, and a colorful, and in many respects tragic, chapter in the history of the Nation's West. Although the litigation comes down to a claim of interest since 1877 on an award of over $17 million, it is necessary, in order to understand the controversy, to review at some length the chronology of the case and its factual setting.

I

For over a century now the Sioux Nation has claimed that the United States unlawfully abrogated the Fort Laramie Treaty of April 29, 1868, in . . . which the United States pledged that the Great Sioux Reservation, including the Black Hills, would be "set apart for the absolute and undisturbed use and occupation of the Indians herein named." The Fort Laramie Treaty was concluded at the culmination of the Powder River War of 1866–1867, a series of military engagements in which the Sioux tribes, led by their great chief, Red Cloud, fought to protect the integrity of earlier-recognized treaty lands from the incursion of white settlers.

The Fort Laramie Treaty included several agreements central to the issues presented in this case. First, it established the Great Sioux Reservation. . . . The United States "solemnly [agreed]" that no unauthorized persons "shall ever be permitted to pass over, settle upon, or reside in [this] territory." . . .

. . . [T]he Sioux agreed to relinquish their rights . . . to occupy territories outside the reservation, while reserving their "right to hunt on any lands north of North Platte, and on the Republican Fork of the Smoky Hill river, so long as the buffalo may range thereon in such numbers as to justify the chase." The Indians also expressly agreed to withdraw all opposition to the building of railroads that did not pass over their reservation lands, not to engage in attacks on settlers, and to withdraw their opposition to the military posts and roads that had been established south of the North Platte River.

. . . [T]he treaty provided: "No . . . cession of any portion or part of the reservation herein described . . . shall be of any validity or force as against the said Indians, unless executed and signed by at least three fourths of all the adult male Indians, occupying or interested in the same."

The years following the treaty brought relative peace to the Dakotas, an era of tranquility that was disturbed, however, by renewed speculation that the Black Hills, which were included in the Great Sioux Reservation, contained vast quantities of gold and silver. In 1874 the Army planned and undertook an exploratory expedition into the Hills, both for the purpose of establishing a military outpost from which to control those Sioux who had not accepted the terms of the Fort Laramie Treaty, and for the purpose of investigating "the country about which dreamy stories have been told." Lieutenant Colonel George Armstrong Custer led the expedition of close to 1,000 soldiers and teamsters, and a substantial number of military and civilian aides. Custer's journey began at Fort Abraham Lincoln on the Missouri River on July 2, 1874. By the end of that month they had reached the Black Hills, and by mid-August had confirmed the presence of gold fields in that region. The discovery of gold was widely reported in newspapers across the country. Custer's florid descriptions of the mineral and timber resources of the Black Hills, and the land's suitability for grazing and cultivation, also received wide circulation, and had the effect of creating an intense popular demand for the "opening" of the Hills for settlement. The only obstacle to "progress" was the Fort Laramie Treaty that reserved occupancy of the Hills to the Sioux.

Having promised the Sioux that the Black Hills were reserved to them, the United States Army was placed in the position of having to threaten military force, and occasionally to use it, to prevent prospectors and settlers from trespassing on lands reserved to the Indians. . . .

Eventually, however, the Executive Branch of the Government decided to abandon the Nation's treaty obligation to preserve the integrity of the Sioux territory. In a letter dated November 9, 1875, to [General Alfred] Terry [Commander of the Department of Dakota], [General Philip] Sheridan [Commander of the Military Division of the Missouri] reported that he had met with President Grant, the Secretary of the Interior, and the Secretary of War, and that the President had decided that the military should make no further resistance to the occupation of the Black Hills by miners, "it being his belief that such resistance only increased their desire and complicated the troubles." These orders were to be enforced "quietly," and the President's decision was to remain "confidential."

With the Army's withdrawal from its role as enforcer of the Fort Laramie Treaty, the influx of settlers into the Black Hills increased. The Government concluded that the only practical course was to secure to the citizens of the United States the right to mine the Black Hills for gold. Toward that end, the Secretary of the Interior, in the spring of 1875, appointed a commission to negotiate with the Sioux. . . . The tribal leaders of the Sioux were aware of the mineral value of the Black Hills and refused to sell the land for a price less than $70 million. The commission offered the Indians an annual rental of $400,000, or payment of $6 million for absolute relinquishment of the Black Hills. The negotiations broke down.

In the winter of 1875–1876, many of the Sioux were hunting in the unceded territory north of the North Platte River, reserved to them for that purpose in the Fort Laramie Treaty. On December 6, 1875, for reasons that are not entirely clear, the Commissioner of Indian Affairs sent instructions to the Indian agents on the reservation to notify those hunters that if they did not return to the reservation agencies by January 31, 1876, they would be treated as "hostiles." Given the severity of the winter, compliance with these instructions was impossible.

On February 1, the Secretary of the Interior nonetheless relinquished jurisdiction over all hostile Sioux, including those Indians exercising their treaty-protected hunting rights, to the War Department. The Army's campaign against the "hostiles" led to Sitting Bull's notable victory over Custer's forces at the battle of the Little Big Horn on June 25. That victory, of course, was short-lived, and those Indians who surrendered to the Army were returned to the reservation, and deprived of their weapons and horses, leaving them completely dependent for survival on rations provided them by the Government.

... In August 1876, Congress enacted an appropriations bill providing that "hereafter there shall be no appropriation made for the subsistence" of the Sioux, unless they first relinquished their rights to the hunting grounds outside the reservation [and] ceded the Black Hills to the United States. ... Congress requested the President to appoint another commission to negotiate with the Sioux. ...

... The commissioners brought with them the text of [an agreement] that had been prepared in advance. The principal provisions ... were that the Sioux would relinquish their rights to the Black Hills and other lands ... in exchange for subsistence rations for as long as they would be needed to ensure [their] survival. In setting out to obtain ... [this] agreement ..., the commission ignored the stipulation of the Fort Laramie Treaty that any cession of the lands contained within the Great Sioux Reservation would have to be joined in by three-fourths of the adult males. Instead, the [agreement] was presented just to Sioux chiefs and their leading men. It was signed by only 10% of the adult male Sioux population.

Congress ... enact[ed] the 1876 "agreement" into law ... [in] 1877. ... The [1877] Act had the effect of abrogating the ... Fort Laramie Treaty. ...

The passage of the 1877 Act legitimized the settlers' invasion of the Black Hills, but throughout the years it has been regarded by the Sioux as a breach of this Nation's solemn obligation to reserve the Hills in perpetuity for occupation by the Indians. ...

II

Prior to 1946, Congress had not enacted any mechanism of general applicability by which Indian tribes could litigate treaty claims against the United States. The Sioux, however, after years of lobbying, succeeded in obtaining from Congress ... a special ... Act which provided them a forum for adjudication of all claims against the United States. ... Pursuant to this statute, the Sioux, in 1923, filed a petition with the Court of Claims alleging that the Government had taken the Black Hills without just compensation, in violation of the Fifth Amendment. This claim was dismissed by that court in 1942. . . . [T]he court concluded that it was not authorized . . . to question whether the compensation afforded the Sioux by Congress in 1877 was an adequate price for the Black Hills, and that the Sioux claim in this regard was a moral claim not protected by the Just Compensation Clause.

In 1946, Congress passed the Indian Claims Commission Act, creating a new forum to hear and determine all tribal grievances that had arisen previously. In 1950, . . . the Sioux resubmitted the Black Hills claim to the Indian Claims Commission. The Commission initially ruled [in 1954] that the Sioux had failed to prove their case. The Sioux . . . alleg[ed] that the Commission's decision had been based on a record that was inadequate. . . . [In] 1958, the Commission . . . announc[ed] that it would reconsider its prior judgment. . . .

Following the Sioux' filing of an amended petition, claiming again that the 1877 Act constituted a taking of the Black Hills for which just compensation had not been paid, there ensued a lengthy period of procedural sparring between the Indians and the Government. . . .

The Commission [finally found, in 1974,] that Congress, in 1877, had made no effort to give the Sioux full value for the ceded reservation lands. . . . [T]he Commission concluded that Congress had acted pursuant to its power of eminent domain when it passed the 1877 Act, rather than as a trustee for the Sioux, and that the Government must pay the Indians just compensation for the taking of the Black Hills.

The Government filed an appeal with the Court of Claims. . . . Without reaching the merits, the Court of Claims held that the Black Hills [unconstitutional taking] claim was barred by the res judicata effect of its 1942 decision. ["Res judicata" is a doctrine generally prohibiting the reopening of a prior lawsuit that has resulted in a final judgment with any appeals exhausted.] . . . [T]he practical impact of [that holding] was limited to . . . whether or not an award of interest would be available to the Indians. This followed from the Government's failure to appeal the Commission's holding that it had acquired the Black Hills through a course of unfair and dishonorable dealing for which the Sioux were entitled to damages, without interest. . . . Only if the acquisition of the Black Hills amounted to an unconstitutional taking would the Sioux be entitled to interest.

The [C]ourt [of Claims] affirmed the Commission's holding that a want of fair and honorable dealings in this case was evidenced, and held that the Sioux thus would be entitled to an award of at least $17.5 million for the lands surrendered and for the gold taken by trespassing prospectors prior to passage of the 1877 Act. The court also remarked upon President Grant's duplicity . . . and the pattern of duress practiced by the Government on the starving Sioux to get them to agree to the sale of the Black Hills. The court concluded: "A more ripe and rank case of dishonorable dealings will never, in all probability, be found in our history. . . ."

Nonetheless, the [C]ourt [of Claims] held that the merits of the [unconstitutional] taking claim had been reached in 1942, and whether resolved "rightly or wrongly," [that] claim was now barred by res judicata. . . . The Sioux petitioned this Court for a writ of certiorari, but that petition was denied [in 1975]. . . .

. . . [In] 1978, Congress passed a statute providing for Court of Claims review of the merits of the Indian Claims Commission's judgment that the 1877 Act effected a taking of the Black Hills, without regard to the defenses of res judicata and collateral estoppel [the latter doctrine prevents relitigation of specific issues decided in prior lawsuits]. The statute authorized the Court of Claims to take new evidence in the case, and to conduct its review of the merits de novo [i.e., to reconsider the case and arrive at a completely fresh decision].

Acting pursuant to that statute, a majority of the Court of Claims [in 1979] . . . affirmed the Commission's holding that the 1877 Act effected a taking of the Black Hills. . . . The court thus held that the Sioux were entitled to an award of interest, at the annual rate of 5% [calculated since 1877], on the principal sum of $17.1 million [the fair market value of the Black Hills in 1877, leaving aside the gold removed prior to then. The total value of the award was more than $100 million in 1980.] . . .

III

. . . Before turning to the merits of the Court of Claims' conclusion that the 1877 Act effected a taking of the Black Hills, we must consider the question whether Congress, in enacting this 1978 amendment, "has inadvertently passed the limit which separates the legislative from the judicial power." . . .

. . . [We conclude that] Congress' mere waiver of the res judicata effect of a prior judicial decision rejecting the validity of a legal claim against the United States does not violate the doctrine of separation of powers.

IV. A

In reaching its conclusion that the 1877 Act effected a taking of the Black Hills for which just compensation was due the Sioux under the Fifth Amendment, the Court of Claims . . . reconcile[d] two lines of cases decided by this Court that seemingly were in conflict. The first line, exemplified by *Lone Wolf v. Hitchcock* (1903), recognizes "that Congress [possesses] a paramount power over the property of the Indians, by reason of its exercise of guardianship over their interests, and that such authority might be implied, even though opposed to the strict letter of a treaty with the Indians." [*Lone Wolf* 1903, 565] The second line, exemplified by the more recent decision in *Shoshone Tribe v. United States* (1937), concedes Congress' paramount power over Indian property, but holds, nonetheless, that "[the] power does not extend so far as to enable the Government 'to give the tribal lands to others, or to appropriate them to its own purposes, without rendering, or assuming an obligation to render, just compensation.'" [*Shoshone* 1937, 497] In *Shoshone Tribe*, . . . Justice Cardozo . . . expressed the distinction between the conflicting principles in a characteristically pithy phrase: "Spoliation is not management." [*Shoshone* 1937, 498] . . .

B

The Government contends that . . . the 1877 Act [did not] effec[t] a taking of the Black Hills . . . [simply because of] Congress's failure to indicate affirmatively that the consideration given the Sioux was of equivalent value to the property rights ceded to the Government. It argues that "the true rule is that Congress must be assumed to be acting within its plenary power to manage tribal assets if it reasonably can be concluded that the legislation was intended to promote the welfare of the tribe." The Government derives support for this rule principally from . . . *Lone Wolf*. . . .

. . . Several [reasons] . . . , however, lead us to doubt whether the *Lone Wolf* Court meant to state a general rule applicable to cases such as the one before us.

First, *Lone Wolf* presented a situation in which Congress "purported to give an adequate consideration" for the treaty lands taken from the Indians. . . . In contrast, the background of the 1877 Act "reveals a situation where Congress did not 'purport' to provide 'adequate consideration,' nor was there any meaningful negotiation or arm's-length bargaining, nor did Congress consider it was paying a fair price."

Second, given the provisions of the Act at issue in *Lone Wolf*, the Court reasonably was able to conclude that "the action of Congress now complained of was but . . . a mere change in the form of investment of Indian tribal property." Under the Act of [Congress at issue in *Lone Wolf*] . . . , each head of a family was to be allotted a tract of land within the reservation of not less than 320 acres, an additional 480,000 acres of grazing land were set aside for the use of the tribes in common, and $2 million was paid to the Indians for the remaining surplus. In contrast, the historical background to the opening of the Black Hills for settlement, and the terms of the 1877 Act itself, . . . would not lead one to conclude that the Act effected "a mere change in the form of investment of Indian tribal property."

Third, it seems significant that the views of the Court in *Lone Wolf* were based, in part, on a holding that "Congress possessed full power in the matter." Earlier in the opinion the Court stated: "Plenary authority over the tribal relations of the Indians has been exercised by Congress from the beginning, and the power has always been deemed a political one, not subject to be controlled by the judicial department of the government." Thus, it seems that the Court's conclusive presumption of congressional good faith was based in large measure on the idea that relations between this Nation and the Indian tribes are a political matter, not amenable to judicial review. That view . . . has long since been discredited. . . .

Fourth, and following up on the political question holding, the *Lone Wolf* opinion suggests that where the exercise of congressional power results in injury to Indian rights, "relief must be sought by an appeal to that body for redress and not to the courts." . . . [T]his case is one in which the Sioux have sought redress from Congress, and the Legislative Branch has responded by referring the matter to the courts for resolution. Where Congress waives the Government's sovereign immunity, and expressly directs the courts to resolve a taking claim on the merits, there would appear to be far less reason to apply *Lone Wolf*'s principles of deference.

. . . More significantly, *Lone Wolf*'s presumption of congressional good faith has little to commend it as an enduring principle for deciding questions of the kind presented here. In every case where a taking of treaty-protected property is alleged, [Fn. 29] a reviewing court must recognize that tribal lands are subject to Congress's power to control and manage the tribe's affairs. But the court must also be cognizant that "this power to control and manage [is] not absolute. While extending to all appropriate measures for protecting and advancing the tribe, it [is] subject to limitations inhering in . . . a guardianship and to pertinent constitutional restrictions."

[Footnote 29: Of course, it has long been held that the taking by the United States of "unrecognized" or "aboriginal" Indian title is not compensable under the Fifth Amendment. [*Tee-Hit-Ton Indians v. United States* 1955, 285] The principles we set forth today are applicable only to instances in which "Congress by treaty or other agreement has declared that thereafter Indians were to hold the lands permanently." [*Tee-Hit-Ton* 1955, 277] In such instances, "compensation must be paid for subsequent taking." [*Tee-Hit-Ton* 1955, 277–78]]

. . . [T]he question whether a particular measure was appropriate for protecting and advancing the tribe's interests, and therefore not subject to the constitutional command of the Just Compensation Clause, is factual in nature. The answer must be based on a consideration of all the evidence presented. We do not mean to imply that a reviewing court is to second-guess, from the perspective of hindsight, a legislative judgment that a particular measure would serve the best interests of the tribe. We do mean to require courts . . . to engage in a thoroughgoing and impartial examination of the historical record. A presumption of congressional good faith cannot serve to advance such an inquiry.

C

. . . [W]e approve [the Court of Claims'] formulation of the inquiry as setting a [legal] standard that ought to be emulated by courts faced with resolving future cases . . . :

"In determining whether Congress has made a good faith effort to give the Indians the full value of their lands . . . , we . . . look to the objective facts as revealed by Acts of Congress, congressional committee reports, statements submitted to Congress by government officials, . . . and similar evidence relating to the acquisition. . . .

" . . . [A] trustee may change the form of trust assets as long as he fairly (or in good faith) attempts to provide his ward with property of equivalent value. If he does that, he cannot be faulted if hindsight should demonstrate a lack of precise equivalence. On the other hand, if a trustee (or the government in its dealings with the Indians) does not attempt to give the ward the fair equivalent of what he acquires from him, the trustee to that extent has taken rather than transmuted the property of the ward. . . ."

D

We next examine the factual findings made by the Court of Claims, which led it to the conclusion that the 1877 Act effected a taking. First, the court found that "[the] only item of 'consideration' that possibly could be viewed as showing an attempt by Congress to give the Sioux the 'full value' of the land the government took from them was the requirement to furnish them with rations until they became self-sufficient." This finding is fully supported by the record, and the Government does not seriously contend otherwise.

Second, the court found, after engaging in an exhaustive review of the historical record, that neither the Manypenny Commission, nor the congressional Committees that approved the 1877 Act, nor the individual legislators who spoke on its behalf on the floor of Congress, ever indicated a belief that the Government's obligation to provide the Sioux with rations constituted a fair equivalent for the value of the Black Hills and the additional property rights the Indians were forced to surrender. This finding is unchallenged by the Government.

... [T]hird[,] ... the conditions placed by the Government on the Sioux' entitlement to rations ... "further show that the government's undertaking to furnish rations to the Indians until they could support themselves did not reflect a congressional decision that the value of the rations was the equivalent of the land the Indians were giving up, but instead was an attempt to coerce the Sioux into capitulating to congressional demands." ...

Finally, the Court of Claims rejected the Government's contention that the fact that it subsequently had spent at least $43 million on rations for the Sioux (over the course of three-quarters of a century) established that the 1877 Act was an act of guardianship taken in the Sioux' best interest. ...

E

The aforementioned findings fully support the Court of Claims' conclusion that the 1877 Act appropriated the Black Hills "in circumstances which involved an implied undertaking by [the United States] to make just compensation to the tribe." [Fn. 32]

[Footnote 32: [Justice Rehnquist's] dissenting opinion suggests that the factual findings of the Indian Claims Commission, the Court of Claims, and now this Court, are based upon a "revisionist" view of history. The dissent fails to identify which materials quoted herein or relied upon by the Commission and the Court of Claims fit that description. The dissent's allusion to historians "writing for the purpose of having their conclusions or observations inserted in the reports of congressional committees," is also puzzling because, with respect to this case, we are unaware that any such historian exists.

The primary sources for the story told in this opinion are the factual findings of the Indian Claims Commission and the Court of Claims. A reviewing court generally will not discard such findings because they raise the specter of creeping revisionism, as the dissent would have it, but will do so only when they are clearly erroneous and unsupported by the record. No one, including the Government, has ever suggested that the factual findings of the Indian Claims Commission and the Court of Claims fail to meet that standard of review.

A further word seems to be in order. [Justice Rehnquist] does not identify a single author, nonrevisionist, neorevisionist, or otherwise, who takes the view of the history of the cession of the Black Hills that [he] prefers to adopt, largely, one assumes, as an article of faith. Rather, [he] relies on the historical findings contained in the [1942] decision [of] the Court of Claims.... [T]hose findings are not before this Court today. Moreover, the [1942] holding ..., to the extent [it] can be read as reaching the merits of the Sioux' taking claim, was based largely on the conclusive presumption of good faith toward the Indians which that court afforded to Congress's actions of 1877. The divergence of results between that decision and the judgment of the Court of Claims affirmed today, which [Justice Rehnquist] would attribute to historical revisionism, is more logically explained by the fact that the former decision was based on an erroneous legal interpretation of ... *Lone Wolf*.]

... [I]t seems readily apparent to us that ... Congress's undertaking of an obligation to provide rations for the Sioux was a quid pro quo for depriving them of their chosen way of life [hunting], and was not intended to compensate them for the taking of the Black Hills.

V

In sum, we conclude that ... the 1877 Act ... effected a taking of tribal property ... which had been set aside for the exclusive occupation of the Sioux by the Fort Laramie Treaty of 1868. That taking implied an obligation on the part of the Government to make just compensation to the Sioux Nation, and that obligation, including an award of interest, must now, at last, be paid....

Justice Rehnquist (dissenting):

... I am convinced that Congress may not constitutionally require the Court of Claims to reopen this proceeding ... and that the Court of Claims' first interpretation [in 1942] of the events in 1877 was by all accounts the more realistic one....

I

. . . [In 1942,] the Court of Claims [fully] considered [this controversy] . . . and found that the United States had not taken the Black Hills from the Sioux within the meaning of the Fifth Amendment. . . . It found that under the circumstances presented in 1877, Congress attempted to improve the situation of the Sioux and the Nation by exchanging the Black Hills for 900,000 acres of grazing lands and rations for as long as they should be needed. The court found that although the Government attempted to keep white settlers and gold prospectors out of the Black Hills territory, these efforts were unsuccessful. . . .

II

Although the Court refrains from so boldly characterizing [Congress's] action, it is obvious . . . that Congress [in 1978] . . . reviewed the decisions of the Court of Claims, set aside the judgment that no taking of the Black Hills occurred, . . . and ordered a new trial. I am convinced that this is nothing other than an exercise of judicial power . . . that may not be performed by the Legislative Branch. . . .

. . . It is quite clear from a comparison of the 1942 decision of the Court of Claims and the opinion of the Court today that the only thing that has changed is an interpretation of the events which occurred in 1877. . . . There has not even been a change in the law, for the Court today relies on decisions rendered long before . . . 1942. It is the view of history, and not the law, which has evolved. . . .

III

Even if I could countenance the Court's decision to reach the merits of this case, I also think it has erred in rejecting the 1942 court's interpretation of the facts. . . .

I think the Court today rejects that conclusion largely on the basis of a view of the settlement of the American West which is not universally shared. There were undoubtedly greed, cupidity, and other less-than-admirable tactics employed by the Government during the Black Hills episode in the settlement of the West, but the Indians did not lack their share of villainy either. It seems to me quite unfair to judge by the light of "revisionist" historians or the mores of another era actions that were taken under pressure of time more than a century ago.

Different historians, not writing for the purpose of having their conclusions or observations inserted in the reports of congressional committees, have taken different positions than those expressed in some of the materials referred to in the Court's opinion. This is not unnatural, since history, no more than law, is not an exact (or for that matter an inexact) science.

But the inferences which the Court itself draws from the letter from General Sheridan . . . reporting on a meeting . . . with President Grant, . . . as well as other passages in the Court's opinion, leave a stereotyped and one-sided impression both of the settlement regarding the Black Hills portion of the Great Sioux Reservation and of the gradual expansion of the [nation] from the Proclamation Line of King George III in 1763 to the Pacific Ocean.

Ray Billington, a senior research associate at the Huntington Library in San Marino, Cal., since 1963, and a respected student of the settlement of the American West, emphasized in his introduction to the [1963] book *Soldier and Brave* that the confrontations in the West were the product of a long history, not a conniving Presidential administration:

"Three centuries of bitter Indian warfare reached a tragic climax on the plains and mountains of America's Far West. Since the early seventeenth century, . . . each advance of the frontier had been met with stubborn resistance. At times this conflict flamed into open warfare. . . .

" . . . In three tragic decades, between 1860 and 1890, the Indians suffered the humiliating defeats that forced them to walk the white man's road toward civilization. Few conquered people in the history of mankind have paid so dearly for their defense of a way of life that the march of progress had outmoded.

"This epic struggle left its landmarks behind, as monuments to the brave men, Indian and white, who fought and died that their manner of living might endure."

[Samuel Eliot Morison's *The Oxford History of the American People* (1965)] highlights the cultural differences which made conflict and brutal warfare inevitable:

"The Plains Indians seldom practiced agriculture or other primitive arts, but they were fine physical specimens; and in warfare, once they had learned the use of the rifle, [were] much more formidable than the Eastern tribes who had slowly yielded to the white man. Tribe warred with tribe, and a highly developed sign language was the only means of intertribal communication. The effective unit was the band or village of a few hundred souls, which might be seen in the course of its wanderings encamped by a watercourse with tipis erected; or pouring over the plain, women and children leading dogs and packhorses with their trailing travois, while gaily dressed braves loped ahead on horseback. They lived only for the day, recognized no rights of property, robbed or killed anyone if they thought they could get away with it, inflicted cruelty without a qualm, and endured torture without flinching."

That there was tragedy, deception, barbarity, and virtually every other vice known to man in the 300-year history of the expansion of the original 13 Colonies into a Nation which now embraces more than three million square miles and 50 States cannot be denied. But in a court opinion, as a historical and not a legal matter, both settler and Indian are entitled to the benefit of the Biblical adjuration: "Judge not, that ye be not judged."

Minnesota v. Mille Lacs Band of Chippewa Indians (1999)

U.S. Supreme Court
March 24, 1999
526 U.S. 172

The Court's opinion was written by Justice Sandra Day O'Connor, appointed by President Ronald W. Reagan in 1981. The decision was 5–4. O'Connor's opinion was joined by Justice John Paul Stevens, appointed by President Gerald R. Ford in 1975; Justice David H. Souter, appointed by President George Bush in 1990; and Justices Ruth Bader Ginsburg and Stephen G. Breyer, appointed by President William J. Clinton in 1993 and 1994, respectively. Chief Justice William H. Rehnquist, appointed as associate justice by President Richard M. Nixon in 1972 and as chief justice by President Reagan in 1986, wrote a dissenting opinion joined by Justices Antonin Scalia and Anthony M. Kennedy, appointed by President Reagan in 1986 and 1988; and Justice Clarence Thomas, appointed by President Bush in 1991. Thomas also wrote a dissenting opinion for himself alone, which is omitted here.

Justice O'Connor (for the Court):

In 1837, the United States entered into a Treaty with several Bands of Chippewa Indians. Under the terms of this Treaty, the Indians ceded land in present-day Wisconsin and Minnesota to the United States, and the United States guaranteed to the Indians certain hunting, fishing, and gathering rights on the ceded land. We must decide whether the Chippewa Indians retain these usufructuary rights today. The State of Minnesota argues that the Indians lost these rights through an Executive Order in 1850, an 1855 Treaty, and the admission of Minnesota into the Union in 1858. After an examination of the historical record, we conclude that the Chippewa retain the usufructuary rights guaranteed to them under the 1837 Treaty.

I.A

In 1837, several Chippewa Bands, including the . . . [Mille Lacs Band], were summoned to Fort Snelling (near present-day St. Paul, Minnesota) for the negotiation of a treaty with the United States. The United States . . . wanted to purchase certain Chippewa lands. . . . The Chippewa agreed to sell the land . . . , but they insisted on preserving their right to hunt, fish, and gather in the ceded territory. . . . [T]he 1837 Treaty . . . guaranteed to the Chippewa the right to hunt, fish, and gather on the ceded lands . . . "during the pleasure of the President of the United States." [Chippewa-U.S. Treaty 1837, 537]

In 1842, many of the same Chippewa Bands entered into another Treaty . . . ceding additional lands to the Federal Government in return for annuity payments of goods and money, while reserving usufructuary rights on the ceded lands. [Chippewa-U.S. Treaty 1842, 591] This Treaty, however, also contained a provision providing that the Indians would be "subject to removal therefrom at the pleasure of the President of the United States." [Chippewa-U.S. Treaty 1842, 592]

In the late 1840s, pressure mounted to remove the Chippewa to their unceded lands in the Minnesota Territory. . . . President [Zachary] Taylor responded to this pressure by issuing an Executive Order [in] 1850 . . . : "The privileges granted temporarily to the Chippewa Indians . . . by the . . . 1837 [and 1842] Treat[ies] . . . are hereby revoked; and all of the said Indians remaining on the lands ceded . . . are required to remove to their unceded lands." The officials charged with implementing this order understood it primarily as a removal order, and they proceeded to implement it accordingly.

The Government hoped to entice the Chippewa to remove to Minnesota by changing the location where the annuity payments—the payments for the land cessions—would be made. The Chippewa were to be told that their annuity payments would no longer be made at La Pointe, Wisconsin (within the Chippewa's ceded lands), but, rather, would be made at Sandy Lake, on unceded lands, in the Minnesota Territory. The Government's first annuity payment under this plan, however, ended in disaster. The Chippewa were told they had to be at Sandy Lake by October 25 to receive their 1850 annuity payment. By November 10, almost 4,000 Chippewa had assembled at Sandy Lake to receive the payment, but the annuity goods were not completely distributed until December 2. In the meantime, around 150 Chippewa died in an outbreak of measles and dysentery; another 230 Chippewas died on the winter trip home to Wisconsin.

The Sandy Lake annuity experience intensified opposition to the removal order among the Chippewa as well as among non-Indian residents of the area. In the face of this opposition, [the] Commissioner of Indian Affairs . . . recommend[ed] that the President's 1850 order be modified to allow the Chippewa "to remain for the present in the country they now occupy." . . . [He stated that] removal of the Wisconsin Bands "is not required by the interests of the citizens or Government of the United States and would . . . be disastrous to the Indians." Three months later, . . . the Secretary of the Interior . . . "suspend[ed] the removal of the Chippeway [*sic*] Indians until the final determination of the President." . . . As the State's own expert historian testified, "federal efforts to remove the Lake Superior Chippewa to the Mississippi River effectively ended in the summer of 1851."

Although [the territorial governor] still hoped to entice the Chippewa to remove by limiting annuity payments to only those Indians who removed to unceded lands, this plan, too, was quickly abandoned. In 1853, Franklin Pierce became President, and he appointed George Manypenny as Commissioner of Indian Affairs. The new administration reversed [course] . . . and in 1853, annuity payments were once again made within the ceded territory[,] . . . thus suggesting that . . . the 1850 removal order had been abandoned.

In 1849, white lumbermen built a dam on the Rum River (within the Minnesota portion of the 1837 ceded Territory), and the Mille Lacs Band of Chippewa protested that the dam interfered with its wild rice harvest. This dispute erupted in 1855 when violence broke out between the Chippewa and the lumbermen, necessitating a call for federal troops. In February 1855, the Governor of the Minnesota Territory, Willis Gorman, who also served as the ex officio superintendent of Indian affairs for the Territory, wrote to Commissioner Manypenny about this dispute. In his letter, he noted that "the lands occupied by the timbermen have been surveyed and sold by the United States and the Indians have no other treaty interests except hunting and fishing." There is no indication that Commissioner Manypenny disagreed with Governor Gorman's characterization of Chippewa treaty rights. In June of the same year, Governor Gorman wrote to Mille Lacs Chief Little Hill that . . . the dam "was put there long before you had any rights there except to hunt and fish." Thus, as of 1855, the federal official responsible for Indian affairs in the Minnesota Territory acknowledged and recognized Chippewa rights to hunt and fish in the 1837 ceded Territory.

On the other hand, there are statements by federal officials in the late 19th century and the first half of the 20th century that suggest that the Federal Government no longer recognized Chippewa usufructuary rights under the 1837 Treaty. . . .

Although the United States abandoned its removal policy, it did not abandon its attempts to acquire more Chippewa land. . . . [In 1855,] Commissioner Manypenny . . . negotiate[d] a[nother] treaty . . . [for] the sale of Chippewa lands to the United States . . . :

"The . . . Chippewa Indians hereby cede, sell, and convey to the United States all their right, title, and interest in . . . [certain defined] lands now owned and claimed by them. . . . And [they] do further fully and entirely relinquish and convey to the United States, any and all right, title, and interest, of whatsoever nature the same may be, which they may now have in, and to any other lands in the Territory of Minnesota or elsewhere." [Chippewa-U.S. Treaty 1855, 1165–1166]

. . . [The 1855 Treaty] set aside lands in the area as reservations for the signatory tribes. The Treaty, however, makes no mention of hunting and fishing rights, whether to reserve new usufructuary rights or to abolish rights guaranteed by previous treaties. The Treaty Journal also reveals no discussion of hunting and fishing rights.

A little over three years after the 1855 Treaty was signed, Minnesota was admitted to the Union. The admission Act [of 1858] is silent with respect to Indian treaty rights.

B

In 1990, the Mille Lacs Band of Chippewa Indians . . . filed suit . . . seeking . . . a declaratory judgment that they retained their usufructuary rights under the 1837 Treaty and . . . prevent[ing] the State's interference with those rights. . . .

II

We are first asked to decide whether President Taylor's Executive Order . . . terminated Chippewa hunting, fishing, and gathering rights under the 1837 Treaty. The Court of Appeals began its analysis of this question with a statement of black-letter law: "The President's power, if any, to issue the order must stem either from an act of Congress or from the Constitution itself." The court considered whether the President had authority to issue the removal order under the 1830 Removal Act. . . . The Removal Act authorized the President to convey land west of the Mississippi to Indian tribes that chose to "exchange the lands where they now reside, and remove there." According to the Court of Appeals, the Removal Act only allowed the removal of Indians who had consented to removal. Because the Chippewa had not consented to removal . . . , the Removal Act could not provide authority for the President's 1850 removal order. . . . We agree. . . .

Because the Removal Act did not authorize the 1850 removal order, we must look elsewhere for a constitutional or statutory authorization for the order. In this Court, . . . the landowners . . . argue that the President's removal order was authorized by the 1837 Treaty itself. There is no support for this proposition, however. The Treaty makes no mention of removal, and there was no discussion of removal during the Treaty negotiations. . . . [Thus,] the 1850 removal order was unauthorized.

The State argues that even if the removal portion of the order was invalid, the 1837 Treaty privileges were nevertheless revoked because the invalid removal order was severable from the portion of the order revoking Chippewa usufructuary rights. . . .

. . . [W]e must determine whether the President would not have revoked the 1837 Treaty privileges if he could not issue the removal order.

We think it is clear that President Taylor intended the 1850 order to stand or fall as a whole. The 1850 order embodied a single, coherent policy, the predominant purpose of which was removal of the Chippewa from the lands that they had ceded to the United States. The federal officials charged with implementing the order certainly understood it as such. . . .

When the 1850 order is understood as announcing a removal policy, the portion of the order revoking Chippewa usufructuary rights is seen to perform an integral function in this policy. The order tells the Indians to "go," and also tells them not to return to the ceded lands to hunt and fish. The State suggests that President Taylor might also have revoked Chippewa usufructuary rights as a kind of "incentive program" to encourage the Indians to remove had he known that he could not order their removal directly. The State points to no evidence, however, that the President or his aides ever considered the abrogation of hunting and fishing rights as an "incentive program." Moreover, the State does not explain how this incentive was to operate. As the State characterizes Chippewa Treaty rights, the revocation of those rights would not have prevented the Chippewa from hunting, fishing, and gathering on the ceded territory; the revocation of Treaty rights would merely have subjected Chippewa hunters, fishers, and gatherers to territorial, and, later, state regulation. The State does not explain how, if the Chippewa were still permitted to hunt, fish, and gather on the ceded territory, the revocation of the Treaty rights would have encouraged the Chippewa to remove to their unceded lands.

There is also no evidence that the Treaty privileges themselves—as opposed to the presence of the Indians—caused any problems necessitating the revocation of those privileges. . . . The only evidence in this regard is . . . that settlers in the Sauk Rapids and Swan River area were complaining about the Chippewa Treaty privileges. But the historical record suggests that the settlers were complaining about the Winnebago Indians, and not the Chippewa. . . . When [the territorial governor] was put in charge of enforcing the 1850 Executive Order, he made no efforts to remove the Chippewa from the Sauk Rapids area or to restrict hunting and fishing privileges there. In fact, his attempts to enforce the order consisted primarily of efforts to move Chippewa from the Wisconsin and Michigan areas to Minnesota—closer to the Sauk Rapids and Swan River settlements. More importantly, . . . [territorial politicians] explicitly tied revocation of the Treaty privileges to removal. Common sense explains the logic of this strategy: If [they were] concerned with ensuring "the security and tranquility of the white settlements," this concern was not addressed by merely revoking Indian Treaty rights; the Indians had to be removed.

We conclude that President Taylor's 1850 Executive Order was ineffective to terminate Chippewa usufructuary rights under the 1837 Treaty. . . . We do not mean to suggest that a President, now or in the future, cannot revoke the Chippewa usufructuary rights in accordance with the terms of the 1837 Treaty. All we conclude today is that the President's 1850 Executive Order was insufficient to accomplish this revocation because it was not severable from the invalid removal order.

III

The State argues that the Mille Lacs Band of Chippewa Indians relinquished its usufructuary rights under the 1855 Treaty with the

Chippewa. Specifically, the State argues that the Band unambiguously relinquished its usufructuary rights by agreeing to the second sentence of Article 1 in that Treaty: "And the said Indians do further fully and entirely relinquish and convey to the United States, any and all right, title, and interest, of whatsoever nature the same may be, which they may now have in, and to any other lands in the Territory of Minnesota or elsewhere." [Chippewa-U.S. Treaty 1855, 1166]

This sentence, however, does not mention the 1837 Treaty, and it does not mention hunting, fishing, and gathering rights. The entire 1855 Treaty, in fact, is devoid of any language expressly mentioning—much less abrogating—usufructuary rights. Similarly, the Treaty contains no language providing money for the abrogation of previously held rights. These omissions are telling because the United States treaty drafters had the sophistication and experience to use express language for the abrogation of treaty rights. In fact, just a few months after Commissioner Manypenny completed the 1855 Treaty, he negotiated a Treaty with the Chippewa of Sault Ste. Marie that expressly revoked fishing rights that had been reserved in an earlier Treaty. . . .

The State argues that despite any explicit reference to the 1837 Treaty rights, or to usufructuary rights more generally, the [1855 Treaty] . . . nevertheless abrogates those rights. But to determine [this] . . . , we look beyond the written words to the larger context that frames the Treaty, including "the history of the treaty, the negotiations, and the practical construction adopted by the parties." In this case, an examination of the historical record provides insight into how the parties . . . understood the terms of the agreement. This insight is especially helpful to the extent that it sheds light on how the Chippewa signatories to the Treaty understood the agreement because we interpret Indian treaties to give effect to the terms as the Indians themselves would have understood them. [*Washington v. Washington State Commercial Passenger Fishing Vessel Association* 1979, 675–676; *United States v. Winans* 1905, 380–381]

The 1855 Treaty was designed primarily to transfer Chippewa land to the United States, not to terminate Chippewa usufructuary rights. . . . [Congress had] authorized treaty negotiations with the Chippewa "for the extinguishment of their title to all the lands owned and claimed by them in the Territory of Minnesota and State of Wisconsin." [Congress was] silent with respect to authorizing agreements to terminate Indian usufructuary privileges, and this silence was likely not accidental. During Senate debate . . . , Senator Sebastian, the chairman of the Committee on Indian Affairs, stated that the treaties to be negotiated . . . would "reserve to them [i.e., the Chippewa] those rights which are secured by former treaties."

In the winter of 1854–1855, Commissioner Manypenny summoned several Chippewa chiefs to Washington, D.C., to begin negotiations over the sale of Chippewa land in Minnesota to the United States. The negotiations ran from February 12 through February 22. Commissioner Manypenny opened the negotiations by telling the Chippewa chiefs that his goal for the negotiations was to buy a portion of their land, and he stayed firm to this proposed course throughout the talks, focusing the discussions on the purchase of Chippewa land. Indeed all of the participants in the negotiations, including the Indians, understood that the purpose of the negotiations was to transfer Indian land to the United States. . . . Chief [Flat Mouth] of the Pillager Band of Chippewa stated: "It appears to me that I understand what you want, and your views from the few words I have heard you speak. You want land." . . .

Like the authorizing legislation, the Treaty Journal, recording the course of the negotiations themselves, is silent with respect to usufructuary rights. The journal records no discussion of the 1837 Treaty, of hunting, fishing, and gathering rights, or of the abrogation of those rights. This silence suggests that the Chippewa did not understand the proposed Treaty to abrogate their usufructuary rights as guaranteed by other treaties. It is difficult to believe that in 1855, the Chippewa would have agreed to relinquish the usufructuary rights they had fought to preserve in 1837 without at least a passing word about the relinquishment.

After the Treaty was signed, President Pierce submitted it to the Senate for ratification, along with an accompanying memorandum from Commissioner Manypenny describing the Treaty he had just negotiated. Like the Treaty and the Treaty journal, this report is silent about hunting, fishing, and gathering rights. . . .

One final part of the historical record also suggests that the 1855 Treaty was a land purchase treaty and not a treaty that also terminated usufructuary rights: the [Chippewa-U.S. Treaty of 1854]. Most of the Chippewa Bands that resided within the territory ceded by the 1837 Treaty were [also] signatories to the 1854 Treaty; only the Mille Lacs Band was a party to the 1855 Treaty. If the United States had intended to abrogate Chippewa usufructuary rights . . . , it almost certainly would have included a provision to that effect in the 1854 Treaty, yet that Treaty contains no such provision. To the contrary, it expressly secures new usufructuary rights to the signatory Bands on the newly ceded territory. The State proposes no explanation—compelling or otherwise—for why the United States would have wanted to abrogate the Mille Lacs Band's hunting and fishing rights, while leaving intact the other Bands' rights to hunt and fish on the same territory.

To summarize, the historical record provides no support for the theory that the . . . [1855 Treaty] was designed to abrogate the usufructuary privileges guaranteed under the 1837 Treaty. . . . At the very least, the historical record refutes the State's assertion that the 1855 Treaty "unambiguously" abrogated the 1837 hunting, fishing, and gathering privileges. Given this plausible ambiguity, we cannot agree with the State that the 1855 Treaty abrogated Chippewa usufructuary rights. We have held that Indian treaties are to be interpreted liberally in favor of the Indians [*Washington v. Washington State Commercial Passenger Fishing Vessel Association* 1979, 675–676], and that any ambiguities are to be resolved in their favor [*Winters v. United States* 1908, 576–577]. . . .

IV

Finally, the State argues that the Chippewa's usufructuary rights under the 1837 Treaty were extinguished when Minnesota was admitted to the Union in 1858. In making this argument, the State faces an uphill battle. Congress may abrogate Indian treaty rights, but it must clearly express its intent to do so. [*United States v. Dion* 1986, 738–740, 90; *Washington v. Washington State Commercial Passenger Fishing Vessel Association* 1979, 690] There must be "clear evidence that Congress actually considered the conflict between its intended action on the one hand and Indian treaty rights on the other, and chose to resolve that conflict by abrogating the treaty." [*United States v. Dion* 1986, 740] There is no such "clear evidence" of congressional intent to abrogate the Chippewa Treaty rights here. The relevant statute—Minnesota's [1858] enabling Act—provides in relevant part: "The State of Minnesota shall be one, and is hereby declared to be one, of the United States of America, and admitted into the Union on an equal footing with the original States in all respects whatever."

This language, like the rest of the Act, makes no mention of Indian treaty rights; it provides no clue that Congress considered the reserved rights of the Chippewa and decided to abrogate those rights when it passed the Act. The State concedes that the Act is silent in this regard, and the State does not point to any legislative history describing the effect of the Act on Indian treaty rights.

With no direct support for its argument, the State relies principally on this Court's decision in *Ward v. Race Horse* (1896). In *Race Horse,* we held that a Treaty reserving to a Tribe "the right to hunt on the unoccupied lands of the United States, so long as game may be found thereon, and so long as peace subsists among the whites and Indians on the borders of the hunting districts" terminated when Wyoming became a State in 1890. [*Race Horse* 1896: 507] This case does not bear the weight the State places on it, however, because it has been qualified by later decisions of this Court.

The first part of the holding in *Race Horse* was based on the "equal footing doctrine," the constitutional principle that all States are admitted to the Union with the same attributes of sovereignty (i.e., on equal footing) as the original 13 States. As relevant here, it prevents the Federal Government from impairing fundamental attributes of state sovereignty when it admits new States into the Union. According to the *Race Horse* Court, because the Treaty rights conflicted irreconcilably with state regulation of natural resources—"an essential attribute of its governmental existence" [*Race Horse* 1896: 516]—the Treaty rights were . . . an invalid impairment of Wyoming's sovereignty. Thus, those rights could not survive Wyoming's admission to the Union on "equal footing" with the original States.

But *Race Horse* rested on a false premise. As this Court's subsequent cases have made clear, an Indian tribe's treaty rights to hunt, fish, and gather on state land are not irreconcilable with a State's sovereignty over the natural resources in the State. [*Washington v. Washington State Commercial Passenger Fishing Vessel Association* 1979] Rather, Indian treaty rights can coexist with state management of natural resources. Although States have important interests in regulating wildlife and natural resources within their borders, this authority is shared with the Federal Government when the Federal Government exercises one of its enumerated constitutional powers, such as treaty making. [*United States v. Winans* 1905, 382–384] Here, the 1837 Treaty gave the Chippewa the right to hunt, fish, and gather in the ceded territory free of territorial, and later state, regulation, a privilege that others did not enjoy. Today, this freedom from state regulation curtails the State's ability to regulate hunting, fishing, and gathering by the Chippewa in the ceded lands. But this Court's cases have also recognized that Indian treaty . . . rights do not guarantee the Indians "absolute freedom" from state regulation. We have repeatedly reaffirmed state authority to impose reasonable and necessary nondiscriminatory regulations on Indian hunting, fishing, and gathering rights in the interest of conservation. [*Puyallup Tribe v. Washington Department of Game* 1968, 398; *Washington v. Washington State Commercial Passenger Fishing Vessel Association* 1979, 682] This "conservation necessity" standard accommodates both the State's interest in management of its natural resources and the Chippewa's federally guaranteed treaty rights. Thus, because treaty rights are reconcilable with state sovereignty over natural resources, statehood by itself is insufficient to extinguish Indian treaty rights to hunt, fish, and gather on land within state boundaries. . . .

The equal footing doctrine was only part of the holding in *Race Horse*, however. We also . . . concluded . . . that the particular rights in the treaty at issue there—"the right to hunt on the unoccupied lands of the United States"—were not intended to survive statehood. [*Race Horse* 1896: 514]

. . . Chief Justice [Rehnquist] reads *Race Horse* to establish a rule that "temporary and precarious" treaty rights, as opposed to treaty rights "which were 'of such a nature as to imply their perpetuity,'" are not intended to survive statehood. But the "temporary and precarious" language in *Race Horse* is too broad to be useful in distinguishing rights that survive statehood from those that do not. In *Race Horse*, the Court concluded that the right to hunt on federal lands was temporary because Congress could terminate the right at any time by selling the lands. [*Race Horse* 1896: 510] Under this line of reasoning, any right created by operation of federal law could be described as "temporary and precarious," because Congress could eliminate the right whenever it wished. . . .

The focus of the *Race Horse* inquiry is whether Congress (more precisely, . . . the Senate) intended the rights secured by the 1837 Treaty to survive statehood. [*Race Horse* 1896: 514–515] The 1837 Treaty itself defines the circumstances under which the rights would terminate: when the exercise of those rights was no longer the "pleasure of the President." There is no suggestion in the Treaty that the President would have to conclude that the privileges should end when a State was established in the area. Moreover, unlike the rights at issue in *Race Horse*, there is no fixed termination point to the 1837 Treaty rights. . . . Treaty rights are not impliedly terminated upon statehood. The *Race Horse* Court's decision to the contrary . . . was informed by that Court's conclusion that the Indian treaty rights were inconsistent with state sovereignty over natural resources and thus that Congress (the Senate) could not have intended the rights to survive statehood. But as we described above, Indian treaty . . . rights are not inconsistent with state sovereignty over natural resources. Thus, . . . *Race Horse* does not compel the conclusion that Minnesota's admission to the Union extinguished Chippewa usufructuary rights guaranteed by the 1837 Treaty. . . .

Chief Justice Rehnquist (dissenting, joined by Justices Scalia, Kennedy, and Thomas):

The Court holds that the various Bands of Chippewa Indians retain a usufructuary right granted to them in an 1837 Treaty. To reach this result, the Court must successively conclude that: (1) an 1850 Executive Order explicitly revoking the privilege as authorized by the 1837 Treaty was unlawful; (2) an 1855 Treaty under which certain Chippewa Bands ceded "all" interests to the land does not include the treaty right to come onto the land and hunt; and (3) the admission of Minnesota into the Union in 1858 did not terminate the discretionary hunting privilege, despite established precedent of this Court to the contrary. Because I believe that each one of these three conclusions is demonstrably wrong, I dissent.

[Part I is omitted.]

II

In 1850, President Taylor expressly terminated the 1837 Treaty privilege by Executive Order. . . .

In deciding that this seemingly ironclad revocation was not effective . . . , the Court [makes] . . . four findings. First, the Court notes that the President's power to issue the order must stem either from an Act of Congress or the Constitution itself. Second, the Court determines that the Executive Order was a "removal order." Third, the Court finds no authority for the President to order the Chippewa to remove from the ceded lands. And fourth, the Court holds that the portion of the Executive Order extinguishing the hunting and fishing rights is not severable from the "removal order" and thus also was illegal. I shall address each of these dubious findings in turn.

The Court's first proposition is the seemingly innocuous statement that a President's Executive Order must be authorized by law in order to have any legal effect. . . . However, the Court neglects to note that treaties, every bit as much as statutes, are sources of law and may also authorize Executive actions. . . . [T]he Executive Order in this case was issued pursuant to a Treaty ratified by the advice and consent of the Senate, and thus became the supreme law of the land. . . .

The Court's second assumption is that the Executive Order was a "removal order"—that its primary purpose was the removal of the Chippewa. This assumption rests upon scattered historical evidence that, in the Court's view, "the officials charged with implementing this order understood it primarily as a removal order, and they moved to implement it accordingly." Regardless of what the President's remote frontier agents may have thought, the plain meaning of the text of President Taylor's order can only support the opposite conclusion. The structure of the Executive Order is not that of a removal order, with the revocation of the hunting privileges added merely as an afterthought. Instead, the first part of the order (not to mention the bulk of its text) deals with the extinguishment of the Indians' privilege to enter onto the lands ceded to the United States and hunt. Only then (and then only in its final five words) does the Executive Order require the Indians to "remove to their unceded lands."

... [W]hat then should we make of the fact that the officials charged with "implementing" the order viewed their task as primarily effecting removal? The answer is simple. First, the bulk of the Executive Order that terminates the hunting privilege was self-executing. Second, while the President could terminate the legal right (i.e., the privilege to enter onto the ceded lands and hunt) without taking enforcement action, a removal order would require actual implementation....

The Court's third finding is that the removal portion of the order is invalid because President Taylor had no authority to order removal. Although the Court sensibly concludes that the Removal Act of 1830 is inapplicable to this case, it then curiously rejects the notion that the 1837 Treaty authorizes removal, largely on the grounds that "the Treaty makes no mention of removal." The Court is correct that the Treaty does not mention removal, but this is because the Treaty was essentially a deed of conveyance—it transferred land to the United States in exchange for goods and money. After the Treaty was executed and ratified, the ceded lands belonged to the United States, and the only real property interest in the land remaining to the Indians was the privilege to come onto it and hunt during the pleasure of the President. When the President terminated that privilege (a legal act that the Court appears to concede he had a right to make), he terminated the Indians' right to come onto the ceded lands and hunt. The Indians had no legal right to remain on the ceded lands for that purpose, and the removal portion of the order should be viewed in this context. Indeed, the Indians then had no legal rights at all with respect to the ceded lands, in which all title was vested in the United States. And this Court has long held that the President has the implied power to administer the public lands. . . . The ceded lands were not a national park, nor did the President have an army of park rangers available to guard Minnesota's wildlife from Chippewa poachers. Removal was the only viable option in enforcing his power under the Treaty to terminate the hunting privilege. Thus, in my view, the final part of the Executive Order discussing removal was lawful.

The fourth element essential to today's holding is the conclusion that if the final part of the Executive Order requiring removal were not authorized, the bulk of the order would fail as not severable. . . . As noted above, this approach to the Executive Order stands it on its head—the order first extinguishes the hunting privilege and only then—in its last five words—orders removal.

But even if I were to assume that the President were without authority to order removal, I would conclude that the removal provision is severable from that terminating the Treaty privileges. There is no dispute that the President had authority under the 1837 Treaty to terminate the Treaty privileges. We have long held that "when the President acts pursuant to an express or implied authorization from Congress, . . . the executive action 'would be supported by the strongest of presumptions and the widest latitude of judicial interpretation, and the burden of persuasion would rest heavily upon any who might attack it.'" Against this deferential standard, the Court musters little more than conjecture and inference, reinforced by its upside-down reading of the Executive Order's plain text. . . . [W]e have only the Court's misguided excursion into historiographical clairvoyance. Accordingly, I would conclude, if necessary, that the termination portion of the Executive Order is severable. . . .

III

Although I believe that the clear meaning of the Executive Order is sufficient to resolve this case, and that it is unnecessary to address the Court's treatment of the 1855 Treaty and the 1858 admission of Minnesota to the Union, I shall briefly express my strong disagreement with the Court's analysis on these issues also.

As the Court notes, in 1855, several of the Chippewa Bands agreed, in exchange for further annuity payments of money and goods, to "fully and entirely relinquish and convey to the United States, any and all right, title, and interest, of whatsoever nature the same may be, which they now have in, and to any other lands in the Territory of Minnesota or elsewhere." [Chippewa-U.S. Treaty 1855, 1166] . . . [U]sing our canons of construction that ambiguities in treaties are often resolved in favor of the Indians, [the Court] concludes that the Treaty did not apply to . . . hunting rights.

I think this conclusion strained, indeed. . . .

IV

Finally, I note my disagreement with the Court's treatment of the equal footing doctrine, and its apparent overruling *sub silentio* of a precedent of 103 years' vintage. In *Ward v. Race Horse* (1896) we held that a Treaty granting . . . Indians [a] "right to hunt . . ." did not survive the admission of Wyoming to the Union since the Treaty right was "temporary and precarious." [*Race Horse* 1896: 515] . . . [T]he Court hints that *[Race Horse]* rested on an incorrect premise—that Indian [hunting] rights were inconsistent with state sovereignty.

Without saying so, this jurisprudential bait-and-switch effectively overrules *[Race Horse]*, a case which we reaffirmed as recently as 1985. . . . *[Race Horse]* held merely that treaty rights which were only "temporary and precarious," as opposed to those which were "of such a nature as to imply their perpetuity," do not survive statehood. [*Race Horse* 1896: 515] Here, the hunting privileges were clearly, like those invalidated in *[Race Horse]*, temporary and precarious . . .

V

The Court today invalidates for no principled reason a 149-year-old Executive Order, ignores the plain meaning of a 144-year-old treaty provision, and overrules *sub silentio* a 103-year-old precedent of this Court. I dissent.

Tribal Criminal Jurisdiction

Oliphant v. Suquamish Indian Tribe (1978)

U.S. Supreme Court
March 6, 1978
435 U.S. 191

The Court's opinion was written by Justice William H. Rehnquist, appointed by President Richard M. Nixon in 1972 (later appointed chief justice by President Ronald W. Reagan in 1986). The decision was 6–2. Rehnquist's opinion was joined by Justice Potter Stewart, ap-

pointed by President Dwight D. Eisenhower in 1958; Justice Byron R. White, appointed by President John F. Kennedy in 1962; Justices Harry A. Blackmun and Lewis F. Powell, Jr., appointed by President Nixon in 1970 and 1972; and Justice John Paul Stevens, appointed by President Gerald R. Ford in 1975. Justice Thurgood Marshall, appointed by President Lyndon B. Johnson in 1967, wrote a short dissenting opinion joined by Chief Justice Warren E. Burger, appointed by President Nixon in 1969. Justice William J. Brennan, Jr., appointed by President Eisenhower in 1956, did not participate, although if he had it seems very likely, based on his voting pattern in other Indian law cases, that he would also have dissented.

Justice Rehnquist (for the Court):

Two hundred years ago, the area bordering Puget Sound consisted of a large number of politically autonomous Indian villages, each occupied by from a few dozen to over 100 Indians. These loosely related villages were aggregated into a series of Indian tribes, one of which, the Suquamish, has become the focal point of this litigation. By the 1855 Treaty of Point Elliott, the Suquamish Indian Tribe . . . agreed to settle on a 7,276-acre reservation near Port Madison, Wash. Located on Puget Sound across from the city of Seattle, the Port Madison Reservation is a checkerboard of tribal community land, allotted Indian lands, property held in fee simple [i.e., by ordinary private ownership] by non-Indians, and various roads and public highways maintained by Kitsap County. [Fn. 1]

[Footnote 1: According to the district court's findings of fact, "[The Port] Madison Indian Reservation consists of approximately 7276 acres of which approximately 63% . . . is owned in fee simple absolute by non-Indians and the remainder 37% is Indian-owned lands subject to the trust status of the United States, consisting mostly of unimproved acreage upon which no persons reside. Residing on the reservation is an estimated population of . . . 2928 non-Indians. . . . There lives on the reservation approximately 50 members of the Suquamish Indian Tribe. . . .]

The Suquamish Indians are governed by a tribal government which in 1973 adopted a Law and Order Code. The Code, which covers a variety of offenses from theft to rape, purports to extend the Tribe's criminal jurisdiction over both Indians and non-Indians. Proceedings are held in the Suquamish Indian Provisional Court. Pursuant to the Indian Civil Rights Act of 1968, defendants are entitled to many of the due process protections accorded to defendants in federal or state criminal proceedings. However, the guarantees are not identical. Non-Indians, for example, are excluded from Suquamish tribal court juries.

Both petitioners are non-Indian residents of the Port Madison Reservation. Petitioner Mark David Oliphant was arrested by tribal authorities during the Suquamish's annual Chief Seattle Days celebration and charged with assaulting a tribal officer and resisting arrest. After arraignment before the tribal court, Oliphant was released on his own recognizance. Petitioner Daniel B. Belgarde was arrested by tribal authorities after an alleged high-speed race along the Reservation highways that only ended when Belgarde collided with a tribal police vehicle. Belgarde posted bail and was released. Six days later he was arraigned and charged under the tribal Code with "recklessly endangering another person" and injuring tribal property. Tribal court proceedings against both petitioners have been stayed pending a decision in this case. . . .

I

[The Tribe] do[es] not contend that [its] exercise of criminal jurisdiction over non-Indians stems from affirmative congressional authorization [i.e., by statute] or [by] treaty provision. Instead, [it] urge[s] that such jurisdiction flows automatically from the "Tribe's retained inherent powers of government over the Port Madison Indian Reservation." Seizing on language in our opinions describing Indian tribes as "quasi-sovereign entities," the Court of Appeals agreed and held that Indian tribes, "though conquered and dependent, retain those powers of autonomous states that are neither inconsistent with their status nor expressly terminated by Congress." . . .

The Suquamish Indian Tribe does not stand alone today in its assumption of criminal jurisdiction over non-Indians. Of the 127 reservation court systems that currently exercise criminal jurisdiction in the United States, 33 purport to extend that jurisdiction to non-Indians. Twelve other Indian tribes have enacted ordinances which would permit the assumption of criminal jurisdiction over non-Indians. . . .

The effort by Indian tribal courts to exercise criminal jurisdiction over non-Indians, however, is a relatively new phenomenon. And where the effort has been made in the past, it has been held that the jurisdiction did not exist. Until the middle of this century, few Indian tribes maintained any semblance of a formal court system. Offenses by one Indian against another were usually handled by social and religious pressure and not by formal judicial processes; emphasis was on restitution rather than on punishment. . . .

It is therefore not surprising to find no specific discussion of the problem before us in . . . [prior Supreme Court decisions]. But the problem did not lie entirely dormant for two centuries. A few tribes during the 19th century did have formal criminal systems. From the earliest treaties with these tribes, it was apparently assumed that the tribes did not have criminal jurisdiction over non-Indians absent a congressional statute or treaty provision to that effect. For example, the 1830 Treaty with the Choctaw Indian Tribe, which had one of the most sophisticated of tribal structures, guaranteed to the Tribe "the jurisdiction and government of all the persons and property that may be within their limits." [Choctaw-U.S. Treaty 1830, art. IV] Despite the broad terms of this governmental guarantee, however, the Choctaws at the conclusion of this [article of the 1830] [T]reaty . . . "express a wish that Congress may grant to the Choctaws the right of punishing by their own laws any white man who shall come into their nation, and infringe any of their national regulations." [Fn. 8] Such a request for affirmative congressional authority is inconsistent with . . . [a] belief that criminal jurisdiction over non-Indians is inherent in tribal sovereignty. Faced by attempts of the Choctaw Tribe to try non-Indian offenders in the early 1800s the United States Attorneys General also concluded that the Choctaws did not have criminal jurisdiction over non-Indians absent congressional authority. According to the Attorney General in 1834, tribal criminal jurisdiction over non-Indians . . . [was] inconsistent with treaty provisions recognizing the sovereignty of the United States over the territory assigned to the Indian nation and the dependence of the Indians on the United States.

[Footnote 8: The history of Indian treaties in the United States is consistent with the principle that Indian tribes may not assume criminal jurisdiction over non-Indians without the permission of Congress. The earliest treaties typically expressly provided that "any citizen of the United States, who shall do an injury to any Indian of the [tribal] nation, or to any other Indian or Indians residing in their towns, and under their protection, shall be punished according to the laws of the United States." While, as elaborated further below, these provisions were not necessary to remove criminal jurisdiction over non-Indians from the Indian tribes, they would naturally have served an important function in the developing stage of United States–Indian relations by clarifying jurisdictional limits of the Indian tribes. The same treaties generally provided that "[i]f any citizen of the United States . . . shall attempt to settle on any of the lands hereby allotted to the Indians to live and hunt on, such person shall forfeit the protection of the United States of America, and the Indians may punish him or not as they please." Far from representing a recognition of any inherent Indian criminal jurisdiction over non-Indians settling on tribal lands, these provisions were instead intended as a means of discouraging non-Indian settlements on Indian territory, in contravention of treaty provisions to the contrary. Later treaties dropped this provision and provided instead that non-Indian settlers would be removed by the United States upon complaint being lodged by the tribe.

As the relationship between Indian tribes and the United States developed through the passage of time, specific provisions for the punishment of non-Indians by the United States, rather than by the tribes, slowly disappeared from the treaties. Thus, for example, none of the treaties signed by Washington Indians in the 1850s explicitly proscribed criminal prosecution and punishment of non-Indians by the Indian tribes. . . .

Only one treaty signed by the United States has ever provided for any form of tribal criminal jurisdiction over non-Indians (other than in the illegal-settler context noted above). The first treaty signed by the United States with an Indian tribe, the 1778 Treaty with the Delawares, provided that neither party to the treaty could "proceed to the infliction of punishments on the citizens of the other, otherwise than by securing the offender or offenders by imprisonment, or any other competent means, till a fair and impartial trial can be had by judges or juries of both parties, as near as can be to the laws, customs and usages of the contracting parties and natural justice: The mode of such trials to be hereafter fixed by the wise men of the United States in Congress assembled, with the assistance of . . . deputies of the Delaware nation. . . ." [Delaware-U.S. Treaty 1778, 14, art. IV] While providing for Delaware participation in the trial of non-Indians, this treaty section established that non-Indians could only be tried under the auspices of the United States and in a manner fixed by the Continental Congress.]

At least one court has previously considered the power of Indian courts to try non-Indians and it also held against jurisdiction. In *Ex parte Kenyon* (1878), Judge Isaac C. Parker, who as District Court Judge for the Western District of Arkansas was constantly exposed to the legal relationships between Indians and non-Indians, held that to give an Indian tribal court "jurisdiction of the person of an offender, such offender must be an Indian" [*Kenyon* 1878: 355] The conclusion of Judge Parker was reaffirmed only recently in a 1970 opinion of the Solicitor of the Department of the Interior. [Footnote 11: The 1970 opinion of the Solicitor was withdrawn in 1974 but has not been replaced. No reason was given for the withdrawal.]

While Congress was concerned almost from its beginning with the special problems of law enforcement on the Indian reservations, it did not initially address itself to the problem of tribal jurisdiction over non-Indians. . . . [T]here was little reason to . . . because of the absence of formal tribal judicial systems. Instead, [the] concern [in the words of President George Washington's Seventh Annual Address to Congress] was with providing effective protection for the Indians "from the violences of the lawless part of our frontier inhabitants." . . . [T]herefore, Congress [in the Indian Country Crimes Act of 1790 provided for punishment of] . . . offenses by non-Indians against Indians which "would be punishable by the laws of [the] state or district . . . if the offense had been committed against a citizen or white inhabitant thereof." In 1817, Congress went one step further and extended . . . [this] law to [crimes by Indians committed in] the Indian country; the only exception [not subject to federal or state law] was for "any offense [in Indian country] committed by one Indian against another." [Indian Country Crimes Act, § 1152] . . .

This unspoken assumption [that Indian tribal courts were without jurisdiction to try non-Indians] was also evident in other congressional actions during the 19th century. In 1854, for example, Congress amended the [law] . . . to proscribe the prosecution in federal court of an Indian who has already been tried [for the same offense] in tribal court. [Indian Country Crimes Act, § 1152] No similar provision, such as would have been required by parallel logic if tribal courts had jurisdiction over non-Indians, was enacted barring retrial of non-Indians. . . .

In a 1960 Senate Report, that body expressly confirmed its assumption that Indian tribal courts are without inherent jurisdiction to try non-Indians, and must depend on the Federal Government for protection from intruders. [Fn. 15] . . .

[Footnote 15: In 1977, a congressional Policy Review Commission, citing the lower court decisio[n] in [this case], concluded that "[t]here is an established legal basis for tribes to exercise jurisdiction over non-Indians." However, the Commission's report does not deny that for almost 200 years . . . , the three branches of the Federal Government were in apparent agreement that Indian tribes do not have jurisdiction over non-Indians. As the Vice Chairman of the Commission, Congressman Lloyd Meeds, noted in dissent, "such jurisdiction has generally not been asserted and . . . the lack of legislation on this point reflects a congressional assumption that there was no such tribal jurisdiction."]

II

. . . [E]ven ignoring treaty provisions and congressional policy, Indians do not have criminal jurisdiction over non-Indians absent affirmative delegation of such power by Congress. Indian tribes do retain elements of "quasi-sovereign" authority after ceding their lands to the United States and announcing their dependence on the Federal Government. [*Cherokee Nation v. Georgia* 1831, 15] But the tribes' retained powers are not such that they are limited only by specific restrictions in treaties or congressional enactments. . . . Indian tribes are prohibited from exercising both those powers . . . that are expressly terminated by Congress and those powers "inconsistent with their status."

Indian reservations are "a part of the territory of the United States." . . . Upon incorporation into the territory of the United States, the Indian tribes thereby come under the territorial sovereignty of the United States and their exercise of separate power is constrained so as not to conflict with the interests of this overriding sovereignty. . . .

We have already described some of the inherent limitations on tribal powers that stem from their incorporation into the United States. In *Johnson v. M'Intosh* [1823, 574], we noted that the Indian tribes' "power to dispose of [their land] at their own will, to whomsoever they pleased," was inherently lost to the overriding sovereignty of the United States. And in *Cherokee Nation v. Georgia* [1831, 17–18], . . . Chief Justice [Marshall] observed that since Indian tribes are "completely under the sovereignty and dominion of the United States, . . . any attempt [by foreign nations] to acquire their lands, or to form a political connexion with them, would be considered by all as an invasion of our territory. . . ."

Nor are the intrinsic limitations on Indian tribal authority restricted to . . . [tribal] power to transfer lands or exercise external political sovereignty. . . . [F]rom the formation of the Union and the adoption of the Bill of Rights, the United States has manifested . . . great solicitude that its citizens be protected by the United States from unwarranted intrusions on their personal liberty. The power of the United States to try and criminally punish is an important manifestation of the power to restrict personal liberty. By submitting to the overriding sovereignty of the United States, Indian tribes therefore necessarily give up their power to try non-Indian citizens of the United States except in a manner acceptable to Congress. This principle would have been obvious a century ago when most Indian tribes were characterized by a "want of fixed laws [and] of competent tribunals of justice." It should be no less obvious today, even though present-day Indian tribal courts embody dramatic advances over their historical antecedents.

In *Ex parte Crow Dog [Kan-Gi-Shun-Ca]* (1883), the Court was faced with almost the inverse of the issue before us here—whether, prior to the passage of the Major Crimes Act [in 1885], federal courts had jurisdiction to try Indians who had offended against fellow Indians on reservation land. [We found] . . . that . . . jurisdiction [over those crimes] was exclusively in the tribe, . . . [and that] [t]he United States was seeking to [prosecute, without congressional authorization] . . . "the members of a community separated by race [and] tradition, . . . to impose upon them the restraints of an external and unknown code . . . which judges them by a standard made by others and not for them. . . . It tries them, not by their peers, nor by the customs of their people, nor the law of their land, but by . . . a different race, according to the law of a social state of which they have an imperfect conception. . . ." [*Kan-Gi-Shun-Ca* 1883, 571] These considerations, applied here to the non-Indian rather than Indian offender, speak equally strongly against the . . . contention that Indian tribes, although fully subordinated to the sovereignty of the United States, retain the power to try non-Indians according to their own customs and procedure.

As previously noted, Congress extended the jurisdiction of federal courts . . . to offenses committed by non-Indians against Indians within Indian Country. In doing so, Congress was careful to extend to the non-Indian offender the basic criminal rights that would attach in non-Indian related cases. Under [the Tribe's] theory, however, Indian tribes would have been free to try the same non-Indians without these careful proceedings unless Congress affirmatively legislated to the contrary. Such an exercise of jurisdiction over non-Indian citizens of the United States would belie the tribes' forfeiture of full sovereignty in return for the protection of the United States. "Indians are within the geographical limits of the United States. The soil and people within these limits are under the political control of the Government of the United States, or of the States of the Union. There exist in the broad domain of sovereignty but these two. There may be cities, counties, and other organized bodies with limited legislative functions, but they . . . exist in subordination to one or the other of these." [*United States v. Kagama* 1886, 379]

We recognize that some Indian tribal court systems have become increasingly sophisticated and resemble in many respects their state counterparts. We also acknowledge that with the passage of the Indian Civil Rights Act of 1968, which extends certain basic procedural rights to anyone tried in Indian tribal court, many of the dangers that might have accompanied the exercise by tribal courts of criminal jurisdiction over non-Indians only a few decades ago have disappeared. Finally, we are not unaware of the prevalence of non-Indian crime on today's reservations which the tribes forcefully argue requires the ability to try non-Indians. But these are considerations for Congress to weigh in deciding whether Indian tribes should finally be authorized to try non-Indians. They have little relevance to the principles which lead us to conclude that Indian tribes do not have inherent jurisdiction to try and to punish non-Indians. The judgments below are therefore reversed.

Justice Marshall (dissenting, joined by Chief Justice Burger):

I agree with the [C]ourt [of Appeals] below that the "power to preserve order on the reservation . . . is a sine qua non [i.e., an inherent or essential element or aspect] of the sovereignty that the Suquamish originally possessed." In the absence of affirmative withdrawal by treaty or statute, I am of the view that Indian tribes enjoy as a necessary aspect of their retained sovereignty the right to try and punish all persons who commit offenses against tribal law within the reservation. Accordingly, I dissent.

Duro v. Reina (1990)

U.S. Supreme Court
May 29, 1990
495 U.S. 676

The Court's opinion was written by Justice Anthony M. Kennedy, appointed by President Ronald W. Reagan in 1988. The decision was

7–2. Kennedy's opinion was joined by Chief Justice William H. Rehnquist, appointed as associate justice by President Richard M. Nixon in 1972 and as chief justice by President Reagan in 1986; Justice Byron R. White, appointed by President John F. Kennedy in 1962; Justice Harry A. Blackmun, appointed by President Nixon in 1970; Justice John Paul Stevens, appointed by President Gerald R. Ford in 1975; and Justices Sandra Day O'Connor and Antonin Scalia, appointed by President Reagan in 1981 and 1986, respectively. Justice William J. Brennan, Jr., appointed by President Dwight D. Eisenhower in 1956, wrote a dissenting opinion joined by Justice Thurgood Marshall, appointed by President Lyndon B. Johnson in 1967.

Justice Kennedy (for the Court):

We address in this case whether an Indian tribe may assert criminal jurisdiction over a defendant who is an Indian but not a tribal member. We hold that the retained sovereignty of the tribe as a political and social organization to govern its own affairs does not include the authority to impose criminal sanctions against a citizen outside its own membership.

I

The events giving rise to this . . . [case] occurred on the Salt River Indian Reservation . . . east of Scottsdale, Arizona, . . . home of the Salt River Pima–Maricopa Indian Community, a recognized Tribe with an enrolled membership. Petitioner in this case, Albert Duro, is an enrolled member of another Indian Tribe, the Torres-Martinez Band of Cahuilla Mission Indians. [Duro] is not eligible for membership in the Pima-Maricopa Tribe. As a nonmember, he is not entitled [under Pima-Maricopa tribal law] to vote in Pima-Maricopa elections, to hold tribal office, or to serve on tribal juries.

[Duro] has lived most of his life in . . . California, outside any Indian reservation. Between March and June 1984, he resided on the Salt River Reservation with a Pima-Maricopa woman friend. He worked for the PiCopa Construction Company, which is owned by the Tribe. On June 15, 1984, [he] allegedly shot and killed a 14-year-old boy within the Salt River Reservation boundaries. The victim was a member of the Gila River Indian Tribe of Arizona, a separate Tribe that occupies a separate reservation. A complaint was filed in United States District Court charging [Duro] with murder . . . [under the Major Crimes Act of 1885,] . . . but the federal indictment was later dismissed without prejudice on the motion of the United States Attorney.

[Duro] then was placed in the custody of Pima-Maricopa officers, and he was taken to stand trial in the Pima-Maricopa Indian Community Court. The tribal court's powers are regulated by [the Indian Civil Rights Act of 1968], which [in 1984] limited tribal criminal penalties to six months' imprisonment and a $500 fine [the limit was raised in 1986 to one year's imprisonment and a $5,000 fine]. [Indian Civil Rights Act, § 1302] The tribal criminal code is therefore confined to misdemeanors. [Duro] was charged with the illegal firing of a weapon on the reservation. After the tribal court denied petitioner's motion to dismiss the prosecution for lack of jurisdiction, he filed a petition for [a writ of] habeas corpus in the United States District Court. . . .

II

Our decisions in [*Oliphant v. Suquamish Indian Tribe* 1978] and [*United States v. Wheeler* 1978] provide the analytic framework for resolution of this dispute. *Oliphant* established that the inherent sovereignty of the Indian tribes does not extend to criminal jurisdiction over non-Indians who commit crimes on the reservation. *Wheeler* reaffirmed the longstanding recognition of tribal jurisdiction over crimes committed by tribe members. The case before us is at the intersection of these two precedents, for here the defendant is an Indian, but not a member of the Tribe that asserts jurisdiction. As in *Oliphant,* the trib[e] do[es] not claim jurisdiction under an affirmative congressional authorization or treaty provision, and [Duro] does not contend that Congress has legislated to remove jurisdiction from the tribes. The question we must answer is whether the sovereignty retained by the tribes in their dependent status within our scheme of government includes the power of criminal jurisdiction over nonmembe[r] [Indians].

. . . [T]he rationale of our decisions in *Oliphant* and *Wheeler,* as well as subsequent cases, compels the conclusion that Indian tribes lack jurisdiction over persons who are not tribe members. . . .

A basic attribute of full territorial sovereignty is the power to enforce laws against all who come within the sovereign's territory, whether citizens or aliens. *Oliphant* recognized that the tribes can no longer be described as sovereigns in this sense. Rather, as . . . *Wheeler* reveals, the retained sovereignty of the tribes is that needed to control their own internal relations, and to preserve their own unique customs and social order. . . ." . . . The areas in which . . . implicit divestiture of [tribal] sovereignty has . . . occurred are those involving the relations between an Indian tribe and nonmembers of the tribe." [*Wheeler* 1978, 326] . . .

It is true that our decisions recognize broader retained tribal powers outside the criminal context. Tribal courts, for example, resolve civil disputes involving nonmembers, including non-Indians. [*Williams v. Lee* 1959] Civil authority may also be present in areas such as zoning where the exercise of tribal authority is vital to the maintenance of tribal integrity and self-determination. [*Brendale v. Yakima Indian Nation* 1989] As distinct from criminal prosecution, this civil authority typically involves situations arising from property ownership within the reservation or "consensual relationships with the tribe or its members, through commercial dealing, contracts, leases, or other arrangements." [*Montana v. United States* 1981, 565] The exercise of criminal jurisdiction subjects a person not only to the adjudicatory power of the tribunal, but also to the prosecuting power of the tribe, and involves a far more direct intrusion on personal liberties.

. . . In the area of criminal enforcement, however, tribal power does not extend beyond internal relations among members. . . . For purposes of criminal jurisdiction, [Duro's] relations with th[e] [Pima Maricopa] Tribe are the same as the non-Indian's in *Oliphant.* We hold that the Tribe's powers over him are subject to the same limitations.

III

[The Tribe] . . . argue[s] that a review of history requires the assertion of jurisdiction here. We disagree. The historical record in this case is somewhat less illuminating than in *Oliphant,* but tends to support the conclusion we reach. [As noted in *Oliphant,*] [e]arly evidence concerning tribal jurisdiction over nonmembers is lacking. . . .

[The Tribe] rel[ies] for [its] historical argument upon evidence that definitions of "Indian" in federal statutes and programs apply to all Indians without respect to membership in a particular tribe. . . . [But] [t]his evidence . . . [merely] reflect[s] the Government's treatment of Indians as a single large class with respect to federal jurisdiction and programs. . . . [It is] not dispositive of [the] question of tribal power. . . .

IV

Whatever might be said of the historical record, we must view it in light of [Duro's] status as a citizen of the United States. Many Indians became citizens during the era of allotment and tribal termination around the turn of the [twentieth] century, and all were made citizens in 1924. . . .

Criminal trial and punishment is so serious an intrusion on personal liberty that its exercise over non-Indian citizens was a power necessarily surrendered by the tribes in their submission to the overriding sovereignty of the United States. We hesitate to adopt a view of tribal sovereignty that would single out another group of citizens, nonmember Indians, for trial by political bodies that do not include them. As full citizens, Indians share in the territorial and political sovereignty of the United States. The retained sovereignty of the tribe is but a recognition of certain additional authority the tribes maintain over Indians who consent to be tribal members. Indians like all other citizens share allegiance to the overriding sovereign, the United States. A tribe's additional authority [under its retained sovereignty] comes from the consent of its members, and so in the criminal sphere membership marks the bounds of tribal authority.

The special nature of the tribunals at issue makes a focus on consent and the protections of citizenship most appropriate. While modern tribal courts include many familiar features of the judicial process, they are influenced by the unique customs, languages, and usages of the tribes they serve. Tribal courts are often "subordinate to the political branches of tribal governments," and their legal methods may depend on "unspoken practices and norms." It is significant that the Bill of Rights does not apply to Indian tribal governments. [*Talton v. Mayes* 1896] The Indian Civil Rights Act of 1968 provides some statutory guarantees of fair procedure, but these guarantees are not equivalent to their constitutional counterparts. There is, for example, no right under the Act to appointed counsel for those unable to afford a lawyer. [Indian Civil Rights Act, § 1302(6)]

Our cases suggest constitutional limitations even on the ability of Congress to subject American citizens to criminal proceedings before a tribunal that does not provide constitutional protections as a matter of right. We have approved delegation to an Indian tribe of the authority to promulgate rules that may be enforced by criminal sanction in federal court [*United States v. Mazurie* 1975], but no delegation of authority to a tribe has to date included the power to punish nonmembers in tribal court. We decline to produce such a result through recognition of inherent tribal authority.

Tribal authority over members, who are also citizens, is not subject to these objections. Retained criminal jurisdiction over members is accepted by our precedents and justified by the voluntary character of tribal membership and the concomitant right of participation in a tribal government, the authority of which rests on consent. This principle finds support in our [older] cases. . . . We held in . . . [1846] that a non-

Indian could not, through his adoption into the Cherokee Tribe, bring himself within the federal definition of "Indian" for purposes of an exemption to a federal jurisdictional provision. But we recognized that a non-Indian could, by adoption, "become entitled to certain privileges in the tribe, and make himself amenable to their laws and usages." [*United States v. Rogers* 1846, 573; *Nofire v. United States* 1897]

With respect to such internal laws and usages, the tribes are left with broad freedom not enjoyed by any other governmental authority in this country. [*Santa Clara Pueblo v. Martinez* 1978] This is all the more reason to reject an extension of tribal authority over those who have not given the consent of the governed that provides a fundamental basis for power within our constitutional system. . . .

The Court of Appeals [in this case] sought to address some of these concerns by adopting a "contacts" test to determine which nonmember Indians might be subject to tribal jurisdiction. But the rationale of the test would apply to non-Indians on the reservation as readily as to Indian nonmembers. Many non-Indians reside on reservations, and have close ties to tribes through marriage or long employment. Indeed, the population of non-Indians on reservations generally is greater than the population of all Indians, both members and nonmembers, and non-Indians make up some 35% of the Salt River Reservation population. The contacts approach is little more than a variation of the argument that any person who enters an Indian community should be deemed to have given implied consent to tribal criminal jurisdiction over him. We have rejected this approach for non-Indians. It is a logical consequence . . . that nonmembe[r] [Indians], who share relevant jurisdictional characteristics of non-Indians, should share the same jurisdictional status.

V

[The Tribe] . . . contend[s] that without tribal jurisdiction over minor offenses committed by nonmember Indians, no authority will have jurisdiction over such offenders[,] . . . the tribes will lack important power to preserve order on the reservation, and nonmember Indians will be able to violate the law with impunity. Although the jurisdiction at stake here is over relatively minor crimes, we recognize that protection of the community from disturbances of the peace and other misdemeanors is a most serious matter. But this same interest in tribal law enforcement is applicable to non-Indian reservation residents, whose numbers are often greater. It was argued in *Oliphant* that the absence of tribal jurisdiction over non-Indians would leave a practical, if not legal, void in reservation law enforcement. The argument that only tribal jurisdiction could meet the need for effective law enforcement did not provide a basis for finding jurisdiction in *Oliphant;* neither is it sufficient here.

For felonies such as the murder alleged in this case . . . , federal jurisdiction is in place under the . . . Major Crimes Act. The tribes also possess their traditional and undisputed power to exclude persons whom they deem to be undesirable from tribal lands. [*Worcester v. Georgia* 1832, 561; *Brendale v. Yakima Indian Nation* 1989, 422] Tribal law enforcement authorities have the power to restrain those who disturb public order on the reservation, and if necessary, to eject them. Where jurisdiction to try and punish an offender rests outside the tribe, tribal officers may exercise their power to detain the offender and transport him to the proper authorities.

[The] major objection to this last point is that, in the circumstances presented here, there may not be any lawful authority to punish the nonmember Indian. State authorities may lack the power, resources, or inclination to deal with reservation crime. Arizona, for example, specifically disclaims jurisdiction over Indian country crimes. And federal authority over minor crime . . . may be lacking altogether in the case of crime committed by a nonmember Indian against another Indian, since . . . general federal jurisdiction over Indian country crime "shall not extend to offenses committed by one Indian against the person or property of another Indian." [Indian Country Crimes Act 1790, § 1152]

Our decision today does not imply endorsement of the theory of a jurisdictional void. . . . States may, with the consent of the tribes, assist in maintaining order on the reservation by punishing minor crime. Congress has provided a mechanism by which the States now without jurisdiction in Indian country may assume criminal jurisdiction. . . . [Public Law 280] Our decision here also does not address the ability of . . . tribal governments . . . to enter into reciprocal agreements giving each jurisdiction over the other's members. As to federal jurisdiction under [the Indian Country Crimes Act], both academic commentators and the dissenting [Court of Appeals] judge [in this case] . . . have suggested that the statute could be construed to cover the conduct here. Others have disagreed. That statute is not before us and we express no views on the question.

If the present jurisdictional scheme proves insufficient to meet the practical needs of reservation law enforcement, then the proper body to address the problem is Congress, which has the ultimate authority over Indian affairs. We cannot, however, accept these arguments of policy as a basis for finding tribal jurisdiction that is inconsistent with precedent, history, and the equal treatment of Native American citizens. . . .

Justice Brennan (dissenting, joined by Justice Marshall):

. . . [Indian] tribes did not "surrender [their] independence . . . [or] self-government, by associating with a stronger [power], and taking its protection." [*Worcester v. Georgia* 1832, 560–561] Tribes have retained . . . "the power to prescribe and enforce internal criminal laws." [*United States v. Wheeler* 1978, 326] I agree with the Court that "[a] basic attribute of full territorial sovereignty is the power to enforce laws against all who come within the sovereign's territory, whether citizens or aliens." I disagree with the Court that *Oliphant v. Suquamish Indian Tribe* (1978) "recognized that the tribes can no longer be described as sovereigns in this sense." In *Oliphant,* the Court held that tribes did not have the power to exercise criminal jurisdiction over non-Indians because such power was inconsistent with the overriding national interest. But it does not follow that because tribes lost their power to exercise criminal jurisdiction over non-Indians, they also lost their power to enforce criminal laws against Indians who are not members of their tribe.

. . . The Court today appears to read *Oliphant* as holding that the exercise of criminal jurisdiction over anyone but members of the tribe is inconsistent with the tribe's dependent status. But *Oliphant* established no such broad principle. Rather, . . . [it] was based on an analysis of Congress' actions with respect to non-Indians. . . .

In *Oliphant,* the Court relied on th[e] [federal] statutory background to conclude that the exercise of tribal jurisdiction over non-Indians was inconsistent with the tribes' dependent status, for from the early days Congress had provided for federal jurisdiction over crimes involving non-Indians. Thus, from these affirmative enactments, it could be inferred that the tribes were tacitly divested of jurisdiction over non-Indians. [*Oliphant,* 199–206] But applying the same reasoning, the opposite result obtains with respect to tribal jurisdiction over nonmember Indians. From the very start, Congress has consistently exempted Indian-against-Indian crimes from the reach of federal or state power. . . . The appropriate inference to be drawn . . . is that tribes retained power over those crimes involving only Indians.

. . . [T]he Court concludes that the federal definition of "Indian" is relevant only to federal jurisdiction and is "not dispositive of a question of tribal power." But this conclusion is at odds with the analysis in *Oliphant* in which the congressional enactments served as evidence of a "commonly shared presumption" that tribes had ceded their power over non-Indians. Similarly, these enactments reflect the congressional presumption that tribes had power over all disputes between Indians regardless of tribal membership.

By refusing to draw this inference from repeated congressional actions, the Court today creates a jurisdictional void in which neither federal nor tribal [nor state] jurisdiction exists over nonmember Indians who commit minor crimes against another Indian. The Court's conclusion that such a void does not counsel in favor of finding tribal jurisdiction misses the point. The existence of a jurisdictional gap is not an independent justification for finding tribal jurisdiction, but rather is relevant to determining congressional intent. The unlikelihood that Congress intended to create a jurisdictional void in which no sovereign has the power to prosecute an entire class of crimes should inform our understanding of the assumptions about tribal power upon which Congress legislated. . . .

The Court also concludes that because Indians are now citizens of the United States, the exercise of criminal jurisdiction over a nonmember of the tribe is inconsistent with the tribe's dependent status. . . . There are several problems with this argument. First, . . . [t]he touchstone in determining the extent to which citizens can be subject to the jurisdiction of Indian tribes . . . is whether such jurisdiction is acceptable to Congress. In *Oliphant,* federal statutes made clear that the prosecution of non-Indians in tribal courts is not acceptable to Congress. By contrast, the same statutes reflect the view that the prosecution of all Indians in tribal courts is acceptable to Congress.

Moreover, this argument proves too much. If tribes were implicitly divested of their power to enforce criminal laws over nonmember Indians once those Indians became citizens, the tribes were also implicitly divested of their power to enforce criminal laws over their own members who are now citizens as well. The Court contends, however, that tribal members are subject to tribal jurisdiction because of "the voluntary character of tribal membership and the concomitant right of participation in a tribal government." But we have not required consent to tribal jurisdiction or participation in tribal government as a prerequisite to the exercise of civil jurisdiction by a tribe [*Williams v. Lee* 1959, 223], and the Court does not explain why such a prerequisite is uniquely salient in the criminal context. Nor have we ever held that participation in the political process is a prerequisite to the exercise of criminal jurisdiction by a sovereign. If such were the case, a State could not prosecute nonresidents, and this country could not prosecute aliens who violate our laws. The commission of a crime on the reservation is all the "consent" that is necessary to allow the tribe to exercise criminal jurisdiction over the nonmember Indian. . . .

More understandable is the Court's concern that nonmembers may suffer discrimination in tribal courts because such courts are "influenced by the unique customs, languages, and usages of the tribes they serve." But Congress addressed this problem when it passed the [Indian Civil Rights Act of 1968 (ICRA)], which extended most of the Bill of Rights to any person tried by a tribal court. In addition, the ICRA provides the remedy of habeas corpus to challenge the legality of any detention order by a tribe. [ICRA, § 1303] The equal protection provision [of ICRA] requires that nonmembers not be subject to discriminatory treatment in the tribal courts. [Fn. 6] In addition, the due process [provision] ensures that each individual is tried in a fundamentally fair proceeding. [ICRA, § 1302] . . .

[Footnote 6: [Duro] argues that the exercise of jurisdiction over a nonmember violates the equal protection provision of the ICRA, because the Tribe does not exercise jurisdiction over non-Indians. This argument is without merit. The statutory equal protection provision requires the Tribe to refrain from denying "to any person within its jurisdiction the equal protection of its laws." [ICRA, § 1302] Thus, [Duro's] argument simply begs the question of who is within the Tribe's jurisdiction. If nonmember Indians are subject to the criminal jurisdiction of the Tribe, the exercise of jurisdiction in this case does not violate . . . equal protection. . . . [Duro] would state a valid equal protection claim, however, if he could show that in the exercise of its jurisdiction, the Tribe treated him differently than others who are also subject to its jurisdiction.]

This country has pursued contradictory policies with respect to the Indians. Since the passage of the Indian Reorganization Act of 1934, however, Congress has followed a policy of promoting the independence and self-government of the various tribes. The Court's decision today not only ignores the assumptions on which Congress originally legislated with respect to the jurisdiction over Indian crimes, but also stands in direct conflict with current congressional policy. . . .

Treaty of Fort Sumner between the United States and the Navajo Nation (1868)

June 1, 1868
15 Stat. 667; Kappler 1904, 1015

Articles of a treaty and agreement made and entered into . . . by and between the United States, represented by its commissioners . . . , and the Navajo Nation or tribe of Indians, represented by their chiefs and head-men. . . .

ARTICLE 1

From this day forward all war between the parties to this agreement shall forever cease. The Government of the United States desires peace, and its honor is hereby pledged to keep it. The Indians desire peace, and they now pledge their honor to keep it.

If bad men among the whites, or among other people subject to the authority of the United States, shall commit any wrong upon the person or property of the Indians, the United States will, upon proof made to the agent [see Articles 3 and 4] and forwarded to the Commissioner of Indian Affairs . . . , proceed at once to cause the offender to be arrested and punished according to the laws of the United States, and also to reimburse the injured persons for the loss sustained.

If the bad men among the Indians shall commit a wrong or depredation upon the person or property of any one, white, black, or Indian, subject to the authority of the United States and at peace therewith, the Navajo tribe agree that they will, on proof made to their agent, and on notice by him, deliver up the wrongdoer to the United States, to be tried and punished according to its laws; and in case they willfully refuse so to do, the person injured shall be reimbursed for his loss from the annuities or other moneys [*sic*] due or to become due to them under this treaty, or any others that may be made with the United States. And the President may prescribe such rules and regulations for ascertaining damages under this article as in his judgment may be proper; but no such damage shall be adjusted and paid until examined and passed upon by the Commissioner of Indian Affairs, and no one sustaining loss whilst violating, or because of his violating, the provisions of this treaty or the laws of the United States, shall be reimbursed therefor.

ARTICLE 2

The United States agrees that [a] . . . district of country [defined in this Article], . . . provided it embraces the outlet of the Canon-de-Chilly [*sic*], which canon is to be all included in this reservation, shall be, and the same is hereby, set apart for the use and occupation of the Navajo tribe of Indians, and for such other friendly tribes or individual Indians as from time to time they may be willing, with the consent of the United States, to admit among them; and the United States agrees that no persons except those herein so authorized to do, and except such officers, soldiers, agents, and employees of the Government, or of the Indians, as may be authorized to enter upon Indian reservations in discharge of duties imposed by law, or the orders of the President, shall ever be permitted to pass over, settle upon, or reside in, the territory described in this article.

ARTICLE 3

The United States agrees to cause to be built, at some point within said reservation, where timber and water may be convenient, the following buildings: a warehouse . . . ; an agency building for the residence of the agent . . . ; a carpenter-shop and blacksmith-shop . . . ; and a schoolhouse and chapel, so soon as a sufficient number of children can be induced to attend school. . . .

ARTICLE 4

The United States agrees that the agent for the Navajos shall make his home at the agency building; that he shall reside among them, and shall keep an office open at all times for the purpose of prompt and diligent inquiry into such matters of complaint by or against the Indians as may be presented for investigation. . . .

ARTICLE 5

If any individual belonging to said tribe . . . shall desire to commence farming, he shall have the privilege to select . . . a tract of land within said reservation. . . .

ARTICLE 6

In order to insure the civilization of the Indians entering into this treaty, . . . they therefore pledge themselves to compel their children, male and female, between the ages of six and sixteen years, to attend school. . . .

ARTICLE 7

When the head of a family shall have selected lands . . . as above directed, and the agent shall be satisfied that he intends in good faith to commence cultivating the soil for a living, he shall be entitled to receive seeds and agricultural implements. . . .

ARTICLE 8

In lieu of all sums of money . . . provided . . . under any treaty . . . heretofore made, the United States agrees to deliver at the agency-house . . . , on the first day of September of each year for ten years, the following articles[:] . . . [C]lothing, goods, or raw materials . . . not exceeding in value five dollars per Indian—each Indian being encouraged to manufacture their own clothing, blankets, *&c.;* to be furnished with no article which they can manufacture themselves. . . . And . . . the sum of ten dollars . . . shall be annually appropriated for . . . ten years, for each person who engages in farming or mechanical pursuits. . . .

ARTICLE 9

In consideration of the advantages and benefits conferred by this treaty, and the many pledges of friendship by the United States, the [Navajos] . . . stipulate that they will relinquish all right to occupy any territory outside their reservation, as herein defined, but retain the right to hunt on any unoccupied lands contiguous to their reservation, so long as the large game may range thereon in such numbers as to justify the chase; and they . . . further expressly agree:

1st. That they will make no opposition to the construction of railroads now being built or hereafter to be built across the continent.

2d. That they will not interfere with the peaceful construction of any railroad not passing over their reservation as herein defined.

3d. That they will not attack any persons at home or travelling, nor molest or disturb any wagon-trains, coaches, mules, or cattle belonging to the people of the United States, or to persons friendly therewith.

4th. That they will never capture or carry off from the settlements women or children.

5th. They will never kill or scalp white men, nor attempt to do them harm.

6th. They will not in future oppose the construction of railroads, wagon-roads, mail stations, or other works of utility or necessity which may be ordered or permitted by the laws of the United States; but should such roads or other works be constructed on the lands of their reservation, the Government will pay the tribe whatever amount of damage may be assessed by three disinterested commissioners to be appointed by the President for that purpose, one of said commissioners to be a chief or head-man of the tribe.

7th. They will make no opposition to the military posts or roads now established, or that may be established, not in violation of treaties heretofore made or hereafter to be made with any of the Indian tribes.

ARTICLE 10

No future treaty for the cession of any portion or part of the reservation herein described, which may be held in common, shall be of any validity or force against said Indians unless agreed to and executed by at least three-fourths of all the adult male Indians occupying or interested in the same; and no cession by the tribe shall be understood or construed in such manner as to deprive, without his consent, any individual member of the tribe of his rights to any tract of land selected by him as provided in article 5 of this treaty.

ARTICLE 11

The Navajos . . . agree that at any time after the signing of [this treaty] they will proceed in such manner as may be required of them by the agent, or by the officer charged with their removal, to the reservation herein provided for, the United States paying for their subsistence en route, and providing a reasonable amount of transportation for the sick and feeble.

ARTICLE 12

It is further agreed . . . that the sum of one hundred and fifty thousand dollars . . . shall be disbursed as follows . . . :

1st. The actual cost of the removal of the tribe from the Bosque Redondo reservation to the [treaty] reservation, say fifty thousand dollars.

2d. The purchase of fifteen thousand sheep and goats, at a cost not to exceed thirty thousand dollars.

3d. The purchase of five hundred beef cattle and a million pounds of corn, to be collected and held at the military post nearest the reservation, subject to the orders of the agent, for the relief of the needy during the coming winter. . . .

ARTICLE 13

The [Navajos] . . . agree to make the reservation herein described their permanent home, and they will not as a tribe make any permanent settlement elsewhere . . . ; and it is further agreed and understood by the parties to this treaty, that if any Navajo Indian or Indians shall leave the reservation . . . to settle elsewhere, he or they shall forfeit all the rights, privileges, and annuities conferred by the terms of this treaty; and it is further agreed by the parties to this treaty, that they will do all they can to induce Indians now away from reservations set apart for the exclusive use and occupation of the Indians, leading a nomadic life, or engaged in war against the people of the United States, to abandon such a life and settle permanently in one of the . . . reservations. . . .

In testimony of all which the said parties have hereunto, on this the first day of June, one thousand eight hundred and sixty-eight, at Fort Sumner, in the Territory of New Mexico, set their hands and seals.

Means v. Chinle District Court (1999)

Navajo Nation Supreme Court
May 11, 1999
7 Nav. Rep. 382; see also http://www.law.harvard.edu/news/courtrules.html

Navajo Nation judges are appointed by the Navajo Nation Council, the tribe's highest legislative body. The Navajo Nation Supreme Court's unanimous opinion in Means *was written by Chief Justice Robert Yazzie, appointed to the Court in 1992, and was joined by Justice Raymond D. Austin, appointed to the Court in 1985, and Justice Irene M. Toledo (sitting by designation), appointed to the Navajo Nation trial court bench in 1989.*

Chief Justice Yazzie (for the Court):

This is an original action for a writ of prohibition . . . to prevent or remedy an act of the Chinle District Court which is allegedly beyond that court's jurisdiction, namely denying Russell Means' . . . motion to dismiss criminal charges against him. Judge Ray Gilmore denied the . . . motion . . . on July 20, 1998. [Means] then sought a writ of prohibition from this Court.

[Means] alleges that the Navajo Nation lacks criminal jurisdiction over [him, as] a member of the Oglala Sioux Nation. Alternatively, [he] requests this Court to prohibit the Chinle District Court from exercising criminal jurisdiction, because a prosecution would violate the equal protection provisions of the 1968 Indian Civil Rights Act, the Navajo Nation Bill of Rights . . . , and the fifth amendment of the United States Constitution. [Means] . . . also broadly asserts that the

Navajo Nation has no criminal jurisdiction over non-Navajo Indians under the Treaty of June 1, 1868 between the United States of America and the Navajo Nation; that [he] has not consented to criminal jurisdiction by virtue of his marriage to a Navajo and residence within the Navajo Nation; and that [the Indian Civil Rights Act,] as amended to recognize Indian nation criminal jurisdiction over nonmember Indians [*Duro* Fix Act, § 1301(2)], is not permissible "preference legislation," but instead . . . violates equal protection of the law. The nub of the equal protection challenge is that while the Navajo Nation "cannot" prosecute non-Indians, the Nation is trying to prosecute [Means] as a nonmember Indian.

. . . [W]e will decide the following questions: [Fn. 3]

1. Does the June 1, 1868 Treaty between the United States of America and the Navajo Nation recognize Navajo Nation criminal jurisdiction over individuals who are not members of the Navajo Nation or Tribe of Indians?

2. Has [Means] consented to the criminal jurisdiction of the Navajo Nation by virtue of his assumption of tribal relations with Navajos?

3. Does the assertion of criminal jurisdiction over [Means] violate equal protection of the law, and is the assertion of such jurisdiction a "political" or a "racial" classification?

[Footnote 3: [Means] invites us to declare that an Act of Congress [the *Duro* Fix Act] is unconstitutional under the fifth amendment to the United States Constitution (equal protection doctrine). While this Court has the authority [under the Navajo Nation Code] to use all "applicable" laws of the United States . . . , and the . . . Constitution is an "applicable" law, we defer to the federal judiciary on the issue of the constitutionality of [the *Duro* Fix Act]. We need not reach the issue . . . to make our decision.]

I.A

The Navajo Nation is the largest Indian nation in the United States in terms of geographic size. It has . . . approximately 25,000 square miles [larger than ten states]. . . . The Navajo Nation membership is the second largest of all Indian nations within the United States, with a total [including those living off the reservation] . . . of 225,298 . . . as of 1990. The 1990 population of the Navajo [reservation] was 145,853 persons of "all races," with 140,749 American Indians, Eskimos and Aleuts, and 5,104 individuals of "other races." Of that population, 96.62% was Indian and 3.38% was "non-American Indian." Of the American Indian population, 131,422 individuals were Navajos and

9,327 were "other Indians." Therefore, the percentage of nonmember Indians [on] the Navajo [reservation] . . . was 6.39%. There were 126 Sioux Indians residing within the Navajo Nation as of 1990.

The Navajo Nation courts had 27,602 criminal cases during Navajo Nation Fiscal Year 1998. . . . The five major categories of offenses were 6,128 driving while intoxicated . . . (22.20% . . .), 6,090 crimes against persons (22.06%), 2,284 offenses against the family (8.27%), 2,208 intoxicating liquor offenses (possession or sale) (7.99%), and 2,167 offenses against the public order (7.85%). The largest single category of civil cases was petitions for domestic abuse protection orders, and there were 3,435 such cases, during the fiscal year.

. . . In sum, the Navajo Nation courts are addressing the serious criminal and social problems of drunk driving, assaults and batteries (including aggravated assault and battery with deadly weapons), sex offenses against children, disorderly conduct, and public intoxication. [Footnote 7: This is a serious matter, because of [intoxicated] people freezing to death in ditches or wandering into traffic.] Many of the crimes against persons are acts of in-family violence, and the civil domestic abuse restraining order numbers show that family violence may be the most serious social problem in the Navajo Nation. [Footnote 8: A survey of Navajos . . . [in 1993–1995] showed that 28.6% of Navajo women age 50 and older and 52.7% of Navajo women under age 50 reported being struck at least once. . . .]

Given the United States Indian education policy of sending Indian children to boarding schools, Indians in the armed services, modern population mobility, and other factors, there are high rates of intertribal intermarriage among American Indians. As noted, at least 9,327 "other" or nonmember Indians resided within the Navajo Nation in 1990. They are involved in some of the 27,000 plus criminal charges in our system and in the 3,435 plus domestic violence cases. The questions are whether nonmember Indians should have de facto immunity from criminal prosecution, given the failure of federal officials to effectively address crime in the Navajo Nation, and whether this Court should rule that thousands of innocent victims, Navajo and non-Navajo, should be permitted to suffer. We must sadly take judicial notice of the fact that, with a few exceptions, non-Indians and nonmember Indians who commit crimes within the Navajo Nation escape punishment. . . .

Recent Justice Department statistics confirm the severity of the situation. As of 1996, Navajos constituted 11.7% of [all] American Indians. The [Department] made these summary findings about crime and American Indians:

American Indians experience per capita rates of violence which are more than twice those of the U.S. resident population.

Rates of violence in every age group are higher among American Indians than that of all races.

Nearly a third of all American Indian victims of violence are between ages 18 and 24. This group of American Indians experienced the highest per capita rate of violence of any racial group considered by age—about 1 violent crime for every 4 persons of this age.

Rates of violent victimization for both males and females are higher among American Indians than for all races. The rate of violent crime experienced by American Indian women is nearly 50% higher than that reported by black males.

At least 70% of the violent victimizations experienced by American Indians are committed by persons not of the same race—a substantially higher rate of interracial violence than experienced by white or black victims.

American Indian victims of violence were the most likely of all races of victims to indicate that the offender committed the offense while drinking.

The 1997 arrest rate among American Indians for alcohol-related offenses (driving under the influence, liquor law violations, and public drunkenness) was more than double that found among all races. Drug arrest rates for American Indians were lower than average.

These are unpleasant facts. However, they point to the need to exercise criminal jurisdiction over all who enter the Navajo Nation. Indian nation courts are at the front line of attempts to control crime and social disruption. They share a common responsibility with police, prosecutors, defenders, and social service programs to address crime and violence for the welfare of not only the Navajo People, but all those who live within the Navajo Nation or reside in areas adjacent to the Navajo Nation. [Footnote 10: State officials frequently complain of the spillover effects of Navajo Nation crime and urge the Nation to take more effective crime prevention actions. There are cooperative efforts to enhance that. . . .] Indian nations cannot rely upon others to address the[se] problems. . . . The Navajo Nation courts have primary jurisdiction to deal with criminal offenses and they must be free to exercise that jurisdiction.

B

[The following paragraph begins Part I, prior to Part I.A, in the original opinion:] On December 28, 1997, the Navajo Nation charged [Means] with three offenses [under the Navajo Nation Criminal Code]: threatening Leon Grant . . . ; committing a battery upon Mr. Grant . . . ; and committing a battery upon Jeremiah Bitsui. . . . Threatening has a maximum potential penalty of imprisonment for a term up to 90 days, a $250 fine, or both, and battery . . . up to 180 days, a $500 fine, or both. The Navajo Nation Criminal Code . . . provides . . . that a defendant found guilty of [multiple] offense[s] may receive . . . multiple sentence[s], with the sentence[s] to run concurrently or consecutively. The petitioner faces a maximum exposure of 450 days incarceration, a fine of $1,250, or both, along with the payment of restitution to the victims of the alleged offenses. . . .

[Means] is a member of the Oglala Sioux Nation. He was 58 years of age as of the date of the [1998 trial court] hearing [on whether to dismiss the charges], and he resided for ten years within the Navajo Nation from 1987 through 1997. He was married to Gloria Grant, an enrolled Navajo woman. Leon Grant, whom [Means] is charged with threatening and battering, is a member of the Omaha Tribe, and Jeremiah Bitsui, whom [Means] is charged with battering, is Navajo. . . . Mr. Grant was [Means's] father-in-law at the time of the incident. [Means] moved from the Navajo Nation to Porcupine, South Dakota within the Pine Ridge Reservation, in December of 1997.

[Means] complained of a lack of hospitality toward him when he resided within the Navajo Nation. He said he could not vote, run for Navajo Nation office (including judicial office), become a Navajo Nation Council delegate, the president, vice-president, or be a member of a farm board. In sum, he could not attain any Navajo Nation political position. He said he could not sit on a jury and received no notice to appear for jury duty. That may be because [he] was not on any Navajo Nation registration or voter list . . . [or] the voter registration list for Apache County, Arizona. He complained at length about his inability to get a job or start a business because of Navajo Nation employment and contracting preference laws.

[Means's] national reputation as an activist is well-known. . . . [After] a 1989 incident when Navajos were shot by Navajos, he led a march to the court house for a demonstration to make a "broad statement" about political activities of the Navajo Nation.

The "facts" [Means] related during his testimony are only partially correct. While it is true that there are preference laws for employment and contracting in the Navajo Nation, they are not an absolute barrier to either employment or the ability to do business. There are many non-Navajo employees of the Navajo Nation (some of whom hold high positions in Navajo Nation government), and non-Navajo businesses operate within the Navajo Nation. The ability to work or do business within the Navajo Nation has a great deal more to do with individual initiative and talent than preference laws. [Means] was most likely not called for jury duty because he did not register to vote in Arizona. Non-Navajos have been called for jury duty since at least 1979. . . . [Footnote 11: . . . Although such is not required by the Indian Civil Rights Act of 1968, criminal defendants in the Navajo Nation court system are entitled to the appointment of counsel if they are indigent, and they are entitled to a jury composed of a fair cross-section of Navajo Nation population, including non-Indians and nonmember Indians. [Means] has all the rights he would have in a state or federal court.]

II

The first issue is whether the June 1, 1868 Treaty between the United States of America and the Navajo Nation gives the Navajo Nation courts criminal jurisdiction over individuals who are not members of the Navajo Nation. . . . We will first discuss the 1868 Treaty as a source of criminal jurisdiction and then apply it.

A

There is a general and false assumption that Indian nations have *no* criminal jurisdiction over non-Indians and nonmember Indians. While the . . . Supreme Court ruled that Indian nations have no inherent criminal jurisdiction over non-Indians in *Oliphant v. Suquamish Indian Tribe* (1978), and that there is no inherent criminal jurisdiction over nonmember Indians in *Duro v. Reina* (1990), criminal jurisdiction over nonmembers can rest upon a treaty or federal statute. The Supreme Court reserved the issues of affirmative congressional authorization or treaty provisions in both cases. [*Oliphant* 1978, 195–197; *Duro* 1990, 684] Therefore, we will examine whether the Navajo Nation Treaty of 1868 is a source of Navajo Nation criminal jurisdiction over nonmember Indians.

The basic canons of treaty construction are:

1. A treaty must be construed as the Indians understood it. [*United States v. Winans* 1905, 380–381] [Footnote 12: We understand this canon to mean that we have the authority to interpret the treaty as

Navajos understand it today. That includes the knowledge passed on to us by our ancestors through oral traditions.]

2. Doubtful or ambiguous expressions in a treaty must be resolved in favor of the given Indian nation. [*Minnesota v. Mille Lacs Band of Chippewa Indians* 1999, 200; *Oliphant v. Suquamish Indian Tribe* 1978, 208, fn. 17; *Winters v. United States* 1908, 576–77]

3. Treaty provisions which are not clear on their face may be interpreted from the surrounding circumstances and history. [*Mille Lacs* 1999, 195–200; *Oliphant* 1978, 208]

4. A treaty is not a grant of rights to Indian nations but a grant of rights from them, with reservations of all rights which are not granted. [*Washington v. Washington State Commercial Passenger Fishing Vessel Association* 1979, 680; *Winans* 1905, 381]

5. Treaties with Indian nations are the law of the land under the treaty clause of the Constitution. [*Worcester v. Georgia* 1832, 558]

B

The Treaty between the Navajo Nation . . . and the United States was negotiated at Fort Sumner, New Mexico Territory, on May 28, 29, and 30, 1868, and it was executed there on June 1, 1868. The United States Senate . . . ratifi[ed it] . . . on July 25, 1868, and President Andrew Johnson proclaimed it on August 12, 1868. We are primarily interested in language found in Article II of the Treaty, which we will call the "set apart for the use and occupation clause," and that in Article I, which we will call the "bad men" clause.

Article II . . . begins with a boundary description and then says that "this reservation" is "set apart for the use and occupation of the Navajo tribe of Indians, and for such other friendly tribes or individual Indians as from time to time they may be willing, with the consent of the United States, to admit among them. . . ." Federal courts use this language as the basis for Navajo Nation civil jurisdiction. [*Williams v. Lee* 1959, 221–23] The Supreme Court held that the Navajo Nation retained its inherent criminal jurisdiction over members in *United States v. Wheeler* [1978, 323].

The plain language of Article II indicates that the Navajo Reservation exists for the exclusive use of not only Navajos, but other Indians, either as tribes or as individuals, where both the Navajo Nation and the United States agree to their admission. Given that the jurisdiction of our courts is recognized in the Article II language, Indians such as [Means] who are permitted to reside within the Navajo Nation fall within the same grouping as Navajo Indians in terms of the Treaty's coverage.

We see this provision applied in the historical record. [In September 1881], . . . Galen Eastman [U.S. agent on the Navajo Reservation] wrote to the Commissioner of Indian Affairs to inform him that about forty Pah-Utes (Paiutes) had arrived in a starving condition and were begging for food. They said "they were going to cease their predatory life and use the hoe thereafter." The Navajo reply was that "if the Great Father is willing, we will try you again and be responsible for your good behavior for we used to be friends and have intermarried with your people and yours with ours . . . but if you return to your bad life, thieving and murdering we (the Navajos) will hang you." Obviously, thinking of the language in Article II of the Treaty, Eastman asked for instructions.

The "bad men" among either "the Indians" or "Whites" language has been litigated in various contexts, but the closest interpretation on the issue of criminal jurisdiction was in the [Ninth Circuit U.S. Court of Appeals] case of *[Arizona] ex rel. Merrill v. Turtle* (1969). There, the State of Arizona arrested a Cheyenne Indian within the Navajo Nation using the "bad men among the Indians" Treaty language as its justification, and the court ruled that the arrest of an Indian had to follow the extradition provision in the "bad men" clause. [*Turtle* 1969, 686] The "bad men" clause has [also] been used [by the Ninth Circuit] as the basis for concurrent civil jurisdiction in the Navajo Nation courts. [*Babbitt Ford, Inc. v. Navajo Indian Tribe* 1983]

Using surrounding circumstances, history, and the "as the Indians understood it" canon of treaty construction, the issue of how to deal with "bad" Indians was the subject of specific discussions at Fort Sumner. Barboncito, the primary Navajo treaty negotiator, gave an opening speech where he outlined the hardships suffered by Navajos at the adjoining Bosque Redondo "reservation." He complained: "I think that all nations around here are against us (I mean Mexicans and Indians) the reason is that we are a working tribe of Indians, and if we had the means we could support ourselves far better than either Mexican or Indian. The Comanches are against us I know it for they came here and killed a good many of our men. In our own country we knew nothing about the Comanches." General William T. Sherman [the leading U.S. negotiator] said this in reply: "The Army will do the fighting, you must live at peace, if you go to your own country the Utes will be the nearest Indians to you, you must not trouble the Utes and the Utes must not trouble you. If, however, the Utes or Apaches come into your country with bows and arrows and guns you of course can drive them out but must not follow beyond the boundary line."

There are two foundations for criminal jurisdiction in the Treaty of 1868 . . . : [T]hose who assume relations with Navajos with the consent of the Navajo Nation and the United States are permitted to enter and reside within the Navajo Nation, subject to its laws, and non-Navajo Indians who enter and commit offenses are subject to punishment. That is what General Sherman told the Navajos who were assembled behind the fort hospital on [May] 28, 1868. [Footnote 15: During that first day of negotiations, General Sherman and Colonel Samuel F. Tappan "negotiated" with all of the approximately 9,500 Navajos present, because Navajo treaty negotiators had not yet been selected.] It is quite obvious from [Agent] Eastman's September . . . 1881 letter . . . that the Navajo leadership was thinking of admitting Paiutes to the Navajo Nation, and if they were admitted, they would be subject to punishment for theft and murder by Navajos.

Therefore, we conclude that the Chinle District Court has criminal jurisdiction over [Means] by virtue of the 1868 Treaty. [Means] entered the Navajo Nation, married a Navajo woman, conducted business activities, engaged in political activities by expressing his right to free speech, and otherwise satisfied the Article II conditions for entry and residence and Article I and II court jurisdiction.

III

It is clear that the Navajo Nation has jurisdiction over its own "members." [*United States v. Wheeler* 1978, 323] The . . . Supreme Court addressed the issue of membership and consent in [*Duro v. Reina* 1990, 694]: . . . "We held in . . . [1846] that a non-Indian could not, through his adoption into the Cherokee Tribe, bring himself within the federal definition of 'Indian' for purposes of an exemption to a federal jurisdictional provision. But we recognized that a non-Indian could, by adoption, 'become entitled to certain privileges in the tribe, and make himself amenable to their laws and usages.' [*United States v. Rogers* 1846, 573; *Nofire v. United States* 1897]" The defendants in the [Supreme Court's] *Nofire* [decision] were "full-blooded Cherokee Indians," but the issue for federal criminal jurisdiction was whether . . . the victim, was an "Indian." The court found that he was married to a Cherokee woman and thus he was a [Cherokee] citizen under Cherokee law. Since he changed his "nationality" to that of the Cherokee Nation, [the case] was under its exclusive jurisdiction and the defendants' convictions were reversed with instructions to surrender them to the Cherokee Nation.

The *[Duro]* Court's endorsement of *Nofire* opens the doors to cases cited in that opinion and cases cited in the other opinions. For example, the *Duro* language is based upon Chief Justice Taney's [1846] observation [quoted above] in *[Rogers]*. . . . In . . . [1891,] the [Supreme] Court ruled that under a provision of an 1866 Treaty, which recognized exclusive Cherokee Nation criminal jurisdiction over cases where parties were members "by nativity or adoption," an adopted . . . defendant could not be tried . . . in federal court. There were similar rulings in other federal criminal cases.

We . . . held, in . . . [1996,] that the Navajo Nation has criminal jurisdiction over individuals who "assume tribal relations." How does that comply with the indications in the *Duro* decision that intermarriage alone does not constitute sufficient consent for criminal jurisdiction? [*Duro* 1990, 679, 695–696]

We have previously ruled that our . . . Navajo Nation Criminal Code will be construed in light of Navajo common law, and the Supreme Court approved Navajo common law in . . . [*United States v. Wheeler* 1978, 312–313]. While there is a formal process to obtain membership as a Navajo, that is not the only kind of "membership" under Navajo Nation law. An individual who marries or has an intimate relationship with a Navajo is a *hadane* (in-law). The Navajo People have *adoone'e* or clans, and many of them are based upon the intermarriage of original Navajo clan members with people of other nations. The primary clan relation is traced through the mother, and some of the "foreign nation" clans include the "Flat Foot–Pima clan," the "Ute people clan," the "Zuni clan," the "Mexican clan," and the "Mescalero Apache clan." . . . A *hadane* or in-law assumes a clan relation to a Navajo when an intimate relationship forms, and when that relationship is conducted within the Navajo Nation, there are reciprocal obligations to and from family and clan members under Navajo common law. Among those obligations is the duty to avoid threatening or assaulting a relative by marriage (or any other person).

We find that [Means], by reason of his marriage to a Navajo, longtime residence within the Navajo Nation, his activities here, and his status as a *hadane*, consented to Navajo Nation criminal jurisdiction. This is not done by "adoption" in any formal or customary sense, but by assuming tribal relations and establishing familial and community relationships under Navajo common law.

There is another aspect to consent by conduct. In *Tsosie v. United States* (1987), the Federal Circuit Court of Appeals discussed the "bad men among the Indians" language, saying that

> [i]t is evident from the negotiations that the Navajos were not to be permanently disarmed, and could defend their reservation. They feared attacks by other Indian tribes, which they could repel, but pursuit and retaliation it was hoped they would refrain from, leaving that to the United States Army. The "bad men" clause is not confined to United States Government employees, but extends to "people subject to the authority of the United States." This vague phrase, to effectuate the purpose of the treaty, could possibly include Indians hostile to the Navajos whose wrongs to the Navajos the United States will punish and pay for: thus the need for Indian retaliation would be eliminated. [*Tsosie* 1987, 396]

Avoidance of retaliation and revenge is clear in the Treaty of 1868. General Sherman urged Navajos to leave the neighboring Mexicans to the Army, but he told Navajos they could pursue Utes and Apaches who entered the Navajo homeland. The Treaty speaks to the admission of Indians from other Indian nations. The thrust of the "bad men" clause was to avoid conflict. We use a rule of necessity to interpret consent under our Treaty. It would be absurd to conclude that our *hadane* relatives can enter the Navajo Nation, offend, and remain among us, and we can do nothing to protect Navajos and others from them. To so conclude would be to open the door for revenge and retaliation. While there are those who may think that the remedies offered by the United States Government are adequate, it is plain and clear to us that federal enforcement of criminal law is deficient. Potential state remedies are impractical, because law enforcement personnel in nearby areas have their own law enforcement problems. We must have the rule of peaceful law rather than the law of the talon, so we conclude that the petitioner has assumed tribal relations with Navajos and he is thus subject to the jurisdiction of our courts.

IV

Now we reach the issue of whether [Means] is denied equal protection of the law because he, as a nonmember Indian, is placed in the classification "Indian" for criminal prosecution, along with Navajos, when non-Indians are not. [Means] is mistaken as to the classification into which he falls. . . . [W]e [have] held that *any* person who assumes tribal relations is fully subject to our law, and that a person who assumes tribal relations is considered to be an "Indian." . . . [Means] belongs to the classification *hadane* and not that of nonmember Indian. One can be of any race or ethnicity to assume tribal relations with Navajos.

Since [Means] insists upon obtaining our ruling on the issue of equal protection, we must decide whether the classification of "nonmember Indian" is a political one or a "racial classification" subject to the strict scrutiny standard. We take our guidance from . . . *United States v. Antelope* (1977), which involved an Indian receiving a disparate penalty under federal criminal law compared to a smaller one under state law. The Supreme Court ruled that the differential treatment of Indians under the federal scheme does not violate equal protection of the law because Indians fall into a political and not a racial classification for purposes of equal protection.

Despite that, there is a fundamental governmental interest in prosecuting nonmember Indians. As mentioned, many Indians marry or enter into intimate relationships with Indians from other Indian nations, and this has been recognized for a long period of time. The [Indian Country Crimes Act] does not distinguish between member and nonmember Indians. . . . We . . . held [in 1973] that the [Indian Country Crimes Act] gives the Navajo Nation the authority to punish any Indian committing an offense in Indian Country. . . .

We stress that [Means] is treated no differently than he would be treated in a state or federal court in a criminal case. At oral argument, [Means's] attorney was asked what . . . rights his client is denied in our judicial system. He could not answer, because there is no difference. The ability to run for public office or to be a judge has utterly nothing to do with a fair criminal trial. Our rules of criminal procedure and our Navajo Nation Bill of Rights make no distinction as to race, ethnicity or membership in the Navajo Nation. The Navajo Nation courts keep no records on the race or ethnicity of any litigant and the justices and judges of our courts understand what equality before the law means. The Navajo Nation has a substantial interest in the welfare and safety of all within its boundaries and the Nation has an obligation to protect all from crime insofar as it can.

V

. . . We return to the basic document which establishes relations between the United States of America and the Navajo Nation. It permitted Navajos to return to their homeland from a concentration camp on the Pecos River in eastern New Mexico. Navajos listened intently on May 28, 1868 when General Sherman explained that they could punish Indians of other nations who entered the Navajo Nation. At the time, oral communications were the primary mode for Navajos to transmit ideas, and our ancestors listened well and had good memories. They knew that they were to return to their own land to have jurisdiction over all their own activities. In fact, General Sherman said this about criminal jurisdiction on May 29, 1868 when the Navajos selected their negotiators and chose Barboncito as "Chief": "[N]ow from this time out you must do as Barboncito tells you, with him we will deal and do all for your good. When we leave here and get to your country you must obey him or he will punish you, if he has not the power to do so he will call on the soldiers and they will do it." Barboncito and his council knew what was expected of them, and in fact the Navajo treaty negotiators at Fort Sumner became the first Navajo police. The Navajo Nation has kept its word to its treaty ally, the United States of America. Accordingly, we call upon the United States of America to support its treaty ally and put to rest the problem of who has the power to deal with crime and social disruption.

. . . This Court finds that the Chinle District Court has jurisdiction under the Treaty of 1868, [that Means] has consented to criminal jurisdiction over him, and that he is not denied the equal protection of the law. Accordingly, . . . this cause is remanded to the Chinle District Court for a prompt trial. . . .

Tribal Civil Jurisdiction

Williams v. Lee (1959)

U.S. Supreme Court
January 12, 1959
358 U.S. 217

The Court's unanimous opinion was written by Justice Hugo L. Black, appointed by President Franklin D. Roosevelt in 1937; joined by Chief Justice Earl Warren, appointed by President Dwight D. Eisenhower in 1953; Justices Felix Frankfurter and William O. Douglas, appointed by President Roosevelt in 1939; Justice Tom C. Clark, appointed by President Harry S. Truman in 1949; and Justices John

Marshall Harlan (the younger), William J. Brennan, Jr., Charles E. Whittaker, and Potter Stewart, appointed by President Eisenhower in 1955, 1956, 1957, and 1958, respectively.

Justice Black (for the Court):

[Lee], who is not an Indian, operates a general store in Arizona on the Navajo Indian Reservation under a license required by federal statute. He brought this action in the Superior Court of Arizona against [the Williamses], a Navajo Indian and his wife who live on the Reservation, to collect for goods sold them there on credit. Over [the Williamses'] motion to dismiss on the ground that jurisdiction lay in the tribal court rather than in the state court, judgment was entered in favor of [Lee]. The Supreme Court of Arizona affirmed, holding that since no Act of Congress expressly forbids their doing so Arizona courts are free to exercise jurisdiction over civil suits by non-Indians against Indians though the action arises on an Indian reservation. . . .

Originally the Indian tribes were separate nations within what is now the United States. Through conquest and treaties they were induced to give up complete independence and the right to go to war in exchange for federal protection, aid, and grants of land. . . . [State] governments sometimes sought to impose their laws and courts on the Indians. Around 1830 the Georgia Legislature extended its laws to the Cherokee Reservation despite federal treaties with the Indians which set aside this land for them. . . . The constitutionality of these laws was tested in *Worcester v. Georgia* [1832]. . . . Rendering one of his most courageous and eloquent opinions, Chief Justice Marshall held that Georgia's assertion of power was invalid. . . .

Despite bitter criticism and the defiance of Georgia which refused to obey this Court's mandate in *Worcester* the broad principles of that decision came to be accepted as law. Over the years this Court has modified these principles in cases where essential tribal relations were not involved and where the rights of Indians would not be jeopardized, but the basic policy of *Worcester* has remained. . . . [S]tate courts have been allowed to try non-Indians who committed crimes against each other on a reservation. But if the crime was by or against an Indian, tribal jurisdiction or that expressly conferred on other courts by Congress has remained exclusive. Essentially, absent governing Acts of Congress, the question has always been whether the state action infringed on the right of reservation Indians to make their own laws and be ruled by them.

Congress has also acted consistently upon the assumption that the States have no power to regulate the affairs of Indians on a reservation. To assure adequate government of the Indian tribes it enacted comprehensive statutes . . . regulating trade with Indians and organizing [an office] of Indian Affairs. Not satisfied solely with centralized government of Indians, it encouraged tribal governments and courts to become stronger and more highly organized. [Indian Reorganization Act 1934] Congress has followed a policy calculated eventually to make all Indians full-fledged participants in American society. This policy contemplates criminal and civil jurisdiction over Indians by any State ready to assume the burdens that go with it as soon as the educational and economic status of the Indians permits the change without disadvantage to them. Significantly, when Congress has wished the States to exercise this power it has expressly granted them the jurisdiction which *Worcester* . . . had denied. [Public Law 280]

No departure from the policies which have been applied to other Indians is apparent in the relationship between the United States and the Navajos. On June 1, 1868, a treaty was signed between General William T. Sherman, for the United States, and numerous chiefs and headmen of the [Navajo]. At the time this document was signed the Navajos were an exiled people, forced by the United States to live crowded together on a small piece of land on the Pecos River in eastern New Mexico, some 300 miles east of the area they had occupied before the coming of the white man. In return for their promises to keep peace, this treaty "set apart" for "their permanent home" a portion of what had been their native country, and provided that no one, except United States Government personnel, was to enter the reserved area. Implicit in these treaty terms, as it was in the treaties with the Cherokees involved in *Worcester* . . . , was the understanding that the internal affairs of the Indians remained exclusively within the jurisdiction of whatever tribal government existed.

Since then, Congress and the Bureau of Indian Affairs have assisted in strengthening the Navajo tribal government and its courts. The Tribe itself has in recent years greatly improved its legal system through increased expenditures and better-trained personnel. Today the Navajo Courts of Indian Offenses exercise broad criminal and civil jurisdiction which covers suits by outsiders against Indian defendants. No Federal Act has given state courts jurisdiction over such controversies. [Fn. 9] In . . . [1953, in Public Law 280,] Congress did express its willingness to have any State assume jurisdiction over reservation

Indians if the State Legislature or the people vote affirmatively to accept such responsibility. To date, Arizona has not accepted jurisdiction, possibly because the people of the State anticipate that the burdens accompanying such power might be considerable.

[Footnote 9: In the 1949 Navajo-Hopi Rehabilitation Bill, ... Congress provided for concurrent state, federal and tribal jurisdiction. President Truman vetoed the bill because he felt that subjecting the Navajo and Hopi to state jurisdiction was undesirable in view of their illiteracy, poverty and primitive social concepts. He was also impressed by the fact that the Indians vigorously opposed the bill. . . .]

There can be no doubt that to allow the exercise of state jurisdiction here would undermine the authority of the tribal courts over Reservation affairs and hence would infringe on the right of the Indians to govern themselves. It is immaterial that [Lee] is not an Indian. He was on the Reservation and the transaction with an Indian took place there. The cases in this Court have consistently guarded the authority of Indian governments over their reservations. Congress recognized this authority in the Navajos in the Treaty of 1868, and has done so ever since. If this power is to be taken away from them, it is for Congress to do it. [*Lone Wolf v. Hitchcock* 1903, 564–566]

Montana v. United States (1981)

U.S. Supreme Court
March 24, 1981
450 U.S. 544

The Court's opinion was written by Justice Potter Stewart, appointed by President Dwight D. Eisenhower in 1958. With regard to the civil jurisdiction issue discussed in the fourth section of Chapter 3, the decision was unanimous, joined by Chief Justice Warren E. Burger, appointed by President Richard M. Nixon in 1969; Justice William J. Brennan, Jr., appointed by President Eisenhower in 1956; Justice Byron R. White, appointed by President John F. Kennedy in 1962; Justice Thurgood Marshall, appointed by President Lyndon B. Johnson in 1967; Justices Harry A. Blackmun and Lewis F. Powell, Jr., appointed by President Nixon in 1970 and 1972; Justice William H. Rehnquist, appointed by President Nixon in 1972 (later appointed chief justice by President Ronald W. Reagan in 1986); and Justice John Paul Stevens, appointed by President Gerald R. Ford in 1975. The

Court in Montana *also considered a separate issue concerning whether the State of Montana or the Montana Crow Tribe held title to part of the bed of the Big Horn River. The Court ruled for the state on that issue by 6–3, with Blackmun (joined by Brennan and Marshall) writing a dissenting opinion and Stevens a concurring opinion. The opinions dealing with the latter issue (including that part of Stewart's majority opinion) are omitted here.*

Justice Stewart (for the Court):

This case concerns the sources and scope of the power of an Indian tribe to regulate hunting and fishing by non-Indians on lands within its reservation. . . .

I

The Crow Indians originated in Canada, but some three centuries ago they migrated to what is now southern Montana. . . . In 1868, the [Crow-U.S.] Treaty of Fort Laramie established a Crow Reservation of roughly 8 million acres, including land through which the Big Horn River flows. By Article II of the treaty, the United States agreed that the reservation "shall be . . . set apart for the absolute and undisturbed use and occupation" of the Crow Tribe, and that no non-Indians except agents of the Government "shall ever be permitted to pass over, settle upon, or reside in" the reservation.

Several subsequent Acts of Congress reduced the reservation to slightly fewer than 2.3 million acres. In addition, the General Allotment Act of 1887 and the Crow Allotment Act of 1920 authorized the issuance of patents in fee [a type of private property title] to individual Indian allottees within the reservation. Under these Acts, an allottee could alienate his land to a non-Indian after holding it for 25 years. Today, roughly 52 percent of the reservation is allotted to members of the Tribe and held by the United States in trust for them, 17 percent is held in trust for the Tribe itself, and approximately 28 percent is . . . [privately owned] by non-Indians. The State of Montana owns . . . 2 percent of the [land in the] reservation, the United States less than 1 percent.

Since the 1920s, the State of Montana has stocked the waters of the reservation with fish, and the construction of a dam by the United States made trout fishing in the Big Horn River possible. The reservation also contains game, some of it stocked by the State. Since the 1950s, the Crow Tribal Council has passed several resolutions respecting hunting and fishing on the reservation. . . . Th[e] resolution [at issue here] prohibits hunting and fishing within the reservation by anyone who is not a member of the Tribe. The State of Montana, however, has continued to assert its authority to regulate hunting and fishing by non-Indians within the reservation.

. . . [In] 1975, . . . the United States endeavored to resolve the conflict between the Tribe and the State by filing the present lawsuit[,] . . . [seeking to] establis[h] that the Tribe and the United States have sole authority to regulate hunting and fishing within the reservation, and. . . . [to] requir[e] Montana to secure the permission of the Tribe before issuing hunting or fishing licenses for use within the reservation. . . .

[Part II is omitted.]

III

Though the parties in this case have raised broad questions about the power of the Tribe to regulate hunting and fishing by non-Indians on the reservation, the regulatory issue before us is a narrow one. The Court of Appeals held that the Tribe may prohibit nonmembers from hunting or fishing on land belonging to the Tribe or held by the United States in trust for the Tribe, and with this holding we can readily agree. We also agree with the Court of Appeals that if the Tribe permits nonmembers to fish or hunt on such lands, it may condition their entry by charging a fee or establishing bag and creel limits. What remains is the question of the power of the Tribe to regulate non-Indian fishing and hunting on reservation land [privately] owned in fee by nonmembers of the Tribe. The Court of Appeals held that, with respect to fee-patented lands, the Tribe may regulate, but may not prohibit, hunting and fishing by nonmember resident owners or by those, such as tenants or employees, whose occupancy is authorized by the owners. The court further held that the Tribe may totally prohibit hunting and fishing on lands within the reservation owned by non-Indians who do not occupy that land. . . .

. . . [T]he Court of Appeals . . . identified [the Tribe's power to regulate non-Indian hunting and fishing on non-Indian lands within the reservation] as an incident of the inherent sovereignty of the Tribe over the entire Crow Reservation. But "inherent sovereignty" is not so broad as to support [this power over] . . . non-Indian lands.

This Court most recently reviewed the principles of inherent sovereignty in *United States v. Wheeler* (1978). . . . [T]he Court was careful to note that, through their original incorporation into the United States as well as through specific treaties and statutes, the Indian tribes have lost many of the attributes of sovereignty. The Court distinguished between those inherent powers retained by the tribes and those divested:

"The areas in which such implicit divestiture of sovereignty has been held to have occurred are those involving the relations between an Indian tribe and nonmembers of the tribe. . . . These limitations rest on the fact that the dependent status of Indian tribes within our territorial jurisdiction is necessarily inconsistent with their freedom independently to determine their external relations. But the powers of self-government, including the power to prescribe and enforce internal criminal laws, are of a different type. They involve only the relations among members of a tribe. Thus, they are not such powers as would necessarily be lost by virtue of a tribe's dependent status." [*Wheeler* 1978, 326]

Thus, in addition to the power to punish tribal offenders, the Indian tribes retain their inherent power to determine tribal membership, to regulate domestic relations among members, and to prescribe rules of inheritance for members. But exercise of tribal power beyond what is necessary to protect tribal self-government or to control internal relations is inconsistent with the dependent status of the tribes, and so cannot survive without express congressional delegation. [*Williams v. Lee* 1959, 219–220; *United States v. Kagama* 1886, 381–382] Since regulation of hunting and fishing by nonmembers of a tribe on lands no longer owned by the tribe bears no clear relationship to tribal self-government or internal relations, the general principles of retained inherent sovereignty d[o] not authorize the Crow Tribe to [do so]. . . .

The Court recently applied these general principles in *Oliphant v. Suquamish Indian Tribe* (1978), rejecting a tribal claim of inherent sovereign authority to exercise criminal jurisdiction over non-Indians. Stressing that Indian tribes cannot exercise power inconsistent with their diminished status as sovereigns, the Court quoted Justice Johnson's words in his concurrence in *Fletcher v. Peck* [1810, 147]—the first Indian case to reach this Court—that the Indian tribes have lost any "right of governing every person within their limits except themselves." [*Oliphant* 1978, 209] Though *Oliphant* only determined inherent tribal authority in criminal matters, the principles on which it relied support the general proposition that the inherent sovereign powers of an Indian tribe do not extend to the activities of nonmembers of the tribe. To be sure, Indian tribes retain inherent sovereign power to exercise some forms of civil jurisdiction over non-Indians on their reservations, even on non-Indian fee lands. A tribe may regulate, through taxation, licensing, or other means, the activities of nonmembers who enter consensual relationships with the tribe or its members, through commercial dealing, contracts, leases, or other arrangements. [*Williams v. Lee* 1959, 223; *Washington v. Confederated Tribes of the Colville Indian Reservation* 1980, 152–154] A tribe may also retain inherent power to exercise civil authority over the conduct of non-Indians on fee lands within its reservation when that conduct threatens or has some direct effect on the political integrity, the economic security, or the health or welfare of the tribe. [*Williams* 1959, 220; *Fisher v. District Court* 1976, 386]

No such circumstances, however, are involved in this case. Non-Indian hunters and fishermen on non-Indian fee land do not enter any agreements or dealings with the Crow Tribe so as to subject themselves to tribal civil jurisdiction. And nothing in this case suggests that such non-Indian hunting and fishing so threaten the Tribe's political or economic security as to justify tribal regulation. The complaint in the District Court did not allege that non-Indian hunting and fishing on fee lands imperil the subsistence or welfare of the Tribe. Furthermore, the District Court made express findings, left unaltered by the Court of Appeals, that the Crow Tribe has traditionally accommodated itself to the State's "near exclusive" regulation of hunting and fishing on fee lands within the reservation. And the District Court found that Montana's statutory and regulatory scheme does not prevent the Crow Tribe from limiting or forbidding non-Indian hunting and fishing on lands still owned by or held in trust for the Tribe or its members. . . .

Nevada v. Hicks (2001)

U.S. Supreme Court
June 25, 2001
533 U.S. 353

The Court's opinion was written by Justice Antonin Scalia, appointed by President Ronald W. Reagan in 1986. The decision was formally unanimous (all justices agreed that the Court of Appeals decision had to be reversed and remanded for further proceedings), but in actual substance, the Court split 6–3. Joining fully in Scalia's majority opinion were Chief Justice William H. Rehnquist, appointed as associate justice by President Richard M. Nixon in 1972 and as chief justice by President Reagan in 1986; Justice Anthony M. Kennedy, appointed by President Reagan in 1988; Justices David H. Souter and Clarence Thomas, appointed by President George Bush in 1990 and 1991, respectively; and Justice Ruth Bader Ginsburg, appointed by President William J. Clinton in 1993. Souter (joined by Kennedy and Thomas) and Ginsburg also wrote concurring opinions. Justice Sandra Day O'Connor, appointed by President Reagan in 1981, wrote an opinion concurring in part and concurring in the judgment but disagreeing strongly with Scalia's reasoning and on how the case should be handled on remand. O'Connor was joined by Justice John Paul Stevens, appointed by President Gerald R. Ford in 1975; and Justice Stephen G. Breyer, appointed by President Clinton in 1994. Stevens (joined by Breyer) also wrote an opinion concurring in the judgment. Stevens's opinion dealt with tribal jurisdiction to hear civil lawsuits under a federal civil rights statute (42 U.S.C. § 1983), an issue somewhat extraneous to the general issue of tribal civil jurisdiction, so his opinion and the part of Scalia's majority opinion dealing with that issue are omitted.

Justice Scalia (for the Court):

This case presents the question whether a tribal court may assert jurisdiction over civil claims against state officials who entered tribal land to execute a search warrant against a tribe member suspected of having violated state law outside the reservation.

I

[Floyd] Hicks is one of about 900 members of the Fallon Paiute–Shoshone Tribes of western Nevada. He resides on the Tribes' reservation of approximately 8000 acres, established by federal statute in 1908. In 1990 Hicks came under suspicion of having killed, off the reservation, a California bighorn sheep, a gross misdemeanor under Nevada law. A state game warden obtained from state court a search warrant "SUBJECT TO OBTAINING APPROVAL FROM THE FALLON TRIBAL COURT . ." According to the [state] judge, this tribal-court authorization was necessary because "[the state court] has no jurisdiction on the Fallon Paiute–Shoshone Indian Reservation." A search warrant was obtained from the tribal court, and the warden, accompanied by a tribal police officer, searched [Hicks's] yard, uncovering only the head of a Rocky Mountain bighorn, a different (and unprotected) species of sheep.

Approximately one year later, a tribal police officer reported to the warden that he had observed two mounted bighorn sheep heads in [Hicks's] home. The warden again obtained a search warrant from state court; though this warrant did not explicitly require permission from the Tribes, a tribal-court warrant was nonetheless secured, and [Hicks's] home was again (unsuccessfully) searched by three wardens and additional tribal officers.

[Hicks], claiming that his sheep-heads had been damaged, and that the second search exceeded the bounds of the warrant, brought [a civil] suit against the [Fallon] Tribal Judge, the tribal officers, the state wardens in their individual and official capacities, and the State of Nevada in the [Fallon] Tribal Court. . . . (His claims against [all the tribal officials] were dismissed by directed verdict and are not at issue here.) [Hicks's] causes of action included trespass to land and chattels, abuse of process, and violation of civil rights. . . . [Hicks] later voluntarily dismissed his case against the State and against the state officials in their official capacities, leaving only his suit against those officials in their individual capacities.

The Tribal Court held that it had jurisdiction over [Hicks's] claims, a holding affirmed by the Tribal Appeals Court. The state officials and Nevada then filed an action in [U.S. District Court] seeking a declaratory judgment that the Tribal Court lacked jurisdiction. The District Court . . . [upheld tribal] jurisdiction, and also held that the state officials would have to exhaust any claims of qualified immunity in the tribal court. The [U.S. Court of Appeals for the] Ninth Circuit affirmed. . . .

II

In this case . . . it is necessary to determine . . . whether the Tribal Court . . . has jurisdiction to adjudicate the alleged tortious conduct of state wardens executing a search warrant for evidence of an off-reservation crime. . . .

A

The principle of Indian law central to this . . . case is our holding in *Strate v. A-1 Contractors* (1997): "As to nonmembers . . . a tribe's adjudicative jurisdiction does not exceed its legislative jurisdiction. . . ." [*Strate* 1997, 453] That formulation leaves open the question whether a tribe's adjudicative jurisdiction over nonmember defendants equals its legislative jurisdiction. [Fn. 2] We will not have to answer that open question if we determine that the Tribes in any event lack legislative jurisdiction in this case. We first inquire, therefore, whether the Fallon

Paiute–Shoshone Tribes—either as an exercise of their inherent sovereignty, or under grant of federal authority—can regulate state wardens executing a search warrant for evidence of an off-reservation crime.

[Footnote 2: In *National Farmers Union Ins. Cos. v. Crow Tribe* (1985) we avoided the question whether tribes may generally adjudicate against nonmembers claims arising from on-reservation transactions, and we have never held that a tribal court had jurisdiction over a nonmember defendant. Typically, our cases have involved claims brought against tribal defendants. [*Williams v. Lee* 1959] In *Strate* . . . , however, we assumed that "where tribes possess authority to regulate the activities of nonmembers, civil jurisdiction over disputes arising out of such activities presumably lies in the tribal courts," without distinguishing between nonmember plaintiffs and nonmember defendants. [*Strate* 1997, 453; *Iowa Mutual Ins. Co. v. LaPlante* 1987, 18] Our holding in this case is limited to the question of tribal-court jurisdiction over state officers enforcing state law. We leave open the question of tribal-court jurisdiction over nonmember defendants in general.]

Indian tribes' regulatory authority over nonmembers is governed by the principles set forth in *Montana v. United States* (1981), which we have called the "pathmarking case" on the subject. [*Strate* 1997, 445] . . . *Montana* observed that . . . "the inherent sovereign powers of an Indian tribe do not extend to the activities of nonmembers of the tribe." [*Montana* 1981, 565] Where nonmembers are concerned, the "exercise of tribal power beyond what is necessary to protect tribal self-government or to control internal relations is inconsistent with the dependent status of the tribes, and so cannot survive without express congressional delegation." [*Montana* 1981, 564] [Fn. 3]

[Footnote 3: Montana recognized an exception to this rule for tribal regulation of "the activities of nonmembers who enter consensual relationships with the tribe or its members, through commercial dealing, contracts, leases, or other arrangements." [*Montana* 1981, 565] Though the wardens in this case "consensually" obtained a warrant from the Tribal Court before searching respondent's home and yard, we do not think this qualifies as an "other arrangement" within the meaning of this passage. . . . [A]n "other arrangement" is clearly another private consensual relationship, from which the official actions at issue in this case are far removed.]

Both *Montana* and *Strate* rejected tribal authority to regulate nonmembers' activities on land over which the tribe could not "assert a landowner's right to occupy and exclude." [*Montana* 1981, 557, 564; *Strate* 1997, 456] . . . [It is] argue[d] that since Hicks's home and yard are on tribe-owned land within the reservation, the Tribe may make its exercise of regulatory authority over nonmembers a condition of nonmembers' entry. Not necessarily. While it is certainly true that the non-Indian ownership status of the land was central to the analysis in both *Montana* and *Strate,* the reason that was so was not that Indian ownership suspends the "general proposition" derived from *Oliphant* that "the inherent sovereign powers of an Indian tribe do not extend to the activities of nonmembers of the tribe" except to the extent "necessary to protect tribal self-government or to control internal relations." [*Montana* 1981, 564–565] *Oliphant* itself drew no distinctions based on the status of land. And *Montana,* after announcing the general rule of no jurisdiction over nonmembers, cautioned that "to be sure, Indian tribes retain inherent sovereign power to exercise some forms of civil jurisdiction over non-Indians on their reservations, even on non-Indian fee lands" [*Montana* 1981, 565]—clearly implying that the general rule of *Montana* applies to both Indian and non-Indian land.

The ownership status of land, in other words, is only one factor to consider in determining whether regulation of the activities of nonmembers is "necessary to protect tribal self-government or to control internal relations." It may sometimes be a dispositive factor. Hitherto, the absence of tribal ownership has been virtually conclusive of the absence of tribal civil jurisdiction; with one minor exception, we have never upheld under *Montana* the extension of tribal civil authority over nonmembers on non-Indian land. Compare, *e.g., Merrion v. Jicarilla Apache Tribe* (1982) (tribe has taxing authority over tribal lands leased by nonmembers) with *Atkinson Trading Co. v. Shirley* (2001) (tribe has no taxing authority over nonmembers' activities on land held by nonmembers in fee); but see *Brendale v. Yakima Indian Nation* (1989) (tribe can impose zoning regulation on that 3.1% of land within reservation area closed to public entry that was not owned by the tribe). But the existence of tribal ownership is not alone enough to support regulatory jurisdiction over nonmembers.

We proceed to consider . . . whether regulatory jurisdiction over state officers in the present context is "necessary to protect tribal self-government or to control internal relations," and, if not, whether such regulatory jurisdiction has been congressionally conferred.

B

In *Strate,* we explained that what is necessary to protect tribal self-government and control internal relations can be understood by looking at the examples of tribal power to which *Montana* referred: [T]ribes have authority "[to punish tribal offenders,] to determine tribal membership, to regulate domestic relations among members, and to prescribe rules of inheritance for members." [*Strate* 1997, 459, quoting *Montana* 1981, 564] These examples show, we said, that Indians have "the right . . . to make their own laws and be ruled by them." [*Strate* 1997, 459, quoting *Williams v. Lee* 1959, 220; *Fisher v. District Court* 1976, 386] Tribal assertion of regulatory authority over nonmembers must be connected to that right of the Indians to make their own laws and be governed by them. [For example, we have held that] . . . "[t]he power to tax is an essential attribute of Indian sovereignty because it is a necessary instrument of self-government," at least as to "tribal lands" on which the tribe "has . . . authority over a nonmember." [*Merrion v. Jicarilla Apache Tribe* 1982, 137, 142]

Our cases make clear that the Indians' right to make their own laws and be governed by them does not exclude all state regulatory authority on the reservation. State sovereignty does not end at a reservation's border. Though tribes are often referred to as "sovereign" entities, it was "long ago" that "the Court departed from Chief Justice Marshall's view that 'the laws of [a State] can have no force' within reservation boundaries." [*White Mountain Apache Tribe v. Bracker* 1980, 141, quoting *Worcester v. Georgia* 1832, 561] "Ordinarily," it is now clear, "an Indian reservation is considered part of the territory of the State." [U.S. Department of Interior 1958, 510, citing *Utah and Northern Railroad Co. v. Fisher* 1885]

That is not to say that States may exert the same degree of regulatory authority within a reservation as they do without. To the contrary, the principle that Indians have the right to make their own laws and be governed by them requires "an accommodation between the interests of the Tribes and the Federal Government, on the one hand, and those of the State, on the other." [*Washington v. Confederated Tribes of the Colville Indian Reservation* 1980, 156] "When on-reservation conduct involving only Indians is at issue, state law is generally inapplicable, for the State's regulatory interest is likely to be minimal and the federal interest in encouraging tribal self-government is at its strongest." [*Bracker* 1980, 144] When, however, state interests outside the reservation are implicated, States may regulate the activities even of tribe members on tribal land, as exemplified by our decision in [*Colville* 1980]. In that case, Indians were selling cigarettes on their reservation to nonmembers from off-reservation, without collecting the state cigarette tax. We held that the State could require the Tribes to collect the tax from nonmembers, and could "impose at least 'minimal' burdens on the Indian retailer to aid in enforcing and collecting the tax." [*Colville* 1980, 151] It is also well established in our precedent that States have criminal jurisdiction over reservation Indians for crimes committed (as was the alleged poaching in this case) off the reservation.

While it is not entirely clear from our precedent whether the last mentioned authority entails the corollary right to enter a reservation (including Indian-[owned] lands) for enforcement purposes, several of our opinions point in that direction. . . . In [*Utah and Northern Railroad Co. v. Fisher* 1885, 31], we observed that " . . . process of [state] courts may run into an Indian reservation . . . , where the subject-matter or controversy is otherwise within [state court] cognizance." . . . [I]n *United States v. Kagama* (1886), . . . [upholding the Major Crimes Act of 1885] giving federal courts jurisdiction over various . . . violent crimes committed by Indians on a reservation within a State[,] . . . [we noted] that the [Act] "does not interfere with the process of the State courts within the reservation, nor with the operation of State laws upon white people found there. Its effect is confined to the acts of an Indian of some tribe, of a criminal character, committed within the limits of the reservation. . . ." [*Kagama* 1886, 383]

The Court's references to "process" in *Utah & Northern* . . . and *Kagama,* and the Court's concern in *Kagama* over possible federal encroachment on state prerogatives, suggest state authority to issue search warrants in cases such as the one before us. ("Process" is defined [by *Black's Law Dictionary*] as "any means used by a court to acquire or exercise its jurisdiction over a person or over specific property," and is equated in criminal cases with a warrant.) It is noteworthy that *Kagama* recognized the right of state laws to "operate . . . upon [non-Indians] found" within a reservation, but did not similarly limit to non-Indians or the property of non-Indians the scope of the process of state courts. This makes perfect sense, since, as we [have] explained in the context of federal enclaves, the reservation of state authority to serve process is necessary to "prevent [such areas] from becoming an asylum for fugitives from justice." [Fn. 6]

[Footnote 6: That this risk is not purely hypothetical is demonstrated by *Arizona ex rel. Merrill v. Turtle* (1969), a case in which the

Navajo Tribal Court refused to extradite a [tribal] member to Oklahoma because tribal law forbade extradition except to three neighboring States. The Ninth Circuit [U.S. Court of Appeals] held [*Turtle* 1969, 685–686] that Arizona (where the reservation was located) could not enter the reservation to seize the suspect for extradition since (among other reasons) this would interfere with tribal self-government.]

We conclude . . . that tribal authority to regulate state officers in executing process related to the violation, off reservation, of state laws is not essential to tribal self-government or internal relations. . . . The State's interest in execution of process is considerable, and even when it relates to Indian-[owned] lands it no more impairs the tribe's self-government than federal enforcement of federal law impairs state government. . . .

C

The States' inherent jurisdiction on reservations can of course be stripped by Congress. But with regard to the jurisdiction at issue here that has not occurred. . . . Nothing in the federal statutory scheme prescribes, or even remotely suggests, that state officers cannot enter a reservation (including Indian-[owned] land) to investigate or prosecute violations of state law occurring off the reservation. . . .

[Parts III and IV are omitted.]

V

Finally, a few words in response to the concurring opinion of Justice O'Connor, which is in large part a dissent from the views expressed in this opinion. [Her] principal point . . . is that our reasoning "gives only passing consideration to the fact that the state officials' activities in this case occurred on land owned and controlled by the Tribe." . . . Even a cursory reading of our opinion demonstrates that this is not so. To the contrary, we acknowledge that tribal ownership is a factor in the *Montana* analysis, and a factor significant enough that it "may sometimes be . . . dispositive." We simply do not find it dispositive in the present case. . . .

[Justice O'Connor] marshals no authority and scant reasoning to support [her] judgment that tribal authority over state officers pursuing, on tribe-owned land, off-reservation violations of state law may be "necessary to protect tribal self-government or to control internal relations." [*Montana* 1981, 564–565] Self-government and internal relations are not directly at issue here, since the issue is whether the Tribes' law will apply, not to their own members, but to a narrow category of outsiders. And [Justice O'Connor] does not . . . explain how allowing state officers to pursue off-reservation violation of state law "threatens or has some direct effect on the political integrity, the economic security, or the health or welfare of the tribe." [*Montana* 1981, 566] That the actions of these state officers cannot threaten or affect those interests is guaranteed by the limitations of federal constitutional and statutory law to which the officers are fully subject.

[Justice O'Connor] exaggerates and distorts the consequences of our conclusion that the term "other arrangements" [with a tribe, subjecting a nonmember to tribal jurisdiction,] in a passage from *Montana[,]* . . . d[oes] not include the state officials' obtaining of tribal warrants in the present case. [Our] conclusion is correct. . . . The *[Montana]* Court . . . was referring to private individuals who voluntarily submitted themselves to tribal regulatory jurisdiction by the arrangements that they (or their employers) entered into. This is confirmed by the fact that all four of the cases in the immediately following citation involved private commercial actors.

[Justice O'Connor] concludes from [our] brief . . . discussion [in footnote 3] that we would invalidate express or implied cessions of regulatory authority over nonmembers contained in state-tribal cooperative agreements, including those pertaining to mutual law-enforcement assistance, tax administration assistance, and child support and paternity matters. This is . . . overreaching. . . . Whether contractual relations between State and tribe can expressly or impliedly confer tribal . . . jurisdiction over nonmembers . . . [is] not at issue here.

Another exaggeration is [Justice O'Connor's] contention that we "give nonmembers freedom to act with impunity on tribal land based solely on their status as state law enforcement officials." We do not say state officers cannot be regulated; we say they cannot be regulated in the performance of their law-enforcement duties. Action unrelated to that is potentially subject to tribal control depending on the outcome of *Montana* analysis. Moreover, even where the issue is whether the officer has acted unlawfully in the performance of his duties, the tribe and tribe members are of course able to invoke the authority of the Federal Government and federal courts (or the state government and state courts) to vindicate constitutional or other federal- and state-law rights.

We must comment upon the final paragraphs of Part II of [Justice O'Connor's] opinion—which bring on stage, in classic fashion, a *deus ex machina* to extract, from the seemingly insoluble difficulties that the prior writing has created, a happy ending. [Justice O'Connor] manages to have [her] cake and eat it too—to hand over state law-enforcement officers to the jurisdiction of tribal courts and yet still assure that the officers' traditional immunity (and hence the State's law-enforcement interest) will be protected—by simply announcing "that in order to protect government officials, immunity defenses should be considered in reviewing tribal court jurisdiction." What wonderful magic. Without so much as a citation (none is available) [Justice O'-Connor] declares the qualified immunity inquiry to be part of the jurisdictional inquiry, thus bringing it within the ken of the federal court at the outset of the case. There are two problems with this declaration. The first is that it is not true. There is no authority whatever for the proposition that . . . immunity defenses pertain to the [tribal] court's jurisdiction. . . . And the second problem is, that . . . it is impossible to know which "immunity defenses" [will apply, if any]. . . . The tribe's law on [official immunity] need not be the same as the State's; indeed, the tribe may decide . . . that there is no immunity defense. . . . One wonders whether, deprived of [her] *deus ex machina,* [Justice O'Connor] would not alter [her] conclusion . . . and agree with us that a proper balancing of state and tribal interests would give the Tribes no jurisdiction over state officers pursuing off-reservation violations of state law. . . .

Because the Fallon Paiute–Shoshone Tribes lacked legislative authority to restrict, condition, or otherwise regulate the ability of state officials to investigate off-reservation violations of state law, [the Tribal Court] lacked adjudicative authority to hear [Hicks's lawsuit] claim[ing] that those officials violated tribal law in the performance of their duties. . . . State officials operating on a reservation to investigate off-reservation violations of state law are properly held accountable for tortious conduct and civil rights violations in either state or federal court, but not in tribal court. . . .

Justice Souter (concurring, joined by Justices Kennedy and Thomas):

I agree that the . . . Tribal Court had no jurisdiction to entertain Hicks's claims against the . . . state officers . . . , and I join the Court's opinion. While I agree with the Court's analysis as well as its conclusion, I would reach that point by a different route. Like the Court, I take *Montana v. United States* (1981), to be the source of the first principle on tribal-court civil jurisdiction. But while the Court gives emphasis to . . . the State's interest in . . . enforc[ing] state law governing off-reservation conduct, I would go right to *Montana*'s rule that a tribe's civil jurisdiction generally stops short of nonmember defendants, subject only to two exceptions, one turning on "consensual relationships," the other on respect for "the political integrity, the economic security, or the health or welfare of the tribe." [*Montana* 1981, 565–566]

Montana applied this presumption against tribal jurisdiction to nonmember conduct on fee land [privately owned by nonmembers] within a reservation; I would also apply it where, as here, a nonmember acts on tribal or trust land, and I would thus make it explicit that land status within a reservation is not a primary jurisdictional fact, but is relevant only insofar as it bears on the application of one of *Montana*'s exceptions to a particular case. . . . [I]t follows for me that, although the holding in this case is "limited to the question of tribal-court jurisdiction over state officers enforcing state law," one rule independently supporting that holding (that as a general matter "the inherent sovereign powers of an Indian tribe do not extend to the activities of nonmembers of the tribe") is not so confined.

I

. . . [T]his Court's . . . pronouncements on [tribal civil jurisdiction over nonmembers] have pointed in seemingly opposite directions. [*Oliphant v. Suquamish Indian Tribe* 1978], however, clarified tribal-courts' criminal jurisdiction (in holding that they had none as to non-Indians), and that decision is now seen as a significant step on the way to *Montana*, "the pathmarking case concerning tribal civil authority over nonmembers." [*Strate v. A-1 Contractors* 1997, 445] The path marked best is the rule that, at least as a presumptive matter, tribal courts lack civil jurisdiction over nonmembers. [Fn. 2]

[Footnote 2: The Court in *[Montana]* referred to "nonmembers" and "non-Indians" interchangeably. In response to our decision in *Duro v. Reina* (1990), in which we extended the rule of *Oliphant* to deny tribal courts criminal jurisdiction over nonmember Indians (i.e., Indians who are members of other tribes), Congress passed a statute expressly granting tribal courts such jurisdiction. [*Duro* Fix Act] Because, here, we are concerned with the extent of tribes' inherent authority, and not with the jurisdiction statutorily conferred on them by Congress, the relevant distinction, as we implicitly acknowledged in *Strate*, is between members and nonmembers of the tribe. . . .]

To be sure, *Montana* does not of its own force resolve the jurisdictional issue in this case. . . . *[Montana]* concerned only the power of an

Indian tribe to regulate the conduct of nonmembers "on reservation land owned in fee by nonmembers of the Tribe." Here, it is undisputed, the acts complained of occurred on reservation land "controlled by a tribe." But although the distinction between tribal and fee land (and, accordingly, between *Montana* and this case) surely exists, it does not in my mind call for a different result. . . .

. . . The *Montana* Court remarked that . . . *[Oliphant]* support[s] a more "general proposition" applicable in civil cases as well, namely, that "the inherent sovereign powers of an Indian tribe do not extend to the activities of nonmembers of the tribe." [*Montana* 1981, 565] Accordingly, . . . *Montana* repeatedly pressed the member-nonmember distinction. . . .

. . . The principle on which *Montana* and [*Strate v. A-1 Contractors* 1997] were decided (like *Oliphant* before them) looks first to human relationships, not land records, and it should make no difference . . . whether acts committed on a reservation occurred on tribal land or on land owned by a nonmember. . . . [Fn. 4]

[Footnote 4: . . . [I]t is not that land status is irrelevant to a proper *Montana* calculus, only that it is not determinative in the first instance. Land status, for instance, might well have an impact under one (or perhaps both) of the *Montana* exceptions.]

II

Limiting tribal-court civil jurisdiction this way . . . serves sound policy. . . . A rule generally prohibiting tribal courts from exercising civil jurisdiction over nonmembers, without looking first to the status of the land on which individual claims arise, . . . makes sense from a practical standpoint, for tying tribes' authority to land status in the first instance would produce an unstable jurisdictional crazy quilt. Because land on Indian reservations constantly changes hands (from tribes to nonmembers, from nonmembers to tribal members, and so on), a jurisdictional rule under which land status was dispositive would prove extraordinarily difficult to administer and would provide little notice to nonmembers, whose susceptibility to tribal-court jurisdiction would turn on the most recent property conveyances.

The ability of nonmembers to know where tribal jurisdiction begins and ends, it should be stressed, is a matter of real, practical consequence given "the special nature of [Indian] tribunals" [*Duro v. Reina* 1990, 693], which differ from traditional American courts in a number of significant respects. To start with the most obvious one, it has been understood for more than a century that the Bill of Rights and the

Fourteenth Amendment do not of their own force apply to Indian tribes. [*Talton v. Mayes* 1896] Although the Indian Civil Rights Act of 1968 (ICRA) makes a handful of analogous safeguards enforceable in tribal courts, "the guarantees are not identical" [*Oliphant* 1978, 194], and [according to a 1998 law review article] there is a "definite trend by tribal courts" toward the view that they "have leeway in interpreting" the ICRA's due process and equal protection clauses and "need not follow the U.S. Supreme Court precedents 'jot-for-jot.'" In any event, a presumption against tribal-court civil jurisdiction squares with one of the principal policy considerations underlying *Oliphant*, namely, an overriding concern that citizens who are not tribal members be "protected . . . from unwarranted intrusions on their personal liberty." [*Oliphant* 1978, 210]

Tribal courts also differ from other American courts (and often from one another) in their structure, in the substantive law they apply, and in the independence of their judges. [According to a 1995 law review article,] [a]lthough some modern tribal courts "mirror American courts" and "are guided by written codes, rules, procedures, and guidelines," tribal law is still frequently unwritten, being based instead "on the values, mores, and norms of a tribe and expressed in its customs, traditions, and practices," and is often "handed down orally or by example from one generation to another." The resulting law applicable in tribal courts is a complex "mix of tribal codes and federal, state, and traditional law," which would be unusually difficult for an outsider to sort out.

. . . [Finally,] there is no effective review mechanism in place to police tribal courts' decisions on matters of non-tribal law, since tribal-court judgments based on state or federal law can be neither removed nor appealed to state or federal courts. The result, of course, is a risk of substantial disuniformity in the interpretation of state and federal law, a risk underscored by the fact that "tribal courts are often 'subordinate to the political branches of tribal governments.'" [*Duro v. Reina* 1990, 693]. . . .

Justice Ginsburg (concurring):

I join the Court's opinion. As the Court plainly states, and as Justice Souter recognizes, the "holding in this case is limited to the question of tribal-court jurisdiction over state officers enforcing state law." The Court's decision explicitly "leaves open the question of tribal-court jurisdiction over nonmember defendants in general," including state officials engaged on tribal land in a venture or frolic of their own . . . "unrelated to [performance of . . . law-enforcement duties]. . . ."

I write separately only to emphasize that *Strate v. A-1 Contractors* (1997) similarly deferred larger issues. *Strate* concerned a highway accident on a [state-controlled] right-of-way over tribal land. . . . [T]he accident site was equivalent to . . . non-Indian land. We held that the nonmember [sued for] negligent driving in *Strate* was not amenable to the Tribe's legislative or adjudicatory authority. But we "expressed no view on the governing law or proper forum" for cases arising out of nonmember conduct on tribal land. The Court's opinion, as I understand it, does not reach out definitively to answer the jurisdictional questions left open in *Strate*.

Justice O'Connor (concurring in part and concurring in the judgment, joined by Justices Stevens and Breyer):

The Court holds that a tribe has no power to regulate the activities of state officials enforcing state law on land owned and controlled by the tribe. The majority's sweeping opinion, without cause, undermines the authority of tribes to "make their own laws and be ruled by them." [*Strate v. A-1 Contractors* 1997, 459, quoting *Williams v. Lee* 1959, 220] I write separately because Part II of the Court's [opinion] is unmoored from our precedents.

I. A

Today, the Court finally resolves that *Montana v. United States* (1981) governs a tribe's civil jurisdiction over nonmembers regardless of land ownership. This is done with little fanfare, but the holding is significant because we have equivocated on this question in the past. . . .

The [Ninth Circuit U.S.] Court of Appeals [below] concluded that *Montana* did not apply in this case because the events in question occurred on tribal land. Because *Montana* is our best source of "coherence in the . . . law of tribal jurisdiction over non-Indians" [*Atkinson Trading Co. v. Shirley* 2001, 659 (Souter, J., joined by Kennedy and Thomas, JJ., concurring)], the majority is quite right that *Montana* should govern our analysis of a tribe's civil jurisdiction over nonmembers both on and off tribal land. I part company with the majority, however, because its reasoning is not faithful to *Montana* or its progeny.

B

. . . We concluded in *[Montana]* that hunting and fishing by nonmembers on reservation land [owned] by nonmembers of the Tribe did not fit within either of the "*Montana* exceptions" that permit jurisdiction over nonmembers. . . . We "readily agreed" with the Court of Appeals in that case, however, that the Tribe "may prohibit nonmembers from hunting or fishing on land belonging to the Tribe or held by the United States in trust for the Tribe," and that "if the Tribe permits nonmembers to fish or hunt on such lands, it may condition their entry by charging a fee or establishing . . . limits." [*Montana* 1981, 557] In the cases that followed, we uniformly regarded land ownership as an important factor in determining the scope of a tribe's civil jurisdiction. . . . [*Merrion v. Jicarilla Apache Tribe* 1982; *Brendale v. Yakima Indian Nation* 1989; *South Dakota v. Bourland* 1993; *Strate v. A-1 Contractors* 1997]

Just last month, we applied *Montana* in a case concerning a tribe's authority to tax nonmember activity occurring on non-Indian [-owned] land. [*Atkinson Trading Co. v. Shirley* 2001] . . . We [held] . . . that the Tribe's inherent power to tax "only extended to 'transactions occurring on trust lands and significantly involving a tribe or its members.'" [*Atkinson* 2001, 653]. . . .

Montana and our other cases concerning tribal civil jurisdiction over nonmembers occupy a middle ground between our cases that provide for nearly absolute tribal sovereignty over tribe members, and our rule that tribes have no inherent criminal jurisdiction over nonmembers. *Montana* recognizes that tribes retain sovereign interests in activities that occur on land owned and controlled by the tribe, and provides principles that guide our determination of whether particular activities by nonmembers implicate these sovereign interests to a degree that tribal civil jurisdiction is appropriate.

C

. . . The Court's reasoning [in this case] suffers from two serious flaws: It gives only passing consideration to the fact that the state officials' activities in this case occurred on land owned and controlled by the Tribes, and it treats as dispositive the fact that the nonmembers in this case are state officials.

Under the first *Montana* exception, a tribe may exercise regulatory jurisdiction where a nonmember enters into a consensual relationship with the tribe. The majority in this case dismisses the applicability of this exception in [footnote 3], concluding that any consensual relationship between tribes and nonmembers "clearly" must be a "private" consensual relationship "from which the official actions at issue in this case are far removed."

The majority provides no support for this assertion. . . . State governments may enter into consensual relationships with tribes, such as contracts for services or shared authority over public resources. . . . [S]uch relationships could provide official consent to tribal regulatory jurisdiction. Some States have formally sanctioned the creation of tribal-state agreements. In addition, there are a host of cooperative agreements between tribes and state authorities to share control over tribal lands, to manage public services, and to provide law enforcement.

Whether a consensual relationship between the Tribes and the State existed in this case is debatable, but . . . there is no need to create a *per se* rule that forecloses future debate as to whether cooperative agreements, or other forms of official consent, could ever be a basis for tribal jurisdiction.

The second *Montana* exception states that a tribe may regulate nonmember conduct where that conduct "threatens or has some direct effect on the political integrity, the economic security, or the health or welfare of the tribe." [*Montana* 1981, 566] The majority concentrates on this aspect. . . . At the outset, the Court recites relatively uncontroversial propositions [to the effect that tribal jurisdiction must accommodate some forms of state authority on the reservation]. . . .

None of [these propositions], however, "accords" with the majority's conclusion that "tribal authority to regulate state officers in executing process related to [an off-reservation violation of state law] is not essential to tribal self-government or internal relations." Our prior decisions are informed by the understanding that tribal, federal, and state governments *share* authority over tribal lands. Saying that tribal jurisdiction must "accommodate" various sovereign interests does not mean that tribal interests are to be nullified through a *per se* rule.

The majority's rule undermining tribal interests is all the more perplexing because the conduct in this case occurred on land owned and controlled by the Tribes. Although the majority gives a passing nod to land status at the outset of its opinion, that factor is not prominent in the Court's analysis. This oversight is significant. *Montana* recognizes that tribes may retain inherent power to exercise civil jurisdiction when the nonmember conduct "threatens or has some direct effect on the political integrity, the economic security, or the health or welfare of the tribe." [*Montana* 1981, 566] These interests are far more likely to be implicated where, as here, the nonmember activity takes place on land owned and controlled by the tribe. If *Montana* is to bring coherence to our case law, we must apply it with due consideration to land status, which has always figured prominently in our analysis of tribal jurisdiction.

This case involves state officials acting on tribal land. The Tribes' sovereign interests with respect to nonmember activities on its land are not extinguished simply because the nonmembers in this case are state officials enforcing state law. Our cases concerning tribal power often involve the competing interests of state, federal, and tribal governments. The actions of state officials on tribal land in some instances may affect tribal sovereign interests to a greater, not lesser, degree than the actions of private parties. In this case for example, it is alleged that state officers, who gained access to Hicks's property by virtue of their authority as state actors, exceeded the scope of the search warrants and damaged Hicks's personal property.

Certainly, state officials should be protected from civil liability for actions undertaken within the scope of their duties. . . . The Court . . . announces . . . that state officials "cannot be regulated in the performance of their law-enforcement duties," but "action unrelated to that is potentially subject to tribal control." Here, Hicks alleges that state officials exceeded the scope of their authority under the search warrants. The Court holds that the state officials may not be held liable in Tribal Court for these actions, but never explains where these, or more serious allegations involving a breach of authority, would fall within its new rule of state official immunity.

The Court's reasoning [is] not . . . faithful . . . [to] *Montana* and its progeny. . . . If the Court were to remain true to [those] principles . . . , [it] would reverse and remand the case to the Court of Appeals for a proper application of *Montana* to determine whether there is tribal jurisdiction. . . .

II

The Court's sweeping analysis gives the impression that this case involves a conflict of great magnitude between the State of Nevada and the Fallon Paiute–Shoshone Tribes. That is not so. At no point did the Tribes attempt to exclude the State from the reservation. At no point did the Tribes attempt to obstruct state officials' efforts to secure or execute the search warrants. Quite the contrary, the record demonstrates that judicial and law enforcement officials from the State and the Tribes acted in full cooperation to investigate an off-reservation crime.

In this case, Hicks attempts to hold state officials (and tribal officials) liable for allegedly exceeding the scope of the search warrants and damaging his personal property. This case concerns the Trib[al

Court's] civil adjudicatory jurisdiction over state officials [i.e., the power to hold them liable as defendants in this civil lawsuit]. The Court concludes that it cannot address adjudicatory jurisdiction without first addressing the Tribes' regulatory jurisdiction [e.g., whether the state officials were required to seek the Tribal Court warrant obtained in this case before carrying out the search]. But there is no need for the Court to decide the precise scope of a tribe's regulatory jurisdiction, or to decide in this case whether a tribe's adjudicatory jurisdiction equals its regulatory jurisdiction.

. . . [Nevada] contend[s] that tribal court jurisdiction over state officials should be determined with reference to officials' claims of immunity [from civil lawsuits]. I agree. . . . The doctrines of official immunity are designed to protect state and federal officials from civil liability for conduct that was within the scope of their duties or conduct that did not violate clearly established law. These doctrines short circuit civil litigation for officials who meet these standards so that [they] are not subjected to the costs of trial or the burdens of discovery. . . .

In this case, the state officials raised their immunity defenses [to Hicks's claims] in Tribal Court as they challenged that court's . . . jurisdiction. [The Tribal Court acknowledged but did not consider the immunity defenses in determining its jurisdiction.] Thus the Tribal Court and the Appellate Tribal Court had a full opportunity to address the immunity claims [but did not do so]. These defendants, like other officials facing civil liability, were entitled to have their immunity defenses adjudicated at the earliest stage possible to avoid needless litigation. It requires no "magic" to afford officials the same protection in tribal court that they would be afforded in state or federal court. I would therefore reverse the [U.S.] Court of Appeals in this case on the ground that it erred in failing to address the state officials' immunity defenses [in making its own determination that the tribal courts have jurisdiction]. It is possible that Hicks's lawsuits would have been easily disposed of on the basis of official . . . immunity.

Tribal Gambling

California v. Cabazon Band of Mission Indians (1987)

U.S. Supreme Court
February 25, 1987
480 U.S. 202

The Court's opinion was written by Justice Byron R. White, appointed by President John F. Kennedy in 1962. The decision was 6–3. White's opinion was joined by Chief Justice William H. Rehnquist, appointed as associate justice by President Richard M. Nixon in 1972 and as chief justice by President Ronald W. Reagan in 1986; Justice William J. Brennan, Jr., appointed by President Dwight D. Eisenhower in 1956; Justice Thurgood Marshall, appointed by President Lyndon B. Johnson in 1967; and Justices Harry A. Blackmun and Lewis F. Powell, Jr., appointed by President Nixon in 1970 and 1972, respectively. Justice John Paul Stevens, appointed by President Gerald R. Ford in 1975, wrote a dissenting opinion, joined by Justices Sandra Day O'Connor and Antonin Scalia, appointed by President Reagan in 1981 and 1986, respectively.

Justice White (for the Court):

The Cabazon and Morongo Bands of Mission Indians, federally recognized Indian Tribes, occupy reservations in Riverside County, California. [Footnote 1: . . . The Cabazon Band has 25 enrolled members and the Morongo Band . . . approximately 730. . . .] Each Band, pursuant to an ordinance approved by the [U.S.] Secretary of the Interior, conducts bingo games on its reservation. The Cabazon Band has also opened a card club at which draw poker and other card games are played. The games are open to the public and are played predominantly by non-Indians coming onto the reservations. The games are a major source of employment for tribal members, and the profits are the Tribes' sole source of income. The State of California seeks to apply to the two Tribes [a California Penal Code provision that] . . . does not entirely prohibit the playing of bingo but permits it [only] when the games are operated and staffed by members of designated charitable organizations who may not be paid for their services. Profits must be kept in special accounts and used only for charitable purposes; prizes may not exceed $250 per game. Asserting that the bingo games on the two reservations violated each of these restrictions, California insisted that the Tribes comply with state law. Riverside County also sought to apply its local [o]rdinance . . . regulating bingo, as well as its [o]rdinance . . . prohibiting the playing of draw poker and the other card games. . . .

I

Th[is] Court has consistently recognized that Indian tribes retain "attributes of sovereignty over both their members and their territory" [*United States v. Mazurie* 1975, 557], and that "tribal sovereignty is dependent on, and subordinate to, only the Federal Government, not the States" [*Washington v. Confederated Tribes of the Colville Indian Reservation* 1980, 154]. It is clear, however, that state laws may be applied to tribal Indians on their reservations if Congress has expressly so provided. Here, the State insists that Congress has . . . given its express consent . . . in [Public Law 280, passed] in 1953. . . . We disagree. . . .

In Public Law 280, Congress expressly granted six States, including California, jurisdiction over specified areas of Indian country within th[ose] States. . . . California was granted broad criminal jurisdiction over offenses committed by or against Indians within all Indian country [i.e., all Indian reservations] within the State. [Public Law 280's] grant of civil jurisdiction was more limited. In *Bryan v. Itasca County* (1976), we interpreted [Public Law 280] to grant [the] States [covered by Public Law 280] jurisdiction over private civil litigation involving reservation Indians in state court, but not to grant general civil regulatory authority. [*Bryan* 1976, 385, 388–390] We held, therefore, that Minnesota could not apply its personal property tax within [an Indian] reservation. Congress's primary concern in enacting Public Law 280 was combating lawlessness on reservations. [*Bryan* 1976, 379–380] [Public Law 280] plainly was not intended to effect total assimilation of Indian tribes into mainstream American society. [*Bryan* 1976, 387] We recognized that a grant to States of general civil regulatory power [e.g., covering taxation, land-use zoning, family law, health, safety, welfare, etc.] over Indian reservations would result in the destruction of tribal institutions and values. Accordingly, when a State seeks to enforce a law within an Indian reservation under the authority of Public Law 280, it must be determined whether the law is criminal in nature, and thus fully applicable to the reservation . . . , or civil in nature, and applicable only as it may be relevant to private civil litigation in state court.

The Minnesota personal property tax at issue in *Bryan* was unquestionably civil in nature. The California bingo statute is not so easily categorized. California law permits bingo games to be conducted only by charitable and other specified organizations, and then only by their members who may not receive any wage or profit for doing so; prizes are limited and receipts are to be segregated and used only for charitable purposes. Violation of any of these provisions is a misdemeanor. California insists that these are criminal laws which Public Law 280 permits it to enforce on the reservations.

[The Ninth Circuit U.S. Court of Appeals], applying what it thought to be the civil/criminal dichotomy [of] *Bryan[,]* . . . [has drawn] a distinction between state "criminal/prohibitory" laws and state "civil/regulatory" laws: [I]f the intent of a state law is generally to prohibit certain conduct, it falls within Public Law 280's grant of criminal jurisdiction, but if the state law generally permits the conduct at issue, subject to regulation, it must be classified as civil/regulatory and Public Law 280 does not authorize its enforcement on an Indian reservation. The shorthand test is whether the conduct at issue violates the State's public policy. Inquiring into the nature of [the California bingo statute], the Court of Appeals held that it was regulatory rather than prohibitory. . . .

We are persuaded that the prohibitory/regulatory distinction is consistent with *Bryan*'s construction of Public Law 280. It is not a bright-line rule [and] . . . an argument of some weight may be made that the bingo statute is prohibitory rather than regulatory. But . . . we are reluctant to disagree with [the Court of Appeals'] view of the nature and intent of the state law at issue here.

There is surely a fair basis for [this] conclusion. California does not prohibit all forms of gambling. California itself operates a state lottery [pursuant to a 1984 state constitutional amendment approved by voter proposition], and daily encourages its citizens to participate in this state-run gambling. California also permits parimutuel horse-race betting. Although certain enumerated gambling games are prohibited under [the California Penal Code], games not enumerated, including the card games played in the Cabazon card club, are permissible. The Tribes assert that more than 400 card rooms similar to the Cabazon card club flourish in California, and the State does not dispute this fact. Also, . . . bingo is legally sponsored by many different organizations and is widely played in California. . . . In light of the fact that California permits a substantial amount of gambling activity, including bingo, and actually promotes gambling through its state lottery, we must conclude that California regulates rather than prohibits gambling in general and bingo in particular. [Fn. 10]

[Footnote 10: Nothing in this opinion suggests that cockfighting, tattoo parlors, nude dancing, and prostitution are permissible on Indian reservations within California [as the dissenting opinion argues]. The applicable state laws governing an activity must be examined in detail before they can be characterized as regulatory or prohibitory.

The lower courts have not demonstrated an inability to identify prohibitory laws. For example, in *United States v. Marcyes* (1977), the [Ninth Circuit U.S.] Court of Appeals adopted and applied the prohibitory/regulatory distinction in determining whether a state law governing the possession of fireworks was made applicable to Indian reservations by the [federal] Assimilative Crimes [Act, which, in conjunction with the Indian Country Crimes Act, applies in those states not covered by Public Law 280]. The court concluded that, despite limited exceptions to the [state fireworks law's] prohibition, [it] was prohibitory in nature.]

California argues, however, that high stakes, unregulated bingo, . . . which attracts organized crime, is a misdemeanor in California and may be prohibited on Indian reservations. But that an otherwise regulatory law is enforceable by criminal as well as civil means does not necessarily convert it into a criminal law within the meaning of Public Law 280. Otherwise, the distinction between [criminal and civil jurisdiction under] that law could easily be avoided and total assimilation permitted. . . . Accordingly, . . . Public Law 280 does not authorize California [or Riverside County] to enforce [the state bingo statute or county bingo and card game ordinances] within the Cabazon and Morongo Reservations. . . .

II

. . . This case . . . involves a state burden on tribal Indians in the context of their dealings with non-Indians since the question is whether the State may prevent the Tribes from making available high stakes bingo games to non-Indians coming from outside the reservations. . . . [S]tate authority . . . "is pre-empted . . . if it interferes . . . with federal and tribal interests reflected in federal law, unless the state interests at stake are sufficient to justify the assertion of state authority." [*New Mexico v. Mescalero Apache Tribe* 1983, 333–334] The inquiry is to proceed in light of traditional notions of Indian sovereignty and the congressional goal of Indian self-government, including its "overriding goal" of encouraging tribal self-sufficiency and economic development. [*Mescalero* 1983, 334–335]

These are important federal interests. They were reaffirmed by [President Ronald Reagan's] 1983 Statement on Indian Policy. More specifically, the Department of the Interior, which has the primary responsibility for carrying out the Federal Government's trust obligations to Indian tribes, [and also the Department of Health and Human

Services and the Department of Housing and Urban Development,] ha[ve] sought to implement these policies by promoting tribal bingo enterprises. . . .

These policies and actions, which demonstrate the Government's approval and active promotion of tribal bingo enterprises, are of particular relevance in this case. The Cabazon and Morongo Reservations contain no natural resources which can be exploited. The tribal games at present provide the sole source of revenues for the operation of the tribal governments and the provision of tribal services. They are also the major sources of employment on the reservations. Self-determination and economic development are not within reach if the Tribes cannot raise revenues and provide employment for their members. The Tribes' interests obviously parallel the federal interests.

California seeks to diminish the weight of these seemingly important tribal interests by asserting that the Tribes are merely marketing an exemption from state gambling laws. In *Washington v. Confederated Tribes of the Colville Indian Reservation* (1980), we held that the State could tax cigarettes sold by tribal smokeshops to non-Indians, even though it would eliminate their competitive advantage and substantially reduce revenues used to provide tribal services, because the Tribes had no right "to market an exemption from state taxation to persons who would normally do their business elsewhere." We stated that "[it] is painfully apparent that the value marketed by the smokeshops to persons coming from outside is not generated on the reservations. . . ." [*Colville* 1980, 155] Here, however, the Tribes are not merely importing a product onto the reservations for immediate resale to non-Indians. They have built modern facilities which provide recreational opportunities and ancillary services to their patrons, who do not simply drive onto the reservations, make purchases and depart, but spend extended periods of time there enjoying the services the Tribes provide. The Tribes have a strong incentive to provide comfortable, clean, and attractive facilities and well-run games in order to increase attendance at the games.

The tribal bingo enterprises are similar to the resort complex, featuring hunting and fishing, that the Mescalero Apache Tribe operates on its reservation through the "concerted and sustained" management of reservation land and wildlife resources. [*New Mexico v. Mescalero Apache Tribe* 1983, 341] The Mescalero project generates funds for essential tribal services and provides employment for tribal members. We there rejected the notion that the Tribe [was] merely marketing an exemption from state hunting and fishing regulations and concluded that New Mexico could not regulate on-reservation fishing and hunting by non-Indians. Similarly, the Cabazon and Morongo Bands are generating value on the reservations through activities in which they have a substantial interest. . . .

The [other] interest asserted by the State to justify the imposition of its bingo laws on the Tribes is in preventing the infiltration of the tribal games by organized crime. To the extent that the State seeks to prevent any and all bingo games from being played on tribal lands while permitting regulated, off-reservation games, this asserted interest is irrelevant. . . . The State insists that the high stakes offered at tribal games are attractive to organized crime, whereas the controlled games authorized under California law are not. This is surely a legitimate concern, but we are unconvinced that it is sufficient. . . . California does not allege any present criminal involvement in the Cabazon and Morongo enterprises. . . . [F]ar from any action being taken [by the Federal Government] evidencing this concern[,] . . . the prevailing federal policy continues to support these tribal enterprises, including those of the Tribes involved in this case.

We conclude that the State's interest in preventing the infiltration of the tribal bingo enterprises by organized crime does not justify state regulation of [those] enterprises in light of the compelling federal and tribal interests supporting them. . . .

Justice Stevens (dissenting, joined by Justices O'Connor and Scalia):

Unless and until Congress exempts Indian-managed gambling from state law and subjects it to federal supervision, I believe that a State may enforce its laws prohibiting high-stakes gambling on Indian reservations within its borders. Congress has not pre-empted California's prohibition against high-stakes bingo games and the Secretary of the Interior plainly has no authority to do so. While gambling provides needed employment and income for Indian tribes, these benefits do not, in my opinion, justify tribal operation of currently unlawful commercial activities. Accepting the majority's reasoning would require exemptions for cockfighting, tattoo parlors, nude dancing, houses of prostitution, and other illegal but profitable enterprises. As the law now stands, I believe tribal entrepreneurs, like others who might derive profits from catering to non-Indian customers, must obey applicable state laws.

In my opinion the plain language of Public Law 280 authorizes California to enforce its prohibition against commercial gambling on

Indian reservations. . . . [Also,] [o]ur . . . recent cases have made it clear . . . that commercial transactions between Indians and non-Indians—even when conducted on a reservation—do not enjoy any blanket immunity from state regulation. . . .

Today the Court seems prepared to acknowledge that an Indian tribe's commercial transactions with non-Indians may violate "the State's public policy." The Court reasons, however, that the operation of high-stakes bingo games does not run afoul of California's public policy because the State permits some forms of gambling and, specifically, some forms of bingo. I find this approach to "public policy" curious, to say the least. The State's policy concerning gambling is to authorize certain specific gambling activities that comply with carefully defined regulation and that provide revenues either for the State itself or for certain charitable purposes, and to prohibit all unregulated commercial lotteries that are operated for private profit. To argue that the tribal bingo games comply with the public policy of California because the State permits some other gambling is tantamount to arguing that driving over 60 miles an hour is consistent with public policy because the State allows driving at speeds of up to 55 miles an hour.

In my view, Congress has permitted the State to apply its prohibitions against commercial gambling to Indian tribes. Even if Congress had not done so, however, the State has the authority to assert jurisdiction over [these] gambling activities [involving non-Indians]. We recognized this authority in *Washington v. Confederated Tribes of the Colville Indian Reservation* (1980) [the tribal smokeshop case]; the Court's attempt to distinguish the reasoning of our decision in that case is unpersuasive. . . . Similarly [to *Colville*], it is painfully obvious that the value of the Tribe's asserted exemption from California's gambling laws is the primary attraction to customers who would normally do their gambling elsewhere. The Cabazon Band of Mission Indians has no tradition or special expertise in the operation of large bingo parlors. Indeed, the entire membership of the Cabazon Tribe—it has only 25 enrolled members—is barely adequate to operate a bingo game that is patronized by hundreds of non-Indians nightly. How this small and formerly impoverished Band of Indians could have attracted the investment capital for its enterprise without benefit of the claimed exemption is certainly a mystery to me. . . .

Moreover, I am unwilling to dismiss as readily as the Court does the State's concern that these unregulated high-stakes bingo games may attract organized criminal infiltration. . . . In my judgment, unless Congress authorizes and regulates these commercial gambling ventures catering to non-Indians, the State has a legitimate law enforcement interest in proscribing them.

[The Tribes] and the Secretary of the Interior may well be correct, in the abstract, that gambling facilities are a sensible way to generate revenues that are badly needed by reservation Indians. But the decision to adopt, to reject, or to define the precise contours of such a course of action, and thereby to set aside the substantial public policy concerns of a sovereign State, should be made by the Congress of the United States. It should not be made by this Court, by the temporary occupant of the Office of the Secretary of the Interior, or by non-Indian entrepreneurs who are experts in gambling management but not necessarily dedicated to serving the future well-being of Indian tribes.

Hotel Employees Union v. Davis (1999)

California Supreme Court
August 23, 1999
21 Cal. 4th 585; 981 P.2d 990; 88 Cal. Rptr. 2d 56

The Court's opinion was written by Justice Kathryn Mickle Werdegar, appointed by California governor Pete Wilson in 1994. The decision was 6–1. Werdegar's opinion was joined by Chief Justice Ronald M. George and Justices Ming W. Chin and Janice Rogers Brown, all appointed by Governor Wilson in 1996; and (sitting by designation) Court of Appeal justices Arthur L. Gilbert, appointed by Governor Jerry Brown in 1982; and Barton C. Gaut, appointed by Governor Wilson in 1997. Supreme Court justices Stanley Mosk, appointed by Governor Pat Brown in 1964, and Marvin R. Baxter, appointed by Governor George Deukmejian in 1991, did not participate. Justice Joyce L. Kennard, appointed by Governor Deukmejian in 1989, wrote a dissenting opinion.

Justice Werdegar (for the Court):

In [the November] 1984 [election], the people of California amended our [State] Constitution to state a fundamental public policy against the legalization in California of casino gambling of the sort then associated with Las Vegas and Atlantic City. . . . In [the November] 1998 . . . [e]lection, the people approved a proposed initiative statute designated on the ballot as Proposition 5—"The Tribal Government Gaming and Economic Self-Sufficiency Act of 1998"—concerning gaming on Indian lands in the State of California. . . . [Proposition 5] purport[s] to authorize various forms of gaming in tribal casinos. . . . [T]o authorize such gaming facilities, however, would be to authorize casinos of the type expressly prohibited by [the 1984 constitutional amendment]. Because Proposition 5, a purely statutory measure, did not amend . . . the Constitution, and because in a conflict between statutory and constitutional law the Constitution must prevail, we conclude Proposition 5's authorization of casino gambling is invalid and inoperative. . . .

DISCUSSION

I. Legal Background. . . .

A. California Gambling Law

Since 1849, the California Constitution has generally prohibited all lotteries and the sale of all lottery tickets. In the original document of 1849, the Constitution prohibited all lotteries and the sale of all lottery tickets. . . . In the current document of 1879, it continues the prohibition, . . . presently in article IV, section 19(a), which declares: "The Legislature has no power to authorize lotteries and shall prohibit the sale of lottery tickets in the State." . . . But since 1984, through the addition of article IV, section 19(d), the California Constitution has provided: "Notwithstanding subdivision (a), there is authorized the establishment of a California State Lottery." . . . [Also] since 1984, through the addition of section 19(e), the California Constitution has declared: "The Legislature has no power to authorize, and shall prohibit casinos of the type currently operating in Nevada and New Jersey." [The 1984 amendments are henceforth referred to as "the Lottery Amendment."]

B. Federal Indian Gaming Law

. . . In 1988, in the wake of [*California v. Cabazon Band of Mission Indians* 1987], Congress enacted [the Indian Gaming Regulatory Act ("IGRA")], with the declared purpose to "provide a statutory basis for the operation of gaming by Indian tribes as a means of promoting tribal economic development, self-sufficiency, and strong tribal governments," while at the same time providing a basis for regulation of Indian gaming so as to shield it from organized crime and corruption, prevent exploitation for non-Indian profit, and ensure fair and honest gaming.

. . . IGRA divides gaming into three categories—"class I," "class II," and "class III." Class I gaming is "social games solely for prizes of minimal value or traditional forms of Indian gaming engaged in by individuals as a part of, or in connection with, tribal ceremonies or celebrations."

Class II gaming is defined to include: "(i) the game of chance commonly known as bingo" and "(ii) card games" that "are explicitly authorized by the laws of the State" or "are not explicitly prohibited by the laws of the State and are played at any location in the State," "but only if such card games are played in conformity with . . . laws and regulations (if any) of the State regarding hours or periods of operation . . . or limitations on wagers or pot sizes. . . ." [IGRA] excludes from its definition of class II gaming: "(i) any banking card games, including baccarat, chemin de fer, or blackjack (21)" and "(ii) electronic or electromechanical facsimiles of any game of chance or slot machines of any kind."

Class III gaming is defined as "all forms of gaming that are not class I gaming or class II gaming" [i.e., class III includes parimutuel race wagering, lotteries, and what are typically regarded as high-stakes casino-style games, including baccarat, chemin de fer, blackjack or 21, other banked card games, craps, roulette, etc., and slot machines or electronic versions thereof].

. . . IGRA provides for the regulation of each of the three categories of gaming—from the lightest regulation for class I, by tribal action alone without federal or state participation; to heavier regulation for class II, by joint federal and tribal participation; to the heaviest regulation for class III, by state and tribal participation through tribal-state compacts plus federal oversight.

. . . IGRA states that class III gaming activities are "lawful . . . only if such activities are . . . authorized by an ordinance or resolution" that, among other things, is adopted by an Indian tribe and approved by the Chairman of the National Indian Gaming Commission; . . . "located in a State that permits such gaming for any purpose by any person, organization, or entity"; and " . . . conducted in conformance with a Tribal-State compact entered into by the Indian tribe and the State." . . . IGRA describes the process whereby the Indian tribe and the state may commence negotiations toward a tribal-state compact: [T]he tribe must "request" that the state "enter into negotiations," and, on receiving such request, the state must proceed to "negotiate with the Indian tribe in good faith. . . ." A compact takes effect only when approved by the Secretary of the Interior.

C. Legal Conflicts Leading up to Proposition 5

Despite IGRA's negotiation and compact framework, several unresolved conflicts have developed between the State of California and Indian tribes surrounding class III gaming and, especially, gaming devices in casinos. Class III gaming . . . is, unquestionably, the "most lucrative kind." . . .

While . . . [legal] proceedings [involving several of these conflicts] . . . were pending, a number of the tribes commenced and continued class III gaming activities without tribal-state compacts; in response, Governor Wilson refused to negotiate further until they ceased such gaming activities. Governor Wilson instead negotiated a compact with the Pala Band of Mission Indians, a tribe previously without gaming facilities, which he intended to serve as a statewide model. In part because of objections to the negotiation procedures and in part because of restrictions the Pala compact placed on the type and number of gaming devices, most of the tribes with existing casinos rejected the Pala compact.

It was to resolve such conflicts between the State of California and Indian tribes relative to class III gaming on Indian lands that Proposition 5 was drafted and circulated by petition. That [Proposition 5] might not meet its purpose was known before the election: [A]fter the measure qualified for the ballot, but prior to the election, the Legislative Counsel issued an opinion concluding . . . that the measure would be invalid under [the Lottery Amendment] because it would authorize "casinos of the type currently operating in Nevada and New Jersey." At the election the people nevertheless approved the measure.

[Part II is omitted.]

III. Proposition 5 and [the Lottery Amendment]

We turn to the claims . . . that Proposition 5 is invalid under the California Constitution, specifically [the Lottery Amendment]. . . . [W]e begin by examining and interpreting each part of [the Lottery Amendment's ban on casinos].

"The Legislature has no power. . . ."

The "power" referred to is, of course, the legislative power. . . . The legislative power may be exercised by either of two legislative bodies. . . . [I]t is "vested" in the Legislature and also "reserve[d]" to the people acting through initiative [and referendum], specifically, initiative statute. [The Lottery Amendment] could, therefore, be taken, relatively narrowly, to deny legislative power to the Legislature alone of the two legislative bodies, or, relatively broadly, to deny legislative power . . . to both legislative bodies. For two reasons, we conclude the broader interpretation is the correct one.

First, as we held in . . . [1983], "[a] statutory initiative is subject to the same state and federal constitutional limitations as are the Legislature and the statutes which it enacts." . . . Second, . . . [f]rom all that appears, [the Lottery Amendment] was designed to proscribe casinos . . . by constitutional force, preventing any future . . . authorization of such casinos without constitutional amendment. It was not designed to proscribe . . . casinos only if they were authorized by the Legislature. [Fn. 2]

[Footnote 2: Unlike the parties, Justice Kennard focuses on the word "authorize" in [the Lottery Amendment], arguing that . . . "it is federal law, not state law, that authorizes Indian gambling. . . ." By [its] terms, however, [Proposition 5] . . . "authorize[s]" various forms of . . . tribal gaming. . . . Moreover, as federal legal authority for class III gaming is, under IGRA, dependent in two ways on state authorization ([by] . . . requiring [that] such gaming be permitted under state law . . . [or by] requiring [the] existence of [a] compact entered into by state and tribe), Justice Kennard's attempt to draw a bright line between federal and state authority in this area is unavailing.]

"Casinos . . . [o]f the type currently operating in Nevada and New Jersey."

. . . What was meant by "the type" of casino "operating in Nevada and New Jersey" in 1984? [The Lottery Amendment] contains no definition of this phrase. Logic and reference to legislative history, however, allow us to see with reasonable clarity what the drafters and voters intended to prohibit in 1984.

The 1984 constitutional amenders must have had in mind a type of gambling house unique to or particularly associated with Nevada and New Jersey, since they chose to define the prohibited institution by reference to those states. On this logic, the "type" of casino referred to must be an establishment that offers gaming activities including banked table games and gaming devices, i.e., slot machines, for in 1984 that "type" of casino was legal only in Nevada and New Jersey. . . .

. . . Proposition 5, including its model tribal-state compact, authorizes what would amount to prohibited casinos. . . .

Against the conclusion that Proposition 5 is invalid . . . [under] the anticasino provision of [the Lottery Amendment], [it is] argue[d] that

IGRA pre-empts the anticasino provision. . . . [The argument] is misplaced because IGRA legalizes only gaming conducted pursuant to a compact validly entered into by both the state and the tribe. . . . To be "entered into" by the state and the tribe means to be "entered into" validly in accordance with state (and tribal) law.

With respect to a tribal-state compact, IGRA balances the interests of the state and the tribe. Its balancing is predicated on a recognition that the state and the tribe are sovereigns, albeit sovereigns subordinate to the federal union. . . . To recognize that the state and the tribe are sovereigns entails an acknowledgment that the law of each operates in its proper sphere and, therefore, that the law of each governs the validity of its own entry into a compact. IGRA would not make lawful particular gaming activities included in a compact if the compact itself were not validly entered into under the law of both the state and the Indian tribe in question. Such is the case here for the model tribal-state compact set forth in Proposition 5: [E]ntry into such a compact is beyond the legislative power under the law of California, conflicting as it would with the anticasino provision of [the Lottery Amendment]. . . .

Justice Kennard (dissenting):

One of the fundamental powers reserved to the people of this state is the power to enact legislation by initiative. . . . At the November 1998 [e]lection, the voters of California exercised their initiative power and enacted into law Proposition 5. The initiative offers Indian tribes a model agreement, or compact, regulating the conditions of gambling on Indian lands. Federal law requires either such a compact, or authorization by the Secretary of the Interior, before tribes may conduct gambling.

Today, the majority rejects the will of the people by invalidating the model compact of Proposition 5. . . . In the majority's view, the model compact authorizes . . . casino gambling and therefore violates [the Lottery Amendment of the California Constitution]. I disagree. . . .

I. The Primacy of Federal Authority over Indian Gambling

As the aboriginal possessors of America, Indian tribes have a unique and sovereign relationship with both the federal government and the states within which they are located. Tribal sovereignty and the federal power over Indian relations greatly limit the power of states to regulate Indian tribes and activities on tribal lands without congressional authorization. . . . From the earliest days of our nation, states have lacked any general sovereign power over Indian tribes and tribal lands. [*Worcester v. Georgia* 1832] . . .

In *California v. Cabazon Band of Mission Indians* (1987), the United States Supreme Court rejected California's argument that . . . Congress had intended to extend all state gambling laws to Indian country. . . . In the wake of that decision, Congress in 1988 enacted a detailed statutory scheme, [IGRA], to regulate gambling on tribal lands. In the structure and scope of IGRA, which comprehensively addresses all forms of gambling on Indian lands, Congress made clear its intent that IGRA pre-empt the field of regulation of Indian gambling . . . [and] preclude state jurisdiction over Indian gambling. . . .

IGRA also removed the power of states, recognized in *[Cabazon]*, to apply to Indian lands those state laws absolutely prohibiting a particular form of gambling. Instead, IGRA included a new federal criminal statute, . . . criminalizing gambling in "Indian country" that is not authorized by IGRA. The federal statute adopts "for purposes of Federal law" state gambling laws, but the federal government has exclusive jurisdiction to prosecute these offenses.

Thus, if a state authorizes class III gaming activities by anyone, federal law authorizes a tribe to engage in those same activities once the tribe adopts an Indian gambling ordinance approved by the Chairman of the National Indian Gaming Commission and enters into a compact with the state. If the state fails or refuses to reach an agreement with the tribe, the Secretary of the Interior may authorize tribal gambling.

Several crucial points emerge from this review of IGRA. First, authorization or prohibition of Indian gambling is exclusively a matter of paramount federal law. Where Indian gambling is authorized, it is authorized by operation of federal law. Where Indian gambling is prohibited, it is prohibited by operation of federal law. Although a state's gambling law may shape the contours of the federal authorization, a state may not directly prohibit Indian gambling as such. A state may not criminalize or prosecute any tribal gambling activities, even for forms of gambling that the state prohibits to everyone [else]. Only the federal government may prosecute gambling that IGRA does not authorize. Nor can a state on its own authorize Indians to engage in gambling, even gambling that it permits everyone else to engage in. For example, even if slot machines were legal everywhere else in California, IGRA would still prohibit their use on a reservation absent an approved tribal ordinance and a tribal-state compact. Even the power of a state to shape the contours of federal authorization is extremely limited. Once a state permits even a single entity (including the state itself) to engage in a class III gaming activity, federal law authorizes all tribes within the state to engage in that form of gambling (once they adopt an approved tribal ordinance and either enter into a compact or, if the state refuses to enter into a compact, receive authorization from the Secretary of the Interior).

II. Does the Model Compact of Proposition 5 Violate the California Constitution?

Do[es] [the Lottery Amendment] . . . bar the state from entering into the model tribal-state compact in accordance with IGRA, as the majority concludes? The answer is no. . . .

By entering into a tribal-state compact the state does not "authorize" . . . gambling. A state may only authorize, or prohibit, acts that are within the limits of its sovereignty. For the reasons stated above, it is utterly beyond the sovereign power of California to authorize or prohibit gambling on Indian lands within the state. California can no more authorize gambling on Indian lands than it can authorize gambling in another state. . . . Although the state may facilitate Indian gambling by negotiating and entering into a compact, doing so does not authorize Indian gambling in the sense of granting permission for an act the state otherwise has the power to prohibit. Nor does a state's failure to enter into a compact have the effect of prohibiting Indian gambling, for in the absence of a compact IGRA directs the Secretary of the Interior to establish procedures governing tribal gambling. The Legislature or, in this case, the voters, cannot sensibly be described as "authorizing" something they lack the power to prohibit.

To be sure, as the majority notes, [Proposition 5] purports to "authorize" tribes to engage in certain forms of class III gaming. Whether a tribe is authorized to engage in class III gaming, however, is a question of federal, not state, law. Whatever [Proposition 5] may say, it cannot [by itself] authorize a tribe to engage in class III gaming. . . .

The parallel case of an interstate compact regulating gambling in another state also illustrates why a tribal-state gambling compact does not unconstitutionally authorize gambling. To further California's interests, the Legislature has entered into a compact with the neighboring State of Nevada, the Tahoe Regional Planning Compact, regulating the number and size of gaming facilities located in Nevada within the Lake Tahoe Basin. That compact has never been considered to be an act by the Legislature authorizing casinos within the meaning of the term "authorize" as used in [the Lottery Amendment].

Indeed, if any act of the State of California may be properly characterized as authorizing Indian gambling, it is the enactment of the constitutional provisions and statutes creating the California state lottery and horse race wagering. These statutes authorizing forms of class III gambling trigger by force of federal law the collateral consequence of authorizing Indian tribes to engage in the same forms of gambling. But these statutes are constitutionally permitted; therefore, if they are the act of authorization of tribal gambling there is nothing unconstitutional about the authorization. . . .

Conclusion

The rise of Indian gambling in the past two decades has stirred deep passions and heated political debate. The voters of California sought to resolve the status of Indian gambling in our state by enacting the model Tribal-State Gaming Compact of Proposition 5. Because the model compact complies both with our state Constitution and with the federal Indian Gaming Regulatory Act, I would uphold the will of the voters. . . .

Gaming Compact between the State of California and California Indian Tribes (2000)

May 16, 2000

see http://www.cfk.com/final%20compact.htm

Following is an edited version of the standard text of the compact signed on September 10, 1999, by California governor Gray Davis and the leaders of fifty-nine California Indian tribes. Some modifications exist in the individual versions of the compact that ultimately took effect between the state and each signatory tribe (some additional tribes have since joined). The compact was approved by the voters of California on March 7, 2000, by passage of Proposition 1A, and took effect on May 16, 2000, upon approval by the U.S. Department of the Interior in accordance with the federal Indian Gaming Regulatory Act of 1988.

This Tribal-State Gaming Compact is entered into on a government-to-government basis by and between . . . [various] federally-recognized sovereign Indian tribe[s] (hereafter "Tribe"), and the State of

California, a sovereign State of the United States (hereafter "State"), pursuant to the Indian Gaming Regulatory Act of 1988 (hereafter "IGRA")....

PREAMBLE

A.... IGRA ... provide[s] a statutory basis for the operation of gaming by Indian tribes as a means of promoting tribal economic development, self-sufficiency, and strong tribal governments; [and] to provide ... regulation of Indian gaming adequate to shield it from organized crime and other corrupting influences....

B.... IGRA rests on an allocation of regulatory jurisdiction among the three sovereigns involved: the federal government, the state in which a tribe has land, and the tribe itself....

D. The State enters into this Compact out of respect for the sovereignty of the Tribe; in recognition of the historical fact that Indian gaming has become the single largest revenue-producing activity for Indian tribes in the United States; out of a desire to terminate pending ... litigation between the Tribe and the State; to initiate a new era of tribal-state cooperation in areas of mutual concern; out of a respect for the sentiment of the voters of California who, in approving Proposition 5, expressed their belief that the forms of gaming authorized herein should be allowed; and in anticipation of voter approval of [Proposition 1A] as passed by the California legislature.

E. The exclusive rights that Indian tribes in California ... will enjoy under this Compact create a unique opportunity for the Tribe to operate its Gaming Facility in an economic environment free of competition.... In consideration for the[se] ... rights ... [and] for the State's willingness to enter into this Compact, the tribes have agreed to provide to the State, on a sovereign-to-sovereign basis, a portion of [their] revenue from Gaming Devices.

F. The State has a legitimate interest in promoting the purposes of IGRA for all federally-recognized Indian tribes in California, whether gaming or non-gaming. The State contends that it has an equally legitimate sovereign interest in regulating the growth of Class III gaming activities in California. The Tribe and the State share a joint sovereign interest in ensuring that tribal gaming activities are free from criminal and other undesirable elements.

Section 1.0. PURPOSES AND OBJECTIVES

The terms of this Gaming Compact are designed and intended to:

(a) Evidence the goodwill and cooperation of the Tribe and State in fostering a mutually respectful government-to-government relationship that will serve the mutual interests of the parties.

(b) Develop and implement a means of regulating Class III gaming. . . .

(c) Promote ethical practices in conjunction with that gaming. . . .

Section 2.0. DEFINITIONS . . .

2.2. "Association" means an association of California tribal and state gaming regulators, the membership of which comprises up to two representatives from each tribal gaming agency of those tribes with whom the State has a gaming compact under IGRA, and up to two delegates each from the state Division of Gambling Control and the state Gambling Control Commission. . . .

2.10. "Gaming Ordinance" means a tribal ordinance or resolution duly authorizing the conduct of Class III Gaming Activities on the Tribe's Indian lands and approved under IGRA. . . .

2.20. "Tribal Gaming Agency" means the person, agency, board, committee, commission, or council designated under tribal law . . . as primarily responsible for carrying out the Tribe's regulatory responsibilities under IGRA and the Tribal Gaming Ordinance. No person employed in, or in connection with, the management, supervision, or conduct of any gaming activity may be a member or employee of the Tribal Gaming Agency. . . .

Section 3.0. CLASS III GAMING AUTHORIZED AND PERMITTED

The Tribe is hereby authorized and permitted to engage in only the Class III Gaming Activities expressly referred to in Section 4.0 and shall not engage in Class III gaming that is not expressly authorized in that Section.

Section 4.0. SCOPE OF CLASS III GAMING

4.1. . . . The Tribe is hereby authorized and permitted to operate the following Gaming Activities under the terms and conditions set forth in this Gaming Compact:

(a) The operation of Gaming Devices [i.e., slot machines or their electronic equivalents].

(b) Any banking or percentage card game.

(c) The operation of any devices or games that are authorized under state law to the California State Lottery, provided that the Tribe will not offer such games through use of the Internet unless others in the state are permitted to do so under state and federal law.

Nothing herein shall be construed to preclude negotiation of a separate compact governing the conduct of off-track wagering at the Tribe's Gaming Facility.

4.2. . . . The Tribe may establish and operate not more than two Gaming Facilities, and only on those Indian lands on which gaming may lawfully be conducted under the Indian Gaming Regulatory Act. . . .

4.3. Authorized Number of Gaming Devices.

4.3.1. The Tribe may operate no more Gaming Devices than the larger of the following:

(a) A number of terminals equal to the number of Gaming Devices operated by the Tribe on September 1, 1999; or

(b) Three hundred fifty (350) Gaming Devices.

4.3.2. Revenue Sharing with Non-Gaming Tribes.

(a) For the purposes of this Section 4.3.2 and Section 5.0, the following definitions apply:

(i) A "Compact Tribe" is a tribe having a compact with the State that authorizes the Gaming Activities authorized by this Compact. Federally-recognized tribes that are operating fewer than 350 Gaming Devices are "Non-Compact Tribes." Non-Compact Tribes shall be deemed third party beneficiaries of this [Compact]. . . .

(ii) The Revenue Sharing Trust Fund is a fund created by the Legislature and administered by the California Gambling Control Commission, as Trustee, for the receipt, deposit, and distribution of monies paid pursuant to this Section 4.3.2.

(iii) The Special Distribution Fund is a fund created by the Legislature for the receipt, deposit, and distribution of monies paid pursuant to Section 5.0.

4.3.2.1. Revenue Sharing Trust Fund.

(a) The Tribe agrees with all other Compact Tribes . . . that each Non-Compact Tribe in the State shall receive the sum of $1.1 million per year. In the event there are insufficient monies in the Revenue Sharing Trust Fund to pay $1.1 million per year to each Non-Compact Tribe, any available monies in that Fund shall be distributed to Non-Compact Tribes in equal shares. Monies in excess . . . shall remain in the Revenue Sharing Trust Fund available for disbursement in future years. . . .

4.3.2.2. Allocation of Licenses.

(a) The Tribe, along with all other Compact Tribes, may acquire licenses to use Gaming Devices in excess of the number they are authorized to use under Section 4.3.1, but in no event may the Tribe operate more than 2,000 Gaming Devices, on the following terms, conditions, and priorities:

(1) The maximum number of machines that all Compact Tribes in the aggregate may license pursuant to this Section shall be a sum equal to 350 multiplied by the number of Non-Compact tribes as of September 1, 1999, plus the difference between 350 and the lesser number authorized under Section 4.3.1.

(2) The Tribe may acquire and maintain a license to operate a Gaming Device by paying into the Revenue Sharing Trust Fund, on a quarterly basis, in the following amounts:

Number of Licensed Devices: Fee Per Device Per Annum

1–350: $0

351–750: $900

751–1250: $1950

1251–2000: $4350. . . .

(e) As a condition of acquiring licenses to operate Gaming Devices, a non-refundable one-time pre-payment fee shall be required in the amount of $1,250 per Gaming Device being licensed, which fees shall be deposited in the Revenue Sharing Trust Fund. The license for any Gaming Device shall be canceled if the Gaming Device authorized by the license is not in commercial operation within twelve months of issuance of the license.

4.3.2.3. The Tribe shall not conduct any Gaming Activity authorized by this Compact if the Tribe is more than two quarterly contributions in arrears in its license fee payments to the Revenue Sharing Trust Fund. . . .

Section 5.0. REVENUE DISTRIBUTION

5.1. (a) The Tribe shall make contributions to the Special Distribution Fund created by the Legislature, in accordance with the following schedule, but only with respect to the number of Gaming Devices operated by the Tribe on September 1, 1999:

Number of Terminals . . . Base Percent of . . . Net Win

1–200: 0%

201–500: 7%

501–1000: 7% applied to the excess over 200 terminals, up to 500 terminals,

plus 10% applied to terminals over 500 terminals, up to 1000 terminals.

1000+: 7% applied to excess over 200, up to 500 terminals,

plus 10% applied to terminals over 500, up to 1000 terminals,
plus 13% applied to the excess above 1000 terminals. . . .

5.2. Use of funds. The State's share of the Gaming Device revenue shall be placed in the Special Distribution Fund, available for appropriation by the Legislature for the following purposes:

(a) grants, including any administrative costs, for programs designed to address gambling addiction;

(b) grants, including any administrative costs, for the support of state and local government agencies impacted by tribal government gaming;

(c) compensation for regulatory costs incurred by the State Gaming Agency and the state Department of Justice in connection with the implementation and administration of the Compact;

(d) payment of shortfalls that may occur in the Revenue Sharing Trust Fund; and

(e) any other purposes specified by the Legislature. It is the intent of the parties that Compact Tribes will be consulted in the process of identifying purposes for grants made to local governments.

5.3. . . . (e) The Tribe shall not conduct Class III gaming if more than two quarterly contributions to the Special Distribution Fund are overdue.

SECTION 6.0. LICENSING

6.1. . . . All Gaming Activities conducted under this Gaming Compact shall, at a minimum, comply with a Gaming Ordinance duly adopted by the Tribe and approved in accordance with IGRA, and with all rules, regulations, procedures, specifications, and standards duly adopted by the Tribal Gaming Agency.

6.2. . . . The Gaming Operations authorized under this Gaming Compact shall be owned solely by the Tribe.

6.3. Prohibition Regarding Minors.

(a) Except as provided in subdivision (b), the Tribe shall not permit persons under the age of 18 years to be present in any room in which Class III Gaming Activities are being conducted unless the person is en-route to a non-gaming area of the Gaming Facility.

(b) If the Tribe permits the consumption of alcoholic beverages in the Gaming Facility, the Tribe shall prohibit persons under the age of 21 years from being present in any area in which Class III gaming activities are being conducted and in which alcoholic beverages may be consumed, to the extent required by the state Department of Alcoholic Beverage Control.

6.4. Licensing Requirements and Procedures.

6.4.1. . . . All persons in any way connected with the Gaming Operation or Facility . . . must be licensed by the Tribal Gaming Agency. . . . [T]he licensing process . . . shall involve joint cooperation between the Tribal Gaming Agency and the State Gaming Agency. . . .

6.4.3. Suitability Standard Regarding Gaming Licenses.

(a) In reviewing an application for a gaming license, . . . the Tribal Gaming Agency shall consider whether issuance of the license is inimical to public health, safety, or welfare, . . . [or] will undermine public trust that the Tribe's Gaming Operations, or tribal government gaming generally, are free from criminal and dishonest elements and would be conducted honestly. A license may not be issued unless . . . the Tribal Gaming Agency is satisfied that the applicant is . . . :

(a) A person of good character, honesty, and integrity.

(b) A person whose prior activities, criminal record (if any), reputation, habits, and associations do not pose a threat to the public interest. . . .

Section 7.0. COMPLIANCE ENFORCEMENT

7.1. On-Site Regulation. It is the responsibility of the Tribal Gaming Agency to conduct on-site gaming regulation and control in order to enforce the terms of this Gaming Compact, IGRA, and the Tribal Gaming Ordinance . . . and to protect the integrity of the Gaming Activities, the reputation of the Tribe and the Gaming Operation for honesty and fairness, and the confidence of patrons that tribal government gaming in California meets the highest standards of regulation and internal controls. . . .

7.2. . . . The Tribal Gaming Agency shall investigate any reported violation of this Gaming Compact and shall require the Gaming Operation to correct the violation. . . . The Tribal Gaming Agency shall be empowered by the Tribal Gaming Ordinance to impose fines or other sanctions within the jurisdiction of the Tribe against gaming licensees or other persons who interfere with or violate the Tribe's gaming regulatory requirements and obligations under IGRA, the Tribal Gaming Ordinance, or this Gaming Compact. The Tribal Gaming Agency shall report significant or continued violations of this Compact or failures to comply with its orders to the State Gaming Agency.

7.3. Assistance by State Gaming Agency. The Tribe may request the assistance of the State Gaming Agency whenever it [appears] reasonably . . . necessary. . . .

7.4. . . . Notwithstanding that the Tribe has the primary responsibility to administer and enforce the regulatory requirements of this Compact, the State Gaming Agency shall have the right to inspect the Tribe's [Class III] Gaming Facility . . . subject to . . . [certain] conditions. . . .

Section 9.0. DISPUTE RESOLUTION PROVISIONS

9.1. . . . In recognition of the government-to-government relationship of the Tribe and the State, the parties shall make their best efforts to resolve disputes that occur under this Gaming Compact by good faith negotiations [or voluntary arbitration] whenever possible. . . . Disagreements that are not otherwise resolved . . . may be resolved in the United States District Court where the Tribe's Gaming Facility is located, . . . and the Ninth Circuit [U.S.] Court of Appeals (or, if those federal courts lack jurisdiction, in any state court of competent jurisdiction and its related courts of appeal). . . .

9.4. Limited Waiver of Sovereign Immunity. . . . In the event that a dispute is to be resolved in . . . court . . . , the State and the Tribe expressly consent to be sued . . . and waive any immunity . . . they may have provided that: (1) The dispute is limited solely to issues arising under this Gaming Compact; (2) Neither side makes any claim for monetary damages. . . .

Section 10.0. PUBLIC AND WORKPLACE HEALTH, SAFETY, AND LIABILITY

10.1. The Tribe will not conduct Class III gaming in a manner that endangers the public health, safety, or welfare; provided that nothing herein shall be construed to make applicable to the Tribe any state laws or regulations governing the use of tobacco.

10.2. Compliance. For the purposes of this Gaming Compact, the Tribal Gaming Operation shall:

(a) Adopt and comply with standards no less stringent than state public health standards for food and beverage handling. . . .

(d) Carry no less than five million dollars ($5,000,000) in public liability insurance for patron claims. . . . [T]he Tribe shall adopt and make available to patrons a tort liability ordinance setting forth the terms and conditions, if any, under which the Tribe waives immunity to suit for money damages resulting from intentional or negligent injuries to person or property at the Gaming Facility or in connection with the Tribe's Gaming Operation . . . ; provided that nothing in this Section shall require the Tribe to waive its immunity to suit except to the extent of the policy limits set out above. . . .

(g) Adopt and comply with standards no less stringent than federal laws and state laws forbidding . . . discriminati[on] in . . . employment . . . on the basis of race, color, religion, national origin, gender, sexual orientation, age, or disability; provided that nothing herein shall preclude the tribe from giving a preference in employment to Indians, pursuant to a duly adopted tribal ordinance.

(h) Adopt and comply with standards that are no less stringent than state laws prohibiting a gaming enterprise from cashing any check drawn against a federal, state, county, or city fund, including but not limited to, Social Security, unemployment insurance, disability payments, or public assistance payments.

(i) Adopt and comply with standards that are no less stringent than state laws, if any, prohibiting a gaming enterprise from providing, allowing, contracting to provide, or arranging to provide alcoholic beverages, or food or lodging for no charge or at reduced prices at a gambling establishment or lodging facility as an incentive or enticement.

(j) Adopt and comply with standards that are no less stringent than state laws, if any, prohibiting extensions of credit. . . .

10.3. Participation in state statutory programs related to employment.

(a) In lieu of permitting the Gaming Operation to participate in the state . . . workers' compensation system, the Tribe may create and maintain a system that provides redress for employee work-related injuries through requiring insurance or self-insurance. . . .

(b) The Tribe agrees that its Gaming Operation will participate in the State's program for providing unemployment compensation [and disability] benefits. . . .

(c) As a matter of comity, with respect to persons employed at the Gaming Facility, other than members of the Tribe, the Tribal Gaming Operation shall withhold all taxes due to the State. . . .

10.6. Possession of firearms shall be prohibited at all times in the Gaming Facility except for state, local, or tribal security or law enforcement personnel authorized by tribal law and by federal or state law to possess firearms at the Facility.

10.7. Labor Relations. Notwithstanding any other provision of this Compact, this Compact shall be null and void if . . . the Tribe has not provided an agreement or other procedure acceptable to the State for addressing organizational and representational rights of Class III Gaming Employees and other employees associated with the Tribe's

Class III gaming enterprise, such as food and beverage, housekeeping, cleaning, bell and door services, and laundry employees. . . .

10.8. Off-Reservation Environmental Impacts.

10.8.1. . . . [T]he Tribe shall adopt an ordinance providing for . . . environmental impact reports concerning potential off-Reservation environmental impacts of any and all Projects to be commenced on or after the effective date of this Compact. In fashioning the environmental protection ordinance, the Tribe will make a good faith effort to incorporate the policies and purposes of the National Environmental Policy Act and the California Environmental Quality Act consistent with the Tribe's governmental interests.

10.8.2.

(a) Prior to commencement of a Project, the Tribe will:

(1) Inform the public of the planned Project;

(2) Take appropriate actions to determine whether the project will have any significant adverse impacts on the off-Reservation environment;

(3) For the purpose of receiving and responding to comments, submit all environmental impact reports concerning the proposed Project to the State Clearinghouse in the Office of Planning and Research and the county board of supervisors, for distribution to the public;

(4) Consult with the board of supervisors of the county or counties within which the Tribe's Gaming Facility is located, . . . and, if the Gaming Facility is within a city, with the city council . . . ;

(5) Meet with and provide an opportunity for comment by those members of the public residing off-Reservation within the vicinity of the Gaming Facility such as might be adversely affected by proposed Project.

(b) During the conduct of a Project, the Tribe shall:

(1) Keep the board or council, as the case may be, and potentially affected members of the public apprized of the project's progress; and

(2) Make good faith efforts to mitigate any and all such significant adverse off-Reservation environmental impacts.

(c) As used [herein], the term "Project" means any expansion or any significant renovation or modification of [a] Gaming Facility. . . .

Section 11.0. EFFECTIVE DATE AND TERM OF COMPACT . . .

11.2.1. . . . (a) Once effective this Compact shall be in full force and effect for state law purposes until December 31, 2020.

(b) Once ratified, this Compact shall constitute a binding and determinative agreement between the Tribe and the State, without regard to voter approval of any constitutional amendment, other than [Proposition 1A], that authorizes a gaming compact.

(c) Either party may bring an action in federal court, after providing a sixty (60) day written notice of an opportunity to cure any alleged breach of this Compact, for a declaration that the other party has materially breached this Compact. Upon issuance of such a declaration, the complaining party may unilaterally terminate this Compact upon service of written notice on the other party. In the event a federal court determines that it lacks jurisdiction over such an action, the action may be brought in the superior court for the county in which the Tribe's Gaming Facility is located. The parties expressly waive their immunity to suit for purposes of an action under this subdivision, subject to [Section 9.4]. . . .

Section 12.0. AMENDMENTS; RENEGOTIATIONS

12.1. The terms and conditions of this Gaming Compact may be amended at any time by the mutual and written agreement of both parties.

12.2. This Gaming Compact is subject to renegotiation in the event the Tribe wishes to engage in forms of Class III gaming other than those games authorized herein and requests renegotiation for that purpose, provided that no such renegotiation may be sought for 12 months following the effective date of this Gaming Compact. . . .

12.4. The Tribe shall have the right to terminate this Compact in the event the exclusive right of Indian tribes to operate Gaming Devices in California is abrogated. . . .

Key People, Laws, and Concepts

Aboriginal Title
See Indian Title

Allotment Act (1887)

Also known as the **Dawes Act**, it was passed by Congress to break up most tribally owned land, distributing small plots to individual Indians and opening much of the remainder to non-Indian settlement.

Allotment Era

See Assimilation Era

American Indian Movement (AIM)

Political movement launched by Indians in 1968. It carried out several major protest actions over the next five years, including occupations of Alcatraz Island, the Bureau of Indian Affairs headquarters, and **Wounded Knee**.

American Indian Religious Freedom Act (1978)

Mostly symbolic law passed by Congress, declaring respect for Native American religious rights.

Articles of Confederation

The first national constitution of the United States, framed and signed in 1777 but not ratified by all thirteen original states, as required for it to take legal effect, until 1781. The articles came to be viewed as providing for a dangerously weak central government and became defunct when the **U.S. Constitution** went into effect in 1789.

Assimilation Era (1871–1933)

Name often given to the period during which the U.S. government, through such laws as the Allotment Act and such court decisions as ***United States v. Kagama*** and ***Lone Wolf v. Hitchcock***, moved toward abolishing Native American sovereignty. Also marked by shocking repression of Indian religious and cultural rights.

Assimilative Crimes Act

Long-standing federal statute, enacted in its modern form in 1948, generally borrowing from and applying state law within federal lands (such as military bases and national parks) located within various states. The Supreme Court has combined this law with the **Indian Country Crimes Act** to "assimilate" most state criminal laws and apply them to crimes within Indian country that involve non-Indians.

Atkinson Trading Co. v. Shirley (2001)

Unanimous U.S. Supreme Court decision, written by Chief Justice **Rehnquist**, rejecting tribal power to tax nonmembers renting hotel rooms on nonmember-owned land within the reservation.

Austin, Raymond D.

Justice of the **Navajo Nation Supreme Court** (1985–present). He joined Chief Justice **Yazzie**'s opinion in ***Means v. Chinle District Court.***

Baldwin, Henry

Justice of the U.S. Supreme Court (1830–1844), appointed by President **Jackson**. He opposed Indian sovereignty in the **Cherokee Cases.**

Bill of Rights

Collective label for the first ten amendments to the **U.S. Constitution**, ratified together in 1791 and mostly providing various guarantees of individual rights, such as freedom of speech and religion and the right to due process and a fair trial. Originally, the Bill of Rights applied only as a limitation on **federal law**, not **state law** or **tribal law**. The **Fourteenth Amendment** has been interpreted, however, to apply most of the Bill of Rights to the states, and Congress, in the **Indian Civil Rights Act**, applied most of it to tribal governments as well.

Black, Hugo L.

Justice of the U.S. Supreme Court (1937–1971), appointed by President Franklin D. **Roosevelt**. He was generally a strong supporter of Indian rights. Although he joined the majority in ***Tee-Hit-Ton Indians v. United States***, he wrote the critically important landmark opinion in ***Williams v. Lee***.

Blackmun, Harry A.

Justice of the U.S. Supreme Court (1970–1994), appointed by President **Nixon**. He was generally a strong supporter of Indian sovereignty. Although he voted with the majority in ***Oliphant v. Suquamish Indian Tribe*** and ***Duro v. Reina***, he wrote the Court's opinion in ***United States v. Sioux Nation*** and a powerful dissent in ***Brendale v. Yakima Indian Nation***.

Brendale v. Yakima Indian Nation (1989)

Split decision by the U.S. Supreme Court, rejecting, 6–3, tribal civil jurisdiction to zone most non–tribal-member-owned property within the reservation. Justice **White** (joined by Chief Justice **Rehnquist** and Justices **Scalia** and **Kennedy**) voted to deny such tribal power over nonmembers throughout the reservation, whereas Justice **Stevens** (joined by Justice **O'Connor**) drew a distinction between different areas of the reservation. Justice **Blackmun** (joined by Justices **Brennan** and Thurgood **Marshall**) strongly disagreed with the reasoning of both White and Stevens and voted to uphold tribal jurisdiction throughout the reservation. The Blackmun and Stevens opinions together created a 5–4 majority that preserved some tribal zoning power over a mostly undeveloped area of the reservation.

Brennan, William J., Jr.

Justice of the U.S. Supreme Court (1956–1990), appointed by President **Eisenhower**. He was a strong supporter of Indian sovereignty and treaty rights, dissenting, for example, in ***Duro v. Reina.***

Breyer, Stephen G.

Justice of the U.S. Supreme Court (1994–present), appointed by President **Clinton**. He is perhaps one of the two most pro-Indian members of the current Court (along with Justice **O'Connor**). He has strongly supported Indian treaty rights and joined O'Connor's separate opinion in ***Nevada v. Hicks.***

***Bryan v. Itasca County* (1976)**

Unanimous U.S. Supreme Court decision, written by Justice **Brennan**, rejecting state power to tax Indians within **Indian country**, even in states governed by **Public Law 280**.

Burger, Warren E.

Chief Justice of the U.S. Supreme Court (1969–1986), appointed by President **Nixon**. He and his Court had a mixed record on Indian sovereignty, in some ways continuing and consolidating the **Warren** Court's record. Burger dissented from his Court's most notable cutback of tribal sovereignty, in ***Oliphant v. Suquamish Indian Tribe.***

Cabeza de Vaca, Álvar Nuñez

Spanish explorer who became the first European (together with the Moroccan slave **Estevánico**) to journey deep within the North American continent and spend substantial time with Indians, in 1528–1536, through what are now Texas, New Mexico, Arizona, and northern Mexico. He wrote a classic account of his travels.

California Supreme Court

Highest state court of California. Like any state supreme court, it has final authority to interpret **state law**, but its judgments may be appealed to the **U.S. Supreme Court** regarding any questions of **federal law**, which includes issues pertaining to Native American sovereignty.

California v. Cabazon Band of Mission Indians (1987)

Six to three U.S. Supreme Court decision, written by Justice **White** (Justice **Stevens** dissenting), upholding the right of tribes in California to conduct at least some gambling enterprises not allowed by state law outside Indian country. Congress codified the ruling the next year in the **Indian Gaming Regulatory Act**, leading eventually to **Proposition 5, Proposition 1A**, and the **California-Tribal Gaming Compact** of 2000.

California-Tribal Gaming Compact (2000)

Agreement entered into between Indian tribes and California Governor **Gray Davis** in 1999, approved by **Proposition 1A** in March 2000, and finalized by approval of the U.S. Department of the Interior in May 2000 under the **Indian Gaming Regulatory Act**. The compact allows almost all forms of casino gambling (except craps and roulette) on participating California Indian reservations.

Canons of Construction

Rules of interpretation followed by courts in deciding legal issues (especially where ambiguity or uncertainty are present) concerning Native Americans, under which there is a presumption in favor of preserving Native American sovereignty and Indian rights, unless the only reasonable interpretation of the language clearly indicates otherwise. Originally developed to interpret Indian **treaty** rights but also applied to other laws affecting Indians.

Cherokee Cases (1831–1832)

U.S. Supreme Court opinions, written by Chief Justice John **Marshall**, upholding limited sovereignty for the **Cherokee Nation** and by extension most Indian tribes. ***Cherokee Nation v. Georgia*** (1831) upheld Cherokee sovereign status 4–2, but also rejected, 4–2, the Cherokee claim to be a "foreign nation" for purposes of invoking the Court's jurisdiction. ***Worcester v. Georgia*** (1832) upheld, 5–1, Cherokee treaty rights to land in Georgia. *Worcester* was not enforced at the time, but the Cherokee Cases have formed the foundation of American Indian law ever since.

Cherokee Nation

The largest Indian tribe in the United States in terms of total membership, based in Oklahoma but with members living throughout the country.

Cherokee Nation v. Georgia (1831)

See **Cherokee Cases**

Cherokee Tobacco Case (1871)

Four to two U.S. Supreme Court decision (three justices not participating), upholding Congress's power to abrogate an Indian **treaty** by passing a later **statute.**

Cherokee-U.S. Treaty of Hopewell (1785)

First in a series of treaties between the **Cherokee Nation** and the United States.

Citizenship

See ***Elk v. Wilkins*** and **Indian Citizenship Act.**

"Civilized Tribes"

Popular term (at one time) for five tribes in the southeastern United States (the Cherokee, Creek, Choctaw, Chickasaw, and Seminole Nations) that had adapted to non-Indian culture to some degree but were nevertheless forcibly removed in the 1830s to **Indian Territory** in what is now Oklahoma.

Clinton, William J.

Forty-second president of the United States (1993–2001). He strongly supported and expanded to some extent the modern federal policy (begun by Presidents **Johnson** and **Nixon** and generally continued since then on a bipartisan basis) of promoting Indian self-determination, Native American sovereignty, and government-to-government relationships with Indian nations.

***Cobell v. Norton* (formerly *Cobell v. Babbitt*; 2001)**

Class-action lawsuit filed in 1996 on behalf of more than 300,000 Indians, claiming up to $10 billion in total damages for the U.S. government's mishandling of trust accounts originating from the **Allotment Act** of 1887.

Cohen, Felix S.

Legal scholar and lawyer for the U.S. Department of the Interior under President Franklin D. **Roosevelt** and **John Collier**. Cohen's *Handbook of Federal Indian Law,* first published in 1941, has been influential in shaping federal Indian policy and court decisions ever since.

Collier, John

U.S. commissioner of Indian affairs under President Franklin D. **Roosevelt**. He was instrumental in the reforms of that era, including the **Indian Reorganization Act** of 1934.

Columbus, Christopher

Italian explorer employed by Spain, who began first sustained encounters of Europeans with Native Americans, starting with his voyage to the Bahamas in 1492. As governor of Hispaniola, he presided over a holocaust in which huge numbers of natives were enslaved, mutilated, and murdered.

Constitution

Highest or fundamental law of a given jurisdiction, such as the U.S. government, a state, or an Indian tribe. A constitution typically trumps any inconsistent lesser law, such as a mere **statute** or **treaty** (*see also* **U.S. Constitution**).

Crazy Horse

Sioux (Lakota) leader who defeated U.S. general **George Armstrong Custer** in the 1876 Battle of Greasy Grass (the Little Bighorn), leading to Congress's abrogation of the **Sioux-Arapaho-U.S. Treaty of Fort Laramie.**

***Crow Dog* Case (1883)**

See ***Kan-Gi-Shun-Ca (Crow Dog), Ex parte***

Curtis Act (1898)

Law passed by Congress extending the **Allotment Act** to the Oklahoma **Indian Territory**.

Custer, George Armstrong

U.S. general defeated by the **Sioux (Lakota) Nation** under **Crazy Horse** in the 1876 Battle of Greasy Grass (the Little Bighorn).

Davis, Gray

Governor of California (1999–present). He has generally supported Indian gambling and signed the **California-Tribal Gaming Compact.**

Dawes Act

See **Allotment Act**

Delaware-U.S. Treaty of Fort Pitt (1778)

First treaty between the United States and an Indian nation.

Dicta

Language in a court opinion that is not essential to the precise bottom-line holding of the case, that is, mere surplusage or editorializing. Dicta has no binding effect on later court decisions; it is not **precedent**, although it may be considered as guidance. "Dicta" is technically the plural form, the singular being "dictum," but the latter is rarely used, since any passage to which the label is applied is likely to consist of more than one word and thus may properly be called "dicta."

Discovery Doctrine

Legal theory embraced by Chief Justice John **Marshall** in ***Johnson v. M'Intosh*** (1823), under which the European power that first encountered any particular area of the Western Hemisphere was conceded to have **sovereignty** over it, exclusive of any other European power, and also trumping the preexisting independence or full sovereignty of any Indian nation or tribe occupying that area.

Domestic Dependent Nation

The term coined by Chief Justice John **Marshall** in the **Cherokee Cases** to describe the legal status of the Native American tribes, somewhere between a foreign nation and a state.

Douglas, William O.

Justice of the U.S. Supreme Court (1939–1975), appointed by President Franklin D. **Roosevelt**. He was an ardent supporter of Indian treaty rights and sovereignty.

"*Duro* Fix" Act (1990)

Law amending the **Indian Civil Rights Act**, passed by Congress on an interim basis in 1990 and then made permanent in 1991, upholding each tribe's criminal jurisdiction over Indians who are nonmembers of that tribe. This act effectively reversed the Supreme Court's decision in ***Duro v. Reina,*** though it remains unclear whether the law will survive legal challenges.

***Duro v. Reina* (1990)**

Seven to two U.S. Supreme Court decision, written by Justice **Kennedy** (Justice **Brennan**, joined by Justice **Thurgood Marshall**, dissenting), rejecting tribal criminal jurisdiction over Indians who are not members of the tribe. Congress quickly overturned the decision in the "***Duro* Fix" Act**, but the legality of that fix remains very much in doubt.

Duvall, Gabriel

Justice of the U.S. Supreme Court (1811–1835), appointed by President Madison. He joined in Chief Justice John **Marshall's** majority opinion in ***Worcester v. Georgia.***

Eisenhower, Dwight D.

Thirty-fourth president of the United States (1953–1961), he presided over a major reversal in federal Indian policy in 1953, under which the U.S. sought **termination** of Native American sovereignty. *See also* **House Resolution 108** and **Public Law 280**.

***Elk v. Wilkins* (1884)**

Seven to two U.S. Supreme Court decision, over the dissent of Justice **Harlan (the elder)**, holding that Indians (even those not maintaining "tribal relations") were not U.S. citizens under the **Fourteenth Amendment**. Such citizenship was later statutorily conferred on all Indians by the **Indian Citizenship Act** of 1924.

Ericsson, Leif

Viking leader, along with Thorfinn Karlsefni, who led first known European encounters with Native Americans, around 1000 C.E.

Estevánico

Moroccan slave who accompanied **Cabeza de Vaca** on his pioneering journey into the interior of North America.

Federal Law

The laws enacted by Congress as the legislative branch of the U.S. government. In a broad sense, "federal law" includes the **U.S. Constitution** itself, although it is often used to refer simply to the body of ordinary federal **statutes**, which cannot be enforced if inconsistent with the U.S. Constitution. The **supremacy clause** of the Constitution declares that federal constitutional and statutory law and also any **treaty** entered into by the United States together constitute "the supreme law of the land," trumping any contrary **state law** (or, by implication, **tribal law**).

Fletcher v. Peck (1810)

U.S. Supreme Court decision, written by Chief Justice John **Marshall** (with a partial dissent by Justice **Johnson**), providing the first (though inconclusive) discussion of **Indian title** or Indian law issues generally by the Court.

Fourteenth Amendment

Amendment to the **U.S. Constitution** ratified in 1868, which guarantees, among other things, citizenship rights, equal protection of the laws, and due process of law, and requires states to abide by most guarantees in the Bill of Rights. It was intended largely to secure the legal rights of the freed African slaves following the Civil War. It was interpreted in ***Elk v. Wilkins*** not to grant citizenship to tribal Indians.

Geronimo

Apache who became the last Indian military leader to surrender to the United States, in 1886.

Ginsburg, Ruth Bader

Justice of the U.S. Supreme Court (1993–present), appointed by President **Clinton**. Although widely considered the most liberal current member of the Court, she has disappointed Indian sovereignty advocates. She has sometimes supported Indian treaty rights (for example, providing one of the critical majority votes in ***Minnesota v. Mille Lacs Band of Chippewa Indians***), but she wrote the Court's opinion in ***Strate v. A-1 Contractors*** and joined Justice Scalia's majority opinion in ***Nevada v. Hicks.***

Harlan, John Marshall (the elder)

Justice of the U.S. Supreme Court (1877–1911), appointed by President Rutherford B. Hayes. He was famous for his powerful but often lonely dissents defending racial equality in cases like *Plessy v. Ferguson* (1896) and defending Bill of Rights guarantees in many other cases. He was the only justice who declined to join the Court's opinion in ***Lone Wolf v. Hitchcock*** (although he concurred in the result without explanation), and he dissented angrily in ***Elk v. Wilkins.***

Harlan, John Marshall (the younger)

Justice of the U.S. Supreme Court (1955–1971), appointed by President **Eisenhower**. A grandson of the elder Justice **Harlan,** he joined the Court's unanimous opinion in ***Williams v. Lee.***

Haudenosaunee Confederacy

Federation of five (later six) tribes in the northeastern United States, also known as the Iroquois. The member tribes are the Oneida, Mohawk, Onondaga, Cayuga, and Seneca, later joined by the Tuscarora. The federation may have been an inspiration for the federal design of the **U.S. Constitution.**

***Hotel Employees Union v. Davis* (1999)**

Six to one California Supreme Court decision, written by Justice **Werdegar** (Justice **Kennard** dissenting), striking down **Proposition 5** under the California state constitution.

House Resolution 108 (1953)

Along with **Public Law 280**, this joint congressional resolution launched the **termination** policy and era. It called for eventual dissolution of tribal governments and abolition of Native American sovereignty.

Indian Child Welfare Act (1978)

Law passed by Congress expanding tribal government powers over Indian children.

Indian Citizenship Act (1924)

Law passed by Congress statutorily conferring U.S. citizenship on all American Indians, thus effectively reversing ***Elk v. Wilkins.***

Indian Civil Rights Act (1968)

Law passed by Congress applying most **Bill of Rights** protections against tribal governmental power (although effective remedies were sharply limited by the Supreme Court's 1978 decision in ***Santa Clara Pueblo v. Martinez***) and prohibiting any further extensions of state jurisdiction under **Public Law 280** without Indian consent (which has not been forthcoming). The law also imposed sharp limitations on the criminal punishments (currently capped at one year in jail and a $5,000 fine) that can be imposed by tribal courts. The act was amended in 1990 and 1991 by the **"*Duro* Fix" Act.**

Indian Claims Commission Act (1946)

Law passed by Congress waiving federal sovereign immunity and allowing tribes to bring claims for compensation for past takings of land, but specifically barring any recovery of lands themselves.

Indian Country

General term for all lands within the United States falling within some degree of Indian control and subject to the federal government's power over Indian affairs. It includes Indian **reservations** composed mostly of "tribal trust" land (i.e., land held communally by the tribes under restrictions imposed by the U.S. government under the **trust relationship**) and allotted lands still owned by individual Indians as a result of the **Allotment Act** and similar laws. It also includes allotted lands now owned by non-Indians, as long as they are located within the outer boundaries of an Indian reservation, although tribal powers over such lands and such non-Indians are greatly restricted.

Indian Country Crimes Act

Originally enacted by Congress as part of the **Trade and Intercourse Act** in 1790, this law provides for federal criminal jurisdiction over crimes in Indian country involving non-Indians. Unlike the **Major Crimes Act** or **Public Law 280**, it does not cover purely "Indian-on-Indian" crimes.

Indian Gaming Regulatory Act (1988)

Law passed by Congress largely codifying ***California v. Cabazon Band of Mission Indians*** (1987) and enlarging potential scope of Indian gambling. It led to, for example, the **California-Tribal Gaming Compact** of 2000 (*see also* **Proposition 1A** and **Proposition 5**).

Indian Reorganization Act (1934)

Also known as the Wheeler-Howard Act, this law was passed by Congress to strengthen and modernize tribal governments, although it has been criticized as heavy-handed and intrusive.

Indian Territory

Specific historical and geographical term for an area in what is now eastern Oklahoma that was set aside for Indians subjected to forcible removal from the east, most notably the **Cherokee Nation** and the other **"Civilized Tribes."**

Indian Title

Also referred to as aboriginal title, this concept was developed in ***Johnson v. M'Intosh*** (*see also* ***Tee-Hit-Ton Indians v. United States***) and based on the **Discovery Doctrine**, under which Indians held their ancestral lands only under a "right of occupancy," subject to termination by the conquering European American sovereign, unless and until such Indian title might be upgraded to secure property title under U.S. law by a **treaty** or **statute.**

Iroquois Confederacy

See **Haudenosaunee Confederacy**

Jackson, Andrew

Seventh president of the United States (1829–1837), Jackson was a renowned Indian fighter and profoundly hostile to continued Native American sovereignty. He declined to enforce the Supreme Court's decisions in the **Cherokee Cases** and was instrumental in implementing the policy of Indian removal reflected in the **Removal Act.**

Jefferson, Thomas

Third president of the United States (1801–1809), he was one of the first to articulate the long-term policy of Indian removal later reflected in the **Removal Act.** His purchase of the Louisiana Territory in 1803 vastly extended U.S. territorial claims over Indian nations.

Johnson, Lyndon B.

Thirty-sixth president of the United States (1963–1969), he delivered the first major presidential address ever devoted solely to Indian affairs in 1968, rejecting **termination** and returning to the policy of promoting Indian sovereignty begun by President Theodore **Roosevelt** in 1933. President **Nixon**'s landmark policy message in 1970 built on this speech.

Johnson v. M'Intosh **(1823)**

Unanimous U.S. Supreme Court decision, written by Chief Justice John **Marshall** and based on **Discovery Doctrine,** holding that Indian tribes may convey land only to, or with the permission of, the European or U.S. sovereign held to have "discovered" and thereby "conquered" the tribe.

Johnson, William

Justice of the U.S. Supreme Court (1804–1834), appointed by President **Jefferson**. He opposed Indian sovereignty in the **Cherokee Cases**.

Judicial Review

Power of courts to strike down a law (**statute**) passed by a legislature or an executive act that the court finds to violate the higher law of a **constitution**.

***Kan-Gi-Shun-Ca (Crow Dog), Ex parte* (1883)**

Unanimous U.S. Supreme Court decision finding that the U.S. government had no jurisdiction over crimes committed within **Indian country** by one Indian against another Indian. Congress quickly reversed this decision by passing the **Major Crimes Act**, which the Court then upheld in ***United States v. Kagama.***

Kennard, Joyce L.

Justice of the California Supreme Court (1989–present), appointed by Governor Deukmejian, who wrote a powerful and interesting dissent supporting Indian sovereignty in ***Hotel Employees Union v. Davis.***

Kennedy, Anthony M.

Justice of the U.S. Supreme Court (1988–present), appointed by President Reagan. He has generally been as hostile as Chief Justice **Rehnquist** to most Indian treaty and sovereignty claims. His most notable Indian law opinion was in ***Duro v. Reina.***

Kiowa Tribe v.
***Manufacturing Technologies, Inc.* (1998)**

Six to three U.S. Supreme Court decision, written by Justice **Kennedy** (Justice **Stevens**, joined by Justices **Thomas** and **Ginsburg**, dissenting), reaffirming tribal sovereign immunity from lawsuits.

Las Casas, Bartolomé de

First Catholic priest to be ordained in the New World. He returned to Spain in 1515 to protest the enslavement and mass murder of the Caribbean Indians.

***Lone Wolf v. Hitchcock* (1903)**

Unanimous U.S. Supreme Court decision upholding Congress's **plenary power** to abrogate an Indian **treaty** and indicating that courts would defer almost totally to Congress on such issues.

Major Crimes Act (1885)

Law passed by Congress in response to the ***Kan-Gi-Shun-Ca (Crow Dog)*** case, extending federal jurisdiction over several serious crimes whenever committed by an Indian within **Indian country** (partly superseded by **Public Law 280**'s extension of some states' criminal jurisdiction over Indian country).

***Marbury v. Madison* (1803)**

Unanimous U.S. Supreme Court decision, written by Chief Justice John **Marshall**, establishing the federal courts' power of **judicial review**.

Marshall, John

Chief justice of the U.S. Supreme Court (1801–1835), appointed by President John Adams. The most influential judge in U.S. history, he wrote the first three critically important Indian law opinions, in ***Johnson v. M'Intosh*** and the **Cherokee Cases**, along with many other major Supreme Court opinions, such as ***Marbury v. Madison.***

Marshall, Thurgood

Justice of the U.S. Supreme Court (1967–1991), appointed by President **Johnson**. The first African American to sit on the Court, he was probably the strongest supporter of Indian sovereignty in the Court's history (with the possible exception of Justice **Douglas**). He dissented in ***Oliphant v. Suquamish Indian Tribe*** and ***Duro v. Reina*** and joined virtually all the Court's pro-Indian decisions during his tenure.

McLean, John

Justice of the U.S. Supreme Court (1830–1861). Although appointed by President **Jackson**, he sided with Chief Justice John **Marshall** in the **Cherokee Cases**.

Means, Russell

Longtime Indian activist and founder of the **American Indian Movement (AIM)**. Means, a member of the Oglala **Sioux (Lakota) Nation**, was charged with domestic assault while living in the **Navajo Nation** in 1997. His challenge to the Navajo tribal court's jurisdiction over him led to the **Navajo Nation Supreme Court**'s decision in ***Means v. Chinle District Court***. The case is now being litigated in the federal courts.

Means v. Chinle District Court (1999)

Unanimous decision by the **Navajo Nation Supreme Court**, written by Chief Justice **Yazzie**, upholding tribal criminal jurisdiction over a nonmember Indian.

Minnesota v. Mille Lacs Band of Chippewa Indians (1999)

U.S. Supreme Court decision, 5–4, written by Justice **O'Connor** (Chief Justice **Rehnquist** dissenting), upholding Indian treaty rights to hunt, fish, and gather outside the reservation.

Montana v. United States (1981)

U.S. Supreme Court decision, written by Justice **Stewart**, involving a treaty claim and an issue of tribal sovereignty over non-Indians owning land within the reservation. The Court rejected the treaty claim 6–3 (Justice **Blackmun**, joined by Justices **Brennan** and Thurgood **Marshall**, dissenting). On the sovereignty issue, the Court unanimously rejected tribal power on the facts of the case. The rule framed by the decision came to be seen as a major turning point and was expanded to cover all non-Indians within Indian country in *Nevada v. Hicks.*

Morton v. Mancari (1974)

Unanimous U.S. Supreme Court decision, written by Justice **Blackmun**, holding that special legal treatment of tribal member Indians is properly based on their political and nationality status, not race, and is therefore consistent with the **Fourteenth Amendment**'s equal protection clause.

Nation

A **polity** having both **sovereignty** and some degree of independence from the control of any other nation. The term has long been applied to Indian **tribes**, even though they now lack full independence.

Native American Graves Protection and Repatriation Act (1990)

Law passed by Congress giving Indian tribes control over many Indian human remains and sacred objects.

Natural Law

Principles (often unwritten) thought to have binding legal force and effect or to be entitled to such effect on the grounds that they are intrinsically right or good or just, even if they are not reflected in laws actually in effect or are not actually followed by those individuals or governments or other entities actually wielding power. *See also* **positivism**.

Navajo (Diné) Nation

Indian tribe with the largest reservation in the United States, an area the size of West Virginia covering northeastern Arizona, northwestern New Mexico, and southeastern Utah. Second-largest tribe in total number of members (more than 200,000), though many do not live on the reservation.

Navajo Nation Supreme Court

Highest court of the **Navajo Nation**, with final authority to interpret tribal law. It decided the major American Indian law case of *Means v. Chinle District Court.*

Navajo-U.S. Treaty of Fort Sumner (1868)

One of the last U.S.-Indian treaties, it guaranteed the **Navajo Nation** the huge reservation (later expanded to an even larger size) where it still governs.

***Nevada v. Hicks* (2001)**

U.S. Supreme Court decision, written by Justice **Scalia**, sharply curtailing tribal civil jurisdiction and seeming to threaten radical changes in the Court's approach to Native American sovereignty. Although formally unanimous, it was effectively 6–3. Justice **O'Connor**'s concurring opinion, joined by Justices **Stevens** and **Breyer**, strongly criticized Scalia's reasoning and disagreed with how the case should be handled on the remand to the lower federal court that all justices agreed was necessary.

New Deal Era

See **Self-Determination Era, First**

Nixon, Richard M.

Thirty-seventh president of the United States (1969–1974). His 1970 message to Congress built on President **Johnson**'s 1968 speech to cement the rejection of termination and remains the bipartisan foundation for the modern policy of Indian self-determination.

O'Connor, Sandra Day

Justice of the U.S. Supreme Court (1981–present), appointed by President Reagan. She has often been a swing vote supporting Indian claims while also voting to restrict Indian sovereignty in certain cases. Probably her most important pro-Indian majority opinion was in *Minnesota v. Mille Lacs Band of Chippewa Indians.* Along with Justice **Breyer**, she is perhaps one of the two most pro-Indian members of the current Court.

Oliphant v. Suquamish Indian Tribe (1978)

Six to two U.S. Supreme Court decision, written by Justice **Rehnquist** (Justice Thurgood **Marshall**, joined by Chief Justice **Burger**, dissenting), rejecting tribal criminal jurisdiction over non-Indians who choose to enter Indian reservations and commit crimes there.

Oneida County v. Oneida Indian Nation (1985)

Five to four U.S. Supreme Court decision, written by Justice **Powell** (joined by Justices **Brennan**, Thurgood **Marshall**, **Blackmun**, and **O'Connor**), with Justice **Stevens** dissenting (joined by Chief Justice **Burger** and Justices **White** and **Rehnquist**). The Court upheld an Indian claim to land transferred by a tribe to New York State in 1795, based on the principle that Indian tribes cannot alienate their lands without U.S. government authorization.

Plenary Power

The supreme authority claimed by the federal government and specifically Congress over Indian affairs, including the power to abrogate prior **treaty** guarantees, as recognized in such cases as *Lone Wolf v. Hitchcock.*

Polity

Any organized political body of people, such as a **nation**, state, **tribe**, or city.

Positivism

An outlook in legal philosophy that holds that "law" properly describes all (and only) rules or principles actually in effect (usually in writing) and recognized as such by those wielding actual power and those actually subject to such power, regardless of how unjust or immoral such rules arguably are. Positivists do not generally disdain the importance or rightness of principles of **natural justice, natural rights**, or **natural law**, but they refuse to call such principles "law" simply because they are morally sound.

Powell, Lewis F., Jr.

Justice of the U.S. Supreme Court (1972–1986), appointed by President **Nixon**. A moderate, he is best known in Indian law for writing the majority opinion in ***Oneida County v. Oneida Indian Nation.***

Precedent

A court holding that is considered binding on later court decisions.

Proposition 1A (2000)

California state constitutional amendment passed by statewide vote of 65 percent to 35 percent in March 2000, authorizing the **California-Tribal Gaming Compact** finalized in May 2000.

Proposition 5 (1998)

Also known as the "Indian Self-Reliance Initiative," this statutory proposal was approved by California voters, 63 percent to 37 percent, in November 1998 but struck down by the **California Supreme Court** in ***Hotel Employees Union v. Davis.*** Proposition 5 would have authorized many but not all types of casino gambling on participating California Indian reservations.

Public Law 280 (1953)

Passed by Congress to extend state criminal jurisdiction and state jurisdiction over civil lawsuits into Indian country within six specified states, including California. Between 1953 and 1968, several additional states assumed jurisdiction over Indian country under Public Law 280, but the **Indian Civil Rights Act** required tribal consent (which has not been forthcoming) for any further extensions.

Realism, Legal

A philosophy of law under which court decisions and other actions by legal actors are considered to be the product of personal or material motivations (including ideology) that can be objectively analyzed, rather than flowing strictly from theoretical principles (whether based on **positivism** or **natural law**) or the logical extension of such principles. Often treated as a "cynical" view of law, legal realism can provide useful insights, even when it may understate the degree to which legal actors are sometimes driven by "pure" logic or theoretical principle.

Rehnquist, William H.

Justice (1972–1986) and chief justice (1986–present) of the U.S. Supreme Court, appointed justice by President **Nixon** and chief justice by President Reagan. He has opposed Indian sovereignty in most cases, most notoriously in his majority opinion in ***Oliphant v. Suquamish Indian Tribe***, although he concurred with ***California v. Cabazon Band of Mission Indians***. He has also dissented against recognition or compensation for Indian treaty rights in cases like ***United States v. Sioux Nation*** and ***Minnesota v. Mille Lacs Band of Chippewa Indians***.

Removal Act (1830)

Passed by Congress to grant western lands to Indians who "chose" to remove there. Sponsored by President **Jackson**, this legislation was a crucial step in what actually became a policy of forced relocation, accompanied by great hardship and many deaths, of thousands of Indians of many different tribes in different parts of the country. The most famous example is the removal of the **Cherokee Nation** from Georgia to what is now Oklahoma.

Reservation

An area of land allocated to a particular Indian tribe or tribes. *See also* **Indian Country**.

Roosevelt, Franklin D.

Thirty-second president of the United States (1933–1945), he presided over a major turnaround in federal Indian policy starting in 1933, especially with the **Indian Reorganization Act** of 1934, under which Native American sovereignty was protected and encouraged to a limited degree.

Santa Clara Pueblo v. Martinez (1978)

Seven to one U.S. Supreme Court decision, written by Justice Thurgood **Marshall**, finding that a tribe could not be sued under the **Indian Civil Rights Act** in a dispute over eligibility standards for tribal membership. The Court applied the **canons of construction** to limit the extent of the Indian Civil Rights Act's restriction of tribal sovereignty. The case aroused controversy, however, because it had the effect of leaving undisturbed a tribal membership policy that blatantly discriminated on the basis of sex.

Scalia, Antonin

Justice of the U.S. Supreme Court (1986–present), appointed by President Reagan. He has joined enthusiastically with Chief Justice **Rehnquist** in cutting back Indian sovereignty (most notoriously in his majority opinion in ***Nevada v. Hicks***) and rejecting Indian treaty claims.

Self-Determination Era, First (1933–1953)

Name often given to first period in which the U.S. government, largely under the administration of President **Roosevelt** and **John Collier**, supported maintaining and even strengthening Native American sovereignty and Indian rights. Sometimes also called the New Deal Era.

Self-Determination Era, Second (1970–present)

Name often given to the modern era from 1970 to the present, launched by the messages to Congress of presidents **Johnson** and **Nixon**, renewing the U.S. government's support for limited Native American sovereignty.

Sequoyah

Great teacher and scholar of the **Cherokee Nation** during its heyday in the 1820s. He invented the Cherokee alphabet, thus making Cherokee the first written Indian language.

Sioux (Lakota) Nation

An Indian nation now legally divided into several different tribes in the Dakotas.

Sioux-Arapaho-U.S. Treaty of Fort Laramie (1868)

One of the last Indian treaties, abrogated by Congress in 1877 when it seized the Black Hills of South Dakota, for which the Supreme Court awarded compensation in ***United States v. Sioux Nation.***

Souter, David H.

Justice of the U.S. Supreme Court (1990–present), appointed by President Bush the elder. He has generally supported Indian treaty rights but also wrote concurring opinions endorsing major cutbacks in tribal authority over non-Indians in ***Atkinson Trading Co. v. Shirley*** and ***Nevada v. Hicks.***

Sovereignty

The power to govern the people within a **polity**, usually reserved to a polity such as a **nation** or a state, rather than a mere city or other unit of local government. Sovereignty implies some degree of independence in the government exercising it, even though the term is still applied to U.S. states and Native American nations obviously lacking full independence.

State Law

The laws or statutes enacted by each of the individual U.S. states for the governance of their own citizens and affairs. Under the **supremacy clause** of the **U.S. Constitution**, state law may not be enforced if inconsistent with **federal law**.

Statute

A law enacted by a legislative body (such as Congress or a state legislature) as distinguished from a **constitution** setting forth the fundamental higher law of a **nation** or **polity**.

Stevens, John Paul

Justice of the U.S. Supreme Court (1975–present), appointed by President Ford. He has often opposed Indian sovereignty while also sometimes supporting Indian treaty rights.

Stewart, Potter

Justice of the U.S. Supreme Court (1958–1981), appointed by President **Eisenhower**. Generally a moderate, he is best known in the field of Indian law for his majority opinions in ***United States v. Wheeler*** and ***Montana v. United States.***

Story, Joseph

Justice of the U.S. Supreme Court (1812–1845), appointed by President Madison. He supported Indian sovereignty even more strongly than Chief Justice John **Marshall** in the **Cherokee Cases.**

***Strate v. A-1 Contractors* (1997)**

Unanimous U.S. Supreme Court decision, written by Justice **Ginsburg,** rejecting tribal civil jurisdiction over a lawsuit against non-Indians arising from an accident on a state highway passing through a reservation.

Supremacy Clause

Provision of the **U.S. Constitution** declaring that **federal law** (and thus Native American sovereignty principles rooted in federal law) trumps any contrary **state law.**

Sycuan Band of the Kumeyaay Nation

Small California tribe that operates a gambling casino near San Diego under the **California-Tribal Gaming Compact.**

Tee-Hit-Ton Indians v. United States (1955)

U.S. Supreme Court decision, 5–3, upholding the U.S. government's power to extinguish **Indian title** without any constitutional duty of compensation.

Termination

Policy launched by Congress in 1953 by passage of **House Resolution 108** and **Public Law 280**, generally calling for ending the separate legal existence of Indian tribes as governments. The **Eisenhower** Administration abandoned efforts to continue the policy without Indian consent by 1959.

Termination Era (1953–1970)

Name often given to period during which the U.S. government pursued the **termination** policy, renewing its push to assimilate Indians into mainstream society and abolish Native American sovereignty (*see also* **Assimilation Era**), and then slowly backed away from that policy prior to decisively abandoning it in 1970 (*see also* **Self-Determination Era, Second**).

Thomas, Clarence

Justice of the U.S. Supreme Court (1991–present), appointed by President Bush the elder. The second African American on the Court, succeeding Justice Thurgood **Marshall**, Thomas's voting record has been dramatically different from Marshall's in Indian law cases. Thomas has joined consistently with Chief Justice **Rehnquist** and Justices **Scalia** and **Kennedy** in rejecting Indian sovereignty and treaty claims.

Thompson, Smith

Justice of the U.S. Supreme Court (1823–1843), appointed by President Monroe. He supported Indian sovereignty even more strongly than Chief Justice John **Marshall** in the **Cherokee Cases**.

Toledo, Irene M.

Trial judge on the **Navajo Nation** tribal court bench (1989–present), she sat by designation on the **Navajo Nation Supreme Court** when it heard ***Means v. Chinle District Court*** and joined Chief Justice **Yazzie**'s opinion.

Trade and Intercourse Act

See **Indian Country Crimes Act**

Trail of Tears

See **Cherokee Nation** and **Removal Act**

Treaty

A legal document reflecting an agreement between two sovereign entities, most typically two independent nations such as the United States and Russia. But the term has also traditionally been applied to many of the agreements reached between the United States and the various Indian **nations** or **tribes**. The U.S. government discontinued any new treaty making with Indian tribes by an act of Congress passed in 1871 but has never legally disavowed most existing treaties.

Treaty Era (1776–1871)

Name often given to period during which U.S.-Indian relations were governed largely by **treaty** making and which was terminated by an act of Congress in 1871.

Tribal Law

The laws (written or unwritten) enacted or followed by each individual Indian tribe for the internal governance of its own members and affairs. It should thus be distinguished from "American Indian law" in the sense used by this book, which concerns the distinct body of law (for the most part an aspect of **federal law**) governing the external relationship of the tribes with the federal and state governments of the United States.

Tribe

Commonly used term for Indian government or **nation**.

Trust Relationship

Legal doctrine related to the **canons of construction**, holding (in theory) that the U.S. government has fiduciary duties toward the Indian tribes in the same way that a trustee has to a ward.

U.S. Constitution

The fundamental law of the United States, framed and signed in Philadelphia in 1787, ratified in 1788, and taking effect in 1789. It has been amended twenty-seven times, starting in 1791 (*see also* **Bill of Rights** and **Fourteenth Amendment**).

U.S. Supreme Court

The highest court of the United States, with final authority to interpret the meaning of **federal law**, including the **U.S. Constitution**, and the power, under ***Marbury v. Madison***, to set aside or strike down any federal or state law or executive action that it finds to be inconsistent with the Constitution. This power has made the Supreme Court the ultimate authority on issues of American Indian law.

United States v. Kagama **(1886)**

Unanimous U.S. Supreme Court decision upholding federal power to enact the **Major Crimes Act**.

United States v. McBratney **(1882)**

Unanimous U.S. Supreme Court decision holding that states have criminal jurisdiction under **state law** over crimes committed within **Indian country** by non-Indians against other non-Indians.

United States v. Sioux Nation (1980)

Eight to one U.S. Supreme Court decision, written by Justice **Blackmun** (Justice **Rehnquist** dissenting), finding the **Sioux (Lakota) Nation** entitled to compensation for the 1877 seizure of the Black Hills of South Dakota and abrogation of the **Sioux-Arapaho-U.S. Treaty of Fort Laramie.**

United States v. Wheeler (1978)

Unanimous U.S. Supreme Court decision, written by Justice **Stewart**, holding that because of inherent tribal sovereignty, tribal, federal, and state governments may bring separate prosecutions against the same person for the same criminal act without violating the double jeopardy clause of the **U.S. Constitution.**

United States v. Winans (1905)

Eight to one U.S. Supreme Court decision upholding Indian **treaty** rights and strongly reaffirming the **canons of construction** originating in the **Cherokee Cases.**

Usufructuary Rights

Legal term referring to hunting, fishing, and gathering rights, such as those often secured to Indians by treaties; literally, the right to "use" the "fruits" of the land.

Ward v. Race Horse (1896)

Eight to one U.S. Supreme Court decision finding that Wyoming statehood effectively abrogated a **treaty** right held by an Indian tribe within the state. The Court rejected the main premise of *Ward* just nine years later in ***United States v. Winans,*** but Chief Justice **Rehnquist** (joined by Justices **Scalia**, **Kennedy**, and **Thomas**) sought unsuccessfully to revive it 103 years later as a general rule of Indian treaty law in ***Minnesota v. Mille Lacs Band of Chippewa Indians.***

Warren, Earl

Chief justice of the U.S. Supreme Court (1953–1969), appointed by President **Eisenhower**. He and his Court generally supported Indian sovereignty and played a major role in reviving the spirit of the **Cherokee Cases** in the pivotal decision of ***Williams v. Lee.***

Washington, George

First president of the United States (1789–1797), he generally sought to enforce Indian treaties and prevent illegal incursions by non-Indians into Indian lands.

Washington v. Confederated Tribes of the Colville Indian Reservation (1980)

Seven to two U.S. Supreme Court decision, written by Justice **White** (Justice **Brennan**, joined by Justice Thurgood **Marshall**, dissenting), upholding state power to tax tribal cigarette sales to non–tribal members on the reservation. The Court unanimously agreed that tribes also had the power to tax such sales, but the majority rendered that power practically useless, given that such double taxation would simply drive business away from the reservation. Only Justice **Stewart** (among the majority) argued that states should at least have to allow a credit for the amount of any tribal tax on such sales.

Werdegar, Kathryn Mickle

Justice of the California Supreme Court (1994–present), appointed by Governor **Wilson**. She wrote the majority opinion in ***Hotel Employees Union v. Davis.***

Wheeler-Howard Act

See **Indian Reorganization Act**

White, Byron R.

Justice of the U.S. Supreme Court (1962–1993), appointed by President John F. Kennedy. He had a mixed record on Indian issues. Although he joined in ***Oliphant v. Suquamish Indian Tribe*** and ***Duro v. Reina***, he also wrote the majority opinion in ***California v. Cabazon Band of Mission Indians***.

White, Edward D.

Justice (1894–1910) and chief justice (1910–1921) of the U.S. Supreme Court, appointed justice by President Cleveland and chief justice by President Taft. He wrote the Court's opinion in ***Lone Wolf v. Hitchcock***.

***Williams v. Lee* (1959)**

Unanimous U.S. Supreme Court decision, written by Justice **Black**, upholding exclusive tribal court jurisdiction over a civil lawsuit brought against a tribal member and arising out of a transaction on the reservation.

Wilson, Pete

Former governor of California (1991–1999). He generally opposed Indian gambling.

Wirt, William

U.S. attorney general (1817–1829) and leading constitutional lawyer of his day. He argued the **Cherokee Cases** on behalf of the **Cherokee Nation** in 1831–1832.

Worcester, Reverend Samuel Austin

White missionary to the **Cherokee Nation** and supporter of tribal sovereignty, he became, in effect, a stand-in for the Cherokee in *Worcester v. Georgia.*

***Worcester v. Georgia* (1832)**

See **Cherokee Cases**

Wounded Knee

A place in South Dakota, on one of the reservations of the **Sioux (Lakota) Nation**, with great significance for Indian history. In 1890, the U.S. military massacred unarmed Indian civilians there, and in 1973 Indian activists engaged in a standoff with federal authorities that ended in violence.

Yazzie, Robert

Chief Justice of the **Navajo Nation** (1992–present). He wrote the **Navajo Nation Supreme Court**'s opinion in ***Means v. Chinle District Court*** and has written several scholarly articles about Navajo Nation **tribal law**.

Chronology

This timeline focuses on key events regarding the interaction of Native American and European American sovereignty in the United States. See "Sources and Further Reading" at the end of Chapter 2 in Part 1.

c. 70,000–10,000 B.C.E.	Migrations from Siberia to North America apparently took place across what are now the Bering Straits. Descendants of these migrations, generally referred to as Native Americans or American Indians, appear to have settled the entire Western Hemisphere from what is now Alaska to Patagonia at the southern tip of South America. Some evidence suggests later migrations continued to more recent times, resulting in distinct population groups of Native Americans.
c. 5000 B.C.E. –600 C.E.	Fragmentary evidence, debated by scholars, suggests possible contacts with the Americas and its original inhabitants by seafarers from, among other places, Indonesia, China, Japan, Africa, and Ireland. The settlement of vast stretches of Polynesia in the South Pacific during this time indicates that such long ocean migrations were certainly feasible long before the modern European voyages that began with the Vikings and Columbus.
c. 980–990	Led by Eric the Red, Norse (Viking) explorers from Norway and Iceland settled in Greenland. These Greenland colonies may have survived as long as 500 years, until around the time of Columbus.
c. 1000–1015	Norse explorers led by Leif Ericsson (son of Eric the Red) and Thorfinn Karlsefni landed in "Vinland" (pos-

sibly Newfoundland) and other places along the northeastern North American coast. They encountered Native Americans but their settlements were short-lived; scholars debate how far into North America they or succeeding Norse explorers ventured.

1492 Christopher Columbus "discovered" America in the first sustained and extensive encounter of non–Native Americans with the Western Hemisphere. In four voyages financed by Spain, Columbus landed in the Bahamas, explored other areas of the Caribbean, and, notably, colonized the island he named "Hispaniola" (on which the present nations of Haiti and the Dominican Republic are located), enslaving and then exterminating most of its native Arawak inhabitants and fueling the intertwined trade in Native American and African slaves.

1497 Explorer John Cabot sailed along the eastern coast of North America, perhaps as far south as Delaware.

1500 Portuguese explorer Gaspar Côrte-Real visited Labrador.

1513–1521 Juan Ponce de Léon led two Spanish expeditions to Florida and was killed in a fight with Indians.

1515 Bartolomé de las Casas, a Spanish Catholic priest (first to be ordained in the New World), returned to Spain to protest the mistreatment of the Indians in the Spanish Caribbean colonies, launching a career as an activist and historian.

1524–1534 French expeditions led by Giovanni da Verrazano (an Italian) and Jacques Cartier explored the Hudson and St. Lawrence Rivers.

1526 The Spanish abandoned a brief settlement attempt in South Carolina, leaving behind African slaves who may have blended into nearby Indian populations, possibly becoming the first non–Native Americans to settle permanently in what is now the United States.

1528–1536 Álvar Nuñez Cabeza de Vaca and the Moroccan slave Estevánico, survivors of a Spanish expedition that began in Florida, completed an odyssey traveling and living among the Indians through what are now Texas,

New Mexico, Arizona, and northern Mexico. Cabeza de Vaca wrote a classic account of the experience.

1540–1542 Francisco Vásquez de Coronado, Hernando de Soto, and Juan Rodríguez Cabrillo led Spanish expeditions through, respectively, the American Southwest (ranging as far north as Kansas), along the Gulf Coast and Mississippi River basin, and up the California Pacific coast. Coronado and de Soto both initiated numerous violent encounters with Native Americans, de Soto's brutality being especially infamous.

1565 First permanent European settlement in what is now the United States, by the Spanish at St. Augustine, Florida. The Spanish massacred a group of French Protestant (Huguenot) exiles who had settled there shortly before.

c. 1580–1610 Spanish invaders and settlers, including some Spanish Jews seeking religious liberty, migrated into what is now New Mexico, culminating in the founding of Santa Fe in 1610.

1584–1591 British explorers financed by Sir Walter Raleigh attempted to settle Roanoke Island, Virginia, but disappeared, becoming the infamous "Lost Colony"; some believe they may have blended into nearby Indian populations from whom the present-day Lumbee Indians of North Carolina are descended.

1605–1608 First sustained French settlements in North America, led by Samuel de Champlain, founded at Port Royal, Nova Scotia, and Québec City. Over the following decades, French explorers, traders, and missionaries fanned out across the Great Lakes region, the Mississippi River basin, and as far west as the Rocky Mountains.

1607 First sustained British settlement in North America founded at Jamestown, Virginia.

1609–1617 The Dutch, employing Englishman Henry Hudson, explored the Hudson River and founded outposts in Manhattan and Albany, New York.

1617–1620 Plague (probably bubonic plague or smallpox) spread by early contacts with European explorers wiped out about 90 percent of the Indians living in southern New

England, one of a long series of epidemics before and since this one, throughout the Americas, that devastated countless Native American populations, who had little immune resistance to diseases prevalent in Europe.

1620 The "Pilgrims" on the *Mayflower* landed at Plymouth Rock, Massachusetts, in the second major British settlement in the United States.

1636–1637 The Pequot War, the first major European-Indian conflict in New England.

1675–1676 King Philip's War, between the New England settlers and the Wampanoags and other Indians, named for the English title given to Wampanoag chief Metacomet. This conflict, like the Pequot War and the Pueblo Revolt, was only one of many between Europeans and Indians during the American colonial period.

1680–1698 Pueblo Indians revolted against Spanish rule in the American Southwest. The Spanish regime fled to El Paso and did not recapture Santa Fe until 1693. Some of the southwestern Indians, like the Hopi, were never completely subdued.

1689–1766 Native Americans and European Americans became enmeshed in the colonial dimensions of four major wars involving Great Britain, France, and Spain: the War of the League of Augsburg (King William's War) (1689–1697), the War of the Spanish Succession (Queen Anne's War) (1702–1713), the War of the Austrian Succession (King George's War) (1739–1748), and the French and Indian War (1754–1763) (the European part of which, known as the Seven Years' War, began in 1756). Pontiac's War (1763–1766), between the British and an alliance of Ohio Indians named for the famous Ottawa chief, was a violent sequel to the last of these; most of the Iroquois (Haudenosaunee) Confederacy of Indians, however, remained allied with the British.

1763 King George III of Great Britain issued a royal proclamation prohibiting the American colonies from encroaching on Indian lands west of the Appalachian Mountains. This aroused great resentment among European American colonists and was a major cause of the discontents leading to the American Revolution.

1769 The Spanish began to settle California with the mission established by Father Junípero Serra in San Diego.

1775–1783 The American Revolution, concluded by the Treaty of Paris.

1776 The U.S. Declaration of Independence was signed, with its famous complaint that the British had incited Indians to attack the European American colonists. Indeed, most eastern Indians, from the Iroquois (Haudenosaunee) in the north to the Cherokee in the south, did side with the British, out of well-founded fear of American expansionism.

1777 The Articles of Confederation, organizing the first formally unified (though weak) U.S. government, were framed but not fully ratified until 1781. The power to manage Indian relations was vested in the new national government.

1778 The Treaty of Fort Pitt, the first of more than 350 treaties between the United States and Indian nations over the next century, was concluded with the Delaware Indians, containing assurances that the United States had no designs on Indian lands.

1785 The Cherokee-U.S. Treaty of Hopewell was signed, the fourth Indian treaty and first of several Cherokee-U.S. treaties.

1787 The present U.S. Constitution was framed. Ratified in 1788 and taking effect in 1789, it vested in Congress the power to regulate "commerce . . . with the Indian tribes," authorized the president to make treaties subject to Senate ratification, and confirmed the validity of prior treaties, including those made with Indian nations.

1791 The first ten amendments to the Constitution, commonly known as the Bill of Rights, were ratified.

1803 The U.S. Supreme Court, in Chief Justice John Marshall's opinion in *Marbury v. Madison,* asserted the power of judicial review, authorizing the Court to strike down legislation or executive acts it finds in violation of the Constitution.

1821 Mexico achieved independence from Spain. At that time, Mexico extended over what is now the American Southwest, including Arizona, California, much of Colorado, Nevada, New Mexico, Texas, and Utah.

1827–1828 The discovery of gold in Cherokee country and the Cherokee Nation's adoption of a written constitution fueled long-standing demands by many European Americans, especially in Georgia, to drive them and other Indians west.

1830 The Removal Act was narrowly passed by Congress and signed by President Andrew Jackson, authorizing removal of Indians to the "Indian Territory" (in what is now Oklahoma) but not abrogating any treaties.

1832 The Supreme Court, in Chief Justice Marshall's opinion in *Worcester v. Georgia,* the second of the great Cherokee cases, upheld the sovereign status of the Cherokee Nation, and by extension all Indian tribes, as "domestic dependent nations" protected by federal treaties and laws against incursion or dissolution by state governments but subject to supreme federal power. But President Jackson and the state of Georgia openly defied the ruling, which only slightly delayed the process of Indian removal.

1832–1842 The five "Civilized Tribes" (Cherokee, Creek, Choctaw, Chickasaw, and Seminole) were forced to migrate from their homelands in Tennessee, North Carolina, Mississippi, Alabama, Georgia, and Florida to the Indian Territory (Oklahoma); the Cherokees' journey in 1838 became known as the "Trail of Tears."

1836–1845 The Republic of Texas, which declared independence from Mexico in 1836, was annexed as a U.S. state in 1845.

1846–1848 The Mexican-American War, concluded by the Treaty of Guadalupe Hidalgo in 1848 and supplemented by the Gadsden Purchase in 1853, resulted in the U.S. conquest of the Southwest, eventually forming the states of California, Nevada, Utah, Colorado, Arizona, and New Mexico. Also in 1846, the United States and Great Britain settled their dispute over the Pacific Northwest, solidifying U.S. control over land later forming the states of Washington, Oregon, and Idaho. These vast territorial expansions brought many powerful Indian nations, including the Nez Percé in the Northwest and the Navajo (Diné) in the Southwest, under U.S. sovereignty.

1861–1865 The U.S. Civil War resulted in the abolition of slavery. Some Indian nations (for example, the Cherokee, many of whom owned slaves) sided with the southern Confederacy because of promises of greater respect for their legal rights.

1864–1868 The U.S.-Navajo War resulted in the "Long Walk" exile of the Navajo (Diné) to Fort Sumner (Bosque Redondo) in New Mexico; they were allowed to return to their homeland by the Treaty of Fort Sumner in 1868, one of the last Indian treaties.

1868 The Treaty of Fort Laramie with the Lakota (Sioux), another of the last Indian treaties, guaranteed them most of what is now South Dakota in perpetuity. The Fourteenth Amendment to the Constitution was ratified, guaranteeing citizenship to all people "born or naturalized in the United States, and subject to the jurisdiction thereof," which was understood to exclude Indians "in a tribal relation."

1871 By act of Congress, the United States terminated treaty making with Indian nations, handling Indian matters thereafter by direct legislation, although treaties remained in effect unless and until abrogated. The Supreme Court indicated, in the *Cherokee Tobacco* case, that Indian treaties may be abrogated by Congress.

1876 Lakota (Sioux) Indians under Crazy Horse defeated General George Armstrong Custer in the Battle of the Little Bighorn (known to the Sioux as the Battle of Greasy Grass), the last major victory by Indians in any military battle with European Americans.

1877 The discovery of gold in the Black Hills in the early 1870s and ensuing conflicts, including Custer's 1876 defeat, led to expropriation of most of the Sioux lands, including the Black Hills, in 1877. The same year, the

	Nez Percé under Chief Joseph fought a valiant but losing war with the U.S. military in the Pacific Northwest.
1881	Helen Hunt Jackson, an early non-Indian activist for Indian rights, published her famous exposé of U.S. government's policies, *A Century of Dishonor*, followed in 1884 by her protest novel *Ramona.*
1885	The Major Crimes Act, extending federal criminal jurisdiction over Indians in Indian country, was enacted in response to the Supreme Court's decision in *Ex parte Kan-Gi-Shun-Ca (Crow Dog)* (1883), which had upheld exclusive tribal jurisdiction over crimes among Indians within recognized Indian nations.
1886	The surrender of the Apache under Geronimo marked the end of organized Indian military resistance to the U.S. government. The Supreme Court upheld the Major Crimes Act in *United States v. Kagama*, reaffirming expansive federal power over Indians.
1887	The Allotment Act was passed by Congress, resulting in expropriation over the next forty years of two-thirds of the Indian tribal land base while allowing some Indians to obtain U.S. citizenship and small plots ("allotments") of individually owned land.
1890	The U.S. military massacred unarmed Indian civilians at Wounded Knee, South Dakota, following hysteria among non-Indians over revival of the Lakota (Sioux) "Ghost Dance." This event is widely viewed as marking the end of the "frontier" era of Indian wars.
1898	The Curtis Act was passed by Congress, imposing allotment of Indian lands in the Indian Territory (in what is now Oklahoma) and abolishing most governmental powers of the five "Civilized Tribes," which had been removed there in the 1830s.
1903	The Supreme Court decided *Lone Wolf v. Hitchcock*, upholding Congress's "plenary power" to abrogate Indian treaties.
1907	Oklahoma, including the former Indian Territory, now with an overwhelmingly non-Indian population after years of white settlement, was granted statehood.
1924	All Indians born in the United States were declared citizens by Congress.

1933 The inauguration of President Franklin D. Roosevelt and reformist Secretary of the Interior Harold Ickes and Commissioner of Indian Affairs John Collier marked a fundamental shift in federal Indian policy from assimilation to promotion of Indian self-determination.

1934 The Indian Reorganization Act was passed, leading to a revival of tribal governments but also to conflicts in many tribes over the European American forms of government promoted under the law.

1941 The most important law book ever about Indians, the *Handbook of Federal Indian Law,* written by Felix S. Cohen, a lawyer for the U.S. Department of the Interior under Roosevelt, Ickes, and Collier, was published by the U.S. government. It strongly supported limited Indian sovereignty and exerted remarkable influence over the following decades.

1953 Congress passed Public Law 280 and House Resolution 108, extending some states' jurisdiction into parts of Indian country and generally embracing the philosophy of terminating Native American sovereignty, marking a basic shift in federal Indian policy away from self-determination and back to assimilation.

1959 The Supreme Court's decision in *Williams v. Lee,* upholding tribal civil jurisdiction over lawsuits arising in Indian country, marked a judicial revival of Native American sovereignty and the spirit of the 1832 *Worcester* decision. The Eisenhower administration abandoned efforts to pursue the termination policy without Indian consent.

1961–1968 The Kennedy and Johnson administrations increased social welfare programs benefiting Native Americans and showed greater concern for Indian civil rights and tribal sovereignty, marking the gradual end of the termination era.

1968 President Lyndon B. Johnson delivered a landmark message to Congress on Indian issues, "The Forgotten American," rejecting the termination policy, stressing "self-determination" and "full participation in the life of modern America," and advocating "freedom of choice" for Indians to develop their tribal homelands and pursue opportunities in urban areas. Congress passed and Johnson signed the Indian Civil Rights Act, extending Bill of Rights guarantees as restrictions on tribal governmental power and prohibiting further extensions of state jurisdiction into Indian country without tribal consent.

1968–1973 The American Indian Movement was formed in 1968, launching a period of Indian activism that included occupations of Alcatraz Island in San Francisco Bay (1969), the Bureau of Indian Affairs headquarters (the culmination of the 1972 "Trail of Broken Treaties" march on Washington, D.C.), and Wounded Knee on the Pine Ridge Sioux Reservation in South Dakota (1973). The latter resulted in a violent confrontation with the Federal Bureau of Investigation.

1970 President Richard M. Nixon delivered a landmark message to Congress, building on Johnson 1968 speech, even more strongly repudiating the termination era and embracing renewed political and economic development of Indian nations on the basis of self-determination. The Johnson and Nixon messages continue to this day to guide federal Indian policy on a bipartisan basis.

1978 The Supreme Court decided *Oliphant v. Suquamish Indian Tribe*, denying tribal criminal jurisdiction over non-Indians within Indian country. The decision, ironically, accompanied a rise in the number and effectiveness of tribal courts as encouraged by federal government policy. Congress passed the Indian Child Welfare Act, expanding tribal authority over the adoption of Indian children, a rare and important legislative reversal in the trend of eroding Native American sovereignty. Congress also passed the mostly symbolic American Indian Religious Freedom Act.

1980 The Supreme Court decided *United States v. Sioux Nation*, finding the Sioux entitled to more than $100 million in compensation for the 1877 seizure of the Black Hills.

1987 The Supreme Court decided *California v. Cabazon Band of Mission Indians*, upholding the authority of

Indian tribes to conduct some gambling operations independent of state law and fueling a nationwide trend of Native American reliance on gambling for economic development. Congress followed up by passing the Indian Gaming Regulatory Act of 1988, largely confirming the *Cabazon* Court's approach.

1990 Congress passed the Native American Graves Protection and Repatriation Act, providing more legal protection for Indian human remains and sacred objects.

1994 President Clinton hosted a historic White House summit conference with Native American leaders and declared his support for "government-to-government" relationships with Indian tribes.

1998–2000 California voters endorsed tribal gambling operations by wide referendum margins in November 1998 and March 2000, leading to the historic California-Tribal Gaming Compact, accelerating the national trend begun by the 1987 *Cabazon* decision, and marking a historic shift in which some state governments and electorates are trending more favorably than the federal government toward Native American sovereignty.

2001 The Supreme Court decided *Atkinson Trading Co. v. Shirley* and *Nevada v. Hicks*, seriously eroding tribal civil jurisdiction over non-Indians within Indian country and making clear that the judiciary, in a historic shift, was now the branch of the federal government most hostile to Native American sovereignty, even more hostile than many state governments and electorates.

Table of Cases and Statutes

Cases

Sources are cited in text by author's name and year; where multiple case reporters are cited here, page references in text are to first reporter cited. For guidance using case reporters, please consult a law librarian. "Cert. denied" refers to the U.S. Supreme Court's refusal to hear an appeal; it does not signify either approval or disapproval of the lower court decision.

Arizona ex rel. Merrill v. Turtle, 413 F.2d 683 (9th Cir. 1969), cert. denied, 396 U.S. 1003 (1970).
Atkinson Trading Co. v. Shirley, 532 U.S. 645 (2001).
Babbitt Ford, Inc. v. Navajo Indian Tribe, 710 F.2d 587 (9th Cir. 1983), cert. denied, 466 U.S. 926 (1984).
Brendale v. Yakima Indian Nation, 492 U.S. 408 (1989).
Bryan v. Itasca County, 426 U.S. 373 (1976).
California v. Cabazon Band of Mission Indians, 480 U.S. 202 (1987).
Cherokee Nation v. Georgia, 30 U.S. (5 Pet.) 1 (1831).
Cherokee Tobacco (207 Half Pound Papers of Smoking Tobacco v. United States), 78 U.S. (11 Wall.) 616 (1871).
Civil Rights Cases, 109 U.S. 3 (1883).
Cobell v. Norton, 240 F.3d 1081 (D.C. Cir. 2001), affirming and remanding *Cobell v. Babbitt*, 91 F. Supp. 2d 1 (D.D.C. 1999).

Duro v. Reina, 495 U.S. 676 (1990).
Elk v. Wilkins, 112 U.S. 94 (1884).
Employment Division v. Smith (see *Oregon Department of Human Resources v. Smith*).
Ex parte Crow Dog (see Ex parte Kan-Gi-Shun-Ca)
Ex parte Kan-Gi-Shun-Ca, 109 U.S. 556 (1883)
Ex parte Kenyon, 14 F. Cas. 353 (W.D. Ark. 1878).
Federal Power Commission v. Tuscarora Indian Nation, 362 U.S. 99 (1960).
Fisher v. District Court, 424 U.S. 382 (1976).
Fletcher v. Peck, 10 U.S. (6 Cranch) 87 (1810).
Hotel Employees Union v. Davis, 21 Cal. 4th 585, 981 P.2d 990, 88 Cal. Rptr. 2d 56 (1999).
Idaho v. United States, 533 U.S. 262 (2001).
Iowa Mutual Ins. Co. v. LaPlante, 480 U.S. 9 (1987).
Johnson v. M'Intosh, 21 U.S. (8 Wheat.) 543 (1823).
Kerr-McGee Corp. v. Navajo Tribe, 471 U.S. 195 (1985).
Kiowa Tribe v. Manufacturing Technologies, Inc., 523 U.S. 751 (1998).
Lone Wolf v. Hitchcock, 187 U.S. 553 (1903).
Marbury v. Madison, 5 U.S. (1 Cranch) 137 (1803).
McClanahan v. Arizona State Tax Commission, 411 U.S. 164 (1973).
McCullough v. Maryland, 17 U.S. (4 Wheat.) 316 (1819).
Means v. Chinle District Court, 7 Nav. Rep. 382 (Navajo Nation Supreme Court 1999).
Menominee Tribe v. United States, 391 U.S. 404 (1968).
Merrion v. Jicarilla Apache Tribe, 455 U.S. 130 (1982).
Minnesota v. Mille Lacs Band of Chippewa Indians, 526 U.S. 172 (1999).
Montana v. United States, 450 U.S. 544 (1981).
Morton v. Mancari, 417 U.S. 535 (1974).
National Farmers Union Ins. Cos. v. Crow Tribe, 471 U.S. 845 (1985).
Nevada v. Hicks, 533 U.S. 353 (2001).
New Mexico v. Mescalero Apache Tribe, 462 U.S. 324 (1983).
Nofire v. United States, 164 U.S. 657 (1897).
Oliphant v. Suquamish Indian Tribe, 435 U.S. 191 (1978).
Oneida County v. Oneida Indian Nation, 470 U.S. 226 (1985).
Oregon Department of Human Resources v. Smith, 494 U.S. 872 (1990).

Plessy v. Ferguson, 163 U.S. 537 (1896).
Puyallup Tribe v. Washington Department of Game, 391 U.S. 392 (1968).
Rumsey Indian Rancheria v. Wilson, 41 F.3d 421 (9th Cir. 1994), amended on denial of rehearing en banc, 64 F.3d 1250 (9th Cir. 1995), amended on denial of rehearing, 99 F.3d 321 (9th Cir. 1996), cert. denied, 521 U.S. 1118 (1997).
Santa Clara Pueblo v. Martinez, 436 U.S. 49 (1978).
Seminole Tribe v. Florida, 517 U.S. 44 (1996).
Shoshone Tribe v. United States, 299 U.S. 476 (1937).
South Dakota v. Bourland, 508 U.S. 679 (1993).
Strate v. A-1 Contractors, 520 U.S. 438 (1997).
Sycuan Band v. Roache, 788 F. Supp. 1498 (S.D. Cal. 1992), affirmed, 54 F.3d 535 (9th Cir. 1994), cert. denied, 516 U.S. 912 (1995).
Talton v. Mayes, 163 U.S. 376 (1896).
Tee-Hit-Ton Indians v. United States, 348 U.S. 272 (1955).
Tsosie v. United States, 825 F.2d 393 (Fed. Cir. 1987).
United States v. Antelope, 430 U.S. 641 (1977).
United States v. Dion, 476 U.S. 734 (1986).
United States v. Enas, 255 F.3d 662 (9th Cir. 2001) (en banc), cert. denied, 122 S. Ct. 925 (2002).
United States v. Kagama, 118 U.S. 375 (1886).
United States v. Marcyes, 557 F.2d 1361 (9th Cir. 1977).
United States v. Mazurie, 419 U.S. 544 (1975).
United States v. McBratney, 104 U.S. 621 (1882).
United States v. Rogers, 45 U.S. (4 How.) 567 (1846).
United States v. Sioux Nation, 448 U.S. 371 (1980).
United States v. Wheeler, 435 U.S. 313 (1978).
United States v. Winans, 198 U.S. 371 (1905).
Utah and Northern Railroad Co. v. Fisher, 116 U.S. 28 (1885).
Ward v. Race Horse, 163 U.S. 504 (1896).
Washington v. Confederated Tribes of the Colville Indian Reservation, 447 U.S. 134 (1980).
Washington v. Washington State Commercial Passenger Fishing Vessel Association, 443 U.S. 658 (1979).
Western Telcon v. California State Lottery, 13 Cal. 4th 475, 917 P.2d 651, 53 Cal. Rptr. 2d 812 (1996).
White Mountain Apache Tribe v. Bracker, 448 U.S. 136 (1980).
Williams v. Lee, 358 U.S. 217 (1959).
Winters v. United States, 207 U.S. 564 (1908).
Worcester v. Georgia, 31 U.S. (6 Pet.) 515 (1832).

Statutes

Sources are cited in text by name and sometimes also by year, unless indicated otherwise here; page references in text are to first source indicated here; section references to statutes are to current codification. For guidance using such legal sources, please consult a law librarian. See Annotated Bibliography for descriptions of Kappler, Prucha, and Urofsky and Finkelman compilations.

Act of Congress, 16 Stat. 544, 566 (1871) (codified in relevant part at 25 U.S.C. § 71) (Prucha 2000, 135) (cited as 1871 Act of Congress).
Allotment Act, 24 Stat. 388 (1887) (Prucha 2000, 170).
American Indian Religious Freedom Act, 92 Stat. 469 (1978) (codified in relevant part at 42 U.S.C. § 1996) (Prucha 2000, 289), amended, 108 Stat. 3125 (1994) (codified at 42 U.S.C. § 1996a) (Prucha 2000, 349).
Articles of Confederation (first U.S. Constitution) of 1777 (Cogan 1999, 40; Urofsky and Finkelman 2002b, *Documents,* 61) (cited as Art. Conf.).
Assimilative Crimes Act, 62 Stat. 686 (1948) (codified at 18 U.S.C. § 13).
California Constitution of 1879 (as amended) (codified in Deering's *California Codes Annotated* and West's *Annotated California Codes*).
Cherokee-U.S. Treaty of Hopewell, 7 Stat. 18 (November 28, 1785) (Kappler 1904, 8; Prucha 2000, 6).
Cherokee-U.S. Treaty of Holston River, 7 Stat. 39 (July 2, 1791) (Kappler 1904, 29).
Cherokee-U.S. Treaty of New Echota, 7 Stat. 478 (December 29, 1835) (Kappler 1904, 439).
Cherokee-U.S. Treaty of Washington, 7 Stat. 195 (February 27, 1819) (Kappler 1904, 177).
Cherokee-U.S. Treaty of Washington, 14 Stat. 799 (July 19, 1866) (Kappler 1904, 942).
Chippewa-U.S. Treaty of La Pointe, 7 Stat. 591 (October 4, 1842) (Kappler 1904, 542).
Chippewa-U.S. Treaty of La Pointe, 10 Stat. 1109 (September 30, 1854) (Kappler, 1904, 648).
Chippewa-U.S. Treaty of St. Peter's, 7 Stat. 536 (July 29, 1837) (Kappler 1904, 491).

Chippewa-U.S. Treaty of Washington, 10 Stat. 1165 (February 22, 1855) (Kappler, 1904, 685).
Choctaw-U.S. Treaty of Dancing Rabbit Creek, 7 Stat. 333 (September 27, 1830) (Kappler 1904, 310; Prucha 2000, 53).
Citizenship Act (see Indian Citizenship Act).
Civil Rights Act, 14 Stat. 27 (1866).
Civil Rights Act of 1968 (see Indian Civil Rights Act).
Comanche-Kiowa-U.S. Treaty (see Kiowa-Comanche-U.S. Treaty).
Crow Allotment Act, 41 Stat. 751 (1920).
Crow-U.S. Treaty of Fort Laramie, 15 Stat. 649 (May 7, 1868) (Kappler 1904, 1008).
Curtis Act, 30 Stat. 495 (1898).
Dawes Act (see Allotment Act).
Delaware-U.S. Treaty of Fort Pitt, 7 Stat. 13 (September 17, 1778) (Kappler 1904, 3).
Duro Fix Act (see Indian Civil Rights Act Amendments of 1990–1991).
General Allotment Act (see Allotment Act).
General Crimes Act (see Indian Country Crimes Act).
House Concurrent Resolution 108, 67 Stat. B132 (1953) (Prucha 2000, 234) (cited as House Resolution 108).
Indian Child Welfare Act, 92 Stat. 3069 (1978) (codified at 25 U.S.C. §§ 1901–1963) (Prucha 2000, 294).
Indian Citizenship Act, 43 Stat. 253 (1924) (codified at 8 U.S.C. § 1401(b)) (Prucha 2000, 218).
Indian Civil Rights Act, 82 Stat. 77 (1968), amended, 100 Stat. 3207 (1986) (raising maximum criminal penalties in tribal court) (codified at 25 U.S.C. §§ 1301–1341) (Prucha 2000, 250).
Indian Civil Rights Act Amendments of 1990–1991, 104 Stat. 1856 (1990), 105 Stat. 646 (1991) (codified at 25 U.S.C. § 1301(2)) (cited as *Duro* Fix Act).
Indian Claims Commission Act, 60 Stat. 1049 (1946) (codified at 28 U.S.C. § 1505) (Prucha 2000, 231).
Indian Country (General) Crimes Act (originally enacted as part of Trade and Intercourse Act), 1 Stat. 137 (1790) (codified at 18 U.S.C. § 1152) (Prucha 2000, 14).
Indian Gaming Regulatory Act, 102 Stat. 2467 (1988) (codified at 25 U.S.C. §§ 2701–2721) (Prucha 2000, 322).
Indian Reorganization (Wheeler-Howard) Act, 48 Stat. 984 (1934) (codified at 25 U.S.C. §§ 461–494) (Prucha 2000, 223).

Indian Self-Determination and Education Assistance Act, 88 Stat. 2203 (1975) (codified at 25 U.S.C. §§ 450–450n).

Kiowa-Comanche-U.S. Treaty of Medicine Lodge Creek, 15 Stat. 581 (October 21, 1867) (Kappler 1904, 977).

Major Crimes Act, 23 Stat. 385 (1885) (codified at 18 U.S.C. § 1153) (Prucha 2000, 166).

Native American Graves Protection and Repatriation Act, 104 Stat. 3048 (1990) (codified at 25 U.S.C. §§ 3001–3013) (Prucha 2000, 332).

Navajo-U.S. Treaty of Fort Sumner, 15 Stat. 667 (June 1, 1868) (Kappler 1904, 1015).

Nez Percé–U.S. Treaty of Washington, 15 Stat. 693 (August 13, 1868) (Kappler 1904, 1024).

Public Law 83-280, 67 Stat. 588 (1953) (codified in relevant part at 18 U.S.C. § 1162 and 28 U.S.C. § 1360) (Prucha 2000, 234) (cited as Public Law 280).

Removal Act, 4 Stat. 411 (1830) (Prucha 2000, 52).

Sioux-Arapaho-U.S. Treaty of Fort Laramie, 15 Stat. 635 (April 29, 1868) (Kappler 1904, 998; Prucha 2000, 109).

Six Nations–U.S. Treaty of Canandaigua, 7 Stat. 44 (November 11, 1794) (Kappler 1904, 34).

Suquamish et al.–U.S. Treaty of Point Elliott, 12 Stat. 927 (January 22, 1855) (Kappler 1904, 669).

Trade and Intercourse Act, 1 Stat. 137 (1790) (Prucha 2000, 14) (see also Indian Country Crimes Act).

U.S. Constitution of 1787 (as amended) (codified in West's U.S. Code Annotated; Urofsky and Finkelman 2002b, *Documents,* 85) (cited as U.S. Const.).

Wheeler-Howard Act (see Indian Reorganization Act).

Executive Documents

Cited in text by author's name, "memorandum," "message," "notice," or "order," and year.

Clinton, President William J. *Executive Memorandum on Government-to-Government Relations with Native American Tribal Governments,* 59 Fed. Reg. 22951 (April 29, 1994) (Prucha 2000, 346).

———. *Executive Order No. 13007 on Indian Sacred Sites,* 61 Fed. Reg. 26771 (May 24, 1996) (Prucha 2000, 357).

———. *Executive Order No. 13084 on Consultation and Coordination with Indian Tribal Governments,* 63 Fed. Reg. 27655 (May 14, 1998).

Gover, Kevin, Assistant Secretary of the Interior for Indian Affairs. *Notice of Approved Tribal-State Compacts,* 65 Fed. Reg. 31189 (May 16, 2000), corrected, 65 Fed. Reg. 34726 (May 31, 2000).

Johnson, President Lyndon B. *Message to Congress on the Problems of the American Indian: "The Forgotten American"* (March 6, 1968) (Prucha 2000, 249).

Nixon, President Richard M. *Message to Congress on Indian Policy,* H.R. Doc. No. 363, 91st Cong., 2d Sess. (July 8, 1970) (Prucha 2000, 256).

Annotated Bibliography

Bailey, Lynn R. 1964. ***The Long Walk: A History of the Navajo Wars, 1846–1868.*** Los Angeles: Westernlore Press.

Classic account of the U.S.-Navajo wars that led to the "long walk" and exile of the Navajo from 1864 to 1868, followed by their repatriation under the treaty of 1868.

Baker, Janet K. 1997. **"Tribal Water Quality Standards: Are There Any Limits?"** *Duke Environmental Law and Policy Forum* 7: 367.

Excellent study of a New Mexico pueblo tribe's efforts to exercise environmental regulatory power in a manner greatly affecting non-Indians outside Indian country.

Baker, Leonard. 1974. ***John Marshall: A Life in Law.*** New York: Macmillan.

Definitive biography of Chief Justice Marshall, with an informative section (pp. 731–746) on his role in the Cherokee Cases.

Benedek, Emily. 1992. ***The Wind Won't Know Me: A History of the Navajo-Hopi Land Dispute.*** New York: Knopf.

Fine account of a long-running land dispute between the Navajo Nation and the Hopi Tribe (a dispute originally caused by inept U.S. government policies), it provides a useful modern perspective on some of the challenges facing the Navajo, the Hopi, and other Indians.

Burke, Joseph C. 1969. **"The Cherokee Cases: A Study in Law, Politics, and Morality,"** *Stanford Law Review* 21: 500 (reprinted in Wunder 1996, 1: 136).

Important analysis of these seminal cases, though debatable in some of its conclusions.

Cabeza de Vaca, Álvar Nuñez. [1542] 1983. ***Adventures in the Unknown Interior of America.*** Reprint, Albuquerque: University of New Mexico Press (translated and annotated by Cyclone Covey; epilogue by William T. Pilkington; first written as *La Relación,* a report to the King of Spain).

Classic account by a survivor of a Spanish expedition that began in Florida, of tremendous historical and anthropological importance because of its detailed descriptions of the first European encounters with

Indians in the interior of North America. Cabeza de Vaca, accompanied by the Moroccan slave Estevánico, wandered among the Indians for eight years, from 1528 to 1536, through what are now Texas, New Mexico, Arizona, and northern Mexico. In notable contrast to the prevailing Spanish attitude, Cabeza de Vaca came to have deep sympathy and respect for the Indians.

Canby, William C., Jr. 1998. ***American Indian Law in a Nutshell.*** 3d ed. St. Paul, MN: West.

West's "Nutshells" are usually regarded as a sort of "Cliff's Notes" series for law students and practitioners. But Canby, an Arizona law professor and expert on Indian law and then judge on the U.S. Court of Appeals for the Ninth Circuit (where he has written many important Indian law decisions), elevated this entry into an art form. Wonderfully concise and readable, it is also amazingly comprehensive. In the field of Indian law, it has the stature of being one of a handful of the best treatises available.

Carr, Waggoner, Attorney General of Texas (with J. S. Bracewell and Milton Richardson). March 3, 1964. ***Memorandum to Governor John Connally Concerning Cherokee Indian Claim Relating to Lands in Texas.***

Report on a Cherokee land claim against the state of Texas, containing fascinating historical details about this aspect of the Cherokee saga.

Carter, Samuel, III. 1976. ***Cherokee Sunset: A Nation Betrayed.*** Garden City, NY: Doubleday.

Beautifully written account of Cherokee history, covering the period from the Treaty of Hopewell (1785) to the aftermath of the Civil War in the 1860s, focusing on the buildup to the Trail of Tears in the 1820s and 1830s.

Clark, C. Blue. 1998. **"How Bad It Really Was before World War II: Sovereignty."** *Oklahoma City University Law Review* 23: 175.

Excellent, concise article summarizing the darkest years for American Indians during the Assimilation Era of 1871–1933.

Clinton, Robert N. 1976. **"Criminal Jurisdiction over Indian Lands: A Journey through a Jurisdictional Maze."** *Arizona Law Review* 18: 503.

Excellent starting point for those with a particular interest in exploring the framework of criminal law in Indian country. Must be updated, however, such as by use of Canby's treatise, to consider recent changes and developments.

———. 2002. **"There Is No Federal Supremacy Clause for Indian Tribes."** *Arizona State Law Journal* 34: 113.

Leading article criticizing the theory and practice of "plenary" federal power over Indian affairs and advocating a treaty-based, government-to-government relationship between Indian nations and the United States.

Cogan, Neil H., ed. 1999. ***Contexts of the Constitution: A Documentary Collection on Principles of American Constitutional Law.*** New York: Foundation.

Useful collection of primary legal documents from the era preceding and contemporary to the U.S. Constitution.

Cohen, Felix S. 1941. ***Handbook of Federal Indian Law.*** Washington, DC: U.S. Government Printing Office.

It is difficult to overstate the importance of this classic book to the field of American Indian law (which Cohen essentially created in its modern form) and to the modern legal status of American Indians. Cohen wrote it while working as a lawyer for the Department of the Interior, and it proved tremendously influential in federal Indian policy and later court decisions. Cohen, a rigorous and brilliant scholar, was fair and balanced in his treatment, not as critical of federal Indian law as many later scholars but strongly defending Indian legal rights and framing his analysis in a way powerfully supportive of Indian claims to continued sovereignty. His prosovereignty views fell out of favor in the U.S. government in the 1950s, and a revised edition of the *Handbook* published in 1958 is widely regarded as an inferior alteration of the original. Hence, it is cited separately below under the authorship of the U.S. Department of the Interior. A panel of eminent Indian law scholars under the leadership of Rennard Strickland prepared the revised and updated 1982 edition, which is more faithful to the tenor and scope of Cohen's original. It is now dated as a legal reference, though still important and useful. Another updated revision is in preparation.

Cornell, Stephen. 1997. **"Sovereignty, Prosperity, and Policy in Indian Country Today."** *Community Reinvestment* (Federal Reserve Bank of Kansas City) 5: 5.

Excellent study of the importance of strong tribal governments in fostering economic development in Indian country.

Debo, Angie. 1970. ***A History of the Indians of the United States.*** Norman: University of Oklahoma Press.

Standard one-volume work on American Indian history; paired with Prucha's abridged volume, *The Great Father*, on U.S.-Indian relations (which provides more insight into legal issues), this history is an excellent starting point for any beginning student.

———. 1984 [1940]. ***And Still the Waters Run: The Betrayal of the Five Civilized Tribes.*** Norman: University of Oklahoma Press.

Classic account of the dispossession of the Cherokee and other Indians settled in "Indian Territory," as Oklahoma was settled by non-Indians and became a state.

Deloria, Philip J. 1998. *Playing Indian.* New Haven, CT: Yale University Press.

Insightful analysis of European American appropriation of Indian dress, customs, and cultural habits.

Deloria, Sam. 2002. **"Commentary on Nation-Building: The Future of Indian Nations."** *Arizona State Law Journal* 34: 55.

Provocative essay on the current challenges facing Indian nations by an experienced legal scholar and advocate (another member of the remarkably productive Deloria family, which includes fellow Indian scholars Vine Deloria, Jr., and Philip J. Deloria; see books listed below under Deloria and Thomas et al.).

Deloria, Vine, Jr. 1988. ***Custer Died for Your Sins: An Indian Manifesto.*** New York: Macmillan, 1969. Reprint, Norman: University of Oklahoma Press.

Very informative survey of modern American Indian culture and politics, focusing on the activist movement just arising at the time of publication. Often highly entertaining, it includes an excellent chapter on the Indian use of humor. This classic is inevitably a bit dated today but not as much as one might think; it is still indispensable reading for any serious student of modern Indian life.

———. 1989. **"Laws Founded in Justice and Humanity: Reflections on the Content and Character of Federal Indian Law."** *Arizona Law Review* 31: 203.

Scathing article on the internal contradictions and systemic problems of American Indian law, especially what Deloria views as the lack of sufficient historical context in much legal analysis.

Deloria, Vine, Jr., and Clifford M. Lytle. 1983. ***American Indians, American Justice.*** Austin: University of Texas Press.

Excellent overview of Indian legal history, focusing on tribal courts and attorneys.

———. 1984. ***The Nations Within: The Past and Future of American Indian Sovereignty.*** New York: Pantheon.

Excellent history of the development of modern federal Indian policy, focusing on the New Deal Era of the 1930s and the renewal of Indian self-determination in the 1960s.

Deloria, Vine, Jr., and David E. Wilkins. 1999. ***Tribes, Treaties, and Constitutional Tribulations.*** Austin: University of Texas Press.

Useful clause-by-clause summary and analysis of constitutional provisions affecting American Indians.

Deloria, Vine, Jr., and Raymond J. DeMallie, eds. 1999. ***Documents of American Indian Diplomacy: Treaties, Agreements, and Conventions, 1775–1979.*** 2 vols. Norman: University of Oklahoma Press.

Indispensable compilation of primary sources, supplementing the classic Kappler collection of Indian treaties.

Dussias, Allison M. 1993. **"Geographically-Based and Membership-Based Views of Indian Tribal Sovereignty: The Supreme Court's Changing Vision."** *University of Pittsburgh Law Review* 55: 1.

Major article exploring how the Supreme Court has slowly shifted the scope of tribal sovereignty from the territorial conception suggested by the Cherokee cases of 1831–1832, to a conception limited mostly to tribal members, thus divesting tribes of much power over nonmembers (see also Frickey 1999).

———. 1997. **"Ghost Dance and Holy Ghost: The Echoes of Nineteenth-Century Christianization Policy in Twentieth-Century Native American Free Exercise Cases."** *Stanford Law Review* 49: 773.

The best and most comprehensive recent law review article on Native American religious freedom issues, especially notable for its thorough effort to place the issue in historical perspective.

Ehle, John. 1988. ***Trail of Tears: The Rise and Fall of the Cherokee Nation.*** New York: Doubleday.

Excellent account of this critically important episode in U.S. history.

Federal Bar Association. 2002. **"27th Annual Indian Law Conference: Reaffirming Tribal Sovereignty in an Era of Judicial Activism: Course Materials."** Albuquerque, NM, April 4–5.

This volume collects a number of useful writings and presentations focusing on the impact of the Supreme Court's decision in *Nevada v. Hicks* (2001).

Forbes, Jack D. 1994. ***Apache, Navaho, and Spaniard.*** 2d ed. Norman: University of Oklahoma Press.

Good study of the early interaction of Europeans and Indians in the American Southwest.

Frickey, Philip P. 1999. **"A Common Law for Our Age of Colonialism: The Judicial Divestiture of Indian Tribal Authority over Nonmembers."** *Yale Law Journal* 109: 1.

One of several key articles (those by Getches in 1996 and 2001 and Dussias in 1993 being other examples) analyzing the Supreme Court's recent erosion of tribal sovereignty under Chief Justice Rehnquist.

Getches, David H. 1996. **"Conquering the Cultural Frontier: The New Subjectivism of the Supreme Court in Indian Law."** *California Law Review* 84: 1573.

Another major article analyzing the anti–tribal sovereignty trend on the Rehnquist Court (see also Frickey 1999).

———. 2001. **"Beyond Indian Law: The Rehnquist Court's Pursuit of States' Rights, Color-Blind Justice and Mainstream Values."** *Minnesota Law Review* 86: 267.

Getches's latest article updating the Rehnquist Court's treatment of Indian law, written just after *Nevada v. Hicks* (2001) was decided (see also Frickey 1999).

Getches, David H., Charles F. Wilkinson, and Robert A. Williams, Jr. 1998. ***Cases and Materials on Federal Indian Law.* 4th ed.** St. Paul, MN: West.

The best law school textbook in the field and really much more than a casebook. It is a comprehensive and remarkably wide-ranging treatise, by its nature providing much more depth than Judge Canby's magnificent "Nutshell," and is much more up-to-date than the revised Cohen treatise. I learned from the second edition of this book as a law student and have taught for years from it myself, gaining more understanding than I could ever sufficiently describe or thank the authors for.

Gibeaut, John. 1999. **"Another Broken Trust."** *American Bar Association Journal* 85 (September): 40.

Good, brief overview of the Indian trust account litigation of *Cobell v. Norton.*

Goldberg, Carole. 1975. **"Public Law 280: The Limits of State Jurisdiction over Reservation Indians."** *UCLA Law Review* 22: 35.

One of the most influential articles in the history of Indian law, Goldberg's analysis was largely adopted by the Supreme Court in *Bryan v. Itasca County* (1976), resulting in a much narrower application of Public Law 280 than the law's text might have suggested.

———. 2002. **"American Indians and 'Preferential' Treatment."** *UCLA Law Review* 49: 943.

Authoritative article elaborating on the issue of Indian racial identity, forming a useful sequel to the 1991 debate between Goldberg and David C. Williams.

Goldberg-Ambrose, Carole. 1991. **"Not 'Strictly' Racial: A Response to 'Indians as Peoples.'"** *UCLA Law Review* 39: 169 (see Williams 1991).

A powerful response to Williams's thoughtful critique of the racial basis for Indian identity.

———. 1997a. ***Planting Tail Feathers: Tribal Survival and Public Law 280.*** Los Angeles: UCLA American Indian Studies Center.

The definitive book about Public Law 280 by the scholar whose 1975 article helped shape the interpretation of the law.

———. 1997b. **"Public Law 280 and the Problem of Lawlessness in California Indian Country."** *UCLA Law Review* 44: 1405.

Informative analysis of the origins and application of Public Law 280, with a particular focus on California.

Gould, L. Scott. 1994. **"The Congressional Response to *Duro v. Reina:* Compromising Sovereignty and the Constitution."** *U.C. Davis Law Review* 28: 53.

Excellent study of the problems raised by the *Duro* Fix Act.

Halbritter, Ray, and Steven Paul McSloy. 1994. **"Empowerment or Dependence? The Practical Value and Meaning of Native American Sovereignty."** *New York University Journal of International Law and Policy* 26: 531.

Informative personal perspective (Halbritter is a leader of the Oneida Indian Nation of New York) on modern issues confronting Indian nations.

Heizer, R. F., and M. A. Whipple. 1971. ***The California Indians: A Source Book.*** Berkeley: University of California Press.

Comprehensive reference source on the histories and cultures of the numerous California Indian tribes.

Huhndorf, Shari M. 2001. ***Going Native: Indians in the American Cultural Imagination.*** Cornell: Cornell University Press.

Penetrating analysis of the role Native Americans have played in popular American culture, including how mainstream European-American culture has often exploited Indians, misappropriated Indian imagery, and echoed historical assaults on Indian sovereignty.

Jackson, Helen Hunt. [1881] 1995. ***A Century of Dishonor: A Sketch of the United States Government's Dealings with Some of the Indian Tribes.*** Reprint, Norman: University of Oklahoma Press.

Classic, powerful, meticulously researched polemic by an early Indian rights activist, inevitably dated but of great historical interest. Jackson went on to write *Ramona,* an 1884 novel often compared to Harriet Beecher Stowe's *Uncle Tom's Cabin,* which may have had even greater impact in raising public awareness about mistreatment of Indians.

Jones, B. J. 1998. **"Welcoming Tribal Courts into the Judicial Fraternity: Emerging Issues in Tribal-State and Tribal-Federal Court Relations."** *William Mitchell Law Review* 24: 457.

Useful analysis of the growing role of tribal courts in the U.S. judicial system.

Jordan, David B. 2000. **"Rolling the Dice on the Cyber-Reservation: The Confluence of Internet Gaming and Federal Indian Law."** *American Indian Law Review* 24: 455.

Useful survey of the interaction between Internet gambling and the growth of tribal casinos.

Kappler, Charles J., ed. 1904. ***Indian Affairs: Laws and Treaties.*** Vol. 2, *Treaties.* Washington, DC: U.S. Government Printing Office.

Classic compilation of Indian treaties; errors and omissions have been corrected in Deloria and DeMallie's recent supplemental collection.

Klein, Christine A. 1996. **"Treaties of Conquest: Property Rights, Indian Treaties, and the Treaty of Guadalupe Hidalgo."** *New Mexico Law Review* 26: 201.

Fascinating article on the issues raised by Indian treaty and property rights in the American Southwest after the Mexican-American War, which was concluded by the 1848 Treaty of Guadalupe Hidalgo.

Kroeber, Theodora. 1961. ***Ishi in Two Worlds: A Biography of the Last Wild Indian in North America.*** Berkeley: University of California Press.

Classic account of the Yahi Indian who was the last survivor of his band, found alone in 1911 after his family had been slaughtered. He was befriended and studied by Alfred L. Kroeber, the author's husband, who was an anthropologist at the University of California at Berkeley.

LaVelle, John P. 2001. **"Strengthening Tribal Sovereignty through Indian Participation in American Politics: A Reply to Professor Porter."** *Kansas Journal of Law and Public Policy* 10: 533.

Impassioned defense of Indian participation in mainstream U.S. politics (see also Porter 1999).

Levy, Guy. 1997. **"*Western Telcon v. California State Lottery:* Will Native Americans Lose Again?"** *Thomas Jefferson Law Review* 19: 361.

Excellent study of the issues facing California gambling tribes during the period following *California v. Cabazon Band of Mission Indians* (1987) and the Indian Gaming Regulatory Act of 1988 but prior to Proposition 5's passage in 1998.

Locke, Raymond Friday. 1992. ***The Book of the Navajo.*** **5th ed.** Los Angeles: Mankind.

Useful reference work on the Navajo Nation.

Loewen, James W. 1995. ***Lies My Teacher Told Me: Everything Your American History Textbook Got Wrong.*** New York: Simon and Schuster.

As vivid and entertaining as it is scholarly, this critical survey of how U.S. history is (or is not) taught in our schools includes, in Chapters 2 through 4 (pp. 37–136), a superb overview of the importance of Indians and Native American perspectives to an understanding of U.S. history.

Mankiller, Wilma, and Michael Wallis. 1993. ***Mankiller: A Chief and Her People.*** New York: St. Martin's.

A lively, highly readable autobiography of the remarkable woman who led the Cherokee Nation from 1985 to 1995. Her account also includes a great deal of very compelling and informative Cherokee history; not to be missed by anyone interested in the Cherokee.

Miller, Robert J. 2001. **"Economic Development in Indian Country: Will Capitalism or Socialism Succeed?"** *Oregon Law Review* 80: 757.

Comprehensive study of the challenges of economic development on Indian reservations and the relative merits of different development models.

Newmyer, R. Kent. 1985. ***Supreme Court Justice Joseph Story: Statesman of the Old Republic.*** Chapel Hill: University of North Carolina Press.

Fine biography focusing on Justice Story's legal philosophy, with a useful section (pp. 211–217) on his role in the Cherokee cases.

Newton, Nell Jessup. 1980. **"At the Whim of the Sovereign: Aboriginal Title Reconsidered."** *Hastings Law Journal* 31: 1215.

Leading scholarly critique of the Supreme Court's treatment of the concept of "Indian title."

———. 1984. **"Federal Power over Indians: Its Sources, Scope, and Limitations."** *University of Pennsylvania Law Review* 132: 195.

Leading scholarly analysis of the origins and scope of the doctrine of federal "plenary" power over Indians.

O'Connor, Sandra Day. 1997. **"Lessons from the Third Sovereign: Indian Tribal Courts."** *Tulsa Law Journal* 33: 1.

Short but intriguing essay about the growing role of tribal courts, especially interesting because of the author's pivotal influence as a Supreme Court justice.

Pommersheim, Frank. 1995. ***Braid of Feathers: American Indian Law and Contemporary Tribal Life.*** Berkeley: University of California Press.

Thoughtful perspectives on Indian law by a longtime scholar and practitioner in the field, especially notable for its superb chapters (pp. 61–135) on tribal court systems.

Porter, Robert B. 1999. **"The Demise of the *Ongwehoweh* and the Rise of the Native Americans: Redressing the Genocidal Act of Forcing American Citizenship upon Indigenous Peoples."** *Harvard BlackLetter Law Journal* 15: 107.

Impassioned argument that Indians should avoid direct participation in U.S. politics and instead focus on government-to-government relations with the United States (see also LaVelle 2001).

Prucha, Francis Paul. 1984. ***The Great Father: The United States Government and the American Indians.*** 2 vols. Lincoln: University of Nebraska Press (abridged 1-vol. ed., 1986).

Comprehensive history of U.S.-Indian relations. A fine companion to Debo's basic history, Prucha's book offers more insight on legal issues. The abridged 1986 edition is more than sufficient for most students; only specialists need to consult the unabridged version.

———. 1994. ***American Indian Treaties: The History of a Political Anomaly.*** Berkeley: University of California Press.

Superb and comprehensive survey of the role of treaty making in the history of U.S. Indian policy.

———, ed. 2000. ***Documents of United States Indian Policy.*** 3d ed. Lincoln: University of Nebraska Press.

Indispensable one-volume collection of most key historical and legal documents pertaining to American Indians.

Rand, Kathryn R. L. 2002. **"There Are No Pequots on the Plains: Assessing the Success of Indian Gaming."** *Chapman Law Review* 5: 47.

Excellent recent study of the impact of Indian gaming on tribal governments and tribal sovereignty.

Rand, Kathryn R. L., and Steven A. Light. 1997. **"Virtue or Vice? How IGRA Shapes the Politics of Native American Gaming, Sovereignty, and Identity."** *Virginia Journal of Social Policy and the Law* 4: 381.

Informative study of the impact of the Indian Gaming Regulatory Act of 1988 on Native American sovereignty.

Richter, Daniel K. 2001. ***Facing East from Indian Country: A Native History of Early America.*** Cambridge: Harvard University Press.

Innovative and provocative account of the history of early eastern North America, told from the standpoint of the tribes who actually controlled most of the continent during this period.

Shattuck, Petra T., and Jill Norgren. 1991. ***Partial Justice: Federal Indian Law in a Liberal Constitutional System.*** New York: Berg.

Powerful analysis of American Indian law and its inherent limitations.

Silko, Leslie Marmon. 1977. ***Ceremony.*** New York: Viking.

Perhaps the greatest novel by any American Indian writer. The quotation at the beginning of Part 1 is taken from p. 260.

———. 1981. ***Storyteller.*** New York: Seaver.

Wonderful collection of short fiction, poetry, and family reminiscences by Silko, a member of the Laguna Pueblo tribe. The quotation at the end of Part 1, in Chapter 4, is taken from p. 247.

Skibine, Alex Tallchief. 2001. **"Making Sense Out of *Nevada v. Hicks:* A Reinterpretation."** *St. Thomas Law Review* 14: 347.

Excellent recent article exploring possible implications and limitations of the Supreme Court's landmark *Hicks* decision.

Thomas, David Hurst, Jay Miller, Richard White, Peter Nabokov, and Philip J. Deloria. 1993. ***The Native Americans: An Illustrated History.*** Atlanta: Turner Publishing.

Magnificent one-volume survey of Indian history and culture, published in connection with the multipart television documentary, "The Native Americans," on the TNT network. Both are of extremely high quality and were sponsored (which is somewhat ironic) by media mogul Ted Turner, who has weathered controversy over his ownership of the Atlanta Braves baseball team, one of many sports franchises exploiting Indian names and imagery in a manner deeply offensive to many.

Urofsky, Melvin I., and Paul Finkelman. 2002a. ***A March of Liberty: A Constitutional History of the United States.*** 2 vols. 2d ed. Oxford and New York: Oxford University Press.

Excellent overview of U.S. constitutional history, highly accessible to nonlawyers.

———, eds. 2002b. ***Documents of American Constitutional and Legal History.*** 2 vols. 2d ed. Oxford and New York: Oxford University Press.

Documentary companion to the authors' two-volume history.

U.S. Department of the Interior. 1958. ***Handbook of Federal Indian Law.*** Washington, DC: U.S. Government Printing Office, 1958 (cited as U.S. Department of Interior 1958) (see Cohen 1941).

Valencia-Weber, Gloria. 1994. **"Tribal Courts: Custom and Innovative Law."** *New Mexico Law Review* 24: 225.

One of a number of excellent recent articles on Indian nation court systems and their development of tribal law.

Wilkins, David E. 1997. ***American Indian Sovereignty and the U.S. Supreme Court: The Masking of Justice.*** Austin: University of Texas Press.

Good overview of leading U.S. Supreme Court decision affecting the development of Indian sovereignty.

———. 2000. **"An Inquiry into Indigenous Political Participation: Implications for Tribal Sovereignty."** *Kansas Journal of Law and Public Policy* 9: 732.

Interesting discussion of the dilemma of mainstream political participation by American Indians (see also Porter 1999 and LaVelle 2001).

———. 2002. ***American Indian Politics and the American Political System.*** Lanham, MD: Rowman and Littlefield.

Excellent recent textbook on Indian governments today, focusing on political issues.

Wilkinson, Charles F. 1987. ***American Indians, Time, and the Law: Native Societies in a Modern Constitutional Democracy.*** New Haven, CT: Yale University Press.

One of the best overall surveys, in concise book-length form, of the history and evolution of American Indian law, by one of the most distinguished scholars of Indian law.

———. 1991. **"To Feel the Summer in the Spring: The Treaty Fishing Rights of the Wisconsin Chippewa."** *Wisconsin Law Review* 1991: 375.

Compelling account of some of the controversies that have arisen over modern revivals of Indian treaty rights.

———. 1997. **"The Role of Bilateralism in Fulfilling the Federal-Tribal Relationship: The Tribal Rights–Endangered Species Secretarial Order."** *Washington Law Review* 72: 1063.

Very interesting article about a modern example of using government-to-government negotiations to resolve legal disputes over Native American sovereignty.

Wilkinson, Charles F., and John M. Volkman. 1975. **"Judicial Review of Indian Treaty Abrogation: 'As Long as Water Flows or Grass Grows**

upon the Earth'—How Long a Time Is That?" *California Law Review* 63: 601.

Classic argument for a strict application of the canons of construction with regard to legislative abrogation of Indian treaties.

Williams, David C. 1991. **"The Borders of the Equal Protection Clause: Indians as Peoples."** *UCLA Law Review* 38: 759.

This article, to which Goldberg-Ambrose responded (see Goldberg-Ambrose 1991, to which Williams responded in turn; see below), is a leading scholarly critique of the dilemma surrounding Indian racial identity (see also Goldberg 2002).

———. 1991. **"Sometimes Suspect: A Response to Professor Goldberg-Ambrose."** *UCLA Law Review* 39: 191 (see Williams's article above and Goldberg-Ambrose 1991).

Williams, Robert A., Jr. 1990. ***The American Indian in Western Legal Thought: The Discourses of Conquest.*** Oxford and: Oxford University Press.

Extremely important study of the roots of U.S. legal doctrine concerning Indians in ancient religious and colonial theories applied by the European powers, both in the Crusades against the Muslims of the Middle East and in the conquest of the Americas.

Wunder, John R. 1994. ***"Retained by the People": A History of American Indians and the Bill of Rights.*** Oxford: Oxford University Press.

Definitive one-volume survey of individual rights issues affecting Indians.

———. **"'Merciless Indian Savages' and the Declaration of Independence: Native Americans Translate the *Ecunnaunuxulgee* Document."** *American Indian Law Review* 25: 65.

Provocative analysis of the meanings of the U.S. Declaration of Independence for American Indians.

———, ed. 1996. ***Native Americans and the Law: Contemporary and Historical Perspectives on American Indian Rights, Freedoms, and Sovereignty.* 6 vols.** New York: Garland.

Very useful collection of leading articles on almost every field of law affecting American Indian life.

Yazzie, Robert. 1994. **"'Life Comes from It': Navajo Justice Concepts."** *New Mexico Law Review* 24: 175.

One of several informative articles by Chief Justice Yazzie of the Navajo Nation Supreme Court on the development of Navajo tribal law and the Navajo court system.

———. 1996. **"'Hozho Nahasdlii'—We Are Now in Good Relations: Navajo Restorative Justice."** *St. Thomas Law Review* 9: 117.

This article explores the longtime Navajo emphasis on restorative justice, a concept that has come back into vogue in the U.S. legal system generally in recent times.

———. 1997. **"Navajo Peacekeeping: Technology and Traditional Indian Law."** *St. Thomas Law Review* 10: 95.

Another fascinating article by Chief Justice Yazzie on the Navajo legal system.

Zelden, Charles L. 2002. ***Voting Rights on Trial: A Handbook with Cases, Laws, and Documents.*** Santa Barbara, CA: ABC-CLIO.

This volume in the On Trial series, focusing generally on the history of voting rights, includes useful sections (pp. 64–67 and 190–193) on the Indian experience in that regard.

Index

About the Author

Bryan H. Wildenthal is associate professor and director of the Center for Law and Social Justice at Thomas Jefferson School of Law in San Diego, California. He has published several major law review articles, mostly on constitutional issues, and is the author of *Nationalizing the Bill of Rights: The Rise, Fall, and Rise of the Fourteenth Amendment Incorporation Doctrine* (forthcoming).

www.ingramcontent.com/pod-product-compliance
Lightning Source LLC
Chambersburg PA
CBHW031415220926
51612CB00004B/48
9781576076248